Sport and Neoliberalism

Edited by David L. Andrews
and Michael L. Silk

Sport and Neoliberalism

Politics, Consumption, and Culture

TEMPLE UNIVERSITY PRESS
PHILADELPHIA

TEMPLE UNIVERSITY PRESS
Philadelphia, Pennsylvania 19122
www.temple.edu/tempress

Library of Congress Cataloging-in-Publication Data

Sport and neoliberalism : politics, consumption, and culture / [edited by]
David L. Andrews.
    p. cm. — (Sporting)
   Includes bibliographical references and index.
   ISBN 978-1-4399-0503-6 (hardcover : alk. paper) — ISBN 978-1-4399-0504-3
(paper : alk. paper) — ISBN 978-1-4399-0505-0 (e-book)   1. Sports—
Political aspects—Cross-cultural studies.   2. Sports—Social aspects—
Cross-cultural studies.   3. Sports and state—Cross-cultural studies.
4. Neoliberalism—Cross-cultural studies.   I. Silk, Michael L.   II. Andrews,
David L.
   GV706.35.S5427 2012
   306.4'83—dc23

                                                                    2012003239

Printed and bound in Great Britain by
Marston Book Services Limited, Didcot

2   4   6   8   9   7   5   3   1

Contents

Part III Consuming Pleasure: Citizenship, Subjectivities, and "Popular" Sporting Pedagogies

1

Sport and the Neoliberal Conjuncture

Complicating the Consensus

MICHAEL L. SILK
DAVID L. ANDREWS

W e begin this book by locating our writing in what are very interesting times. We are but a stone's throw into the new millennium, yet we are in a moment dominated by perpetual war; financial crises; enhanced security; terror threats; the seeming ubiquitous celebration of the free market; an increased emphasis on individual responsibility for all facets of everyday life; a rampant media and culture industry that entertains us and educates us in how to act, behave, and live; higher education systems that increasingly act as handmaidens for government and corporations; and the downgrading and diminished import of any public and social services (health services, education, transportation, and so on). As popular cultural forms—both in terms of popularity and in the sense that Stuart Hall (1981) proposed, with respect to how they function as a continuing tension (relationship, influence, and antagonism) to the dominant culture—sporting practices, experiences, and structures are far from distinct from this context. As Giardina (2005, 7) proposes, contemporary sport finds itself sutured into and through this context; "global (cultural) sporting agents, intermediaries, and institutions actively work as pedagogical sites to hegemonically re-inscribe and re-present (hetero)-normative discourses on sport, culture, nation, and democracy throughout an ascendant global capitalist order." Thus, this book offers an insight into how sport, as a component of popular culture, acts as a powerful educational force that, through pedagogical relations and practices, organizes identity, citizenship, and agency within a neoliberal present (Giroux and Giroux 2006). We begin by thinking through the current neoliberal moment, both in the United States and, to some degree, beyond (specifically the United Kingdom and Canada). It is our contention that neoliberalism has its ideological and figurative core in the United States—hence the focus of this project. Nonetheless, it equally possesses a truly international reach. This signposts our future work examining the relationship between sport and neoliberalism in a variety of national contexts (settings that differ in terms of geography, level of economic development, and mode of governance, and thus the precise way that the sport and neoliberalism relation is enacted). Having spatially and historically located the trajectory of neoliberalism in its seemingly relentless march toward becoming an ascendant ordering logic of contemporary societies, we then begin to sketch how such processes have been manifest in sport, suggesting that much work is needed to begin to understand the variety of ways that neoliberalism (in its various mutations) has been both understood and mobilized within sporting contexts. This leads to introducing each of the chapters solicited for this text, contributions that begin to fill the void in our understandings of the articulations between the heterogeneous complexities of neoliberal ideology, political praxis, pedagogy, and sport.

Our Contested Present

On October 14, 2008, in the final throes of his presidency, George W. Bush delivered a statement in the Rose Garden of the White House that promised "unprecedented" and "aggressive" steps to address the financial crisis that had devastated the global economy over the previous year (and indeed continues unabated at the current time of writing). In a move that doubtless proved an anathema to the legions of free-marketers who had dominated American economic and political life in the preceding three decades, Bush vowed to save *American* capitalism by taking the unprecedented step of partially nationalizing nine of the country's largest banking institutions:

> This weekend, I met with finance ministers from the G7 and the G20—organizations representing some of the world's largest and fastest-growing economies. We agreed on a coordinated plan for action to provide new liquidity, strengthen financial institutions, protect our citizens' savings, and ensure fairness and integrity in the markets. Yesterday, leaders in Europe moved forward with this plan. They announced significant steps to inject capital into their financial systems by purchasing equity in major banks. And they announced a new effort to jumpstart lending by providing temporary government guarantees for bank loans. These are wise and timely actions, and they have the full support of the United States. Today, I am announcing new measures America is taking to implement the G7 action plan and strengthen banks across our country. . . .
>
> They will make clear that the government's role will be limited and temporary. And they will make clear that these measures are not intended to take over the free market, but to *preserve* it. ("Bush: Moves Made" 2008; emphasis added)

As the final sentence of Bush's statement of intention makes plain—far from signaling an epochal shift and the demise of the largely unregulated, free-market approach to economic structuration and development—this was a policy announcement that couched government intervention into the floundering economy in almost apologetic terms and promised a swift return to the political-economic order that had brought the American, and indeed global, economy to this perilous state. This was not an effort by the Bush administration to disrupt the sovereignty of a new logic and structure of rule, an empire, centered on a global market and global circuits of production (Hardt and Negri 2000) and to imagine, as Hardt and Negri (2000) might, an alternative power structure or political strategy that resurrects the nation-state against capitalism. Clearly, the Bush administration was continuing to exist and operate under the assumption that, however dire the financial situation might appear, the current parlous state of the economy was merely a *temporary correction* in the neoliberal political-economic modus operandi that characterized his presidency. Therefore, and much like the justification for the wars on Afghanistan and Iraq, the actions were part of the effort of *preservation* of a system of structures and values on which his entire regime was founded. The Bush administration's myopic intransigence simply would not allow it to be distracted from its unwavering belief in the managerial rectitude *and* moral righteousness of a system of neoliberal economic and political governance centered on free-market capital, state disinvolvement, and structure deregulation. Following Robbins (2009, 473) then, it appears that "the cure for a jaundiced neoliberal market order is a moderately revised market order where the government actively socializes the costs and consequences of the care for the diseased and dangerous patient while privatizing the profits."

The inauguration of President Barack Hussein Obama on January 20, 2009, promised much change from the previous administration. Within his first week of office, President Obama began to reverse many of the repressive policies of the Bush administration. The announced closure of the Guantánamo Bay prison camp, the lifting of restrictions on U.S. government funding for groups involved with abortion overseas, and moves toward reversal of Bush's climate change policies all signaled a conscious decision to publicly and strategically distance the regime from its predecessor. However, and without being the harbingers of doom for the *new* era, we would be somewhat naïve were we to think of Obama's presidency as a teleological fault line, a complete rupture, from the last forty years of economic, political, military, domestic, and international "policy." Indeed, less than a week into his presidency, Obama ordered his first military action, a strike against "suspected" militants in rural Pakistan that killed at least eighteen people. Further, he has been critiqued for his deafening silence on Gaza, a stance that shows little distance from that which has gone before and, indeed, one that may well threaten his perception among Muslims throughout the world (Tisdall 2009). On February 17, 2009, as testimony to the continued reliance on and support of financial markets as the primary vehicle for ensuring sustainable economic growth and the preservation of economic stability, Obama signed a $787 billion stimulus bill: the American Recovery and Reinvestment Act. While cloaked in neo-Keynesian rhetoric, Obama's general approach to the current fiscal crisis is steeped in the neoliberal *underpinnings* of the Bush regime, which clearly continue to frame popular and policy consciousness regarding the appropriate form of economic structure and development. As Robbins (2009) suggests, what is interesting and perhaps most disturbing about the Obama administration—the self-styled "change" administration—is that many of the elements of the previous order still hold sway. Without characterizing it too simplistically, in the early stages of the Obama presidency, J. Maynard Keynes *and* Milton Friedman have seemingly become the unlikeliest of economic policy bedfellows.

While there is much cause for optimism in the Obama regime, it is unlikely that he will distance himself from some forty years of a "triumphant" free market. On one hand, this is not wholly surprising. Unlike the near anarchic turmoil created by the spiraling and biting economic depression in the early 1930s—which necessitated the economic and social radicalism of FDR's Keynes-informed New Deal—Obama has inherited an America bathed in the afterglow of decades of consumer-propelled economic growth but now in the midst of seemingly unprecedented economic decline. However, as profound as the current *crisis* may in fact be, it has yet to reach the scale and scope of the depression, largely because of the levels of *relative* affluence attained by many (if by no means all) sectors of the American populace. Thus, economic decline within a "postscarcity" society (and we use the term advisedly and with necessary caveats) results in real economic consequences in terms of people's spending power and lifestyle choices, but it does not have the same degree of catastrophic impact regarding levels of poverty, hardship, and, indeed, starvation that characterized economic downturns within societies in which the "scarcity" of basic requirements for individual and familial sustenance was a widespread concern (e.g., the United States in the early 1930s). As a consequence, the factors that arguably led to the current crisis continue to be viewed as the roots of the economy's salvation. Obama has consequently inherited an America whose economic existence continues to be prefigured on the primacy of free markets, deregulation, and unfettered international trade (Sassen 2000); is institutionalized within the formation of transnational political structures, alliances, and treaties (such as the World Trade Organization, the International Monetary Fund, and the North American Free Trade Agreement); and is expressed through the ability, and indeed the inalienably perceived requirement, of individuals to define themselves within and through their forays into the consumer marketplace.

So the present moment—at least in a U.S. context—can be characterized as a specific stage in the evolution of the liberal capitalist order that has (in various guises) dominated U.S. society for at least 150 years (post–Civil War, in approximate terms). In its present iteration, the Obama regime has inherited a pernicious and regressive social formation instantiated and materialized through the "overlapping" (Frow and Morris 2000) discourses of neoliberalism, neoconservatism, neoimperialism, and neoscientism that have both emerged from and helped to institutionally frame the subjective and material experience of the current moment. No matter the cogency of Obama's reaction to this moment, academically, there has yet to be adequate critical explication that has fully developed and understood how the various tentacles of economic and political policy have been and continue to be manifest in everyday life. That is, the ramifications of the cultural tentacles of these overlapping discourses needs to be interrogated; any semblance of progressive change can take place only once the moment has been understood, lest the history books show little in terms of change within the cultural realm of everyday life.

Our focal point for this intellectual project and its sites of critical intellectual engagement are ground within understanding how the sociopolitical-economic trajectories of certain neoliberal regimes and administrations became and continue to be mapped onto and appropriated within popular forms of culture. Specifically, our focus is on the multiple iterations of sporting cultures, experiences, expressions, and structures. For it is from this interdiscursive assemblage that the physical cultural realm comes to exude the "boundaries and limits of tolerable politics" (Hall 1989, 13), through "events" such as the post-Katrina accelerated renovation of the Louisiana Superdome and the popular media's celebration thereof; the crass mobilization of sport spectacles in support of neoimperialist agendas; the social and racial containment enacted as part of the governance of spectacularized city spaces predicated on sporting consumption; or the personalization and individualization of medical discourses through reality television (see Couldry 2008) that act as powerful forms of public pedagogy correcting the ways in which we should eat, exercise, act, discipline children and pets, behave toward our neighbors, consume, and so on.

In this respect, given the relative importance of ideology and affect in the construction and experiencing of everyday (neoliberal) life, there has never been a greater need to expand "the tools of ideology critique to include a range of sites in which the production of knowledge takes place (including, but not limited to, television, Hollywood films, video games, newspapers, popular magazines, and Internet sites)" (Giroux 2001a, 14). Clearly, we can and should add sport and exercise cultures to this partial list. That is, through locating or articulating sport as an element of the cultural terrain within a wider cultural politics, critical interrogation can begin to understand it as a site through which various discourses are mobilized in regard to the organization and discipline of daily life in the service of particular political agendas (Andrews 1995; Giroux 2001a, 2001b; Grossberg 1992, 1997). In this regard we can begin to understand how sport serves as an economy of affect through which power, privilege, politics, and position are (re)produced. Before sketching out these relationships, however, and contrary to the many standard commentaries that treat neoliberalism as a largely uniform and undifferentiated identity, we highlight the heterogenous complexity of neoliberal ideology and political praxis.

Our Neoliberal Present

While neoliberalism has been manifest in complex and multiple ways within sporting contexts, it is important to offer a sense of what the term means and from where it emerged—no matter how contested and how it is experienced, with different intensities, in specific parts of the world and at different times (and many of the contributions to this volume offer variations on our efforts to explicate the term). Our understanding of the extant neoliberal mantra is that of a populist political and economic ideology and praxis manifest in the reappropriation of the poststructuralist leitmotif pertaining to the *death of the social* (Giroux 2000a, 2000b, 2001a, 2003a, 2003b, 2004a, 2004b, 2004c). For Giroux (2001a), the defining essence of neoliberalism is the morbidity of the social sphere, evidenced from the hegemony of a cynicism toward all things public and collective, the corollary of which has been the rise of a virulent contempt for the notion of social welfare provision; an equally pernicious and questioning attitude toward its recipients; and a individualizing culture of surveillance, accountability, and resentment. Of course, this palpable shift in the political landscape—what Stuart Hall (1983) referred to as the "Great Moving Right Show"—emerged from particular sociostructural conditions. Specifically, the political landscape became profoundly altered in response to intensifying conditions of local and global recession, the related decline of mass-manufacturing economies and industries, and the precipitated crisis of Keynesian welfarism (see Harvey 2007). Thus, coming to the fore in the late 1970s and early 1980s after a considerable incubation period, within most Western democracies, an alternative political philosophy was strategically advanced, prefigured on the need to dismantle the basic institutional components of the postwar social welfare consensus and to mobilize policies intended to extend market discipline, competition, and commodification throughout society (Brenner and Theodore 2002a, 2002b; Hobbs et al. 2000; Jessop 2002). The increasing worldwide ascendancy of neoliberalism in the early 1980s was closely intertwined with a pervasive rescaling of capital-labor relations, intercapitalist competition, financial and monetary regulation, state power, international configuration, and uneven development throughout the world economy (Brenner and Theodore 2002a). Subsequently, the loosening or dismantling of the various institutional constraints on marketization, the logics of competitiveness and commodification, the hyperexploitation of workers, the deconstruction of labor unions and social welfare programs, and the discretionary power of private capital, processes of deregulation, liberalization, and state retrenchment (or, more accurately, reorganization) became manifest in an alarming range of spaces, institutions, and policies (Brenner and Theodore 2002a, 2002b; Peck and Tickell 2002). This ideologically and economically based form of political revisionism provoked an "epochal shift" away from the supposed "social mentality" proclivities underpinning the role of the state (Rose 1999)—a shift that saw the state relieved of its powers of obligation to answer for all society's needs for order, health, security, and productivity. For Nikolas Rose, this involved a "double movement of autonomization and responsibilitization [in which] [p]opulations once under the tutelage of the social state are to be made responsible for their destiny and for that of society as a whole. Politics is to be returned to society itself, but no longer in a social form: in the form of individual morality, organizational responsibility, and ethical community" (2000a, 1400).

The global hegemony of this mode of political rationality has led many to suggest that it has become a commonsense "nebulous phenomena" (Peck and Tickell 2002, 381), a "new planetary vulgate" (Bourdieu and Wacquant 2001, 2), or an ideological "thought virus" (Beck 2000, 122). Despite there being different inf(l)ections impacted by the particularities of various locales, neoliberalism can be seen as a new political consensus that became materialized via new, deeply interventionist forms of institutional hardware and invasive social policies, congealed around "social" issues such as crime, immigration, policing, welfare reform, urban order, surveillance, and community regeneration (Peck and Tickell 2002). While the doses vary, the basic prescription of neoliberalism is the same: purge the system of obstacles to the functioning of free markets; celebrate the virtues of individualism (recast social problems as individual problems, such as drug use, obesity, or inadequate health insurance) and competitiveness; foster economic self-sufficiency; abolish or weaken social programs; include the marginalized (often by this shift in the role of government) or the poor into the labor market, on the market's terms (such as through the workfare scheme); and criminalize the homeless and the urban poor (subject this population to curfew orders, increased surveillance, or "zero-tolerance" policing) (Giroux 2004b; Peck 2003; Rose 1999, 2000b).

This emergent and active period of "roll-out neoliberalism," predicated on the technocratic embedding of routines of neoliberal governance, the extension of neoliberal institutions, and the erosion of pockets of political and institutional resistance, has meant that particular attention needs to be directed toward the "purposeful construction and consolidation of neoliberalized state forms, modes of governance, and regulatory relations" (Peck and Tickell 2002, 384). Critical scholarship then, as Peck (2003) proposes, needs to interrogate what the reorganized state is doing, and to whom, and thereby expose the causes and consequences of neoliberalism across a range of spaces (Katz 2001).

The extension of the domain of economics into politics affords neoliberal market rationality the "responsibility" to organize, regulate, and define the basic principles and workings of the state. As opposed to assuming responsibility for a range of social needs, the state is instead interested in pursuing a wide range of deregulations, privatizations, and abdications of responsibility to the market and private philanthropy (Giroux 2008; Steinmetz 2003). Yet as the forces of neoliberalism dismantle the historically guaranteed social provisions provided by the welfare state—profit becoming defined as democracy—a growing disjuncture emerges between the ideology of self-regulating markets and the everyday reality of persistent economic stagnation, manifest in a growing apparatus of social control, intensifying inequality, generalized social insecurity, and a battered citizenry (Giroux 2004b, 2008). As a diverse political, economic, and pedagogic project, Giroux (2004b, 2008) argues, the state has been transformed from a social state to a punishing state manifest through the "proto fascism" of the present—the cult of traditionalism, the corporatization of civil society, a culture of fear and "patriotic correctness," the collapse of the separation between church and state, a language of official "Newspeak," and the ownership and control of the media. The normalization of an authoritarian neoliberal ideology, then, has meant that the ever-expanding militarized neoliberal state, marked by the interdependence of finance capital, authoritarian order, a vast war machine, and a "culture of force," now serves as a powerful pedagogical influence that shapes the lives, memories, and daily experiences of most Americans, waging an internal, domestic war against the poor, youth, women, and the elderly, especially those further marginalized by class and color (Giroux 2003a, 2004b, 2008). In this sense, the agenda that positions abject bodies in the degraded borderlands of the broken promises of capitalism projects class and racial anxieties onto the "abject," polices and governs the presence of disposable populations in an increasingly gentrified *urbanité*, weakens support for citizens' rights, downgrades social services, and creates an increasingly criminogenic public school, a militarized popular culture, and a surveillance-dominated cityscape (Giroux 2003a, 2003b, 2004b, 2004c).

We would argue that we can set down multiple manifestations of inequality as markers of a neoliberal conjuncture centered on bolstering the logics of the marketplace as opposed to the welfare of the citizenry. For example, a variety of traditionally public health issues and concerns have become incorporated into the reach of the private sector: disease prevention, health promotion, latchkey children, personal and public health, juvenile curfews, medical services, day care, nutrition, substance abuse prevention, mental health and family counseling, teen pregnancy, services for the homeless, family and community revitalization, family abuse, arts and cultural awareness, education, recreation, career structures, improvement of infrastructures, and economic revitalization (Andrews, Silk, and Pitter 2008). Indeed, health disparities may constitute the most concrete disadvantages associated with the social and racial patterns of polarization and postwar neglect (Hillier 2008; Squires and Kubrin 2005), given that poverty causes poor health by its connection with inadequate nutrition, substandard housing, exposure to environmental hazards, unhealthy lifestyles, and decreased access to and use of health care services (U.S. Department of Health and Human Services, Department of Disease Control and Prevention 2005). As an indicator of the shift of the role of government away from social provision, the ratio of black to white infant mortality increased from 1.6 to 2.4 between 1950 and the 1990s (Kington and Nickens 2001; Squires and Kubrin 2005). Disparities in health and wellness of populations disadvantaged by class, race, and social and spatial location are well established; for example, access to clean air and water, exposure to lead paint, stress, obesity, smoking habits, diet, social isolation, availability of public spaces (such as parks and recreation facilities), proximity to hospitals and other medical treatment facilities, and availability of health insurance are all traceable to the withdrawal of welfare (compare Bullard 1996; Dreier, Mollenkopf, and Swanstrom 2001; Kington and Nickens 2001; Klinenberg 2002; Squires and Kubrin 2005, 52). In this sense, neoliberalism produces, legitimates, and exacerbates the existence of persistent poverty, the absence of employment opportunities, inadequate health care, and substandard housing and education—an extant racial apartheid created by ever-increasing "problems of social dislocation in the inner city" (Wilson 1987, 22), leading to growing inequalities between the rich and the poor (Giroux 2004b, 46). Such disparities—concentrated poverty, the restoration of class power, and racial segregation and (health) inequality—were perhaps most vividly exposed in the racially skewed death toll of Hurricane Katrina, particularly with regard to the loss of life in New Orleans (Gibson 2006; see also Denzin 2006 and Molotch 2006).

Our neoliberal conjecture, then, drawing on Sheller and Urry (2003), indicates a power shift from democratic local governing regimes to a constellation of public/private institutions that operate largely independently from democratic politics, with little public accountability and less of a commitment to extend social justice to the whole of society. In this regard, as the state becomes keyed on bolstering the logics of the market and more closely aligned with capital,

> politics is defined largely by its policing functions rather than as an agency for peace and social reform. As the state abandons its social investments in health, education, and the public welfare, it increasingly takes on the functions of an enhanced security or police state, the signs of which are most visible in the increasing use of the state apparatus to spy on and arrest its subjects, the incarceration of individuals considered disposable (primarily poor people of color), and the ongoing criminalization of social policies. (Giroux and Giroux 2006, 26)

What then of the complex relationships between different forms of sporting experiences, structures, and organizations and the conceptualization of the destructive and creative moments of neoliberal policy, politics, economics, praxis, and ideology? In what ways have these relationships been formed, contested, played out, and framed in, through, and by sport? How has sport been affected by, and indeed affected, the role of the state, the market, or the subject within a neoliberal conjuncture? Do sporting institutions, organizations, and forms bolster or reject the advancement of the free market, and how do individuals experience sport within our neoliberal present? What of the place of sport in the multiple manifestations of social inequality and the citizenry alluded to previously? Complex debates can be held around each of these initial questions, discussions that form the essence of this text as we consider how sport has been appropriated and mobilized within the major institutional arenas in which capital accumulation and regulation occurs.

Sport in Our Neoliberal Present

This book emerges from an intellectual and political project that has occupied our work and that of a number of other scholars in recent years. Along with our colleagues, we have been equally fascinated and perturbed by nationalist assaults and war cries; growing economic disparities and social inequalities; the increasing pathologization of the poor, the black, and the welfare recipient; the urban apartheid manifest in "smart"-growth initiatives; the demonization of schooling; the seeping corporate ideologies that frame the "scholarship" of academics; and the "blame the victim" cultures all mobilized in and appropriated through the seemingly apolitical and banal sporting world. With others, we have questioned the normalization of war in the construction and experience of everyday life through various mediated sporting spectacles and products that opine a myopic expression of American jingoism, militarism, and geopolitical imperial domination (see, e.g., Hogan 2003; Silk and Falcous 2005; Falcous and Silk 2005); the neoconservative appropriation of NASCAR dads and the privileging of patriarchal masculinity, the Republican Party, Christianity, and corporate consumerism (Vavrus 2007; see also Giardina 2009 and Newman 2007); and the "innocent" Disney-produced Little League World Series children's baseball tournament that acts to reinforce the notion that America is "a morally superior, righteous" place and that any critical attacks on it are misguided at best and criminally unsubstantiated at worst (White, Silk, and Andrews 2008). Some have centered on the putative scientific hegemony of the corporatized university, the corollary of which is a "methodological fundamentalism" (House 2005) that privileges the randomized experiment as that which "counts" (see Freshwater and Rolfe 2004)—social and economic conditions that privilege a science that is embedded within, and looks to expand, economic modes of governance and efficiency (Murray et al., 2007; Murray, Holmes, and Rail 2008). With critics of "state" science (i.e., Denzin and Giardina 2006; Giroux 2004a; House 2005, 2006), we sit in a field that points to the politics of evaluation, narrowly understood, as a manifestation of the neofundamentalisms evident within the Bush regime and we decry a "scientific knowledge" that is political through and through, a knowledge ground within our contemporary social and political conditions that authorize particular regimes of truth (Murray et al. 2007; Silk, Bush, and Andrews 2010).

All of these projects and works—which have framed our embryonic thinking about sport and the neoliberal conjuncture—have been part of a wider moment of cultural critique that has, at its heart, the aim of exposing how the project of the right has been nurtured and expressed in and through the affective realm of popular culture and within the structures and institutions of the state, of which the sporting economy is a significant component. Yet while all of these projects have endeavored to interrogate cultural texts through a focus on how they operate within the material and institutional contexts that structure everyday life (Giroux 2001a), a lacuna of work has explicitly centered on critical explication of how, in various guises and often in highly localized contexts, the tentacles of neoliberalism have been manifest, experienced, appropriated, and mobilized within multifarious iterations of sporting experiences, expressions, and structures. Thus, when viewed in toto, the book is our effort to highlight the diverse ways in which neoliberalism has been understood and mobilized within sporting contexts.

Much historically grounded empirical, theoretical, and political work re-mains to be done in order to decode and ultimately dismantle the everyday vio-lence of neoliberalism, the "utopia of unlimited exploitation" (Bourdieu 1998, quoted in Brenner and Theodore 2002b, 345). This is certainly the case with regard to teasing out the nuances in the relationships between sport and neo-liberalism. To date, there has been a relative dearth of work that has critically engaged this relationship. Further, and at least in the extant sport literature, those who have attempted to address this relationship have taken a rather uni-form and superficial approach. We see this text as one small step toward fill-ing this void as we attempt to understand, expose, oppose, and think through alternatives to the deleterious social consequences of neoliberalism (Wacquant 2009). While focusing largely on the United States (and to a lesser extent the United Kingdom and Canada), we have nonetheless sought contributions that engage a range of empirical sites and dimensions (including the relationship between sport and the state, sport and the environment, and sport and the city and the relationships among institutions, practices, and agencies with regard to sporting experiences and with respect to different types of sporting prac-tices). In the chapters that follow, the contributors to this volume explicate the entrenchment of neoliberal discourse, technologies, disparities, and policies as they are operationalized and institutionalized within a diverse array of sport-ing structures, experiences, spaces, and technologies—including neoliberal state sporting policy; the corporatized university sport system; urban renewal; the governance of play in urban space; discourses of health; articulations with gender and sexuality, national identity, race, and class; "corporatized sportain-ment"; media spectacles and cultural technologies; and physical embodiments of the end of neoliberalism. As a result, we have a collection of chapters from a wide range of extremely well-respected academics that address sport and neolib-eralism, from macro through micro levels, including discussions of social struc-ture and individual experience and the relationship between both realms of existence. To capture the essence of these multifarious contributions within the book, we have divided the contributions into three thematic/conceptual parts.

In Part I, "Structures, Formations, and Mechanics of Neoliberalism," the emphasis is on the multiple architectures of neoliberalism and the institutions through which it is manifest. Embracing a simultaneously theoretical, political, performative, and pedagogical challenge concerned with the often localized conception and characterization of neoliberal sporting cultures, the identifi-cation of its local/global command centers, explicating its mechanisms of im-position and reproduction, and exposing its flanks of vulnerability (Peck and Tickell 2002; see also Giroux 2001a, 2004a), Part I offers multifarious under-standings and mechanisms of neoliberalism. In Chapter 2, Toby Miller exca-vates the origins of the neoliberal market and the associated impacts on the polis, a mantra of economic citizenship in which each individual assumes the "responsibility" for his or her own material fortunes and destiny. Emphasizing the triumph of the free market and consumerism, Miller charts transformations

in consumption of sport (from spectator to producer), commercial entrenchment, the crisis of televised sport, and sport labor exploitation. Focusing more
explicitly on the ways in which citizens are governed under the logics of neoliberalism, in Chapter 3, Mick Green addresses the growing significance of sport
policy interventions (related to education, health, crime, social inclusion, social
cohesion, and citizenship) for the construction of a social investment state. In
Chapter 4, Michael D. Giardina and C. L. Cole investigate the proliferation of
new social meanings that translate from neoliberal economic forms to the conduct of organizations and individuals. Through juxtaposing the place of the
Louisiana Superdome in post-Katrina narratives and sporting narratives (and
indeed how these narratives conflated), Giardina and Cole reveal the latent and
systemic racisms inherent in neoliberal architectures, suggesting that the problems of inner-city life have become the new targets of self-management, regulation, restraint of individual appetites, responsibility, and morality. Chapter 5,
by Samantha King, moves the debate from the inner city to the university. In
particular, through excavating the corporate university, King suggests that the
marketing strategies enshrined in contracts between universities and athletic
apparel corporations are helping to reconfigure, both materially and ideologically, the culture of the university as part of a broader shift toward a branded,
privatized society. The focus of Chapter 6, by Brian Wilson, is the deregulation
and reregulation practices inherent in neoliberalism that leave environmental
issues to be addressed through market-related mechanisms and nongovernmental partners/monitors. Wilson reveals some of the tensions inherent in the
"carbon-offsetting" practices that have become standardized in the hosting of
major sporting events, questioning the essence of discourse that understands
nature as being "owned" by humans—not least, what happens when such
"ownership" is driven in the pursuit of profit. Chapter 7, by Grant Farred, concludes Part I by musing on the "end" of neoliberalism. Farred offers a trajectory
through two swimming phenomena, Mark Spitz and Michael Phelps, arguing
that Spitz metaphorically and physically embodied the emergence of neoliberalism during the 1972 Olympic Games in Munich, while Phelps emerged as the
epitome of the "end" of a neoliberal order (during the tumult of economic crisis
during the 2008 Beijing Olympic Games) founded on the premise that only the
free market can produce the kind of competition that enables individuals (released from all unnecessary constraints imposed by the state) in all walks of life
to achieve their full potential.

In Part II, "Government, Governance, and the Cultural Geographies of
Neoliberalism," contributors consider the systematic geographies of neoliberalism. Drawing on Brenner and Theodore (2002b), many of these chapters address "actually existing neoliberalism" that is particularly pronounced on the
urban scale, frequently with profound and often contrasting consequences for
private capital and public interests. Each contribution reconceptualizes how
the destructive and creative moments of neoliberalism have been mobilized
through distinctly geographical strategies. In Chapter 8, the editors offer a theoretical purview of the multidiscursive (political, economic, social, juridical, and

architectural) constitution of new urban glamour zones and associated populations. They offer a theoretical account of the various neoliberal policies and practices underpinning the discursive constitution of belonging and difference—categories of inclusion and exclusion—in the construction and management of powerful symbolic spaces of urban representation (Soja 2000). They propose that brutalizing injustices result from the advancement of profoundly divisive neoliberal social geographies (incorporating interdependent social and spatial dimensions)—processes and practices of social governance through which both valorized and pathologized urban bodies are made visible, regulated, and managed that contribute to materializing the differentiated (and indeed differentiating) new urban landscape. In Chapter 9, Caroline Fusco extends this base, focusing on the ways in which discourses of "healthification"— which "encourage" individuals to take responsibility for their own health and well-being and/or the health of others—have become manifest within the reproduction of space. Fusco proposes that neoliberal urban imaginaries and moral geographies of healthification are centered on life, health, and well-being, which, despite being set against the omnipresent backdrop of risk and degenerating urban landscapes, operate as powerful technologies designed to manage youth's conduct through choices to *re*imagine oneself as a consumer and citizen of the city. The securitization of city space, a theme that runs throughout many chapters in Part II, is given critical examination in Chapter 10, where Kimberly S. Schimmel explores the relationships between the escalating economic expenditures devoted to major sport infrastructure and the intensifying militarization of urban space. Schimmel focuses on one of the central trajectories of neoliberal ideology and policy—the military-industrial complex—arguing that "security" has become the justification for measures that contribute to downgrading the quality of life for urban residents. Focused on an even more localized scale of neoliberal consumerism, in Chapter 11, Leslie Heywood and Mark Montgomery discuss the significant changes to localism, and the surf economy, under the aegis of neoliberalism. They point to the contestations of *the* local surfing space, consumerism, differing groups of (gendered) subjects, and the life cycle in the understanding of surfing as part of a globalized neoliberal economy. Chapter 12, by Michael Atkinson, concludes Part II by causing us to reflect on the overemphasis on the logics and practices of mainstream power and performance sports. He instead focuses on what he terms a "post-sport" physical culture, one that subverts modernist ideologies and practices outright and in which corporeal dichotomies between sacred and profane bodies are smashed through subaltern and autonomous forms of athletic movement. His focus on free-running encourages us to think about how "post-sport" can challenge the modalities of life regulated by anesthetizing market-consumptive logics and governmentally disciplining risk discourses.

Part III, "Consuming Pleasure: Citizenship, Subjectivities, and 'Popular' Sporting Pedagogies," considers the often subtle ways in which citizens become subject to and complicit within the technologies of government. Here we emphasize the various technologies of self-governance—"cultural technologies"

(Ouellette and Hay 2008a, 2008b)—concerned with the conduct of conduct or, specifically, the calculated *direction of conduct* to shape behavior to certain desirable ends (Palmer 2003). The focus is on the array of practices for shaping identities and forms of life (Rose 1999): advertising, marketing, the proliferation of goods, the multiple stylizations of the act of purchasing, mediation, celebrity, sporting consumerism, and reality television. In this sense, Part III addresses the convergence and transformation of programs, strategies, and techniques for the conduct of conduct, the "rationalities and technologies underpinning a whole variety of more or less rationalized and calculated interventions that have attempted to govern the existence and experience of contemporary human beings and to act on human conduct to direct it to certain ends" (Rose 2000b, 322). In true neoliberal fashion, these cultural technologies circulate techniques for a government of the self—a central component in the neoliberal reinvention of "welfare" that promotes choice, personal accountability, consumerism, and self-empowerment as ethics of citizenship while, at the same time, masking social forces (Ouellette and Hay 2008a, 2008b). These neoliberal technologies educate subjects, discipline the noncompliant, and become part of a moral economy that differentiates between "good" and "bad" citizens. The chapters in Part III then discuss powerful and public sporting forms, experiences, and consumption as highly educative sporting discourses, one component of popular culture that serves as an economy of affect through which power, privilege, politics, and position are (re)produced. As powerful public pedagogies (Giroux 2004a), educators of sorts (Leonard 2009; Lugo-Lugo and Bloodsworth-Lugo 2009; O'Riordan 2007), the chapters point to how "popular" sporting pleasures—mediated sporting discourses, events, spectacles, and (hi)stories and technologies of corporeal recollection and embodiment—become ingrained with the discourses of nation, subjectivity, regulation, and consumption (Giroux 2000a) that frame the cultural present. In Chapter 13, Mary G. McDonald addresses the marketing discourses—and the embodied accoutrements in the form of the players—of the Women's National Basketball Association (WNBA). In so doing, the chapter centers on the naturalization of heteronormativity and the contested sexual politics of neoliberalism. In Chapter 14, Jessica Francombe and Michael L. Silk interrogate what Nick Couldry (2008) has called the "secret theatre" of neoliberalism: reality television. They argue that the reality show *The Biggest Loser* is a powerful, militarized, neoliberal form of public (bio)pedagogy, a normalizing cultural technology in the formation, shaping, and production of good consumer-citizens, the program's focus on personal responsibility for "health" and "well-being" acting as a key pedagogical site framed by the massive retrenchment of social welfare sensibilities and programs. In Chapter 15, Joshua I. Newman furthers the understanding of the normalized neoliberal subjectivity through consideration of the sporting U.S. South as an "incubator" containing pedagogies attendant to the neoliberal imperative. Through a focus on NASCAR and the spectacles surrounding the University of Mississippi's intercollegiate football team, Newman contemplates the ways in which myths of the neoliberal nation have been dialectically articulated through the identity politics and bodily practices of a normalized (conservative, white, masculine, Christian, working-class, hetero-normative) "southern" subject position. Farther north and above the forty-ninth parallel, Jay Scherer and Lisa McDermott (Chapter 16) lament the "hijacking" of Canadian identity by the right-wing Harper government. Explicating the relationships between the apparent "ordinaryness" of hockey and the neolib-eral mantra, Scherer and McDonald discuss how Canadian national identity is grounded in a neoliberal subject (Harper), who is positioned as an independent, self-actualizing individual committed to a belief in the "freedom" of "choice" and who is imagined to be the "ordinary" Canadian. Finally, Chapter 17, by Ted Butryn, turns to what is perhaps the eponymous exemplar of neoliberalism: World Wrestling Entertainment (the WWE), which operates overtly for profit and with far less pretense than many equivalent "sporting" institutions. Butryn exposes the WWE as a neoliberal poster child, offering a reading that places the WWE firmly within the "Bush gang's" rampant militarized, corporatized, globalized, neoconservative, and Viagra-fueled neoliberal conjuncture.

We hope that this collection, taken as a whole, "simultaneously create[s] and sustain[s] a critical dialogue focused on history and politics as they unfold in front of us" (Denzin and Lincoln 2003, xv) by making sense of neoliberal sport, illuminating and exposing the practices, policies, and processes respon-sible for the normalization of neoliberal sporting cultures—processes that are clearly anchored in power relations that serve particular ends and thereby per-petuate structural inequalities. We thus hope that the collection is seen sim-ply as embracing a position that fosters a "spirit in opposition, rather than in accommodation . . . in dissent against the status quo" (Said 1994, 12). In this regard, explicating the articulations between neoliberal sporting practices, cul-tures, expressions, and structures allows us to contribute a part, however small, toward the production of scholarship as social endeavor—scholarship that is *meaningful* through connecting private troubles and public concerns and that extends its critical, performative, and utopian impulses to address urgent so-cial issues in the interests of promoting social change (Giroux 2001a; Giroux and Giroux 2006). To this end, and with deference, we leave the final words on this volume (at least, at this juncture, for we are sure there will be many other readings) to our esteemed colleague, Norm Denzin, who provides an evocative afterword to our humble efforts to explicate the relationships between sport and neoliberalism.

REFERENCES

Andrews, D. 1995. "Excavating Michael Jordan: Notes on a Critical Pedagogy of Sporting Representation." In *Sport and Postmodern Times: Culture, Gender, Sexuality, the Body and Sport*, ed. G. Rail and J. Harvey, 185–220. Albany: State University of New York Press.

Andrews, D. L., M. Silk, and R. Pitter. 2008. "Sport and the Polarized American City." In *Sport in Society*, ed. B. Houlihan, 284–304. London: Sage.

Beck, U. 2000. *What Is Globalisation?* Cambridge, UK: Polity Press.

Bourdieu, P. 1998. *Acts of Resistance: Against the Tyranny of the Market.* New York: New Press.

Bourdieu, P., and L. Wacquant. 2001. "Neoliberal Speak: Notes on the New Planetary Vulgate." *Radical Philosophy* 105:2–5.

Brenner, N., and N. Theodore. 2002a. "Cities and the Geographies of 'Actually Existing Neoliberalism.'" *Antipode* 34 (3): 349–379.

——. 2002b. "Preface: From the New Localism to the Spaces of Neoliberalism." *Antipode* 34 (3): 341–347.

Bullard, R. D. 1996. *Unequal Protection: Environmental Justice and Communities of Color.* San Francisco: Sierra Club Books.

"Bush: Moves Made to 'Preserve Free Market.'" 2008. *Wall Street Journal*, October 14. Available at http://blogs.wsj.com/washwire/2008/10/14/bush-moves-made-to-pre serve-free-market/.

Couldry, N. 2008. "Reality TV or the Secret Theatre of Neoliberalism." *Review of Education, Pedagogy, and Cultural Studies* 30 (1): 3–13.

Denzin, N. 2006. "Katrina and the Collapse of Civil Society in New Orleans." *Space and Culture* 9 (1): 95–99.

Denzin, N., and M. Giardina, eds. 2006. *Qualitative Inquiry and the Conservative Challenge.* Walnut Creek, CA: Left Coast Press.

Denzin, N. K., and Y. S. Lincoln. 2003. *9/11 in American Culture.* Lanham, MD: Altamira Press.

Dreier, P., J. Mollenkopf, and T. Swanstrom. 2001. *Place Matters: Metropolitics for the Twenty-First Century.* Lawrence: University Press of Kansas.

Falcous, M., and M. Silk. 2005. "Manufacturing Consent: Mediated Sporting Spectacle and the Cultural Politics of the 'War on Terror.'" *International Journal of Media and Cultural Politics* 1 (1): 59–65.

Freshwater, D., and G. Rolfe. 2004. *Deconstructing Evidence-Based Practice.* New York: Routledge.

Frow, J., and M. Morris. 2000. "Cultural Studies." In *Handbook of Qualitative Research*, ed. N. Denzin and Y. Lincoln, 315–346. 2nd ed. Thousand Oaks, CA: Sage.

Giardina, M. 2005. *Sporting Pedagogies: Performing Culture and Identity in the Global Arena.* New York: Lang.

——. 2009. *From Soccer Moms to NASCAR Dads: Sport, Culture, and Politics since 9/11.* Boulder, CO: Paradigm.

Gibson, T. 2006. "New Orleans and the Wisdom of Lived Space." *Space and Culture* 9 (1): 45–47.

Giroux, H. 1994. *Disturbing Pleasures: Learning Popular Culture.* New York: Routledge.

——. 2000a. *Impure Acts: The Practical Politics of Cultural Studies.* New York: Routledge.

——. 2000b. "Public Pedagogy as Cultural Politics: Stuart Hall and the 'Crisis' of Culture." *Cultural Studies* 14 (2): 341–360.

——. 2001a. "Cultural Studies as Performative Politics." *Cultural Studies ↔ Critical Methodologies* 1 (1): 5–23.

——. 2001b. "Private Satisfactions and Public Disorders: 'Fight Club,' Patriarchy, and the Politics of Masculine Violence." *JAC: A Journal of Composition Theory* 21 (1): 1–31.

——. 2003a. *The Abandoned Generation: Democracy beyond the Culture of Fear.* New York: Palgrave.

——. 2003b. *Public Spaces, Private Lives: Democracy beyond 9/11.* Lanham, MD: Rowman and Littlefield.

——. 2004a. "Cultural Studies, Public Pedagogy, and the Responsibility of Intellectuals." *Communication and Critical/Cultural Studies* 1 (1): 59–79.

——. 2004b. *The Terror of Neoliberalism: Authoritarianism and the Eclipse of Democracy.* Boulder, CO: Paradigm.

———. 2004c. "War on Terror: The Militarising of Public Space and Culture in the United States." *Third Text* 18:211–221.

———. 2008. "The Militarization of US Higher Education after 9/11." *Theory, Culture and Society* 25 (5): 56–82.

Giroux, H., and S. Giroux. 2006. "Challenging Neoliberalism's New World Order: The Promise of Critical Pedagogy." *Cultural Studies ↔ Critical Methodologies* 6 (1): 21–32.

Grossberg, L. 1992. *We Gotta Get Out of This Place: Popular Conservatism and Postmodern Culture*. New York: Routledge.

———. 1997. *Bringing It All Back Home: Essays on Cultural Studies*. Durham, NC: Duke University Press.

Hall, S. 1981. "Notes on Deconstructing the Popular." In *People's History and Socialist Theory*, ed. R. Samuel, 21–33. London: Routledge.

———. 1983. "The Great Moving Right Show." In *The Politics of Thatcherism*, ed. S. Hall and M. Jacques, 19–39. London: Lawrence and Wishart.

———. 1989. "The 'First' New Left: Life and Times." In *Out of Apathy: Voices of the New Left Thirty Years On*, ed. Oxford University Socialist Discussion Group, 11–38. London: Verso.

Hardt, M., and A. Negri. 2000. *Empire*. Cambridge: MA: Harvard University Press.

Harvey, D. 1989. *The Condition of Postmodernity: An Inquiry into the Origins of Cultural Change*. Oxford: Blackwell.

———. 2007. "Neoliberalism and the City." *Studies in Social Justice* 1 (1): 2–13.

Hillier, A. 2008. "Childhood Obesity and the Built Environment: Making Technology Part of the Solution Rather Than Part of the Problem." *Annals of the American Academy of Political and Social Science* 61 (5): 56–82.

Hobbs, D., S. Lister, P. Hadfield, S. Winslow, and S. Hall. 2000. "Receiving Shadows: Governance and Liminality in the Night-Time Economy." *British Journal of Sociology* 51 (4): 701–717.

Hogan, J. 2003. "Staging the Nation: Gendered and Ethnicized Discourses of National Identity in Olympic Opening Ceremonies." *Journal of Sport and Social Issues* 27 (2): 100–123.

House, E. R. 2005. "Qualitative Evaluation and Changing Social Policy." In *The Sage Handbook of Qualitative Research*, ed. N. K. Denzin and Y. S. Lincoln, 1069–1082. 3rd ed. Thousand Oaks, CA: Sage.

———. 2006. "Methodological Fundamentalism and the Quest for Control(s)." In *Qualitative Research and the Conservative Challenge*, ed. N. Denzin and M. Giardina, 93–108. Walnut Creek, CA: Left Coast Press.

Jessop, B. 2002. "Liberalism, Neoliberalism, and Urban Governance: A State-Theoretical Perspective." *Antipode* 34 (3): 452–472.

Katz, C. 2001. "Hiding the Target: Social Reproduction in the Privatized Urban Environment." In *Postmodern Geography: Theory and Praxis*, ed. C. Minca, 93–110. Oxford: Blackwell.

Kington, R. S., and H. W. Nickens. 2001. "Racial and Ethnic Differences in Health: Recent Trends, Current Patterns, Future Directions." In *America Becoming: Racial Trends and Their Consequences*, ed. N. J. Smelser, W. J. Wilson, and F. Mitchell, vol. 2, 253–310. Washington, DC: National Academies Press.

Klinenberg, E. 2002. *Heat Wave: A Social Autopsy of Disaster in Chicago*. Chicago: University of Chicago Press.

Leonard, D. 2009. "Young, Black (and Brown) and Don't Give a Fuck: Virtual Gangstas in the Era of State Violence." *Cultural Studies ↔ Critical Methodologies* 9 (2): 248–272.

Lugo-Lugo, C., and M. Bloodsworth-Lugo. 2009. "'Look Out New World, Here We Come'? Race, Racialization, and Sexuality in Four Children's Animated Films by Disney, Pixar, and Dreamworks." *Cultural Studies* ↔ *Critical Methodologies* 9 (2): 166–178.

Molotch, H. 2006. "Death on the Roof: Race and Bureaucratic Failure." *Space and Culture* 9 (1): 31–34.

Murray, S. J., D. Holmes, A. Perron, and G. Rail. 2007. "No Exit? Intellectual Integrity under the Regime of 'Evidence' and 'Best-Practices.'" *Journal of Evaluation in Clinical Practice* 13:512–516.

Murray, S. J., D. Holmes, and G. Rail. 2008. "On the Constitution and Status of 'Evidence' in the Health Sciences." *Journal of Research in Nursing* 13 (4): 272–280.

Newman, J. 2007. "A Detour through 'NASCAR Nation': Ethnographic Articulations of a Neoliberal Sporting Spectacle." *International Review for the Sociology of Sport* 42 (3): 289–308.

O'Riordan, K. 2007. "Technologized Bodies: Virtual Women and Transformations in Understandings of the Body as Natural." In *Physical Culture, Power, and the Body*, ed. J. Hargreaves and P. Vertinsky, 232–253. London: Routledge.

Ouellette, L., and J. Hay. 2008a. *Better Living through Reality TV*. Oxford: Blackwell.

———. 2008b. "Makeover Television, Governmentality and the Good Citizen." *Continuum: Journal of Media and Cultural Studies* 22 (4): 471–484.

Palmer, G. 2003. *Discipline and Liberty Television and Governance*. Manchester, UK: Manchester University Press.

Peck, J. 2003. "Geography and Public Policy: Mapping the Penal State." *Progress in Human Geography* 27 (2): 222–232.

Peck, J., and A. Tickell. 2002. "Neoliberalizing Space." *Antipode* 34 (3): 380–404.

Robbins, C. 2009. "Searching for Politics with Henry Giroux: Through Cultural Studies, Public Pedagogy and the 'Terror of Neoliberalism.'" *Review of Education, Pedagogy, and Cultural Studies* 31 (5): 428–478.

Rose, N. 1999. *Powers of Freedom: Reframing Political Thought*. Cambridge: Cambridge University Press.

———. 2000a. "Community, Citizenship, and the Third Way." *American Behavioral Scientist* 43 (9): 1395–1411.

———. 2000b. "Government and Control." *British Journal of Criminology* 40 (2): 321–339.

Said, E. 1994. *Representations of the Intellectual*. New York: Pantheon.

Sassen, S. 2000. *The Global City: New York, London, Tokyo*. Princeton, NJ: Princeton University Press.

Sheller, M., and J. Urry. 2003. "Mobile Transformations of Public and Private Life." *Theory, Culture and Society* 20 (3): 107–125.

Silk, M., A. Bush, and D. Andrews. 2010. "Contingent Intellectual Amateurism, or, the Problem with Evidence-Based Research." *Journal of Sport and Social Issues* 34 (1): 105–128.

Silk, M., and M. Falcous. 2005. "One Day in September/A Week in February: Mobilizing American (Sporting) Nationalisms." *Sociology of Sport Journal* 22 (4): 447–471.

Soja, E. 2000. *Postmetropolis: Critical Studies of Cities and Regions*. Oxford: Blackwell.

Squires, G. D., and C. E. Kubrin. 2005. "Privileged Places: Race, Uneven Development and the Geography of Opportunity in Urban America." *Urban Studies* 42 (1): 47–68.

Steinmetz, G, 2003. "The State of Emergency and the Revival of American Imperialism: Toward an Authoritarian Post-Fordism." *Public Culture* 15 (2): 323–346.

Tisdall, S. 2009. "Obama Is Losing a Battle He Doesn't Know He's In." *The Guardian*, January 4. Available at http://www.guardian.co.uk/commentisfree/2009/jan/04/obama-gaza-israel.

U.S. Department of Health and Human Services, Centers for Disease Control and Prevention. 2005. *Chartbook on Trends in the Health of Americans.* Hyattsville, MD: National Center for Health Statistics. Available at http://www.cdc.gov/nchs/data/hus/hus05.pdf.

Vavrus, M. 2007. "The Politics of NASCAR Dads: Branded Media Paternity." *Critical Studies in Communication* 24 (3): 245–261.

Wacquant, L. 2009. *Punishing the Poor: The Neoliberal Government of Social Insecurity.* Durham, NC: Duke University Press.

White, R., M. Silk, and D. Andrews. 2008. "Revisiting the Networked Production of the 2003 Little League World Series: Narrative of American Innocence." *International Journal of Media and Cultural Politics* 4 (2): 183–202.

Wilson, W. 1987. *The Truly Disadvantaged: The Inner City, the Underclass, and Public Policy.* Chicago: University of Chicago Press.

I

Structures, Formations, and Mechanics of Neoliberalism

2

A Distorted Playing Field

Neoliberalism and Sport through the Lens of Economic Citizenship

TOBY MILLER

Neo-liberalism is not Adam Smith; neo-liberalism is not
market society, neo-liberalism is not the Gulag on the
insidious scale of capitalism . . . but . . . taking the formal
principles of a market economy and . . . projecting them
on to a general act of government.
    —MICHEL FOUCAULT, *The Birth of Biopolitics*

Neoliberalism was one of the most successful attempts to reshape individuals in human history. Its achievements rank alongside such productive and destructive sectarian practices as state socialism, colonialism, nationalism, and religion. Neoliberalism's lust for market regulation was so powerful that its prelates opined on every topic imaginable, from birth rates to divorce, from suicide to abortion, from performance-enhancing drugs to altruism. Rhetorically, it stood against elitism (for populism), against subvention (for markets), and against public service (for philanthropy) (Hall and Massey 2010; Gorbachev 2009).

Neoliberalism's "whole way of being and thinking" (Foucault 2008, 218) was promoted by an elect who knew everything and spared no one their analyses and prescriptions. Many of us looked on, bemused, as neoclassical economists denounced or ignored work done by sociologists, anthropologists, and historians while promoting their own capacity to comprehend the totality of human life without reference to class, gender, race, culture, ideology, or collective identity, other than as acts of individual rationality. Given the fervor accompanying this extraordinary self-appointed claim to omniscience and omnipotence, it comes as no surprise that economics has a religious origin. When the Trinity was being ideologized within Christianity, something had to be done to legitimize the concept at the same time as dismissing and decrying polytheistic and pagan rivals to the new religion's moralistic monotheism. Hence *oikonomia*, a sphere of worldly arrangements that was to be directed by a physical presence on Earth representing theology's principal superstition, the deity. God gave Christ "the economy" to manage, so "the economy" manifested Christianity (Agamben 2009, 9–10).

Neoliberalism sought to create "an enterprise society" (Foucault 2008, 218) through the pretense that the latter was a natural (albeit never-achieved) state of affairs. Paradoxically, this attempt flourished by imposing competition as a framework to regulate everyday life through the most subtly comprehensive statism imaginable (Foucault 2008, 145). Michel Foucault's recently translated (2008) insights on neoliberalism's birth in the 1970s provide "a way of thinking about this problem before it became actual," before it "ruined people's lives and wrecked social, political and economic institutions" (Tribe 2009, 694). Foucault did not simply equate the concept with a stage of economic development; nor did he fall for the canard that it sought to withdraw the state from economic activity. Rather, he explained that neoliberalism governed populations through market imperatives, invoking and training them as ratiocinative liberal actors. Today, even though neoliberalism is "on the ropes" after suffering multiple blows to the head from the global financial crisis, its legacy as a mode of thought and practice remains powerful.

It seems to me that the neoliberal right won many struggles enacted over culture, sometimes in concert with the new right of cultural studies—the prelates of creative industries and their doctrine of "prosumption"—and sometimes in concert with conservatives, when making nationalism into a cultural and commercial norm (Ritzer and Jurgenson 2010). This was possible because while there are superficial differences between a collectivist ethos and individualistic utilitarianism, they share the precept that ethico-aesthetic exercises are necessary to develop responsible individuals, amenable to both niche cultural commodification and self-governance. Neoliberalism ultimately sank under the weight of these contradictions, buried beneath its own blend of individuation and authoritarianism. The wealthy world descended into an ongoing economic crisis in 2008, via the delayed disasters of derivatives deregulation and the New International Division of Labor. The result has forced the clerisy, from Beijing to the Bourse, to pick over the social ruins they had overseen. But even as its wreckage is everywhere to be seen, neoliberal ideology continues to bob about and hinder reform. Sport is its most spectacular embodiment, through the dual fetish of competition and control, individualism and government.

The backdrop to neoliberalism was the anthropomorphization of the economy and the intensification of globalization via a global division of labor, regional trading blocs, globally oriented cities, and an antilabor ethos of deregulation. Such developments made the market "a 'test,' a locus of privileged experience" that could "identify the effects of excessive governmentality" (Foucault 1997, 76). Neoliberalism provided more than "a political alternative" to mixed-market social welfare. Its singular triumph over thirty years was to sustain a "many-sided, ambiguous, global claim with a foothold in both the right and the left" (Foucault 2008, 218) through a seeming rejection of tyranny and promotion of transparency.

The neoliberal clerisy enlisted philosophical liberals and conservatives alike by opposing labor and welfare, remaining agnostic about elections other than when governmental outlays were at stake, and maintaining that individuals could govern themselves (Newell 2001; Miller 1993). Citizenship was said to entail "voluntary actions of the people in managing their lives" (Vigoda and Golembiewski 2001, 274). The paradox claimed by neoliberal mavens at the *Economist* was that the "standard of living people in the West enjoy today is due to little else but the selfish pursuit of profit" because of the paradoxical way that struggle binds groups together in mutual dependency ("The Good Company" 2005).

In what follows, I offer a history of neoliberalism in general terms, with particular reference to its almost-identical twin in sport. The terrible twosome shared a mutually supportive lexicon that legitimated each half of the pair via such powerful clichés as "level playing field," "fair play," "moving the goalposts," "take a good look at yourself," "respect the ref," "the gaffer/coach is in charge," "the best side won today," "we just weren't competitive," and "you'll have to talk to my agent." This chapter looks at the political-economic and philosophical underpinnings of economic citizenship, which became the core of neoliberalism, and draws links to the field of play, arguing that the apparent desire to shrink the state and remove it from everyday life is not what neoliberalism was really about. I conclude with a proposal for dealing with the detritus of neoliberalism's hegemonic status through revived, revised discourses of economic citizenship and human rights as wedges against the tumult of sporting capitalism.

Economic Citizenship

Economic citizenship has been alive for a long time, via the collection and dissemination of information about the public through the census and related numerical devices. Such governmental action became an interventionist category following what Karl Polanyi (2001) called "the discovery of society"—the nineteenth-century transformation of capitalism when paupers came to be marked as part of the social, and hence deserving of aid and inclusion, critique and exclusion. Their well-being was incorporated into collective subjectivity as a right, a problem, a statistic, and a law, juxtaposed to the self-governing worker or owner. The positive side of this statistical pauperization, when merged with class activism and philanthropic moralism, was that society was held to be simultaneously more and less than the promises and precepts of the market. Along came public education, mothers' pensions, and U.S. Civil War benefits (Miller 2007).

Welfarist economic citizenship really took off in the Global North during the Depression and in the Global South during decolonization. It addressed employment, health, and retirement security through the redistribution of capitalist gains, at the same time as the state assisted capitalist innovation in areas of market malfunction. For instance, the great task of the New Deal was "to find through government the instrument of our united purpose" against "blind economic forces and blindly selfish men," via "a new chapter in our book of self government" that would "make every American citizen the subject of his country's interest and concern" (Roosevelt 1937). This governmentality took the form of guaranteeing rights and investing in capacities. In World War II, the state effectively said, "We are asking you to get yourselves killed, but we promise you that when you have done this, you will keep your jobs until the end of your lives" (Foucault 2008, 216).

From that moment, two historic promises were made by established and emergent governments: to secure the political sovereignty and economic welfare of citizens. Universal sovereignty required concerted international action to convince the extant colonial powers that the peoples whom they had enslaved should be accorded self-determination, with nationalism a powerful ideology of political mobilization as a supposed precursor to liberation. When this promise was made good, the resulting postcolonial governments undertook to deliver on the economy. Economic welfare seemed locally deliverable, via state-based management of supply and demand and the creation of industries that would substitute imports with domestically produced items. Most followed capitalism in one country, known as import-substitution industrialization (ISI), frequently via state enterprises or on the coattails of multinational corporations that established local presences (Miller 2007).

Economic citizenship also popularized the notion of "the economy." English-language media references to it as a living subject, with needs and desires, derive from coverage of the Depression. Press attention shifted at that time from relations between producers and consumers of goods (a labor-process discourse of the popular newspapers) and onto relations between different material products of labor, with a similar change in emphasis from use-value to exchange-value. The discursive commodities "the economy" and "the market" were given life and value first through being textualized and then through being fetishized as empirical realities (Emmison 1983; Emmison and McHoul 1987). In other words, with the crisis of the 1930s and the diffusion of Keynesianism, "the economy" entered popular knowledge. It referred to actual material practices but, like all statistical forms, textualized interests and conflicts. The discursive framework "the economy" came to be theorized anthropomorphically as a being, complete with needs and emotions. This invention was *constructed* rather than merely *described* by economics (Arminen 2010).

As we shall see, neoliberalism relied on a double movement: once the economy became a person, people became consumers. The first of these prerequisites was met at this early stage. For Keynesian retextualization ultimately led, along with the microeconomic ideology that displaced it, to twenty-first-century derivative instruments—the inevitable outcome of the mathematicization of economics and its seduction of and by capital.

Neoliberalism's Advent

For decades after Keynes's intervention, economic citizenship was turned on its head through historic policy renegotiations conducted by capital, the state, and their rent-seeking intellectual servants in political science and economics.

Foucault focuses on prominent 1970s coin-operated think tanks such as the American Enterprise Institute. These intellectual hand-servants of neoliberalism mounted a "permanent criticism of government policy" (Foucault 2008, 247). Anxieties over unemployment trumped anxieties over profits, labor pieties displaced capital pieties, and workers identified as stakeholders in business or as consumers, rather than as combatants with capital. The prior achievements of Keynesian reconstruction became logocentrically interdependent yardsticks against which neoliberalism measured its success. As each welfare program was unraveled in the name of privatization and deregulation, a paradox unfurled: neoliberalism revealed itself to be both at the heart of state projects *and* their severest critic (Foucault 2008, 217).

There had always been a negative aspect to the pauperization explained by Polanyi, because it forged an enduring nexus between poverty and crime. Now, that production was used to criminalize the poor and justify ongoing inequality as a result of their failure to invest appropriately in human capital (Venn 2009, 208, 221). This produced successive moral panics about domestic and global security. At the micro level within the Global North, statistics about theft and violence were articulated to statistics about immigration and indigence. When Britain's neoliberal prime minister Margaret Thatcher countered Polanyi in the 1980s, claiming there was no such thing as "society" (Keay 1987), her remark signified a massive shift toward legitimizing not the poor but the wealthy. The market became "the interface of government and the individual" (Foucault 2008, 253). Each person was intelligible through the precepts of selfishness, a ratiocinative liberal actor who could be governed through market imperatives.

Associated reforms redistributed income back to bourgeoisies and metropoles. Corporations became privileged economic citizens, with individual citizens conceived of as self-governing consumers. The neoliberal trend may have reached its rhetorical apogee when Vicente Fox, the president of Mexico from 2000 to 2006, challenged reporters who were querying the record of neoliberalism with "*¿Yo por qué? . . . ¿Qué no somos 100 millones de mexicanos?* [Why ask me? . . . Aren't there 100 million other Mexicans?]" (quoted in Venegas 2003). In other words, each person must assume responsibility for his or her material fortunes. The fact that not every one of the other hundred million Mexicans exercised control over the country's money supply, tariff policy, trade, labor law, and exchange rate might have given him pause. Similarly, George W. Bush's presidential mantra was "making every citizen an agent of his or her own destiny" (quoted in Miller 2007).

At the macro level across the third world, postcolonial states suffered underdevelopment in the 1970s and 1980s because of their dependent relations with the core and were unable to grow economically. Public-private partnerships intervened to destabilize threats to U.S. economic dominance, via clandestine and overt funding and advice from agencies such as the perversely named National Endowment for Democracy and "economic hit men," who tied developing countries to antisocialist politics, improbable infrastructural investments, and colossal debt regimes (Perkins 2004). Formal *political* postcoloniality rarely became *economic*, apart from some Asian states that pursued permanent capitalism. Export-oriented industrialization (EOI) and service-based expansion drew on authoritarian control and favorable trading deals in exchange for cold war docility and collusion. After the capitalist economic crises of the 1970s, even Western states that had bourgeoisies with sufficient capital formation to permit a welfare system found that stagflation undermined their capacity to hedge employment against inflation. They selectively turned away from ISI and required less-developed countries to do the same. Development policies of the 1950s and 1960s were problematized and dismantled from the 1970s, a tendency that grew in velocity and scope with the erosion of state socialism (Miller 2007).

Financial and managerial decisions made in one part of the world increasingly took rapid effect elsewhere. New international currency markets proliferated with the demise of a fixed exchange rate, matching regulated systems with piratical financial institutions that crossed borders. Speculation brought greater rewards than production, as the trade in securities and debts outstripped profits from selling cars or building houses. The world circulation of money created the conditions for imposing international creditworthiness tests on all countries. With productive investment less profitable than financial investment, marketing, labor, and administration were reconceived on an international scale. Of course, these neoliberal positions remained highly contingent. When it suited U.S. steel or farm subsidies, market moralists became unrepentant protectionists, and corporate welfare thrived, while the dread work of imperialism saw public subvention of entire "private" industries such as those of aerospace and telecommunications. But the notion of indoctrinating citizens into the dogma of self-governance continued regardless.

The corollary was that national governments in the Global South could not guarantee the economic well-being of their citizens. The loan-granting power of the World Bank and the International Monetary Fund forced a shift away from the local provision of basic needs, redirecting public investment toward sectors supposedly endowed with comparative advantage. Neoliberalism did not offer an end to center-periphery inequalities, competition between states, or macro decision making by corporations; it just cut the capacity of the state system to control such transactions and relegated responsibility for the protection and welfare of the workforce to multinational corporate entities and financial institutions. Even in the Global North, the state fell under constant critique, its legitimacy whittled away other than as a regulator and a site for endowing people with skills. For example, in 1996, Bill Clinton outlined five key policy precepts: a family orientation for workers, health care and retirement systems, safety on the job, training for productivity, and employee participation (Hemphill 2004, 343–344). The idea was to endow the population with capacities by investing in their human capital in a way that would feed markets and provide vestigial but diminished welfare provision.

To repeat, the grand paradox of neoliberalism was its passion for intervention in the name of nonintervention. It pleaded for investments in human

capital at the same time as it derided social engineering. It called for the generation of more and more markets by the state while insisting on fewer and fewer
democratic controls. It hailed freedom as a natural basis for life that could
function only with the heavy hand of policing by government to administer
property relations. Neoliberalism said that it freed the disabled from confine-
ment, encouraged new subjectivities, rewarded intellect and competitiveness,
linked people across cultures, and allowed billions of flowers to bloom in a
postpolitical cornucopia. It was a kind of Marxist/Godardian wet dream, where
people fished, filmed, fucked, and financed from morning to midnight under
the duplicitous signage of laissez-faire. Nothing could be left outside the market, and nothing left to the chance that market relations might falter without
massive policing.

Sporting Neoliberalism

The notion of consumption was turned on its head by neoliberalism. Everyone
was creative; no one was simply a spectator. Sporting fans were manufacturing pleasure from activities they had paid to watch. When you sat in Yankee
Stadium, you were making the game happen. Internally divided—but happily
so—you were "a consumer on the one hand, but . . . also a producer" (Foucault
2008, 226). Neoliberalism deployed the notion of individual investment in human capital through aptitude, choice, and training to explain sporting prowess
and organization. The dominant logic asked "how the person uses the means
available to him" (Foucault 2008, 223).

Was this an accurate account? Figurational and Marxist-Foucauldian studies of athletic migrants (Maguire 1999, 2005; Miller et al. 2001, 2003) suggest
otherwise. A small labor aristocracy experiences genuine class mobility, underpinned by a huge reserve army of labor and ancillary workers, each subject to
massive exploitation.

It is significant that Foucault's 1970s lectures on neoliberalism were close
partners with his investigations of how colonialism remade Europe by pauper-
izing the rest of the world (2003, 2007). Association football (soccer) is the major site of labor mobility in sport, because its media audience promises huge
global revenue. Footballers move in accordance with several factor endow-
ments, beyond issues such as talent and money. There is a clear link between
imperial history and job destination in the case of Latin Americans going to
Spain, Portugal, and Italy, or Africans playing in France, while cultural links
draw Scandinavians to Britain (Giulianotti 2002).

Neoliberalism may have become a governing ideology, but it is not a real
description of this phenomenon by contrast with the New International Division of Cultural Labor. And neoliberalism's disciplining drive and dependence
on the state were core, if unacknowledged, features. Hence sport in the United
States is a matter of private initiative *and* team membership, an opponent of
state intervention *and* a beneficiary of tax relief, and a sign of laissez-faire *and* a
dependent of antitrust exemptions and educational largesse.

Neoliberalism's triumphs of deregulation and profit making have reached a fascinating point in cricket. The game's imperial remnants are under erasure now that Indian money runs it. The toppling of international cricket's white Australian chief executive in 2008 was one in a series of moments when racial and international tensions were resolved through Indian hegemony. India's cricket administrators denied TV rights sales in 2007 to the highest bidder, as per the struggle for rights that led to chaos across different fractions of the ruling class in the 1970s in Australia, when media money supplanted old boys' clubs. The response was to set up a rival league (Miller 1989; Gupta 2009).

But that provocation was of minor moment next to private Indian capital's next intervention, undertaken in concert with local administrators. It took the recent English invention of 20/20, whereby the game is quicker than baseball, and set up urban franchises across India via the Indian Premier League (IPL). The IPL used a draft system. Players were bid for as per U.S. pro sports—but as established stars rather than rookies. Cricketers flocked from across the globe to sign up for unprecedented sums (Mehta, Gemmell, and Malcolm 2009).

A poignant subtext surrounded the most expensive player in the first draft, Andrew Symonds. An Afro-Caribbean, Symonds was born in Britain and adopted by teachers who then migrated to Australia. Immediately before the first 20/20 competition in India, he was incensed when an Indian opponent, Harbhajan Singh, allegedly used a racial epithet to describe him during a match in Australia. Harbhajan claimed he was using a non-English word that was not racist. Symonds was attacked in the Indian press for braggadocio and ignorance. The referee found in favor of Symonds, deciding that he had been racially pilloried. That referee was a stalwart of apartheid-era white South African cricket, Mike Procter. In later twists, Harbhajan was suspended for the entire 20/20 season for slapping a teammate on the field and reducing him to tears, while Symonds was dumped after the IPL by the Australian national side during a tour for going fishing rather than practicing before a game against Bangladesh—a sign in each case of poor self-control, inopportune squandering of human capital, and unworthy selfishness ("Harbhajan Singh" 2008).

The IPL is a rush by capital obsessed with conduct as well as profit. It signifies the mixture of an enterprise culture and an audit culture that was typical of neoliberalism's Janus face, at once turned toward liberty and control (Venn 2009, 219). Sport's mix of youthfulness, hypermasculinity, global popularity, commodification, governance, and nationalism exemplified neoliberalism in limit cases such as plundering players from other commitments, then disciplining them for behavioral breaches. But by 2010, the league was under severe stress through terrorism and corruption ("India Steps Up Tax Probe" 2010). Neoliberalism's dual forces—the drive for total control over populations and absolute freedom for capital—were making a perfect storm. Sleeper issues included the unsustainable nature of a draft system without a nursery and management that refused to recognize collective bargaining. What were the implications in terms of the nurturance of young players provided by the longer, less-profitable version of the game? And what would happen to national identification? As usual, neoliberalism had failed to create an infrastructure of any robustness.

Meanwhile, threats were emerging to neoliberal sport's poster child: TV. The idea of an endlessly expanding universe of televised sport, a recession-proof genre that would keep going and going, was resembling a fantasy. Morgan Stanley says the major U.S. television networks lost US$1.3 billion on sport between 2002 and 2006. This led to an expected US$3 billion dollar write-down of the rights they had bought. The U.S. National Football League (NFL) suffered a 13 percent decrease in TV ratings in the five seasons from 1997 to 2002. Because of falling audience numbers, in 2006 Disney exiled *Monday Night Football* from its broadcast network (ABC) to a niche cable channel (ESPN), where it succeeded at a much lower ratings threshold (Miller 2010).

During the first five years of association football's English Premier League, which commenced in 1992, sixty matches were screened per season; by 2006, the number was 138. Games remained popular with viewers, but there were few competitors for rights. The European Commission expressed major concerns about the prospects for new bidders because of price. That opened the way to Setanta, a satellite channel that was moving from Irish pubs around the world to private homes. Between them, Setanta and Sky paid £2.7 billion for national and international rights between 2007 and 2010. With the major rights holders through 2013 being a subsidiary of News Corp, which had manifold debts, and Setanta, which operated under serious financial strictures, and with many teams themselves owned by debtors, the bubble grew tighter yet more tumescent. Then Setanta U.K. and U.S. collapsed, and many teams that were highly geared faced similar futures. More and more mavens and pundits thought the entire sport of football would trip, stumble, and perhaps even fall, as its owners, players, and broadcasters lost capitalization because advertising revenue was diminishing (Miller 2010).

In addition to this crisis of televised sport, we have also witnessed the appalling impact on athletes of sporting capital exploiting pauperization. In the United States, the NFL, notorious for having the weakest, most pliant union among the country's major professional sports, is being exposed for its record of worker health. There is an alarming correlation of NFL careers with poor fitness, early death, substance abuse, depression, obesity, arthritis, neurodegeneration, metabolic syndrome, and cardiovascular mortality (Selden et al. 2009; Wojtys 2009; Amen et al. 2011; Harp 2005; Cottler et al. 2011; National Institute for Occupational Safety and Health 1994; Nack 2001). The science makes the league's vaunted contributions to charities and neurological research (Halchin 2008) look like tokenistic corporate social responsibility of the most brazen kind.

U.S. baseball offers a different model of exploitation in the era of neoliberal globalization. Between 1974 and 1991, the proportion of revenue spent on Major League Baseball (MLB) salaries increased from 17.6 percent to 42.9 percent, because baseball players achieved free agency in 1975, following court and union action. That stimulated the desire to develop players beyond the U.S.

college system in order to cut beginners' compensation. In 1970, fewer than 10 percent of MLB players were born outside the United States; the 2009 season featured 229 players from fifteen nations and territories. That was 28 percent of the total roster: the epitome of internationally competitive, "free" human capital. But as with cricket, what was the infrastructure? This time, it was built to last—but not for the players (Marcano Guevara and Fidler 1999, 517–518; Brown 2005, 1117; "Opening Day Rosters" 2009).

MLB teams set up academies across Latin America in the 1980s that continue today. They sign up young men (defined as age 11 and older) for much less than equivalently gifted players domiciled in the United States. Academy members are outside the U.S. amateur draft's protection of wages and conditions. Teams discourage young boys from attending school and require them to avoid agents (whose bargaining skills have been so important in the domestic arena). The biggest source is the Dominican Republic, with Puerto Rico, Venezuela, and Mexico of increasing importance. MLB teams have thirty academies in the Dominican Republic, where baseball ranks among the top five national industries. Life in the academies is brutish and short, and there are many tragic stories of players destined for the equivalent of a wrecking yard if injuries or talent militate against their success. Rejected in their early twenties, they lack marketable skills (Gmelch 2006; Klein 2006; Marcano Guevara and Fidler 1999).

Conclusion

In Kenya, football is vastly popular with sporting fans. But whereas there are just two world-class soccer stadia, dozens of private golf courses cater to domestic and overseas elites, with further development urged by neoliberal tourism authorities and U.S. aid advisers—the dread work of EOI. This is typical across the Global South. But so are organic movements of resistance to neoliberal sport: Malaysia's Asia-Pacific People's Environmental Network, Thailand's Asian Tourism Network, and the Global Network for Anti–Golf Course Action. The latter has a node in Mexico, where actions by a disgruntled populace in Tepoztlán brought down the entire municipal government a decade ago in reaction against the environmental despoliation of this most atrocious example of land misuse ("Kenya's Golf Courses" 2007; Winter and Dillon 2004; Stolle-McAllister 2004).

So there are alternatives to the hypocrisy of neoliberalism. James Truslow Adams, a Latino who coined the expression "the American Dream" seventy years ago, disparaged a focus on economics that did not consider distribution in the face of "very marked injustice." Echoing the Edwardian Fabian Graham Wallas (1967)—and anticipating Lyndon Johnson—he called for the "Dream" to be made real through a "Great Society" that would elevate the population "not merely economically, but culturally." Adams lit on the Library of Congress as an institution that "exemplifies the dream," because it comes "straight from the heart of democracy"—a public entity that serves the population through freely available knowledge. He quoted an indigent migrant, Mary Antin, who wrote, perched on the steps of the Boston Public Library, that its treasures offered her a "shining future" to go with its own "majestic past" (Adams 1941, 410–411, 413–414, 416–417). During the same period, Wallas's former student Walter Lippmann spoke of "a deep and intricate interdependence" that came with "living in a Great Society" and countered the dehumanizing tendencies of "the incessant and indecisive struggle for domination and survival" (Lippmann 1943, 161, 376).

Half a century later, Bruno Latour thinks that global interdependence generated by life in a risk society may be shifting us "to a time of co-existence," where senses of, and capacities for, historicity and commonality prevail (Latour and Kastrissianakis 2007). Not surprisingly, opinion polls indicate that people across the world do not think capitalism works absent state intervention ("Wide Dissatisfaction with Capitalism" 2009). They recognize that crises are endemic to any system built on selfishness and exploitation.

We need to address economic ideas that come to us through alternative routes to the discredited ones that led to neoliberalism (Ruccio 2008), such as the post-autistic economics movement (http://paecon.net), gender and queer economics (the journal *Feminist Economics*; Jacobsen and Zeller 2007), and postmodern economics (the journals *Rethinking Marxism* and *Review of Radical Political Economics*). In terms of activism, we need an alternative to the antipolitics of neoliberalism.

The discourse of human rights draws on neoliberalism, in that it is traditionally dominated by the bourgeois-individualist ethos of U.S. definitions. But human rights also transcend neoliberalism, thanks to a robust and developing collectivist strain that has been pushed for decades by the Global South's doctrine of basic needs, and is embraced by Amnesty International ("Economic, Social and Cultural Rights," n.d.). Neoliberals are often enchanted by human rights, provided that the discourse stays clear of economic and social issues and firmly inside the third sector. So Kofi Annan and Nelson Mandela trumpet sport's capacity to counter discrimination through hope, merit, universality, peace, justice, and tolerance, at the same time as they accept its corporate and governmental dominance (Donnelly 2008, 382).

It seems to me that sporting progressives can find a tool in human rights that will resist both corporate hegemony and individualistic rhetoric. The 1948 United Nations Declaration of Human Rights guarantees "the right to rest and leisure" and "to participate in the cultural life of the community." Yet conventional competitive sport operates contra many precepts of the declaration. Consider these binaries. Whereas the declaration promotes freedom, equality, and dignity, sport prefers inequality and humiliation; human-rights concerns for safety can be juxtaposed with sport's taste for violence; the declaration's promulgation of open judgment sits poorly alongside sport's preference for closed tribunals of good old boys and plutocrats; calls for freedom of expression and information are opposed to sport's repeated attempts to outlaw political activity by athletes; the declaration's support for freedom of association negates sport's distaste for unions and third-sector activism; and the stress of human rights on education finds uncomfortable *frottage* with sport's desire for teen-aged professionalism and thought control.

The contradictions multiply when one examines the International Covenants on Political, Social and Cultural Rights and Civil and Political Rights (1966), the European Sport for All Charter (1976), UNESCO's International Charter of Physical Education and Sport (1978), the UN's Convention on the Elimination of All Forms of Discrimination against Women (1979) and Convention on the Rights of the Child (1989), the International Olympic Committee's Fundamental Principles (1997), the UN Convention on the Rights of Persons with Disabilities (2008), and successive related UN declarations (1998, 2002, and 2006). Human rights formed the core of black power protests against U.S. racism and imperialism at the 1968 summer Olympics, and the campaign to destabilize apartheid drew crucially on human rights and sport—by 1985, South Africa was effectively isolated from international competition through a UN Convention (United Nations, n.d.; Giulianotti 2004; Giulianotti and McArdle 2006; Donnelly 2008).

We are often told that in addition to being scarred by its individualistic connotations, the discourse on human rights is marked as a concern of the Global North. But in Latin America, human rights have been, and continue to be, a major bulwark against the rightist forces of darkness that tortured and assassinated thousands under U.S. direction in the 1970s and 1980s. Many signatories to the Sports for Peace petition in 2008 that called for human rights in Tibet before the Beijing summer Olympics petition were athletes from the Global South. Of course, the Chinese state denounces all human-rights critics as illegitimate and inaccurate. But this is a new tactic. It is hypocritical in terms of China's own 2004 constitution, the claims made by China to the International Olympic Committee to gain the games, and the state's own history. Until 1989, the government used human-rights discourse freely in propaganda and international fora to argue against imperialism, colonialism, apartheid, Zionism, the American war in Vietnam, the USSR, the United States, capitalism, sexism, racism, and the Kuomintang (Hunter 2009; Amnesty International 2008; Worden 2008).

Reforming sport by drawing on human rights necessitates understanding that "state-phobia" (Foucault 2008, 76) masks a hypergovernmentalization that underpins competition; we can expose the love of discipline that is the Janus face of individual excellence (Foucault 2008, 67). To reveal the calumny, the selfishness, the inequitable outcomes, the lies, and the solipsism that form neo-liberalism's beating heart, we should return, albeit critically and carefully, to the origins of economic citizenship—coupled with a strategic engagement with human rights that emphasizes its collective, economic side as well its individual, political side—and the precarious nature of sporting labor.

REFERENCES

Adams, J. T. 1941. *The Epic of America.* New York: Triangle Books.

Agamben, G. 2009. *What Is an Apparatus?* trans. D. Kishik and S. Pedatella. Stanford, CA: Stanford University Press.

Amen, D. G., J. C. Wu, D. Taylor, and K. Willeumier. 2011. "Reversing Brain Damage in Former NFL Players: Implications for Traumatic Brain Injury and Substance Abuse Rehabilitation." *Journal of Psychoactive Drugs* 43 (1): 1–5.

Amnesty International. 2008. *People's Republic of China: The Olympics Countdown—Broken Promises.* ASA 17/089/2008.

Arminen, I. 2010. "Who's Afraid of Financial Markets?" *International Sociology* 25 (2): 170–183.

Brown, S. F. 2005. "Exceptionalist America: American Sports Fans' Reaction to Internationalization." *International Journal of the History of Sport* 22 (6): 1106–1135.

Cottler, L. B., A. B. Abdallah, S. M. Cummings, J. Barr, R. Banks, and R. Forchheimer. 2011. "Injury, Pain, and Prescription Opioid Use among Former National Football League (NFL) Players." *Drug and Alcohol Dependence* 116 (1–3): 188–194.

Donnelly, P. 2008. "Sport and Human Rights." *Sport in Society* 11 (4): 381–394.

"Economic, Social and Cultural Rights: Access to Justice for All." n.d. Amnesty International. Available at http://amnesty.org/en/economic-social-and-cultural-rights (accessed February 12, 2012).

Emmison, M. 1983. "'The Economy': Its Emergence in Media Discourse." In *Language, Image, Media*, ed. H. Davis and P. Walton, 139–155. Oxford: Blackwell.

Emmison, M, and A. McHoul. 1987. "Drawing on the Economy: Cartoon Discourse and the Production of a Category." *Cultural Studies* 1 (1): 93–111.

Foucault, M. 1997. *Ethics: Subjectivity and Truth: The Essential Works of Foucault 1954–1984*, vol. 1, ed. P. Rabinow, trans. R. Hurley, L. Davis, J. Johnston, J. O'Higgins, B. Lemon, A. Forster, W. Smock, et al. New York: New Press.

———. 2003. *"Society Must Be Defended": Lectures at the Collège de France 1975–1976*, ed. M. Bertani and A. Fontana, trans. David Macey. New York: Picador.

———. 2007. *Security, Territory, Population: Lectures at the Collège de France 1977–1978*, ed. M. Senellart, trans. G. Burchell. Basingstoke, UK: Palgrave.

———. 2008. *The Birth of Biopolitics: Lectures at the Collège de France, 1978–79*, ed. M. Senellart, trans. G. Burchell. Houndmills, UK: Palgrave Macmillan.

Giulianotti, R. 2002. "Soccer Goes Glocal." *Foreign Policy* 131:82–83.

———. 2004. "Human Rights, Globalization and Sentimental Education: The Case of Sport." *Sport in Society* 7 (3): 355–369.

Giulianotti, R., and D. McArdle, eds. 2006. *Sport, Civil Liberties and Human Rights.* London: Taylor and Francis.

Gmelch, G., ed. 2006. *Baseball without Borders: The International Pastime.* Lincoln: University of Nebraska Press.

"The Good Company." 2005. *The Economist*, January 22, 11.

Gorbachev, M. 2009. "Bring Back the State." *New Perspectives Quarterly* (Spring): 53–55.

Gupta, A. 2009. "India and the IPL: Cricket's Globalized Empire." *Round Table* 98 (401): 201–211.

Halchin, L. E. 2008. *Former NFL Players: Disabilities, Benefits, and Related Issues: CSR Report for Congress.* Washington, DC: Congressional Research Service.

Hall, S., and D. Massey. 2010. "Interpreting the Crisis." In *After the Crash: Reinventing the Left in Britain*, ed. R. S. Grayson and J. Rutherford, 37–46. London: Soundings/Social Liberal Forum/Compass.

"Harbhajan Singh Called Andrew Symonds a 'Monkey God.'" 2008. *Courier Mail*, January 6. Available at http://www.couriermail.com.au/sport/cricket/singh-called-him-a-monkey-god/story-e6frepmo-1111115265006.

Harp, J. B. 2005. "Obesity in the National Football League." *Journal of the American Medical Association* 293 (9): 1061–1062.

Hemphill, T. 2004. "Corporate Citizenship: The Case for a New Corporate Governance Model." *Business and Society Review* 109 (3): 339–361.

Hunter, A. 2009. "Soft Power: China on the Global Stage." *Chinese Journal of International Politics* 2:373–398.

"India Steps Up Tax Probe into IPL Corruption." 2010. BBC.com, April 21. Available at http://news.bbc.co.uk/2/hi/south_asia/8633923.stm.

Jacobsen, J., and A. Zeller, eds. 2007. *Queer Economics: A Reader*. London: Routledge.

Keay, D. 1987. "AIDS, Education and the Year 2000!" Interview with Margaret Thatcher. *Woman's Own*, October 31, 8–10.

"Kenya's Golf Courses: A Threat to the Environment?" 2007. *Kenvironews*, August 21. Available at http://kenvironews.wordpress.com/2007/08/21/kenya%E2%80%99s-golf-courses-a-threat-to-the-environment/.

Klein, A. M. 2006. *Growing the Game: The Globalization of Major League Baseball*. New Haven, CT: Yale University Press.

Latour, B., with K. Kastrissianakis. 2007. "We Are All Reactionaries Today." *Re-Public: Re-Imagining Democracy*, March 22. Available at http://www.re-public.gr/en/?p=129.

Lippmann, W. 1943. *The Good Society*. New York: Grosset and Dunlap.

Maguire, J. 1999. *Global Sport: Identities, Societies, Civilizations*. Cambridge, UK: Polity Press.

———. 2005. *Power and Global Sport: Zones of Prestige, Emulation and Resistance*. London: Routledge.

Marcano Guevara, A. J., and D. P. Fidler. 1999. "The Globalization of Baseball: Major League Baseball and the Mistreatment of Latin American Baseball Talent." *Indiana Journal of Global Legal Studies* 6:511–577.

Mehta, N., J. Gemmell, and D. Malcolm. 2009. "'Bombay Sport Exchange': Cricket, Globalization and the Future." *Sport in Society* 12 (4–5): 694–707.

Miller, T. 1989. "World Series Sound and Vision." *Meanjin* 48 (3): 591–596.

———. 1993. *The Well-Tempered Self: Citizenship, Culture, and the Postmodern Subject*. Baltimore: Johns Hopkins University Press.

———. 2007. *Cultural Citizenship: Cosmopolitanism, Consumerism, and Television in a Neoliberal Age*. Philadelphia: Temple University Press.

———. 2010. *Television Studies: The Basics*. London: Routledge.

Miller, T., G. Lawrence, J. McKay, and D. Rowe. 2001. *Globalization and Sport: Playing the World*. London: Sage.

———. 2003. "The Over-Production of US Sports and the New International Division of Cultural Labor." *International Review for the Sociology of Sport* 38 (4): 427–440.

Nack, W. 2001. "The Wrecking Yard." *Sports Illustrated*, May 7. Available at http://sportsillustrated.cnn.com/si_online/news/2002/09/11/wrecking_yard.

National Institute for Occupational Safety and Health. 1994. *NFL Mortality Study*. Washington, DC: U.S. Department of Health and Human Services.

Newell, P. 2001. "Environmental NGOs, TNCs, and the Question of Governance." In *The International Political Economy of the Environment: Critical Perspectives*, ed. D. Stevis and V. J. Assetto, 85–107. Boulder, CO: Rienner.

"Opening Day Rosters Feature 229 Players Born outside the U.S." 2009. MLB.com, April 6. Available at http://mlb.com/news/press_releases/press_release.jsp?ymd=20090406 &content_id=4139614&vkey=pr_mlb&fext=.jsp&c_id=mlb.

Perkins, J. 2004. *Confessions of an Economic Hit Man*. San Francisco: Berrett-Koehler.

Polanyi, K. 2001. *The Great Transformation: The Political and Economic Origins of Our Time*. Boston: Beacon Press.

Ritzer, G., and N. Jurgenson. 2010. "Production, Consumption, Prosumption: The Nature of Capitalism in the Age of the Digital 'Prosumer.'" *Journal of Consumer Culture* 10 (1): 13–36.

Roosevelt, F. D. 1937. "Second Inaugural Address." January 20. Available at http://www.bartleby.com/124/pres50.html.

Ruccio, D. F., ed. 2008. *Economic Representations: Academic and Everyday*. London: Routledge.

Selden, M. A., J. H. Helzberg, J. F. Waeckerle, J. E. Browne, J. H. Brewer, M. E. Monaco, F. Tang, and J. H. O'Keefe. 2009. "Cardiometabolic Abnormalities in Current National Football League Players." *American Journal of Cardiology* 103 (7): 969–971.

Stolle-McAllister, J. 2004. "Contingent Hybridity: The Cultural Politics of Tepoztlán's Anti-Golf Movement." *Identities: Global Studies in Culture and Power* 11 (2): 195–213.

Tribe, K. 2009. "The Political Economy of Modernity: Foucault's Collège de France Lectures of 1978 and 1979." *Economy and Society* 38 (4): 679–698.

United Nations. n.d. "UN Conventions." Available at http://un.org/wcm/content/site/sport/home/resourcecenter/conventions (accessed February 12, 2012).

Venegas, J. M. 2003. "¿Yo por Qué?, Insiste Fox; ¿Qué No Somos 100 Millones de Mexicanos?" *La Jornada: Politica*, August 2, 3.

Venn, C. 2009. "Neoliberal Political Economy, Biopolitics and Colonialism: A Transcolonial Genealogy of Inequality." *Theory, Culture and Society* 26 (6): 206–233.

Vigoda, E., and R. T. Golembiewski. 2001. "Citizenship Behavior and the Spirit of New Managerialism: A Theoretical Framework and Challenge for Governance." *American Review of Public Administration* 31 (3): 273–295.

Wallas, G. 1967. *The Great Society: A Psychological Analysis*. Lincoln: University of Nebraska Press.

"Wide Dissatisfaction with Capitalism—Twenty Years after Fall of Berlin Wall." 2009. BBC World Service, November 9. Available at http://globescan.com/news_archives/bbc2009_berlin_wall.

Winter, J. G., and P. J. Dillon. 2004. "Effects of Golf Course Construction and Operation on Water Chemistry of Headwater Streams on the Precambrian Shield." *Environmental Pollution* 133 (2): 243–253.

Wojtys, E. M. 2009. "Big Hits." *Sports Health: A Multidisciplinary Approach* 1 (6): 459.

Worden, M., ed. 2008. *China's Great Leap: The Beijing Games and Olympian Human Rights Challenges*. New York: Seven Stories Press.

3

Advanced Liberal Government, Sport Policy, and "Building the Active Citizen"

MICK GREEN

Following a period of sustained economic growth and vitality during which most of us living in developed nations experienced some of the fruits of (virtually) unregulated capitalism and neoliberal free-market thinking, and during which a minority enjoyed very large financial rewards for their work in the banking and financial sectors, we are now facing a rather gloomier set of circumstances: economic downturn, a "credit crunch," real concerns about homes and negative equity, reduced opportunities for employment, and ultimately exclusion from the "good life" so easily promised by politicians of different persuasions. Since the early 1970s, the broad thrust and predominance of neoliberal politics swept across much of the Western world and beyond (Harvey 2007; Powell 2007). Such ideas had greatest impact in the United Kingdom and the United States, where they were articulated in, and embedded by, the New Right Conservative policies of Prime Minister Margaret Thatcher and in the so-called "Reaganomics" of President Ronald Reagan, respectively. While the rise of neoliberalism as "a global narrative of development" (Powell 2007, 1) provides the social and political backdrop to this chapter, the Anglo-Foucauldian writings that draw on Foucault's account of "governmentality" (Dean 1999, 2007; Miller and Rose 2008; Rose 1999) are used to help us make sense of some of the changes occurring in the ways in which we are governed in the early twenty-first century. Specifically, in this chapter, we concentrate on what has been termed "advanced liberalism"[1] (Dean 1999, 209; see also Rose 1993), and especially on some of the ramifications of this mode of governing for sport policy in the United Kingdom.

New Labour's election victory in 1997 ended eighteen years of Conservative rule in the United Kingdom. It also announced the emergence of Third Way[2] politics and the construction of a new social welfare policy architecture. In line with these developments, a number of writers (e.g., Dobrowolsky 2002; Dobrowolsky and Jenson 2005; Dobrowolsky and Lister 2008; Featherstone 2006;

Jenson 2005; Jenson and Saint-Martin 2003, 2006; Lister 2003, 2004) provide insights into and critiques of Anthony Giddens's (1998) articulation of a "social investment state" and the valorization of the "active citizen." Recently, Giddens has argued that this amounts to "State-provided or regulated investments in human or social capital" (2007, xiii). Although Giddens played a prominent role in communicating to New Labour the salience of Third Way politics and social investment strategies, the antecedents of the party's embrace of social investment thinking can be traced back to the truncated leadership of the late John Smith and the report by the Commission on Social Justice (CSJ) in 1992. The CSJ (1994) report "advanced now familiar policy positions that shaped the identity of New Labour" (Dobrowolsky and Jenson 2005, 207). Spending on programs for employment rather than welfare, lifelong learning, the comple-mentarity of economic and social policy, and a child focus for social investment have all been identified with New Labour policy positions.

The idea of the social investment state, then, has been used "to capture a politics in which future welfare costs are to be contained through the focus-ing and targeting of social investment" (Newman and McKee 2005, 658). Run-ning through these developments, over the past decade or so a modernizing program of political and policy reform has been at the heart of "New Labour's social and political project" (Finlayson 2003, 66). For the purposes of this chap-ter, an important strand of this project is "the constitution of new subjects— self-reliant and responsible, moral and familial, community-centred and at the same time seeking new opportunities for themselves as individuals" (Newman 2001, 143): in short, the building of the "active citizen." From a governmentality perspective, this line of thinking echoes Rose's (1999, 154) elaboration of one vector of governing under advanced liberalism—namely, "autonomisation plus responsibilisation" (see also Dean 1999; Watson 2000). Or, as the leader of the Labour Party, Tony Blair, put it before his electoral victory in 1997, "The rights we receive should reflect the duties we owe. With the power should come the responsibility" (1995, 5).

Against this complex and dynamic sociopolitical landscape, academic analyses have interrogated particular developments and distinct issues in the government's key social welfare policy-related sectors (and subsectors) of ed-ucation (Dobrowolsky and Jenson 2005), citizenship (Dwyer 1998), the fam-ily (Featherstone 2006), health, and poverty/employment (Jenson 2005; Lister 2004). However, an account of the ways in which the political salience of sport policy has emerged, since 1997, as a key contributor to New Labour's social in-vestment strategies is notable by its absence. This chapter's primary objective, therefore, is to interrogate and register the growing significance of sport policy interventions for the construction of a social investment state under conditions of advanced liberalism. In so doing, the literature about governmentality is drawn on to inform the analysis of the place of sport policy in New Labour's ongoing configuration of a social investment state and to examine the argu-ment that the latter is characterized by a "double-sided nature . . . it can be facilitative but also regulatory and coercive" (Dobrowolsky 2002, 57; see also

Dobrowolsky and Lister 2008). Importantly, given New Labour's rhetoric of joined-up policy development that cross-cuts hard-to-break-down major departmental boundaries, sport policy interventions traverse sectors/issues such as education, health, crime, social inclusion, social cohesion, and citizenship (Collins and Kay 2003).

Few would now dispute the view that sport policy now matters in ways in which it never mattered in the past and, crucially, that it matters at the highest political levels. As the then prime minister Tony Blair stated in a foreword to *Game Plan*, a major government review of sport policy and structures in the United Kingdom, "Sport is a powerful and often under-used tool that can help Government to achieve a number of ambitious goals" (quoted in Department for Culture, Media and Sport [DCMS]/Strategy Unit 2002, 5). Blair noted the large amount of financial resources allocated for the realization of these ambitions: "Over £2bn of money from Government and the Lottery will be going into sport over the next three years. This is more than ever before" (5). Blair also highlighted children as a key policy target: "We have prioritised young people, and committed ourselves to ensuring that, by 2005, at least 75% of children will have the chance to participate in two hours of high quality sport and PE [physical education] every week" (5). This target was increased to 85 percent by 2008 and "was met a year early, with 86% doing at least 2 hours in 2006/07" (DCMS 2008, 10). School sport, PE, and physical activity more generally are therefore clearly areas that Tony Blair and his successor, Gordon Brown, have endorsed as having the capacity to achieve not only key educational objectives—New Labour's paramount policy priority (Bache 2003)—but also policy objectives in important domains such as health, crime, and social inclusion (DCMS/Strategy Unit 2002).

Space precludes analysis of the broad range of governmental objectives to which sport policy is now being applied. Instead, we concentrate on an investigation of the ways in which sport policy is being utilized in the key policy sectors of education and health, both of which are cornerstones of New Labour's social investment strategies (Dobrowolsky and Jenson 2005). For example, promoting healthier communities and tackling health inequalities is a shared priority of local, regional, and national governmental authorities across the United Kingdom (Sport England 2006c). The "growing epidemic of obesity" (Department of Health [DoH] 2004, iii; see also DoH 2002) is at the heart of these governmental concerns. More important, perhaps, for this chapter, is the acknowledgment by the Chief Medical Officer that a "major focus on the health gains that could be achieved through increased participation in [sport] and physical activity" is currently "receiving serious attention" at the highest levels of government (DoH 2004, iv).

The chapter's analysis draws on three empirical studies. The first explored elite (Olympic) sport development and, in particular, policy change in Australia, Canada, and the United Kingdom (Green and Houlihan 2005). The second provided an account of the changing status of school sport and PE in England and Wales (Houlihan and Green 2006). The third study reviewed and analyzed the (potential) consequences of New Labour's modernizing agenda for Sport England[3] and UK Sport[4] (Houlihan and Green 2008). These studies did not set out to engage, specifically, with the relationship between sport policy and the construction of a social investment state. However, evidence from all three studies reveals that there is a relationship, and an interrogation of that relationship is the main objective of this analysis.

The next section of this chapter provides a brief account of the broader context of governing under advanced liberalism within which ideas about the social investment state have gained prominence in the United Kingdom; the literature about governmentality informs this section. The subsequent section outlines the key characteristics of and developments in the construction of a social investment state in the United Kingdom and analyzes the ways in which sport and physical activity policies are contributing to these developments. The conclusions reflect on the salience of the theoretical insights discussed throughout in relation to the increasingly instrumental ways in which sport and physical activity programs have emerged as salient mechanisms through which New Labour "delivers" on its most pressing social welfare policy objectives.

Advanced Liberal Government

The Political Context

The broader political landscape against which analyses of the emergence of social investment strategies in the United Kingdom (and elsewhere, notably Canada and Australia) are grounded is the decline over the past three decades of left-wing Labour parties and the emergence of neoliberal programs of government (Dean and Hindess 1998; Frankel 1997; Newman 2001, 2004; Powell 2007). Indeed, Newman (2001) suggests that New Labour has continued some strands of Conservative reform, such as the emphasis on quality and efficiency and recourse to the tenets of "new public management." However, a key aspect of New Labour's 1997 electoral platform was an attempt to soften "the outright assault on public services" (Newman 2001, 52) that took place under successive Conservative administrations. While the political rationalities of the Thatcher and Major Conservative governments focused on the benefits of competition, New Labour placed greater emphasis on collaborative arrangements both at the level of policy (in the rhetoric of "joined-up" government) and management (building partnerships and strategic alliances across the public, private, and voluntary sectors). Interestingly, as a signpost for the analysis in the next section ("The Rise of Sport Policy in New Labour's Social Investment State"), McDonald's (2005, 594) investigation of governance, partnerships and sport policy found that despite New Labour's program of devolution and regionalization, central government, UK Sport, and the national Sports Councils remain the dominant actors in the sport domain, controlling the agenda and seeking "to influence the behaviours of others accordingly" (see also Green and Houlihan 2006).

In line with the preceding work, writers drawing on Foucault's work on governmentality provide us with useful insights for exploring the emergence of social investment strategies within modes of advanced liberal governing. Rose uses the term *advanced liberalism* to denote shifts in the political rationalities of governments that help in part to explain the emphasis now placed on the close association of economic and social policy: "Social government must be restructured in the name of an economic logic, and economic government must create and sustain the central elements of economic well-being such as the enterprise form and competition" (1999, 141). And, importantly, as Lister notes, one of the key elements of social investment state strategies is an "integration of social and economic policy, but with the former still the 'handmaiden' of the latter" (2004, 160). What marks out this vector of neoliberalism from that promoted in Britain under Margaret Thatcher's New Right Conservative administrations during the 1980s, for Dean (1999) at least, is the representation—by center-left parties such as New Labour—of objectives in terms of "citizenship" and the "active society." Dean also argues that these are "notions which go beyond participation in the market to include participation in other social spheres, including leisure [and thus sport], domestic work, family caring and politics itself" (1999, 163).

Moreover, and perhaps more importantly, this version of "neo-liberalism has given rise to the concept of self-regulated forms of 'governmentality'" (Frankel 1997, 75), which have replaced centralized, statist-bureaucratic forms of government. Analyses along these lines seek to interrogate governmental techniques for "shaping and guiding the behaviour of subjects who, in modern liberal society, are formally free yet still objects of social policy" (Finlayson and Martin 2006, 168). Under this schema, in order to act freely, the subject must first be shaped, guided, and molded into one capable of responsibly exercising that freedom through systems of domination. Here, we have subjection and subjectification overlaid one upon the other. And, as Dean notes, at times these are separated and made relatively autonomous, providing an illusion of agency, for example, "(in practices of self-help and self-development, in the taking up of physical exercise) so that the relations of subjection involved are obscure and distant" (1999, 165). Thus in a whole variety of practices—educational, medical, economic, and sport—"government seeks not to govern society per se, but to promote individual and institutional conduct that is consistent with governmental objectives" (Raco and Imrie 2000, 2191). This is a particular strategy, redolent of advanced liberal democracies, of "government at a distance" (Rose 1999, 49).

Toward Self-Regulation?

Thus "new systems of control" (Finlayson 2003, 94) are emerging "based on the apparent 'empowerment' of subjects to regulate themselves" (Newman 2001, 22). Newman's emphasis on the "apparent" nature of empowerment provides "a sharp contrast with the normative view of the 'self-governing subject' or the 'self-regulating network' as autonomous social agents" (22). The new systems of control incorporate disciplinary practices which seek to "reshape the ways in which each individual, at some point, will conduct him- or herself in a space of regulated freedom" (Rose 1999, 22). Moreover, Rose also suggests that "discipline is constitutively linked to the emergence of new ways of thinking about the tasks of political rule in terms of the government of the conduct of the population" (22). In other words, as Daly argues, for the realization of a socially inclusive society, New Labour promotes modernization "as an end in itself and the impetus of reform is for people [and institutions and organisations] to be active in their own self-government" (2003, 121).

In line with this argument, poststructuralist perspectives on power direct attention to the kinds of knowledge and technologies through which social activity (such as sport) is regulated, and through which actors—in our case institutions, citizens, and parents and young people especially—are constituted as self-disciplining subjects. The comment by Rose and Miller (1992, 174) that "power is not so much a matter of imposing constraints upon citizens as of 'making up' citizens capable of bearing a kind of regulated freedom" provides a valuable perspective from which to make sense of neoliberal-informed and Third Way thought that characterizes political discourse in the United Kingdom (Finlayson 2003). Indeed, Hall argues that Labour's neoliberal New Managerialism privileges "in its moral discourse the values of self-sufficiency, competitiveness and entrepreneurial dynamism" (1998, 11). Rather than the "smaller government" promised by such political thinking (for example, deregulation, privatization, individual autonomy, and new public management) and by the literature on governance that points to self-organizing networks or participatory approaches, such changes can be conceived of as the diffusion of government power across new sites of action within civil society and the "private" sphere (Newman 2004). Government power is enhanced through new strategies and techniques that seek to exert control within these domains without formally undermining their autonomy.

Calculative Technologies

Programs, such as modernization, depict or represent spheres of activity in ways which are essentially self-validating. In this regard, Rose and Miller argue that "they make the objects of government thinkable in such a way that their ills appear susceptible to diagnosis, prescription and cure by calculating and normalising intervention" (1992, 183). Programs are operationalized through the application of various technologies of government including audit, benchmarking, public service agreements, target-setting, and performance reviews and measurement. Audit, for example, is the process of producing auditable objects, a normative commitment that "hardens into the routines of practice a new regulatory common sense" (Power 1997, 138). Lister's (2003, 427) analysis of New Labour's social investment state and the associated prioritization of children as "citizen-workers of the future" rather than "citizen-child[ren] of the present" is pertinent in this respect. Lister argues that "in the target-filled world of the managerial state, education is reduced to a utilitarian achievement-oriented measurement culture of tests and exams, with little attention paid to the actual educational experience" (434).

Lister's critique of these technologies points to potential tensions, and as yet unresolved issues, in the bringing together of (social investment) interventions around education, health, sport, and indeed social inclusion, in order to realize—in large part—*future* health and economic benefits. Schools clearly play an important role in this respect. However, Kay highlights at least one tension in this regard in arguing that "although the present New Labour political rhetoric is of a citizenship based on *social inclusion* with sport at its heart, the very nature of sport is to exclude and eliminate the many until the elite are found" (2003, 7). This critique rests on the argument that, unlike the skill-based focus of coaching, PE teaching is founded on the principle of a pupil-centered rationale. Enhancing performance is clearly important in raising levels of self-esteem but if "performance is the only measure of improvement then, for many, this will damage rather than develop self-esteem" (7). Therefore, as MacPhail, Kirk, and Eley argue, the incentives for young people to participate in sport are diminished "if they are merely there to make up the numbers and later to be discarded while their more talented, and often socially privileged, peers progress" (2003, 69). A disengagement with sport and physical activity is the likely outcome of such a scenario. Paradoxically, given this critique, the reversal of such outcomes was at the heart of New Labour's PE, School Sport and Club Links (PESSCL)[5] strategy, introduced in 2002–2003 (Department for Education and Skills[6] [DfES]/DCMS 2003), and continued in the transition to the new PE and Sport Strategy for Young People (PESSYP), which commenced in January 2008 (Youth Sport Trust [YST] 2008). These strategies and other sport and physical activity programs are interrogated in more depth in the next section.

The net effect of the application of these technologies is to ensure that individuals and organizations—in our case, for example, national governing bodies (NGBs), local authorities, County Sport Partnerships, and schools—are instrumental in their own self-government and engaged in the reflexive monitoring of their actions such that they are able to "account for what they do when asked to do so by others" (Giddens 1995, 35). Thus power is exercised not only by the "ability to demand accounts" (Power 1997, 146) but also in the deep sense of obligation to provide them. The reality of highly constrained choices of both strategy and practice is masked by the illusion of agency, producing what Rose (1999, 154) refers to as a double movement of responsibilization and autonomization. Dobrowolsky's analysis of an emerging social investment state in the United Kingdom is indicative of this argument: "Here the double-sided nature of the social investment state is exposed: it can be facilitative but also regulatory and coercive" (2002, 57).

Yet what remains unsaid here is that running in parallel to New Labour's exhortations for us all to become active, responsible, autonomous citizens is the threat of inspection and the fear of failure. Two examples help to make the point. First, in a statement to announce the government's latest sport strategy—*Playing to Win* (DCMS 2008)—the Secretary of State for Culture, Media and Sport offered the following "advice" to NGBs:

> In return for public money and the new freedom comes responsibility. Governing bodies will be expected to operate to high standards of internal organisation and democracy, ensuring that the voice of all levels and participant groups can be heard. This should be the standard of good governance for the modern governing bodies. School and youth sports centre stage, women and girls' games, and disability sport, not an optional extra, but a vital part of what governing bodies will be required to do. And if any sport does not wish to accept the challenge, funding will be switched to those that do. (Quoted in DCMS 2008, 4)

The second example concerns the implementation of a performance framework—Towards an Excellent Service (TAES)—for sport and recreation services in local authorities. A senior Sport England official captures the prevailing conditions of "demarcated freedom" within which local authorities are currently working:

> [We are] trying to encourage improvement through self-assessment, validate that self-assessment, where self-assessment is validated through peer review. [If a local authority] . . . under-achieves we inspect and where inspection shows it's not delivering, you [local authority] go in special measures and that's the agenda we're running with. (Green 2007b, 62)

In sum, the preceding discussion draws attention to a growing awareness of, interest in, and policies designed for social investment strategies in the United Kingdom over the past decade or so. The political backdrop within which this shift toward social investment strategies has emerged is one that has been termed an advanced liberal mode of government. Characteristic of this mode of government are "activities directed at shaping, channelling, and guiding the conduct of others" (Raco and Imrie 2000, 2189), which provides a valuable perspective from which we can start to make sense of the strong rights and responsibilities agenda in current government policy. With these thoughts in mind, the next section provides a brief overview of the key principles underlying the emergence of a social investment state before interrogating the underacknowledged role that New Labour policies for sport and physical activity are now playing in the realization of these strategies.

The Rise of Sport Policy in New Labour's Social Investment State

Esping-Andersen's (2000) analysis of changing social models of welfare reform across Europe provides a clear statement of the underlying premise on which

New Labour grounded social investment policy development. Esping-Andersen argues that "a revised social model requires a future-oriented perspective, and must therefore focus on those who will become tomorrow's adults" (31). In short, concrete investments in children today will reduce welfare problems among future working adults. Here, social investment ideas are captured in microcosm: a future-oriented focus, the central status of children and young people, and the alignment of economic and social policy goals. In line with this assessment, and in relation to the focus of the chapter, numerous analyses of the social investment state point to not only the significance of investing in children (Jenson and Saint-Martin 2003, 93) in general but also the promotion of healthy lifestyles (Jenson and Saint-Martin 2006, 444) and "good quality education" (Dobrowolsky 2002, 51) in particular. Investment in children is premised on the argument that they clearly hold the promise of the future and that such investment will benefit society overall because of the hoped-for reduction in future social welfare costs.

At the heart of New Labour social investment ideas, then, is a rethinking of the notion of equality (Lister 2004). The focus for public policy concerned with equality and social justice along these lines must take account of Esping-Andersen and colleagues' observation that "opportunities and life chances in today's society remain as powerfully rooted in social inheritance as in the past" (Esping-Andersen et al. 2002, 27). For Lister, the aim for public policy now is to achieve "redistribution of opportunity to promote social inclusion rather than of income to promote equality" (2004, 160). Taken together, these observations point to a clear emphasis on education, health, children, young people, and future economic benefits as ways in which public policy interventions may begin to redress some of the negative consequences of continuing privileged social inheritance for children and young people.

It is at the juncture of all these perspectives that policies for sport and physical activity have emerged since 1997 to play an increasingly important role in the realization of New Labour's social investment aspirations (DCMS/Strategy Unit 2002; Sport England 2006a, 2006b, 2006c, 2008). For example, in the latest of a new series of publications—*Sport Playing Its Part*—a new Children's Plan is given some prominence. School sport is to play a significant part. With funding of £1 billion between 2008 and 2011, the Department for Children, Schools and Families (DCSF, formerly Education and Skills) aims to realize education, health, and community benefits through school sport and PE (Sport England 2008, 4). In an earlier publication, Sport England's chief executive captures the core (social investment) rationale for this new series of publications in arguing that sport has "a much larger part to play in achieving other outcomes, building stronger safer communities, strengthening the economy and developing the skills of local people, meeting the needs of children, as well as the associated health benefits" (quoted in Sport England 2006c, 2).

In a 1999 lecture, Tony Blair not only encapsulated these ideas on the prioritization of social investment but also reflected our earlier elaboration of governing under advanced liberalism. On the former, the then prime minister argued for "radical welfare reform" (Blair 1999, 1), where "the concept of social welfare had to fit economic policy. . . . But above all our welfare reform programme will give children—all children—the support they need" (3, 8). In line with those who argue that we are now governed under advanced liberal principles, Blair maintained that "social justice is about mutual responsibility . . . [and] a welfare state that is just about 'social security' is inadequate. It is passive where we now need it to be active. It encourages dependency where we need to encourage independence, initiative, enterprise for all" (2, 6). The prime minister also echoed New Labour's 1997 manifesto focus in stating that "education is our number one priority" (8) and added, "That is why we're driving up school standards, tackling failing schools . . . giving children the basic skills of reading, writing and numeracy. . . . But we also want them to have worthwhile activities to go to outside school" (8). These are all core policy goals of continuing investment in New Labour's strategy for school sport and PE (DCMS 2008). Building on the PESSCL strategy, the new PE and Sport Strategy for Young People cements government's focus on "early years" intervention. With an investment of £755 million over three years (2008–2011), the aim is to provide all five- to nineteen-year-olds with five hours of PE and sport within and beyond the curriculum (YST 2008).

A social investment focus on children has been maintained throughout New Labour's three terms in office. The 2003 Green Paper, *Every Child Matters*, is a clear example of this focus, in which the Chief Secretary to the Treasury stated that "since 1997, we have tried to put children first" (quoted in DfES 2003, 3). *Every Child Matters* set out five aspirational outcomes for children and young people, two of which were "being healthy: enjoying good physical and mental health and living a healthy lifestyle . . . [and] enjoying and achieving: getting the most out of life and developing the skills for adulthood" (6). Improved health benefits and educational attainment, and thus greater preparedness for life after childhood, are clearly signaled in these aspirational outcomes. It is therefore perhaps unsurprising that New Labour has (now) embraced sport and physical activity initiatives as mechanisms for realizing these policy ambitions. A senior civil servant at the DfES, commenting on the ongoing investment of more than £1 billion into school sport and PE, helps to make the point: "It's not simply about PE and school sport. If what we end up with at the end of this is lots of kids having lots of fun [but] making no difference perhaps to behaviour, attitude, motivation and achievement, then actually we will have failed" (quoted in Houlihan and Green 2006, 86).

Following the publication of *Every Child Matters* in 2003, a plethora of government policy documents have been published that address specific issues relating to children and young people, including youth justice, children in the care of the state, child poverty, and parents' responsibilities (for more detail, see DfES 2004, E7). For example, in 2004, *Every Child Matters: Change for Children* reported on the "progress to date of improving outcomes for children and young people" (DfES 2004, E5). Among eighteen listed outcomes, the report highlighted the PESSCL strategy and the importance of sport: "Physical education and school sport play an important role in young people's lives. It helps to raise standards, improve behaviour and health, increase attendance and develop social skills" (E5).

The 2006 budget speech maintained New Labour's social investment focus. Again, children, young people, education, and health were among the chief beneficiaries. The budget speech also heralded unprecedented (for the Treasury) statements on and increased resource allocations for sport and physical activity that were in part indicative of these strategies (Brown 2006). Alongside the £200 million of public money allocated for the 2012 Olympic Games, the chancellor committed £34 million for a new National Sports Foundation as well as £2 million "to offer young people evening sports and to tackle anti-social behaviour" (Brown 2006). Moreover, the clear desire to encourage responsibilities in us all, and in children and young people in particular, is evident in the budget statement on volunteering. Once again sport is called on to help achieve this goal. Acknowledging that 47 percent of volunteering takes place in sport, the government aims to create one million new volunteers over the next five years. Opportunities to achieve this aim will be created in "sport, the arts, media and the environment" (HM Treasury 2006, 113).

In sum, the embrace of policies for sport and physical activity by government to the degree evident over the past decade or so is unprecedented. As Houlihan and Green (2006) note, historically, government interest in sport, PE and physical activity has at best been one of intermittent action and, at worst, neglect and indeed outright disdain. In order to illustrate the nature of shifting governmental rationales for sport policy, the next section first (briefly) acknowledges previous government interventions in sport policy in relation to social welfare objectives from the 1970s, and second, presents evidence of the contemporary political salience of sport with respect to the (potential) social investment benefits to be accrued through the realization of policy objectives for education and health.

Shifting Policy Priorities for Sport

From Welfare to the "Active Citizen"

The role of sport and recreation policy as an element of social welfare, which emerged during the 1970s, has been well documented (see, e.g., Coalter, Long, and Duffield 1988; Henry 2001) and we do not wish to rehearse in any depth those accounts here. Various targeted or "disadvantaged groups," notably, young people, the elderly, women, ethnic minorities, disabled people, and lower socioeconomic groups, were at the heart of government concerns at this time (Sports Council 1982). A shift toward a more pragmatic promotion of sport and leisure, on the basis of the externalities that accrue from such provision, found expression in programs aimed at reducing boredom and urban frustration based on the premise that "participation in active recreation contributes to the reduction of hooliganism and delinquency among young people" (Department of the Environment 1975, 2). In this respect, the "shock waves" from the urban (inner city) riots in England in the early 1980s shaped, profoundly, the Conservative government's (elected in 1979) policy priorities for inner city sport and leisure spending (Henry 2001).

The shift away from spending on targeted groups, which was rationalized on the basis of alleviating recreational disadvantage and the fostering of community development, and toward the use of sport and leisure as a form of "benign policing," realigned political priorities for sport, recreation, and physical activity policy. Greater prominence was thus given to concentrating resources on the symptoms, rather than the causes, of social unrest in the inner cities. As a consequence, what characterized political and policy responses to sport "policy problems," at least until the early 1990s, was their relative passivity or reactive nature. With the advent of social investment ideas, policies designed around sport and physical activity gradually became increasingly proactive and heralded the valorization of the "active citizen" (Raco 2004), with government seeking to enhance the capacities of individuals and communities through which they were to take greater responsibility for their own actions and future welfare.

Sport Policy and the Social Investment State

Until relatively recently, it would have been difficult to sustain the argument that sport and physical activity was a domain of significant political importance in the United Kingdom. As discussed, this is not the case in the early twenty-first century. On the one hand, New Labour has presided over the construction of what is now a highly regarded and well-funded system for the development of elite athletes (Green and Houlihan 2005)—developments that culminated in the successful London bid for the 2012 Olympic Games. On the other hand, it is in the area of school sport and PE where we see not only the largest investment ever in the sector (Houlihan and Green 2006) but also the seeds of social investment policy development. As one senior civil servant at the DfES explained, the emphasis on school sport and PE in recent years "came about . . . because the Secretary of State [for the DCMS] at the time was trying to respond to the Prime Minister's desire to do something about school sport. Now what exactly that was, was up for negotiation really but [there was] a desire to do something" (quoted in Houlihan and Green 2006, 81).

Proactive government rationalities and social investment ideas in the realm of sport and physical activity were first set out in a robust manner in *Game Plan*, which outlined a long-term aim for 2020 "to increase significantly levels of sport and physical activity, particularly among disadvantaged groups" (DCMS/Strategy Unit 2002, 80). A target was set "for 70% (currently ~30%) of the population to be reasonably active (for example 30 minutes of moderate exercise five times a week) by 2020" (80). In the context of this chapter, what is noticeable is that, in the government's prioritization of "disadvantaged groups," greatest prominence is placed on children and young people (women, older people, and people from lower socioeconomic groups are also mentioned). Crucially, New Labour locates its strategy for increasing participation (for all targeted groups) within a set of four criteria, one of which is whether it "fit[s] with other overarching objectives (crime reduction, education, social cohesion, etc.)" (95). To this list, we can add health objectives, as each campaign for the targeted groups is required to "achieve health benefits [which] can be articulated quite simply with the '5×30mins' message" (104).

Thus *Game Plan*'s focus on lifelong opportunity, social inclusion, and a child-centered sport and physical activity agenda clearly mirrors social investment objectives in other policy sectors. For example, in charting the markedly altered thinking in recent years with respect to social policy, Jenson and Saint-Martin (2006, 430–431) argue that "attention has shifted from the supposedly passive spending on social protection to social investments that will generate an 'active society' and 'active citizenship.' . . . Associated with the altered patterns of spending is explicit attention to children." Indeed, in *Game Plan* the Secretary of State for Culture, Media and Sport argues that sport and physical activity projects help "to improve all round educational performance, to build confidence, leadership and teamwork in our young people, to combat social exclusion, reduce crime and build stronger communities" (quoted in DCMS/Strategy Unit 2002, 7). Moreover, the secretary of state goes on to note the hoped-for lifelong gains in such an approach: "A 10% increase in adult activity would prevent around 6,000 premature deaths not to mention bringing economic benefits worth at least £2 billion a year" (7). Here, we begin to see more clearly the linkages to Lister's (2003; see also Dobrowolsky 2002) analysis of the social investment state, the growing relationship between social and economic policy, and the focus on children as "citizen-workers of the future." Lister's (2003, 433) critique of such an approach hinges in part on concerns that children become "valued" merely as "cipher[s] for future economic prosperity," with the well-being or enjoyment of children as children overshadowed.

Associated with such concerns is the unease regarding the "progress" of young athletes, which is one, if not the most, major concern to emerge from an increased prioritization on elite sport development in the United Kingdom over the past decade (Green and Houlihan 2005). For example, a former senior official at the British Athletic Federation drew attention to talent identification mechanisms with regard to young athletes, and argued that "Nobody cares what happens to them if they aren't successful. Nobody seems to be asking the question at all about how people put together their lives when they have failed to make it through the talent ID [identification and development] process" (quoted in Green 2007a, 438). These comments do not rest easily with a Social Exclusion Unit (SEU) report, which stated that it is imperative to "listen to what young people are saying, take their views into consideration, treat young people as equals, let them be involved in the discussion about them, explain things clearly" (SEU 2005, 7). Yet, as MacPhail, Kirk, and Eley note, the disavowal of a voice for children is not unusual: "The voices of young people are rarely heard in educational research, even though they are important to the educational process and directly affect it. . . . A similar argument could be made in relation to the development of policy for youth sport" (2003, 58). These are somewhat damning indictments, especially so given the political rhetoric surrounding children and young people in *Game Plan*, Sport England's *Sport Playing Its Part*, and New Labour's social investment strategies more generally.

However, the embedding of social investment ideas and their relationship with sport and physical activity is clearly deepening. In this respect, *Sport Playing Its Part: The Contribution of Sport to Meeting the Needs of Children and Young People* (Sport England 2006b) is instructive. Here, attention is drawn to a recent government Green Paper (*Youth Matters*) that explores the issues facing young people and teenagers. Sport England's publication not only cites the Green Paper's acknowledgment of "the positive contribution of sport to the health and well being of young people" (5) but also, and especially, states that "for such benefits for children and young people to be realised through sport there is a need to take a *proactive* approach" (5; emphasis added). In these observations from Sport England, as well as from the DCMS and the Strategy Unit in *Game Plan*, we have powerful evidence of what Foucault (1982, 220–221) referred to as the "conduct of conduct," or the rationalities and techniques of government that seek to shape and guide those who are the object of government "to particular sets of norms and for a variety of ends" (Dean 1999, 10).

These rationalities and techniques are about shaping behavior constitutive of "active" citizens, in both senses of the word: active in the sense of "becoming active," or genuinely taking part in sport and physical activity, and active in taking responsible steps for their own well-being and health. And government will measure this activity, creating calculable spaces within which citizens can be judged (DCMS/Strategy Unit 2002, 112). In this respect, these policy interventions are in many ways about risk aversion (Jenson and Saint-Martin 2006). One of the ways, therefore, in which New Labour seeks—at an early stage—to intervene and avert "risky behaviors" for health, and other social policy objectives, is to target schools; children and young people are thus center-stage in New Labour's social investment strategies for sport and physical activity interventions.

Conclusion

This chapter has explored and registered the growing salience of sport and physical activity policy for New Labour's social investment strategies within the broader political context of governing under advanced liberalism. There can now be little argument that policies for sport and physical activity—especially with respect to education and health goals but also in relation to social inclusion and social cohesion objectives—have emerged as vital mechanisms for New Labour's reconstruction of welfare objectives and the prioritization of resources for citizen welfare in general, and for children and young people in particular. The aim of situating the analysis within the broader political context of governing under advanced liberalism was to (begin to) help make sense of the political rationalities of and technologies employed by New Labour in this reconstruction. In particular, the "building" of the normative idea of the "active citizen," who has both rights and responsibilities, is one that elides analyses of advanced liberalism and examinations of social investment strategies. In her examination of New Labour's "strategic social investment state," Dobrowolsky argues that "New Labour championed active, responsible citizens . . . [where] [i]ndividuals would get something from the state only if they met certain criteria and fulfilled certain duties and behaviours" (2002, 50). Compare Dobrowolsky's examination with Rose and Miller's analysis of the political rationalities of governing under advanced liberalism, where "the political subject is less a social citizen with powers and obligations deriving from membership of a collective body, than an individual whose citizenship is active. This citizenship is to be manifested not in the receipt of public largesse, but in the energetic pursuit of personal fulfilment and the incessant calculations that are to enable this to be achieved" (1992, 201).

The argument that the social investment state is not only facilitative but also regulatory and coercive (Dobrowolsky 2002; Dobrowolsky and Lister 2008) also resonates with writers who draw on governmentality analyses. On the one hand, under advanced liberalism, governmental power is contingent on freedom of choice and the autonomy of the individual, not simply by command and control from the center. On the other hand, autonomy is made possible by governments that have utilized policy initiatives and reforms of institutional arrangements to endorse certain patterns of behavior and lifestyle in the "making up" of citizens who are self-regulating and responsible—but within a demarcated space of illusory freedom. As Dobrowolsky and Lister observe, there is "a coercive side to social investment that [involves] compulsion and control directed toward some young people" (2008, 126). The use of calculative technologies of audit, assessment, performance review, and inspection mark out and "often impose limits over what it is possible to do" (Dean 1999, 31). In this respect, Daly argues that a key characteristic of New Labour "in practice is a great deal of central steering of decentralised networks and agencies" (2003, 122). From our analysis, the clearest manifestation of "central steering" is Sport England's reconfiguration of its remit in line with DCMS objectives for the realization of instrumentally explicit goals related to education, health, social inclusion, and so on (Sport England 2006a, 2006b, 2006c).

To sum up, the social investment state has the power to decide where and for whom investment is deserving (Jenson and Saint-Martin 2006). While children are deserving, there may be other groups who are deemed less so, for example, older people who, unlike children and young people, have marginal currency in a future-oriented world. For example, Craig argues that "older people are denied some of the fundamentals of citizenship important to their inclusion in society . . . and the ability to participate as fully as possible in society on terms of their choosing" (2004, 112). More recently, in the *Times*, Halpin reported on the rising costs of evening classes, noting that further education colleges are contemplating closure "in the evenings because of the reduction in adult learning and the focus on younger people" (2006, 1). Not only is this a "potentially morally censorious" (Dobrowolsky 2002, 66) way of thinking, but also some inequality becomes an inevitable consequence.

Thus, despite the compelling evidence that children and young people have emerged as a clear governmental priority over the past decade or so, two (quite different) issues in particular are highlighted for consideration by sport policy makers, management professionals, and practitioners alike: (1) the particular needs of children and young people, and their involvement, as far as is practicable, in all stages of policy interventions, and (2) that the needs of children and young people should not be overvalorized to the detriment of other groups in society. If realized, then New Labour will have taken important steps toward its ambitious goals for sport and physical activity policy. Of course, and to return to our opening lines, the broader question that remains unanswered at the time of writing is whether the chill winds of change blowing through the capillaries of global capitalism will serve to reorder the ways in which we are governed. Is it possible that the meta-narrative of neoliberalism may be challenged (Harvey 2007)? And is it possible that what may evolve out of the current economic malaise is a world where virtue is not defined in terms of individual agency, and where welfare is not just a matter of personal responsibility?

NOTES

1. Dean outlines the key characteristics of advanced liberalism as the types of discourses and rationalities of government that have emerged in the United Kingdom, Australia, and North America over the past fifteen to twenty years. These include the introduction of market-led reforms to former public-sector services; indirect forms of calculative technologies of regulation such as auditing, inspection, and accounting; the promotion of citizens as self-responsibilizing; and, somewhat paradoxically, the growth of "paternalistic and coercive measures for those deemed not to display the capacities of responsible and prudential autonomy" (1999, 209).

2. Giddens (1998) suggests that there are six components of Third Way politics: (1) a renewal of public institutions, (2) a search for a different relationship between government and civil society, (3) the active involvement of government with economic life, (4) the structural reform of the welfare state, (5) ecological issues to have a central role in politics, and (6) a strong recognition of the importance of transnational politics.

3. Sport England is the brand name for the English Sports Council. It is categorized as a nondepartmental public body (NDPB) that operates on the "arm's length" principle in its relationship with the DCMS—the central government department responsible for sport. From April 1, 2006, Sport England's remit changed from one that, in the past, covered a broad elite sport–mass sport range to one with a much tighter focus on what is being termed "Community Sport."

4. The UK Sports Council (UK Sport) was created in 1996–1997 and, like Sport England, is an NDPB under the auspices of the DCMS. It has a tight focus on supporting elite athlete development, promoting the hosting of major sporting events, controlling anti-doping procedures, and using sport for international development purposes.

5. The PESSCL strategy was launched in October 2002 and, over a three-year period beginning in April 2003, the government invested more than £1 billion on the delivery of eight programs—Specialist Sports Colleges, School Sport Coordinators, the Gifted and

Talented initiative, PE and School Sport Investigation (through the Qualifications and Curriculum Authority), Step into Sport, Professional Development, School/Club Links, and Swimming—as well as improvements to school sport facilities across England (DfES/DCMS 2003, 1).

6. The Department for Education and Skills is now known as the Department for Children, Schools and Families.

REFERENCES

Bache, I. 2003. "Governing through Governance: Education Policy Control under New Labour." *Political Studies* 51 (2): 300–314.

Blair, T. 1995. "The Rights We Enjoy Reflect the Duties We Owe." Spectator Lecture, London, March 22.

———. 1999. Beveridge Lecture, Toynbee Hall, London, March 18.

Brown, G. 2006. "Chancellor of the Exchequer's Budget Statement." HM Treasury, March 22. Available at http://www.hm-treasury.gov.uk/budget/budget_06/bud_bud06_speech.cfm.

Coalter, F., with J. Long and B. Duffield. 1988. *Recreational Welfare*. Aldershot, UK: Gower.

Collins, M. F., with T. Kay. 2003. *Sport and Social Exclusion*. London: Routledge.

Commission on Social Justice. 1994. *Social Justice: Strategies for National Renewal*. London: Vintage Books.

Craig, G. 2004. "Citizenship, Exclusion and Older People." *Journal of Social Policy* 33 (1): 95–114.

Daly, M. 2003. "Governance and Social Policy." *Journal of Social Policy* 32 (1): 113–128.

Dean, M. 1999. *Governmentality: Power and Rule in Modern Society*. London: Sage.

———. 2007. *Governing Societies: Political Perspectives on Domestic and International Rule*. Maidenhead, UK: Open University Press.

Dean, M., and B. Hindess, eds. 1998. *Governing Australia: Studies in Contemporary Rationalities of Government*. Cambridge: Cambridge University Press.

Department for Culture, Media and Sport. 2008. *Playing to Win: A New Era for Sport*. London: DCMS.

Department for Culture, Media and Sport/Strategy Unit. 2002. *Game Plan: A Strategy for Delivering Government's Sport and Physical Activity Objectives*. London: DCMS/Strategy Unit.

Department for Education and Skills. 2003. *Every Child Matters* (Cm. 5860). London: Stationery Office.

———. 2004. *Every Child Matters: Change for Children*. London: Stationery Office.

Department for Education and Skills/Department for Culture, Media and Sport. 2003. *Learning through PE and Sport: A Guide to the Physical Education, School Sport and Club Links Strategy*. London: DfES/DCMS.

Department of the Environment. 1975. *Sport and Recreation*. London: HMSO.

Department of Health. 2002. *Health Check: On the State of Public Health*. London: DoH.

———. 2004. *At Least Five a Week: Evidence on the Impact of Physical Activity and Its Relationship to Health*. London: DoH.

Dobrowolsky, A. 2002. "Rhetoric versus Reality: The Figure of the Child and New Labour's Strategic 'Social Investment State.'" *Studies in Political Economy* 69 (Autumn): 43–74.

Dobrowolsky, A., and J. Jenson. 2005. "Social Investment Perspectives and Practices: A Decade in British Politics." In *Social Policy Review 17: Analysis and Debate in Social Policy 2005*, ed. M. Powell, L. Bauld, and K. Clarke, 203–230. Bristol, UK: Policy Press.

Dobrowolsky, A., and R. Lister. 2008. "Social Investment: The Discourse and the Dimensions of Change." In *Modernising the Welfare State: The Blair Legacy*, ed. M. Powell, 125–142. Bristol, UK: Policy Press.

Dwyer, P. 1998. "Conditional Citizens? Welfare Rights and Responsibilities in the Late 1990s." *Critical Social Policy* 18 (57): 493–517.

Esping-Andersen, G. 2000. "A Welfare State for the 21st Century." Report to the Portuguese Presidency of the European Union. Available at http://www.nnn.se/seminar/pdf/report.pdf.

Esping-Andersen, G., D. Gallie, A. Hemerijck, and J. Myles. 2002. *Why We Need a New Welfare State*. Oxford: Oxford University Press.

Featherstone, B. 2006. "Rethinking Family Support in the Current Policy Context." *British Journal of Social Work* 36 (5): 5–19.

Finlayson, A. 2003. *Making Sense of New Labour*. London: Lawrence and Wishart.

Finlayson, A., and J. Martin. 2006. "Poststructuralism." In *The State: Theories and Issues*, ed. C. Hay, M. Lister, and D. Marsh, 155–171. Basingstoke, UK: Palgrave Macmillan.

Foucault, M. 1982. "The Subject and Power." In *Michel Foucault: Beyond Structuralism and Hermeneutics*, ed. H. Dreyfus and P. Rabinow, 208–226. Brighton, UK: Harvester.

Frankel, B. 1997. "Confronting Neo-liberal Regimes: The Post-Marxist Embrace of Populism and Realpolitik." *New Left Review* 226 (November/December): 57–92.

Giddens, A. 1995. *A Contemporary Critique of Historical Materialism*. Cambridge, UK: Polity Press.

———. 1998. "Equality and the Social Investment State." In *Tomorrow's Politics: The Third Way and Beyond*, ed. I. Hargreaves and I. Christie, 25–38. London: Demos.

———. 2007. *Europe in the Global Age*. Cambridge, UK: Polity Press.

Green, M. 2007a. "Policy Transfer, Lesson Drawing and Perspectives on Elite Sport Development Systems." *International Journal of Sport Management and Marketing* 2 (4) 426–441.

———. 2007b. "Governing under Advanced Liberalism: Sport Policy and the Social Investment State." *Policy Science* 40:55–71.

Green, M., and B. Houlihan. 2005. *Elite Sport Development: Policy Learning and Political Priorities*. London: Routledge.

———. 2006. "Governmentality, Modernisation and the 'Disciplining' of National Sporting Organisations: Athletics in Australia and the United Kingdom." *Sociology of Sport Journal* 23 (1): 47–71.

Hall, S. 1998. "The Great Moving Nowhere Show." *Marxism Today* (November/December): 9–14.

Halpin, T. 2006. "Evening Classes to Double Charges." *The (London) Times*, March 28, 1–2.

Harvey, D. 2007. *A Brief History of Neoliberalism*. Oxford: Oxford University Press.

Henry, I. P. 2001. *The Politics of Leisure Policy*, 2nd ed. Basingstoke, UK: Palgrave.

HM Treasury. 2006. *Budget 2006* (HC 968). London: Stationery Office.

Houlihan, B., and M. Green. 2006. "The Changing Status of School Sport and Physical Education: Explaining Policy Change." *Sport, Education and Society* 11 (1): 73–92.

———. 2008. "Modernization and Sport: The Reform of Sport England and UK Sport." *Public Administration* 87 (3): 678–698.

Jenson, J. 2005. "Social Investment for New Social Risks: Consequences of the LEGO™ Paradigm for Children." Available at http://www.cccg.umontreal.ca/pdf/Social%20 investment%20Jane%20Jenson.pdf.

Jenson, J., and D. Saint-Martin. 2003. "New Routes to Social Cohesion? Citizenship and the Social Investment State." *Canadian Journal of Sociology* 28 (1): 77–99.

———. 2006. "Building Blocks for a New Social Architecture: The LEGO™ Paradigm of an Active Society." *Policy and Politics* 34 (3): 429–451.

Kay, W. 2003. "Physical Education, RIP?" *British Journal of Teaching Physical Education* 34 (4): 6–9.

Lister, R. 2003. "Investing in the Citizen-Workers of the Future: Transformations in Citizenship and the State under New Labour." *Social Policy and Administration* 37 (5): 427–443.

———. 2004. "The Third Way's Social Investment State." In *Welfare State Change: Towards a Third Way?* ed. J. Lewis and R. Surender, 157–181. Oxford: Oxford University Press.

MacPhail, A., D. Kirk, and D. Eley. 2003. "Listening to Young People's Voices: Youth Sports Leaders' Advice on Facilitating Participation in Sport." *European Physical Education Review* 9 (1): 57–73.

McDonald, I. 2005. "Theorising Partnerships: Governance, Communicative Action and Sport Policy." *Journal of Social Policy* 34 (4): 579–600.

Miller, P., and N. Rose. 2008. *Governing the Present: Administering Economic, Social and Personal Life.* Cambridge, UK: Polity Press.

Newman, J. 2001. *Modernising Governance: New Labour, Policy and Society.* London: Sage.

———. 2004. "Modernising the State: A New Style of Governance?" In *Welfare State Change: Towards a Third Way?* ed. J. Lewis and R. Surender, 69–88. Oxford: Oxford University Press.

Newman, J., and B. McKee. 2005. "Beyond the New Public Management? Public Services and the Social Investment State." *Policy and Politics* 33 (4): 657–674.

Powell, F. 2007. *The Politics of Civil Society: Neoliberalism or Social Left?* Bristol, UK: Policy Press.

Power, M. 1997. *The Audit Society: Rituals of Verification.* Oxford: Oxford University Press.

Raco, M. 2004. "Whose Gold Rush? The Social Legacy of a London Olympics." In *After the Gold Rush: A Sustainable Olympics for London*, ed. A. Vigor, M. Mean, and C. Tims, 33–49. London: Institute for Public Policy and Research/Demos.

Raco, M., and R. Imrie. 2000. "Governmentality and Rights and Responsibilities in Urban Policy." *Environment and Planning A* 32 (1):, 2187–2204.

Rose, N. 1993. "Government, Authority and Expertise in Advanced Liberalism." *Economy and Society* 22 (3): 283–299.

———. 1999. *Powers of Freedom: Reframing Political Thought.* Cambridge: Cambridge University Press.

Rose, N., and P. Miller. 1992. "Political Power beyond the State: Problematics of Government." *British Journal of Sociology* 43 (2): 172–205.

Social Exclusion Unit. 2005. *Transitions: Young Adults with Complex Needs.* London: Office of the Deputy Prime Minister.

Sport England. 2006a. *Sport Playing Its Part: The Contribution of Sport to Healthier Communities.* London: Sport England.

———. 2006b. *Sport Playing Its Part: The Contribution of Sport to Meeting the Needs of Children and Young People.* London: Sport England.

———. 2006c. *Sport Playing Its Part: Executive Summary.* London: Sport England.

———. 2008. *Sport Playing Its Part (Issue 5).* London: Sport England.

Sports Council. 1982. *Sport in the Community: The Next Ten Years.* London: Sports Council.

Watson, S. 2000. "Foucault and the Study of Social Policy." In *Rethinking Social Policy*, ed. G. Lewis, S. Gewirtz, and J. Clarke, 66–77. London: Sage.

Youth Sport Trust. 2008. *PE and Sport Strategy for Young People.* Loughborough, UK: YST.

4

Race, Class, and Politics in Post-Katrina America

MICHAEL D. GIARDINA
C. L. COLE

The Hurricane Katrina disaster . . . revealed a vulnerable and destitute segment of the nation's citizenry that conservatives not only refused to see, but had spent the better part of two decades demonizing.
> —HENRY A. GIROUX, "Violence, Katrina, and the Biopolitics of Disposability"

A racially divided, disorganized . . . falling-apart-at-the-seams New Orleans: this is George W. Bush and Karl Rove's gift to America.
> —NORMAN K. DENZIN, "Katrina and the Collapse of Civil Society in New Orleans"

Proem

It is the images that strike you first: the lifeless body of a fellow citizen cast off to the side of a street, a starving dog gnawing at a bloody limb. A mother gripping onto her infant daughter at the New Orleans Convention Center, begging—*pleading*—for someone, anyone, to whisk them away from their uncertain future. An elderly man in a wheelchair, clinging to his last shards of breath. A news reporter breaking down into frustrated tears on national television. People—fellow human beings—rummaging in garbage cans or blown-out storefronts for food because the Federal Emergency Management Agency (FEMA) had yet to realize that New Orleans was, in fact, a city located in the United States.[1] The collapse of civil society: live and in unliving color.

The mood is somber. Reflective. Harsh. Sad. Depressing. Frustrating. A collision of emotions ready to explode. Kim Segal, a segment producer at CNN caught in New Orleans, recalls the scene unfolding through her journalistic eyes: "It was chaos. There was nobody there, nobody in charge. And there was nobody giving even water. The children, you should see them—they're all just in tears. There are sick people. We saw . . . people who are dying in front of you"

("The Big Disconnect on New Orleans" 2005). A photojournalist from NBC concurs, declaring that a third world country he once covered was in much better shape than the ramshackle conditions downtown. CNN's Sanjay Gupta, a medical doctor by trade, relays the shocking brute force of horror in one of New Orleans's hospitals: "When patients die in the hospital, there is no place to put them, so they're in the stairwells. It is one of the most unbelievable situations I've seen as a doctor, certainly as a journalist as well. There is no electricity. There is no water. There's over 200 patients still here remaining" ("The Big Disconnect on New Orleans" 2005). And hardened journalists such as CNN's Anderson Cooper and Fox News Channel's Shepard Smith break down numerous times during live shots, the former snapping viciously at U.S. senator Mary Landrieu (D-LA) during an on-air interview,[2] the latter barking unexpectedly at his colleagues for not "getting" what he was physically witnessing and psychologically experiencing as they sat back in the comfort of their broadcast studio.

As the days turned to weeks, and the situation on the ground turned from atrocious to horrific to absurd, satirical headlines such as "Iraq to Deploy Troops in Louisiana, Mississippi"—which appeared in *Flak Magazine* and included such hard-hitting musings as "The Iraqi National Assembly, in an amazing display of solidarity between Kurds, Shiites, and Sunnis, unanimously voted to send 10,000 of its troops into America" and "The victims of the flood will greet [them] as liberators"—seemed almost plausible in the wikiality of Bush World (see Scott, n.d.).

Contextualizing Katrina

Hurricane Katrina and the overwhelming flooding that followed has been called the most devastating natural disaster in recent U.S. history (on par with only the Deepwater Horizon oil spill in the Gulf of Mexico during the summer of 2010), as well as arguably its most devastating bureaucratic disaster (the Iraq and Afghanistan misadventures notwithstanding). For most Americans, it was television (and later digital video available online at sites such as YouTube and Google Video) that drew attention to the crisis with shocking images—primarily from New Orleans—of people suffering in nightmarish conditions. Viewers watched live as more than twenty thousand people, many from the city's historically black, working-class Ninth Ward, were stranded—in some cases abandoned—without food, water, or sanitation; witnessed people who were sick and dying; saw homes and lives literally being destroyed in real time: the scene could very well have mirrored that of conditions in Baghdad, Kabul, or Darfur. With the massive, imposing structure of the famed Louisiana Superdome (home to the New Orleans Saints of the National Football League, now corporately sponsored as the Mercedes-Benz Superdome) as a soaring architectural backdrop, the world watched as one of the most vulnerable populations in the United States—poor urban blacks—were left without even the crudest necessities of life.

Most provocatively, the image of the black mother and child, photographed in stark relief against the looming Superdome, figured prominently in cable media's 24/7 live coverage. Indeed, the Superdome became the national media's reproductive stage for the very violences (racism, poverty, and federal neglect) it is typically deployed to conceal on any given Sunday. Some commentators appealed to discourses already in place to attempt to make sense of the scene; the repetition of the traumatized mother and child—the black mother, helpless to do anything other than comfort her hungry infant—stood in for the poor black community in distress. But the narrative of suffering was countered by a mediated spectacle of upheaval signaled by the apparent breakdown of law and order in and around the Superdome. A long familiar trope in the United States—the always-already pathologized bodies of black men—was used to signal "incomprehensible crimes." Some cable news pundits repeated and then repeated again stories about "looters" who were stealing guns, alcohol, sneakers, athletic wear, and electronics (not to mention groceries—i.e., *food*—which figured prominently in one racialized story line).[3] Others claimed the city was under siege by "roving gangs" who were shooting at rescue helicopters, hospital supply trucks, and workers trying to evacuate the sick in hospitals. And still others repeated stories of children being raped in the Superdome, along with other atrocities normally reserved for dystopian horror movies.

To listen to a medley of cable news reports, a *Mad Max*-meets-*New Jack City* shroud had become draped over a dark, twisted, evil city languishing in chaos. Along this line, and on his highly rated Fox News Channel spinfest *The O'Reilly Factor*, host Bill O'Reilly blatantly inferred that most of the Katrina victims of New Orleans—particularly those trapped in the Superdome—were uneducated, poor drug addicts who lived a "gangsta" lifestyle akin to that of the *Grand Theft Auto* video game world:

> Every American kid should be required to watch videotape of the poor in New Orleans and see how they suffered, because they couldn't get out of town. And then, every teacher should tell the students, "If you refuse to learn, if you refuse to work hard, if you become addicted, if you live a gangsta-life, you will be poor and powerless just like many of those in New Orleans." (O'Reilly 2005)

And all of it was a pack of lies. As Pulitzer Prize–winning *Washington Post* columnist Eugene Robinson pointed out, the prevailing mediated pedagogy of urban destruction and black male violence dominating the Katrina landscape just was not *entirely* true in any such empirical reality:

> I got there five days after the deluge, when the story, as the whole world understood it, was one of *Mad Max* depravity and violence. Hoodlums were raping and pillaging, I just "knew"—even shooting at rescue helicopters trying to take hospital patients to safety. So it was a surprise when I rolled into the center of the city, with all my foreign-correspondent antennae bristling, and found the place as quiet as a tomb. The next day I drove into the French Quarter and was struck by how pristine St. Louis Cathedral

looked, almost like the castle at Disney World. I got out of the car and walked around the whole area, and I wrote in my notebook that except for the absence of tourists, it could have been just an ordinary Sunday morning in the Big Easy. Then I got back into the car, and on the radio a caller was breathlessly reporting that, as she spoke, a group of policemen were "pinned down" by snipers at the cathedral. I was right there; nobody was sniping at anybody. But the reigning narrative was *Mad Max*, not Magic Kingdom. Thanks to radio, television and the Internet, everyone "knew" things that just weren't true. (2005, A23)

However, as liberal wunderkind blogger turned *Washington Post* essayist Ezra Klein reminded us at the time, it is not enough to simply point out that incendiary news coverage was just spotty work done by lazy or inept reporters, or even the product of ratings-driven decisions on the part of various cable news directors and editors. He stated:

Those horror stories, now proved [mostly] untrue, were not simply mistaken, they were racist. From the widely reported but never confirmed rapes in the Superdome all the way to the false accounts of sniped rescue workers and roving gangs of looting blacks, Katrina exposed a latent cultural racism that many Americans assumed had vanished. These were tropes more suited to the Deep South of the 1800s than the cable networks of the 21st century. (2005)

So let us cut to the chase: as Governor Howard Dean (2006), then chairman of the Democratic National Committee, stated in his address to the National Baptist Convention of America on the impact of Katrina, "We must . . . come to terms with the ugly truth that skin color, age, and economics played a deadly role in who survived and who did not."[4] William Jelani Cobb (2009) put it in more direct language: "Filter through the spin and you will meet a brutal truth: there are people who have died and people who are dying in Louisiana because they are black and they are poor" (n.p.). Correlatively, Mark Anthony Neal (2005) is correct in his observation that this sentiment is one we must complicate: "The initially tepid and lazy response to Katrina in New Orleans wasn't *just* a product of racist neglect, [but] it was *also* the product of the devaluation of whole communities because they didn't possess political capital." His strong words were echoed by former U.S. senator and ambassador to New Zealand Carol Moseley Braun (D-IL), who spoke out about the general neglect of poor and underprivileged citizens in New Orleans: "I think it's a sin of omission more than anything. They don't see poor people. They don't even think about them, they don't plan for them. How do you tell people to evacuate and then turn your back on those who don't have money for cab fare or who don't have cars?" (Bradley 2005).[5] On this point, Cobb's (2009) words again rang true: "The truth is that neglect is the racial default setting—which is why those people were left behind in the city literally and metaphorically."

Yet despite the federal neglect and disastrous bureaucratic rescue attempts by FEMA, an outpouring of charity came full-force from the American (and, indeed, world) public in droves not seen since the immediate aftermath of the September 11, 2001, attacks on the Pentagon and World Trade Center. *How do we make sense of this apparent paradox?* Perhaps it was the finely honed Madonna image that limited the impact of the criminalized looter image, as racialized pleas for help were translated into mainstream American compassion. In part, what made the Madonna-child image so powerful is both its long, political career and, given the recent coverage of the famine in Niger or the political unrest in Darfur, its immediacy in the collective imaginary of the United States. As scholars such as Christina Klein, Wendy Kozol, and Laura Briggs have illustrated, that image has figured prominently in U.S. images of third world poverty and hunger. Briggs summarizes its effects in her recent genealogy of the image:

> [The image] directs attention away from structural explanations of poverty, famine, and other disasters, including international, political, military, and economic causes. . . . It has played a powerful role in shaping support in the US for a variety of public policy and foreign policy initiatives, from IMF loans to the globalization of an international force to US debates about the family. . . . The visual and familial practices worked together to produce an ideology of rescue by white people of non-white people inside and outside the United States. (2003, 180–181)

The prominent association of the image with the third world can help us begin to make sense of America's confounded puzzlement about the geopolitical context of the image. And the historic political work performed by the image helps us account for the atypical entrance of black women as celebrated mothers into the U.S. public sphere. As well, it helps of make sense of the narrative of rescue that followed and facilitated the dramatic consumption of the event.

Already profoundly and intimately woven into the traumatized Madonna image, the narrative of rescue took its form in a national discourse of heroic *white* masculinity. White men, in sharply creased military uniform, openly displaying weapons of war, stood in for the state as a moral actor meeting its obligations. Again with the Superdome in the background, rescuers were represented as all-American action heroes (in much the same fashion as first responders on 9/11 or U.S. Marines in Iraq have been portrayed in news stories and political orations of national import). Rescues took on an extreme sport aesthetic as they appeared to be overcoming and redefining their bodily limits as they maneuvered through the wreckage, rappelled from helicopters, or sped through flooded neighborhoods in powerboats.[6]

While we obviously do not want to dismiss the efforts of those who helped people to safety, we do want to draw attention to the way that the rescue efforts were *framed* to highlight an heroic white masculinity. The reader will no doubt recognize such a trope in charity, development, and aid campaigns as diverse as (Product)[RED], Charity:Water, and the United Nations Mine Action Service. In each of these instances, wealthy white men (e.g., Bill Gates, Bono, Michael Dell), upscale urbanites, or suburban nuclear families (soccer dads) respectively are deployed to both invoke a feeling of distant pity (what philosopher Hannah Arendt would term as the activation of a *politics* of pity) toward the less fortunate and recuperate a sense of faith in the neoliberal state to care for those very same individuals (see Giardina 2009). Or to put it more simply, *white masculinity mediated the social relations between the spectators and those who were suffering.*

These masculine images quickly replaced what had begun dangerously as a threat to the American myth of colorblind plenty with a smug sense of white heroics and charitable opportunity. Most especially, sport—or, perhaps more appropriately, physicality and the site of the body—was front and center in these narratives. In one particularly striking example, framed under the guise of providing "never-before-seen" footage of the crisis, Discovery Channel debuted its October 2005 *SOS: Coast Guard Rescue Series* with three hours of Katrina rescues, or what it called "close-up, you-are-there video," made possible by helmet-mounted cameras. Viewers, according to Discovery Channel, "swing through the window of a flooded house" and are there "as a desperate family reach[es] out to embrace [the rescuer]." And, the show's press materials continue, when the rescuer "climbs into the attic looking for a way to get the family onto the roof, viewers will find themselves peering into the darkness for an ax or a crowbar on anything that might help." "Viewers" coded as would-be heroic white men are helped by the Discovery Channel to overcome what was first played out as shock and even shame at the plight of Americans in poverty. This retelling—in fact, revisioning—of the Katrina story is symptomatic of yet another form of protecting the white public from so-called damaging media images—it is the story that will salvage *white* American innocence and allow for a cathartic adventure experience in place of activism and social awareness to change the historical and political circumstances that led to such a crisis in the first place.

Racialized (Sporting) Bodies

The representation of black bodies before, during, and after the hurricane hit is of further relevance when we consider, for a moment, the Louisiana Superdome during Katrina as itself a transient site for the mediation of blackness in the United States. For a few fleeting days, the Superdome found itself openly officiating between two seemingly warring camps about "urban" blackness: the story of *productive* black male bodies disciplined through sport to entertain and profit privileged fans and owners, and that of *undisciplined* black male bodies that threaten the social good and burden the U.S. economy. Never mentioned was the irony that those people who were typically priced out of the Superdome as sport spectators were now trapped within it, being treated like caged animals, contained by armed National Guard troops. Indeed, the sort of taxing and finance priorities that build and maintain stadiums like the Superdome, rather than using resources for the entire public's good, are at least partially responsible for the continued poverty of evacuees such as these in the first place.

That is to say, both public and popular disposition toward U.S. urban centers has over the years followed a contradictory hypermoral impulse. As Michael D. Giardina and Cameron R. McCarthy (2005) have argued, "urban" America throughout the last twenty years has been discursively oriented between "all-out decay" and the possibility of social and economic "renewal," at various times emphasizing cold disinterest, at other times seen as the object of almost laboratory-like social experimentation and intervention. This pendulum of neglect and intervention continually swings, they argue, sometimes frenetically, one way or another, as the urban context continues to be viewed by bureaucratic and cultural elites through a paradigm of cultural deficit and moral underdevelopment (see, for example, CNN's recent multipart exposé "CNN Presents: Black in America," which received widespread criticism despite its laudable efforts, primarily due to the perceived disconnection between the exposé's commentators and those they were commenting about: the urban poor). Since the high point of the civil rights era and its culminating fruition in the ameliorative social programs of the Great Society/War on Poverty era, the urban centers of the United States have been the consistent target of revisionary strategies of both policy makers and policy intellectuals (on both sides of the political spectrum). This revisionary disposition has been, to give but one example, operationalized in the policies of benign neglect found during the Nixon/Ford/Carter years and the aggressive disinvestment of social programs begun during the Reagan/George H. W. Bush era and rapidly increasing during the George W. Bush years (Giardina and McCarthy 2005, 157).

Up until the 1990s, argue Giardina and McCarthy, the dominant framework around which both public policy and the surplus popular social meanings were generated was the Keynesian formula of (more or less) social welfarism:

> In the early 1990s, this overwhelming paradigm of Keynesianism was both rhetorically and practically overturned as the newly inaugurated Clinton administration sought to connect urban centers to its broad-scale global neoliberal initiatives vis-à-vis universalizing entrepreneurship. As the administration implemented or backstopped such decidedly free-market friendly endeavors as the North American Free Trade Agreement (NAFTA), General Agreement on Tariffs and Trade (GATT), and the World Trade Organization (WTO), it simultaneously turned its newly embraced public-private partnership gaze on the inner city by speaking the language of enterprise zones, self-help, personal responsibility, and community voluntarism [the key signposts of Clinton's "Third Way" political rationality of attaining liberal means through conservative ends]. The urban center—both in the real and discursive sense—was/is thus a piece of a much larger puzzle of the proliferation of new social meanings that "translate the capitalist enterprise form of modern conduct to the conduct

of organizations (e.g., charter schools, corporate partnerships, and voucher programs in education) and the conduct of individuals; the problems of inner-city life have become the new targets of self-management, regulation, the restraint of individual appetites, and the moral purposive voluntaristic investment of the inner-city dweller himself or herself. (2005, 158)

We see this governing practice instantiated within public policy maneuvers such as those related to so-called Empowerment Zones generally and the Gulf Opportunity Zone (or GO Zone; H.R. 4400) as related to Katrina-afflicted areas specifically, the latter of which portended in its implementation to offer lower tax rates, expand private investment incentives, and promote regulatory relief in the hurricane-devastated region. If the neoliberal economic policies/politics that have informed empowerment zones heretofore are carried through in the GO Zone, issues of crime and criminality will be centrally located within its makeup. Such was the language of the 1993 *Building Communities Together: Guidebook for Community-Based Strategic Planning for Empowerment Zones and Enterprise Communities*, authored by President Clinton's Community Enterprise Board, which stated in part:

If this program is to stabilize and reinvigorate neighborhoods, residents must be free from the fear of crime and violence. Job creation, improved housing, and enhanced service delivery are crucial in most potential empowerment zones and enterprise communities, but a commitment to the reduction of crime and violence through coordinated law enforcement is necessary to community stability, the delivery of health education, and other social services and economic development . . . *Unchecked violence, gun and drug trafficking, drug use, and other serious felonies will stifle investment, development and community building emphasis of the initiative.* (President's Community Enterprise Board 1993, 45–46; emphasis added)

Yet, on closer inspection of such supposedly high-minded rhetoric, as we point out in our case-study analysis of the New York City/Upper Manhattan Empowerment Zone project (Giardina and Cole 2005), such (de)moralizing jingoism is eerily reminiscent of something President Reagan said in 1982:

We must make America safe again, especially for women and elderly who face so many moments of fear. . . . Study after study shows that most serious crimes are the work of a relatively small group of hardened criminals. Let me give you an example—subway crime in New York City. Transit police estimate that only 500 habitual criminal offenders are responsible for nearly half of the crimes in New York's subways last year. . . . It's time to get these hardened criminals off the street and into jail. . . . We can and must make improvements in the way our courts deal with crime. . . . These include revising the bail system so that dangerous offenders, and especially big-time drug pushers, can be kept off our streets. (Reagan 1983, 2)

Though David L. Andrews was writing in response to Reagan's quote, his words remain applicable to the 1993 guidebook: "Without ever referring to race or ethnicity, it is manifest that the threat to American society he vocalized was a black male inhabitant of American's anarchic urban jungles" (1993, 114–115). The outcome is that security becomes mobilized around economic stability and corporate investment opportunities: incarcerating or evicting young black (or Latino) men becomes the naturalized, accepted—in some cases, even promoted—outcome of "cleaning up" or "revitalizing" the so-called inner city and paving the way for corporate expansionary measures (a fate we have witnessed in empowerment zones from New York to Cleveland to Los Angeles).

While New Orleans will most certainly be rebuilt (at least, from a structural point of view), does anyone expect the "new" Big Easy to be anything more than an expansion of the Times Square Lite, consumerist façade that already existed—a place where jazz music, Cajun/Creole food, and French historical inflections are reduced to banal touristic caricatures that see "neighborhood radicalism and protest as entertainment, myth, human-interest story, or a peculiar spectacle to be gazed at by a curious middle-class" (Mele 2000, 308)? Of course not! If anything, the new branding dynamic sure to take place in New Orleans will be "embedded in highly marketable, sanitized styles and signs of subversion, anti-authoritarianism, and experimentation that designate it as an 'alternative' space" (Cole 2001, 117). As Friedman, Andrews, and Silk (2004) contend, one of the primary results of such "consumption-based, visitor-oriented redevelopment could be in creating little more than a veneer of change and vitality within the city" in which, beneath the shiny new façade of an improved national image, "the underlying realities of urban life frequently remain unaltered" (130). Sarah Vowell (2003) got it right when she said, "There are few creepier moments in cultural tourism than when a site tries to rewrite its past" (36).

Not only that, but the initial political responses to the tragedy telegraphed the problematic engagement and rebuilding efforts that were to come in the years in that followed—most notably, the imposition of a direction in which *New* New Orleans was not going to look much like *Old* New Orleans. Rep. Richard Baker (R-LA) admitted as much when he crassly told the *Wall Street Journal*, "We finally cleaned up public housing in New Orleans. We couldn't do it, but God did" (quoted in Hamill 2005). Of course, by "cleaned up public housing," Rep. Baker means that he is thankful that the hurricane displaced those (largely poor, primarily black) residents who were living in impoverished dwellings, in effect making the now-abandoned or destroyed land prime for real estate (re)development. In fact, Alphonso R. Jackson, Secretary of Housing and Urban Development at the time, openly (a cynic might say giddily) predicted that New Orleans would be "whiter" following the dispersal of a large segment of five hundred thousand pre-Katrina African Americans across the country, many to Houston, Texas, and other neighboring areas.

The stakes of this callous attitude for the cultural history of New Orleans (as well as the political orientation of the state in national politics) are high. As

Mark Krasnof, a cofounder of the Civic Center Shelter on the Louisiana-Texas border, which helped house many who were lucky to escape Katrina's wrath, remarked in the immediate aftermath of the storm, "The very soul of Louisiana is now at stake. . . . If our 'leaders' have their way this whole goddamn region will become either a toxic graveyard or a big museum where jazz, zydeco and Cajun music will still be played for tourists but the cultures that gave them life are defunct or dispersed" (quoted in Davis and Fontenot 2005, 1).[7] Fighting against this possibility, Glen Ford and Peter Gamble of the *Black Commentator* pleaded:

> Priority must be given to the right to preserve and continue the rich and diverse cultural traditions of the city, and the social experiences of Black people that produced the culture. The second line, Mardi Gras Indians, brass bands, creative music, dance foods, language and other expressions are the "soul of the city." The rebuilding process must preserve these traditions. THE CITY MUST NOT BE CULTURALLY, ECONOMICALLY OR SOCIALLY GENTRIFIED INTO A "SOULLESS" COLLECTION OF CONDOS AND tract home NEIGHBORHOODS FOR THE RICH. (2005; formatting in original)

These diverse traditions, Matt Sakakeeny points out, can be found in the fact that

> as a French, Spanish, and American city, New Orleans has always maintained a significant Black population that has continuously and resourcefully created a coherent yet flexible collective identity through the combination of what Stuart Hall (2003) calls "presences": the *présence Africaine, présence Européene*, and *présence Américaine*. (2006, 42)

Likewise, if recent history was to hold true, economic marginalization in the vein of underpaid or temporary laborers were to be the arms of capital "sanitizing" New Orleans for the foreseeable future. In fact, and in the weeks and months that followed, firms were at the ready to capitalize on what Naomi Klein (2008) refers to as "disaster capitalism" (the profit-based privatization of relief efforts in disaster-stricken environs). Ever beholden to the "free market," the Bush administration even went so far as to temporarily suspend the Davis-Bacon Act of 1931 for the Gulf Coast reconstruction effort (see "Proclamation by the President" 2005).[8] In response to this suspension of Davis-Bacon, Edward C. Sullivan, president of the Building and Construction Trades Department of the AFL-CIO, criticized President Bush for taking away critical wage protections from struggling Gulf State workers. He stated in a press release, "Once again the poorest workers are exploited in this disaster. This Administration's continued disregard for the victims of this tragedy is evident in the President's proclamation suspending Davis-Bacon protection for workers in the hurricane torn Gulf" (Corbett 2005). Sullivan further stated:

Once again this Administration is looking out for corporations eager to profit from a national emergency. They want to pay the poorest workers the lowest wages to do the most dangerous jobs. Suspending Davis-Bacon protections for financially distressed workers in the Gulf States amounts to legalized looting of these workers who will be cleaning up toxic sites and struggling to rebuild their communities while favored contractors rake in huge profits from FEMA reconstruction contracts. This is a shameful action and a national disgrace. It's time for this Administration and those members of Congress who blatantly carry the water for corporate gougers during a disaster to realize that denying fair wages to Gulf State workers is no way to help them get back on their feet.[9] (Quoted in Corbett 2005)

In line with proposals such as the suspension of Davis-Bacon, Paul Teller, legislative director of the House Republican Study Committee, circulated an e-mail containing a list of pro-free-market ideas for responding to Katrina. Included among the suggestions were making the entire area a flat-tax free-enterprise zone; waiving the so-called death tax for anyone in the affected area who died between August 20, 2005, and December 31, 2005; repealing or waiving environmental regulations for building contractors; eliminating faith-based regulatory blocks; giving school-choice vouchers to displaced children and their families (this was especially promoted by the guru of neoliberalism, Milton Friedman, in the *Washington Post*); and making the entire region an economic competitiveness zone.[10]

And so there we have it: At the core of this nascent form of disaster capitalism emerges the overriding market logic of the Bush administration as revealed during and after Hurricane Katrina. As Adolph Reed Jr. suggests, "The goal of this [neoliberal ideological position] is acceptance, as the unquestioned natural order of things, that *private* is always better than *public*, and that the main functions of government are to enhance opportunities for the investor class and suppress wages for everyone else. Hurricane Katrina and reactions to it throw into relief how successful that program has been" (2006, 1).

Returning for a moment to the Superdome itself, we would do well to remember how its "rebirth" was heralded when, a year after Katrina, the stadium reopened to national fanfare, with the Saints football team and its players depicted as shining beacons of a redeveloped New Orleans. The gathered, partying throng of 68,000-plus fans—primarily white—jammed the stadium, this time in celebration. Signs could be seen bearing phrases such as "Dome Is Where the Heart Is," "Welcome Home!" "America's Help: Priceless," "Thanks, Y'all," "Our Home, Our Team," and "No Place Like Dome." Sports reporters and television news crews were in abundance (hundreds of media credentials were made available), all promoting a "successful" if not landmark event—quite a departure from the last assembly of bodies in the Superdome.

Additionally, and as part of the $185 million in repairs, FEMA contributed $115 million (out of an initial $1.2 billion in funds awarded to Louisiana by

FEMA in the year following Katrina). Federal coordinating officer Scott Wells said, "[The Superdome's] rehabilitation is *essential* to New Orleans' recovery" ("FEMA Provides $6.3 Million" 2006; emphasis added). Yet the Superdome was not just *repaired*: it received numerous technology upgrades in the form of state-of-the-art LED scoreboards; fan comfort was stressed, as club-level seats (among the most expensive in the stadium) were replaced with leatherette seats; all 137 luxury suites were remodeled (including the addition of plasma televisions in each); and so forth. How is this outlay "essential" to New Orleans? Perhaps one can make the civic pride argument (and when the Saints won the Super Bowl a few years later and gained a national following, it would have been hard to deny such an argument), but remodeling luxury suites owned by corporations and wealthy patrons while schools remained closed in the Ninth Ward raises questions regarding such a, to spin a word, development—the racialized juxtaposition of aid could not be more stark. And, as Christopher Caldwell has noted, moments such as these "make explicit the privileges of the haves and the envy of the have-nots in a way that is embarrassing for both" (quoted in N. Klein 2008, 509).

Thus, and although one could credibly argue that the preceding is a particularly striking example of sport development gone *wrong*, we would side with Naomi Klein in stating that this is, sadly, disaster capitalism at its best (which, of course, means the very worst). And, increasingly, it is getting harder and harder to tell the two apart!

Conclusion

As the days following Katrina turned into weeks, and the weeks into months, two more powerful hurricanes slammed into the southern coast of the United States. This time, the discourse was in place, the hero narratives well planned. The appearance of law and order was back, up and running, organized. News reports focused on federal help that actually managed to arrive. Racial issues were soon ignored once again by the mainstream media. Critical discussions about poverty and class silently receded into the mist as attention was once again focused on such pressing infotainment issues as the Tom Cruise–Katie Holmes marriage or supermodel Kate Moss's arrest on drug charges.

In working through and unmasking this latent, systemic cultural racism, we must reject outright such outlandish claims that the people of New Orleans brought this tragedy on themselves, or that those who did not have the means to vacate the city failed of their own volition. Alongside O'Reilly in the domain of public demagoguery, Senator Rick Santorum (R-PA) heartlessly suggested *punishing* those who are unable to leave a disaster-stricken area, as when he stated: "I mean, you have people who don't heed those warnings and then put people at risk as a result of not heeding those warnings. So there may be a need to look at tougher penalties, candidly, on those who decide to ride it out and understand there are consequences to not leaving" (Hamill 2005). These statements cannot be allowed to stand without strong push-back.

Additionally, we must also be mindful of the disturbing corollary to Rep. Baker's aforementioned theoconservative "blame-the-victim" statement that, in effect, "God cleaned up public housing in NOLA": a nationwide poll of 1,003 Americans conducted several weeks after Katrina hit found that 23 percent of Americans believe that "hurricanes are a *deliberate* act of God" (see also Miller 2007).[11] This absurd implication—that Katrina was a *deliberate*, punitive act by "God" unleashed against the citizens of New Orleans—was propagated en masse by those on the far right, such as Michael Marcavage, director of Repent America (a Philadelphia-based ministry), who stated in a press release: "Although the loss of lives is deeply saddening, this act of God destroyed a wicked city. From 'Girls Gone Wild' to 'Southern Decadence,' New Orleans was a city that had its doors wide open to the public celebration of sin" (Marcavage 2005).[12]

A year after Katrina came ashore, New Orleans remained an empty shell of its past glory. As Spike Lee's documentary *When the Levees Broke* (Lee and Nevins 2006), so powerfully details, decomposed bodies were still being pulled from the wreckage, garbage and debris remained strewn in the streets, and the local economy continued its faltering slide. To mark the one-year anniversary, President Bush spun empty platitudes about how the hurricane launched "a moment of great sadness" and how "although a year has gone by, it's really the beginning of the renewal and rebuilding" ("Bush Sees Rebirth from 'Sadness' of Katrina" 2006).

And now *five* years after Katrina, the racial politics of disaster (and disaster capitalism) continue unabated, this time with the implication that the BP oil spill in the Gulf of Mexico is "Obama's Katrina"—that is, a disaster in which a president is at fault for not doing enough to "fix" things on the ground. Consumed by propagandistic images on Fox News of struggling *white* fishermen neglected by a *black* president, this time the narrative was turned on its head. Obama, already the target of ongoing racist attacks by the conservative right for everything from health care reform to financial regulation, was presented in some quarters as doing intentional harm to small businesses and corporations by either neglecting the region (which he was not) or levying hefty fines against BP for their part in the disaster.[13] Here the engines of capitalism and those who allegedly fuel them (i.e., white men) were presented as the economic victims, and the public narrative actually began to coalesce around them, with calls to divert hundreds of millions of dollars of Katrina relief to the oil spill and its victims (see McClelland 2010).[14]

In the end, to quote Tim Wise, "Let us acknowledge that these racial disparities *matter*, and that they tell us how far removed we are from the equal opportunity society we profess to be, against all evidence to the contrary" (2006). And let us resolve ourselves to do something about it.

NOTES

Acknowledgments: We thank Laura Vaughan (née Hess) for our conversations regarding her time spent volunteering and providing humanitarian relief in Louisiana in the aftermath of Katrina. This chapter draws on, updates, and revisits arguments in Giardina and Hess 2007 and Cole and Giardina 2005.

1. The *New York Times*, among other media outlets, reprinted former FEMA director Michael Brown's shocking e-mails from the time when New Orleans was first under siege. These e-mails contained, among other statements, Brown's telling one staffer, "If you'll look at my lovely FEMA attire you'll really vomit. I am a fashion god." Other e-mails revealed that Brown and his staffers were more concerned with his dinner reservations in Baton Rouge and a dog sitter for his house than with anything of any consequence. Brown was also credited with perhaps the most bizarre comment of the situation when he stated, "Considering the dire circumstances that we have in New Orleans, virtually a city that has been destroyed, things are going relatively well."

2. After introducing Sen. Landrieu (D-LA), Cooper immediately asked her, "Does the federal government bear responsibility for what is happening now? Should they apologize for what is happening now?" Landrieu responded, "There will be plenty of time to discuss those issues" and proceeded to begin thanking various government officials for their disaster relief support. Cooper then interrupted her and passionately stated, "Senator, I'm sorry. . . . [F]or the last four days, I have been seeing dead bodies here in the streets of Mississippi and to listen to politicians thanking each other and complimenting each other—I have to tell you, there are people here who are very upset and angry, and when they hear politicians thanking one another, it just, you know, it cuts them the wrong way right now, because there was a body on the streets of this town yesterday being eaten by rats because this woman has been laying in the street for 48 hours, and there is not enough facilities to get her up. Do you understand that anger? . . . There are people that want answers, and people want someone to stand up and say, 'We should have done more'" ("Cooper to Landrieu" 2005).

3. The sharply mediated divide of public opinion toward "black" and "white" survivors was vividly captured in the main of America's popular-public sphere when the Agence France-Presse and Associated Press news agencies became embroiled in a case of image captioning that set off a mini-firestorm of debate. The first photo, from Agence France-Presse, highlighted a picture of two white individuals (a man and a woman) wading through water carrying bags of food with the description "Two residents wade through chest-deep water after *finding* bread and soda from a local grocery store after Hurricane Katrina came through the area in New Orleans, Louisiana." The second photo, from the Associated Press, highlighted a picture of an African American man carrying similar items with the description "A young man walks through chest-deep flood water after *looting* a grocery store in New Orleans on Tuesday, Aug. 30, 2005" ("Controversy over New Orleans Photo Captions" 2005).

4. According to the 2000 census, the per capita annual income for "whites" in New Orleans, $31,971, was $10,000 above the national average. The per capita income for African Americans, $11,332, was $10,000 below the national average. This $20,000 gap between white and black residents of New Orleans compared to a gap of less than $10,000 nationwide.

5. Former first lady Barbara Bush summed up the view of many on the right when she callously stated with respect to evacuees who had fled to Houston, Texas, "What I'm hearing which is sort of scary is that they all want to stay in Texas. Everybody is so overwhelmed by the hospitality. And so many of the people in the arena here, you know, were underprivileged anyway so this [*chuckle*]—this is working very well for them." A close second in terms of callousness can be attributed to George W. Bush himself who, in touring the region several days later, stated: "We've got a lot of rebuilding to do. . . . The good news

is—and it's hard for some to see it now—that out of this chaos is going to come a fantastic Gulf Coast, like it was before. Out of the rubbles of [Senator] Trent Lott's house—he's lost his entire house—there's going to be a fantastic house. And I'm looking forward to sitting on the porch [*Laughter*]" ("Bush Sees the Bright Side" 2005).

6. Indeed, one coffee table book sold in various souvenir shops in New Orleans one year after Katrina hit featured a U.S. military Black Hawk rescue helicopter as the cover's *focal* image, prominently drawing attention away from four other images of destruction.

7. Let us not forget, as Gloria Ladson-Billings (2003) reminded us in her recent address to the American Educational Researchers Association meetings in New Orleans, that the cultural history of New Orleans has *already* been whitewashed numerous times over, renarrated through capitalism's ghoulish eyes: "They sold slaves in this city. They made a tourist stop out of the place where they sold slaves!"

8. The Davis-Bacon Act of 1931 established the requirement for paying the "prevailing wage" on public works projects. All federal construction contracts and most contracts for federally assisted construction over $2,000 must include provisions for paying workers on site no less than the "locally prevailing wages," including fringe benefits. it is recognized by workers both inside and outside the construction industry as an important milestone in the history of organized labor.

9. Pressured by numerous sides, Bush eventually relented and dropped the suspension of Davis-Bacon.

10. For a full list, see Teller 2005.

11. It is important to point out that the division between income/education levels and responses is quite stark: 31 percent of respondents with a high school diploma or less reported believing that hurricanes are a *deliberate* act of God (compared with 61 percent, who said no), whereas only 11 percent of those with a college degree or higher reported believing that hurricanes are a *deliberate* act of God (79 percent said no). (The key word here is *deliberate*.)

12. Rev. Bill Shanks, pastor of the New Covenant Fellowship of New Orleans, touched a similar chord: "New Orleans now is abortion free. New Orleans now is Mardi Gras free. New Orleans now is free of Southern Decadence and the sodomites, the witchcraft workers, false religion—it's free of all of those things now . . . God simply, I believe, in His mercy purged all of that stuff out of there—and now we're going to start over again" (quoted in Aravosis 2005). And, not to be outdone, the Irreverend Pat Robertson claimed on his September 12 broadcast of *The 700 Club* cable program that Katrina was punishment for the "legalization of abortion." For more on the collision of religion and politics during the Bush era, see Goldberg 2006, Hedges 2007, Kaplan 2005, and Phillips 2006.

13. Most noteworthy was Rep. Joe Barton (R-TX), who went so far as to *apologize* to BP CEO Tony Hayward for the "shakedown" the Obama administration had "forced" on the company (i.e., the $20 billion in funds BP is to contribute to the cleanup of the Gulf Coast region).

14. This at a time when a visitor to New Orleans can still take "disaster tours" around the Ninth Ward starting at $34.95 per person.

REFERENCES

Andrews, D. L. 1993. *Deconstructing Michael Jordan: Popular Culture, Politics, and Postmodern America*. Ph.D. dissertation. University of Illinois, Urbana-Champaign.

Aravosis, J. 2005. "Lead Religious Right Group Promotes Theory That God Wiped Out NOLA on Purpose." *America Blog*, September 2. Available at http://www.americablog .com/2005/09/lead-religious-right-group-promotes.html.

"The Big Disconnect on New Orleans." 2005. CNN.com, September 2. Available at http://
    www.cnn.com/2005/US/09/02/katrina.response/.
Bradley, B. 2005. "Reverend Jesse Jackson Criticizes Hurricane Response." ABC7
    News, September 3. Available at http://abclocal.go.com/wls/story?section=news/
    local&id=3411462.
Briggs, L. 2003. "Mother, Child, Race, Nation: The Visual Iconography of Rescue and
    the Politics of Transnational and Transracial Adoption." *Gender and History* 15 (2):
    179–200.
"Bush Sees Rebirth from 'Sadness' of Katrina: As Bells Toll on Anniversary, President Says
    New Orleans 'Still a Mess.'" 2006. MSNBC/NBC, August 29. Available at http://www
    .msnbc.msn.com/id/14567350/.
"Bush Sees the Bright Side." 2005. *Wonkette*, September 2. Available at http://wonkette
    .com/123665/bush-sees-the-bright-side.
Cobb, W. J. 2009. "It Is about Race." *Essence*, December 16. Available at http://www.essence
    .com/2005/09/12/it-is-about-race.
Cole, C. L., and M. D. Giardina. 2005. "Revelation at the Superdome: The 'Other' America."
    Paper presented at the annual conference of the North American Society for the
    Sociology of Sport, Winston-Salem, NC, October.
"Controversy over New Orleans Photo Captions." 2005. WikiNews Service, September 2.
    Available at http://en.wikinews.org/wiki/Controversy_over_New_Orleans_photos_
    captions.
"Cooper to Landrieu: Americans Want Answers." 2005. *ThinkProgress*, September 1.
    Available at http://thinkprogress.org/politics/2005/09/01/1716/cooper-to-landrieu-
    americans-want-answers/?mobile=nc.
Corbett, H. 2005. "Building Trades Blast Administration for Suspension of Worker
    Wage Protections in Hurricane Stricken Gulf Counties." Building and Construction
    Trades Department press release, September 9. Available at http://www.thefreeli
    brary.com/Building+Trades+Blast+Administration+for+Suspension+of+Worker+
    Wage...-a0135984859.
Davis, M., and A. Fontenot. 2005. "Hurricane Gumbo." *The Nation*, October 20. Available
    at http://www.thenation.com/doc/20051107/davis/6.
Dean, H. 2006. Speech to the Democratic National Committee. Chicago, August 18.
"FEMA Provides $6.3 Million for Superdome Repairs." 2006. FEMA, January 30. Available
    at http://www.fema.gov/news/newsrelease.fema?id=23040.
Ford, G., and P. Gamble. 2005. "The Battle for New Orleans: Only a Real Movement Can
    Win This War." *Black Commentator*, October 27. Available at http://www.blackcom
    mentator.com/156/156_cover_battle_for_no.html.
Friedman, M., D. L. Andrews, and M. L. Silk. 2004. "Sport and the Façade of Redevelopment
    in the Post-industrial City." *Sociology of Sport Journal* 21 (2): 119–139.
Giardina, M. D. 2009. "One Day, One Goal? PUMA, Corporate Philanthropy, and the
    Cultural Politics of Brand 'Africa.'" *Sport in Society* 13 (1): 130–142.
Giardina, M. D., and C. L. Cole. 2005. "Magic Johnson's Urban Renewal: Empowerment
    Zones and the National Fantasy of *HarlemUSA*." In *Race, Identity, and Representation
    in Education*, 2nd ed., ed. C. McCarthy, W. Crichlow, G. Dimitriadis, and N. Dolby,
    379–392. London: Routledge.
Giardina, M. D., and L. A. Hess. 2007. "If Not Us, Then Who? Performing Pedagogies
    of Hope in Post-Katrina America." *Cultural Studies* ↔ *Critical Methodologies* 7 (2):
    169–187.
Giardina, M. D., and C. R. McCarthy. 2005. "The Popular Racial Order of Urban America:
    Sport, Identity, and the Politics of Culture." *Cultural Studies* ↔ *Critical Methodologies*,
    5 (2): 145–173.

Goldberg, M. 2006. *Kingdom Coming: The Rise of Christian Nationalism.* New York: Norton.

Hall, S. 2003. "Cultural Identity and Diaspora." In *Theorizing Diaspora: A Reader,* ed. J. E. Braziel and A. Mannur, 233–246. Malden, MA: Blackwell.

Hamill, S. D. 2005. "Santorum Retreats on Evacuation Penalty Remarks." *Pittsburgh Post-Gazette,* September 7. Available at http://www.post-gazette.com/pg/05250/566844 .stm.

Hedges, C. 2007. *American Fascists: The Christian Right and the War on America.* New York: Free Press.

Kaplan, E. 2005. *With God on Their Side: George W. Bush and the Christian Right.* New York: Free Press.

Klein, E. 2005. "The Media of 100 Years Ago, Today." *American Prospect,* October 30.

Klein, N. 2008. *The Shock Doctrine: The Rise of Disaster Capitalism.* New York: Picador.

Ladson-Billings, G. 2003. Egon Guba Distinguished Lecture. Presented at the annual meeting of the American Educational Research Association, New Orleans, LA, April.

Lee, S., dir., and S. Nevins, exec. prod. 2006. *When the Levees Broke: A Requiem in Four Acts.* New York: 40 Acres and a Mule Filmworks.

Marcavage, M. 2005. "Hurricane Katrina Destroys New Orleans Days before 'Southern Decadence.'" *Repent America,* August 31. Available at http://www.repentamerica.com/ pr_hurricanekatrina.html.

McClelland, M. 2010. "Robbing New Orleans to Pay for BP's Spill." *Mother Jones,* July 14. Available at http://motherjones.com/rights-stuff/2010/07/katrina-recovery-new-orleans-BP.

Mele, C. 2000. *Selling the Lower East Side: Culture, Real Estate, and Resistance in New York City.* New York: New York University Press.

Miller, T. 2007. "The American People Cannot Be Trusted." In *Contesting Empire, Globalizing Dissent: Cultural Studies after 9/11,* ed. N. K. Denzin and M. D. Giardina, 121–135. Boulder, CO: Paradigm.

Neal, M. A. 2005. "Race-ing Katrina." *NewBlackMan,* September 6. Available at http:// newblackman.blogspot.com/2005/09/race-ing-katrina.html.

O'Reilly, B. 2005. "Government Cannot Protect Us: Part Two." FoxNews.com, September 8. Available at http://www.foxnews.com/story/0,2933,168777,00.html.

Phillips, K. 2006. *American Theocracy: The Peril and Politics of Radical Religion, Oil, and Borrowed Money in the 21st Century.* New York: Viking Press.

President's Community Enterprise Board. 1993. *Building Communities, Together: Guidebook for Community-Based Strategic Planning for Empowerment Zones and Enterprise Communities.* Washington, DC: U.S. Government Printing Office.

"Proclamation by the President: To Suspend Subchapter IV of Chapter 31 of Title 40, United States Code, within a Limited Geographic Area in Response to the National Emergency Caused by Hurricane Katrina." 2005. Office of the Press Secretary of the President of the United States, September 8. Available at http://georgewbush-white house.archives.gov/news/releases/2005/09/20050908-5.html.

Reagan, R. 1983. *Public Papers of the Presidents of the United States: Ronald Reagan, 1982.* Washington, DC: U.S. Government Printing Office.

Reed, A., Jr. 2006. "Undone by Neoliberalism." *The Nation,* August 31. Available at http:// www.thenation.com/doc/20060918/reed.

Robinson, E. 2005. "Instant Revisionism." *Washington Post,* October 7, A23.

Sakakeeny, M. 2006. "Resounding Silence in the Streets of a Musical City." *Space and Culture* 9 (1): 41–44.

Scott, A. n.d. "Iraq to Deploy Troops to Louisiana, Mississippi." *Flak Magazine.* Available at http://www.flakmag.com/rejected/louisiana.html (accessed February 12, 2012).

Teller, P. 2005. "Pro-Free-Market Ideas for Responding to Hurricane Katrina and High Gas." *Shock Doctrine*, September 13. Available at http://www.naomiklein.org/shock-doctrine/resources/part7/chapter20/pro-market-ideas-katrina.

Vowell, S. 2003. *The Partly Cloudy Patriot.* New York: Simon and Schuster.

Wise, T. 2006. "'Eracing' Katrina: Historical Revisionism and the Denial of the Obvious." TimWise.org, July 25. Available at http://www.timwise.org/2006/07/eracing-katrina-historical-revisionism-and-the-denial-of-the-obvious/.

5

Nike U

Full-Program Athletics Contracts and the Corporate University

SAMANTHA KING

O ver the past three decades, universities in the United States have become key battlegrounds in a broader struggle over how and by whom socioeconomic relations should be managed and regulated. While education has never been independent of the market, this period has witnessed an intensified encroachment of commercial principles into every aspect of higher learning (Giroux 2007; Hanley 2001; Washburn 2005). In the "corporate university," as this institutional formation is often described (Nelson and Watt 1999), faculty are increasingly imagined as entrepreneurs, students as consumers, and college campuses as hybrid organizations that wed the revenue-producing goals of the business park with the ubiquitous promotion of brand-name goods more commonly associated with the shopping mall.

While these shifts have been widespread and enduring, they have not gone unopposed. Indeed, the 1990s were characterized by a resurgence of campus activism in which staff and faculty unions, student activists, and concerned members of the public have fought to maintain the distinction between democratic values and market interests, between education and job training, and between knowledge and commodity (Benjamin 2000; Giroux 2007; Shaw 1999; White and Hauck 2000). Intercollegiate sport has emerged as a focal point of these struggles as issues such as the multimillion-dollar salaries awarded to some coaches and the labor practices of the corporations that make team apparel have prompted the emergence of an array of social movement organizations. Some of these groups are devoted primarily to reforming college sport to

An earlier version of this chapter appeared as Samantha King and Sheila Slaughter, "Sports 'R' Us: Contracts, Trademarks, and Logos," in *Academic Capitalism and the New Economy: Markets, State, and Higher Education*, edited by S. Slaughter and G. Rhoades, 256–278 (Baltimore: Johns Hopkins University Press, 2004).

bring it in line with the educational mission of higher education (for example, the Drake Group), while for others college sport represents the vehicle through which broader questions related to wage exploitation and global inequalities can be addressed (for example, Students against Sweatshops). Both sets of issues and approaches are the subject of substantial bodies of academic work (Benjamin 2000; Duderstadt 2000; Klein 2002; Sack and Staurowsky 1998; Sage 1999; Shaw 1999; Shulman and Bowen 2001; Sperber 1990, 2001; Thelin 1994; Thelin and Wiseman 1989; Zimbalist 2001).

The focus of this chapter, "full-program" or "multisport" contracts between Division 1A universities and athletic apparel corporations, transects these concerns. I share with scholars of intercollegiate sport a concern with the effects of commercialization on the values, structure, and purpose of college athletics, and on the educational mission of the university. But my main goal here is to explore how the marketing strategies enshrined in full-program contracts are helping to reconfigure, both materially and ideologically, the culture of the university as part of a broader shift toward a branded, privatized society (Chomsky 1998; Comaroff and Comaroff 2000; Duggan 2003; Ewen 2001; Frank 1997; Goldman and Papson 1996; Klein 2002; Rose 1999; Savan 1994; Twitchell 1996). That is, I seek to show how the undermining of intercollegiate athletics and a university education as public goods that are circulated in public spaces through public relationships is both a symptom of and vehicle for the ascent of neoliberal discourse and practice.

Neoliberalism, like any descriptor mobilized by a diverse range of actors to describe a complex set of forces, is a contested and unstable term. I use it to refer to a philosophy and a set of economic and political policies aimed at cutting expenditures on public goods such as education, health care, and income assistance in the name of "free enterprise" and in the service of enhanced corporate profit. Under the auspices of bodies such as the International Monetary Fund, the World Bank, the U.S. Treasury, and the World Trade Organization, the most common strategies used to implement this goal include fiscal austerity, privatization, and deregulation. In Lisa Duggan's words, the general effect of this "wide-ranging political and cultural project" has been to encourage the dramatic "upward redistribution of a range of resources" and a widespread tolerance of increasing inequality in the context of a gradual elimination of a concept of the public good (2003, xi).

The aspects of neoliberalism that form my focus here are privatization and the ongoing encroachment of market principles into almost every facet of everyday life in the United States. In the first two sections of this chapter, I contextualize my argument within the literature on neoliberalism and the corporate university and explore the history of full-program contracts. From there I move to a close reading of eight agreements that make companies like Nike and Adidas the sole suppliers of apparel and equipment to university athletics programs. In exchange for advertising space on the clothing and footwear of players, coaches, trainers, and administrators and on signage across campus, corporations provide varying amounts of free equipment and, in some instances, rewards in cash. Drawing on Naomi Klein's succinct summary of such relationships, I argue that the breadth and depth of the privileges that stem from these contracts enables corporations not simply to *sponsor* the university but to *be* the university (Klein 2002). This phenomenon is evidenced in the hyperpolicing of logos and trademarks, ceding of substantial tracts of campus space to corporate partners, growing corporate influence over athlete and nonathlete recruitment, and nondisparagement clauses that ban criticism of business partners by members of the university community. The exploitative labor practices of these business partners, rightfully the subject of much critical activism and research, are thus also implicated in the fundamental transformation of U.S. higher education and the public sphere of which it is part.

The Corporate University

Research on changes to the economic structure and social functions of higher education suggests that this key realm of public life is being divorced from its role in producing critically engaged citizens (Giroux 2007; Washburn 2005). Like other sites transformed by the implementation of neoliberal philosophies, the corporate university is operated "more like a profit-making business than a public or philanthropic trust" (Ohmann 2003, 131). In the realm of teaching, full-time tenure-track faculty are increasingly replaced with low-paid part-time and temporary workers and by computerized and distance learning schemes (Nelson and Bérubé 1995). In the name of efficiency, and in the face of massive decreases in government funding for higher education, class sizes have grown and face-to-face interaction with research professors has diminished (Washburn 2005). At the same time, fewer lower-income students have the opportunity to enter the university at all, as grants have been slashed and the debt load for students who do manage to attend has increased substantially (Giroux 2007).

The physical environments of campuses have also been transformed as corporate brand names and logos increasingly adorn classrooms, student unions, athletics facilities, museums and galleries, modes of transportation, bathrooms, and cafeterias, the naming rights to which are sold off to the highest bidder. The subcontracting of a variety of services including dining, health care, physical plant services, and textbook retail has added to the increasingly private and profit-oriented structure of campuses (Kniffin 2000). Among the key actors in these shifts are college administrators who are now more often hired for their role as fund-raisers and their ability to bridge the world of academe and business than for their intellectual capacities and experience in public service.

The disconnect between university administrations and the educational function of higher education is further evidenced by the application of productivity and performance measures, by the introduction of interdepartmental competition for resources, and by a focus on efficiency rather than critical thought and intellectual culture (Giroux 2007). In this new regime, high value is placed on vocational and technical disciplines, whereas degree programs that do not translate directly into jobs, located mostly in the humanities and fine arts, find themselves fighting for legitimacy and sometimes even survival (Nelson and Bérubé 1995).

The work of Sheila Slaughter and Gary Rhoades (2004) on what they call "academic capitalism" offers a theoretical framework for understanding how and why these changes have occurred. Their research reveals how groups of actors—faculty, students, administrators, and academic professionals—employ a variety of public resources to create new circuits of knowledge that link institutions of higher education to the new economy. They emphasize that corporatization is not a product of external forces acting on a defenseless university culture but a set of relations produced, in part, by the "investment, marketing and consumption behaviors" of members of the university community (Slaughter and Rhoades 2004, 15). One major effect of this new regime is the commodification and privatization of knowledge exemplified by the gradual replacement of peer-reviewed, federally funded grants with corporate backing for research (Nelson and Watt 1999), corporate ownership of laboratory research results, and university patenting and licensing of faculty inventions. Jennifer Washburn (2005) notes that these shifts have meant that less emphasis is placed on research that offers little immediate financial return but may impact millions of lives, or on the risk-taking experimentation and unconventional inquiry that has historically characterized university research. As Henry Giroux argues, "Such corporatization affects not only the culture of the campus but also the very content delivered by the university, as academic labor is increasingly based on corporate needs rather than on the demands of research for the public good or on education designed to improve public life" (Giroux 2007, 103). Hence, what was once known as the hidden curriculum—the subordination of education to capital—is now open and much vaunted (Giroux 2007).

A Brief History of Full-Program Contracts

These shifts have been nowhere more profound than in the context of intercollegiate athletics, where the connection between universities and their corporate sponsors has been so firmly established that institutions of higher education are often now known as "Nike schools" or "Adidas schools." It did not take long for these symbolic relationships to take hold. In the early 1990s, full-program contracts were practically nonexistent. Indeed, in 1993, the year before the University of Michigan entered into one of the first of such agreements, its legendary "fab five" men's basketball team had no logos whatsoever (beyond the university M) on their uniforms.

The roots of the full-program strategy go back to 1977 when the Converse Corporation signed a deal with Jerry Tarkanian, men's basketball coach at the University of Nevada, Las Vegas, giving Tarkanian two free pairs of shoes for every pair he bought for his team. Nike soon caught on to the idea and in 1978 offered Tarkanian free shoes and warm-up suits for the entire team and $2500 for himself; they also signed Lefty Driesell of the University of Maryland under a similar arrangement (Zimbalist 2001). A year later, sixty more coaches were brought into the Nike fold. The terms of these sponsorships have increased substantially since that time, especially after Nike hired Sonny Vaccaro to recruit coaches as endorsers of its products.[1] John Thompson of Georgetown University was one of the first signees, reportedly earning several thousand dollars in the early 1980s in exchange for requiring his team to wear Nike shoes (Slater and Lloyd 2004). By the late 1990s, Nike was paying top coaches such as Mike Krzyzewski of Duke University more than $1 million a year, plus stock options, a range of perquisites, and assistance in their recruiting efforts (Zimbalist 2001).

Because new corporations depend so heavily on marketing for their success, they must continually build their brands through the appropriation of new spaces on which to imprint their logos, hence the growth of these contracts to include more teams and in many cases entire athletics departments. When Michigan signed a six-year, $7 million contract with Nike in 1994, the athletics director at the time, Joe Roberson, claims that he was motivated not by the money (Michigan's athletics department was running a healthy surplus at the time) but by a desire for transparency in terms of what his coaches were receiving and giving away in their individual contracts with corporate sponsors, for equalization across sports, and for maximization of the financial benefits that he says he did not need (Herbert 2004). The motivations for signing full-program agreements are less significant to my argument than their outcomes, but it is nonetheless important to note here that when Nike pulled out of renewal negotiations with Michigan over the university's desire to include in the contract language consistent with their code of conduct that would apply to working conditions for Nike's overseas factories, the athletics department, now under the stewardship of Tom Goss, was in a less healthy fiscal state. After paying $1.8 million out of the department budget for equipment that the university had been accustomed to receiving as part of their contract with Nike, a new athletics director, Bill Martin, was hired and charged with persuading Nike to enter into a second contract, a task in which he succeeded (Herbert 2004).

In the present moment, it would be unheard of for a school with a large and prominent athletics program to be without a major apparel and equipment sponsor, but this does not mean that such universities operate without regard for competitive pressures. Indeed, there was (unconfirmed) speculation that Michigan transferred its allegiances to Adidas in 2007 not simply because the German company outbid Nike but also because Nike was weary of continuing its relationship with a losing men's basketball program (Rovell 2007). The university's new arrangement with Adidas is much more generous than what it had with Nike and included a $6.5 million signing bonus (the first in college sports history) and a "most favored program clause," which means that no other "Adidas school" can receive more money or goods from the company (Carty 2007).

For their part, corporations like Nike and Adidas view their primary purpose as making not products but images of their brand (Klein 2002). These companies retain control of the cultural capital represented by their logos and brand image, while the raw materials that constitute their shoes and clothes are assembled by low-paid overseas workers. These workers frequently labor under poor conditions in factories owned by subcontractors who seek to outbid one another in order to offer companies the lowest manufacturing costs. Rather than compete on the basis of price, however, Nike and Adidas have actually driven up the amounts consumers must pay by pouring money into their marketing budgets, which pay for huge endorsement contracts for star athletes and sponsorship arrangements for universities.

Placing logos on the uniforms of athletes and coaching staff guarantees exposure to future star endorsees, to students, to live audiences at games, and, crucially, to television audiences. Students are a prime market segment that spent an estimated $80 billion in 1998 on goods and services. They constitute a particularly significant portion of the market for the "athleisure wear" that is sold in college bookstores and adorned with a swoosh or the three Adidas stripes in exchange for a licensing fee paid to the university. Live audiences also provide a great deal of exposure; in 2006 close to 37 million people attended Division I football games, and 48.1 million tuned into the men's National Collegiate Athletic Association (NCAA) basketball championship game in 2010. The particular fans such programming draws are dominated by men in the coveted eighteen-to-thirty-five-year-old market segment. Adding a logo to the uniforms of athletes can thus be more cost effective than buying a thirty-second commercial slot. For instance, when the Ohio State men's football team played Louisiana State University in the Bowl Championship Series title game in January 2008 before a television audience of 23 million, the prominently placed swooshes on the uniforms of the athletes of both teams transformed the game into a four-hour advertisement for Nike.

Full-Program Contracts

While the logos of Nike and Adidas are hypervisible to anyone walking around the grounds of a full-program school, the specific terms of the contracts remain closely guarded secrets, and even very basic information about which schools have contracts, when they were signed, and their monetary value is difficult to obtain. Attributing their confidentiality to concerns about competitive advantage, the major sponsors of college athletics were not willing to reveal to me the names of the schools with which they had contracts when I first contacted them in 2002. On the basis of the results of a simple survey sent to the top level of the 110 schools in Division 1A, telephone calls to schools that did not reply, and media coverage of contract signings, I was able to ascertain that at least twenty-three universities had full-program contracts at that time (fifteen with Nike, seven with Adidas, and one with Reebok). I then filed Freedom of Information Act requests for copies of the contracts of the nineteen public universities in the sample. The analysis presented here focuses on eight contracts that were in effect in 2003, the second year of the research project: Adidas's agreements with Arizona State University (ASU) (Arizona State University 1999), the University of Louisville (University of Louisville Athletic Association 1998), and the

University of Wisconsin–Madison (University of Wisconsin–Madison 2001) and Nike's agreements with the University of Arizona (University of Arizona 1998), the University of Kentucky (University of Kentucky 1997), the University of Michigan (University of Michigan 1994), Texas A&M University (Texas A&M University 1997), and the U.S. Air Force Academy (U.S. Air Force Academy Athletic Association 2002).[2]

The Nike contracts in my sample are remarkably similar. They all involve a form of base compensation, ranging from $82,500 over five years for the U.S. Air Force Academy, to $8.4 million over the course of seven years for the University of Michigan, to $13.5 million over the course of ten years for the University of Kentucky. In addition to base compensation, Nike agreements include the provision of clothing and equipment for all teams. The now expired University of Michigan contract specified the retail value of products at $14 million over seven years, but other Nike contracts specify only the number of items—jackets, shoes, and so forth—allotted to each team, university-sponsored camps, and, in some contracts, a onetime cash payment to the university (University of Kentucky 1997) or the university president's office (Texas A&M University 1997).

In addition to support in the form of cash and products, both corporations pay the universities for the license to manufacture and sell their products bearing university trademarks. The amount of royalties paid ranges from 7.5 percent (for example, ASU) to 10 percent (for example, the University of Michigan). In return, corporations receive a range of perquisites including free tickets to home games, VIP parking passes, space for hospitality events, use of university golf courses for tournaments, access to university facilities for "community programming" events, and a range of other guarantees and benefits discussed shortly.

Although the Adidas contracts share many similarities with those of the company's rival, there are some important differences. The yearly base compensation paid by the corporation to the universities is lower: $275,000 per annum for ASU and $200,000 for the University of Wisconsin–Madison for the first year and $250,000 for the next three. Adidas pays no base compensation in this contract to the University of Louisville. In the context of the increasing disparities between rich and poor programs decried by critics of the commercialization of college sport, the demand that some universities in the sample purchase a minimum number of products from Adidas is particularly interesting. The University of Wisconsin–Madison contract requires that the university order $40,000 worth of Adidas products per year for its camps and clinics in addition to paying a onetime "transition and start-up cost" of $525,000. Similarly, the ASU contract obliges the university to purchase a minimum number of products to be sold on campus in exchange for the free products supplied to the athletics department and team coaches. If the university does not meet the minimum requirement, it must pay Adidas 35 percent of the total shortfall.

A 1998 article in the *Phoenix New Times*, written before the signing of the ASU-Adidas contract, offers some important context for understanding the terms of this agreement (Dougherty 1998). According to its author, John Dougherty, the top marketing goal of ASU's then athletics director, Kevin White, was to "convince Nike to sign an agreement that would put ASU in the company of 18 other universities that have all-school agreements with one of three major sports-apparel manufacturers—Nike, Reebok and Adidas" (1998). Without such an agreement, ASU would struggle to hire a big-time men's basketball coach or to recruit the star talent that White claimed would follow a Nike contract: "The best way to promote the school to young athletes, White says, is to allow Nike or another company to market ASU sports apparel." White continued, "The kids today are driven by brand identification, and it's only going to become more and more prevalent in that regard, in our view" (quoted in Dougherty 1998). While such reasoning is not in itself surprising, what is notable about this story is the lengths to which ASU was willing to go in order to secure an agreement with Nike. For example, in a March 17, 1997, letter to the company, White made the following offer: "In order to further justify (from the Nike perspective) the enhanced relationship, ASU will consider several inordinately large (mammoth) and well-placed venue signage opportunities, i.e., the roof of the University Activity Center and on the respective straight-aways on our new track" (Dougherty 1998). He also "reiterated previous pledges that ASU would be a strong 'political' friend of Nike's" (Dougherty 1998). As Dougherty notes, White's offers strengthened Nike's hand. They now knew that neither Reebok nor Adidas had responded to ASU's request for proposals (RFP), and instead of the $1-million-a-year contract ASU expected when it prepared the RFP *in consultation with Nike*, Nike offered a $565,000-a-year annual package for five years. After much back-and-forth, the negotiations stalled for good, and ASU eventually signed an agreement with Adidas, the terms of which were starkly less generous than those offered to higher-profile programs and considerably more enabling of corporatization. In addition to the promise of minimum purchases outlined previously, Adidas received a twenty-five-year lease on a three-acre site adjacent to the school's softball stadium where a company that tests Adidas products, Athletes' Performance, was built; "access" to players, player locker rooms, and university mailing lists; and a nondisparagement clause preventing criticism of the corporation from members of the campus communities. Although the ASU negotiations represent just one case, they powerfully illustrate how full-program contracts are not simply the outcome of competition between corporations to offer schools the best set of conditions but the result of schools doing what they can to attract corporations and offer them the most lucrative deals—in this case, at the expense of public space and, potentially, academic freedom.

Policing of Logos

The contracts include an inordinate amount of detail about where, when, and how corporate logos must be displayed. All contracts stipulate that athletics department coaches, athletes, and staff must wear official Nike or Adidas clothing and shoes in all program activities (e.g., practices, games, exhibitions, clinics, sports camps, photo sessions, and interviews) and may not wear products bearing brand identification other than that of their corporate partners. In addition, the contracts allow no change to the size, placement, design, or number of logos on any particular product. Products must not be altered to resemble a nonpartner product, and personnel may not wear nonpartner products that have been altered to resemble partner products.

The exceptional circumstances described in the contracts illustrate the extent to which the appearance of logos is micromanaged. If a university needs products that the corporation does not make, the university has to ask permission to use an alternative supplier and that supplier's logo must be removed. Several contracts allow coaches to wear dress shoes rather than official sneakers when a particular public appearance requires more formal dress. In addition, athletes who must wear other products because of a "bona fide" medical condition require a physician's note and must cover competing logos "so as to completely obscure such manufacturer's identification" (University of Kentucky 2001, 9). Injured athletes are also prohibited from wearing tape or bandages that hide a logo. These stipulations prevent small acts of resistance among athletes who do not want to act as walking billboards for corporations, but they also reshape athletics training practices. In most cases, athletes are required to obtain medical certification before they can tape over a logo, and some contracts prohibit taping regardless of medical conditions. The contracts are actively enforced by corporate representatives who visit campuses on a regular basis to ensure that universities are complying with the terms of the contract. On game days, these representatives often join with university "logo cops," officials from the licensing agencies that most universities employ to operate their trademark licensing programs, and law enforcement officials to hunt for trademark infringers to cite or arrest (King and Slaughter 2004).

The Creeping Commercialization of Campus Space and Employees' Time

A reading of full-program agreements reveals how they enable the creeping commercialization of public space. Standard features oblige universities to supply radio and program advertisements, electronic message board endorsements, and public address system announcements on behalf of corporate sponsors, as well as camera-visible signage in the form of billboards, website banners, goalpost pads, basketball bench chair backs, hockey dasher boards, and backlit concourse signs. In three cases, universities must help corporations secure retail outlets on campus if the corporation so desires. In four cases they must help their partners place products in their bookstores and in one case must provide office space and near-campus housing if asked to do so. In the University of Wisconsin–Madison's first full-program contract with Reebok, like ASU's contract with Adidas, the corporation was allowed access to university mailing lists. The University of Kentucky agreement contains a clause to ensure that when future spaces for signage become available, Nike will have first refusal to occupy the space.

The colonization of space is accompanied by the infiltration of employees' workloads by obligations to the corporate partner. In seven contracts, head coaches are required to make a minimum number of appearances for the corporation each year. The number of appearances ranges from two to four, but for University of Wisconsin–Madison coaches the obligation is set at eight eight-hour days per year. The function of university athletics departments and their employees and athletes has thus become increasingly blurred. They not only help market the school (a role they have played for more than a hundred years) but are also now increasingly enlisted as marketing representatives and strategists for the sponsoring corporations. In addition to undertaking appearances for Nike and Adidas, at three schools in the sample, university staff members are required to act as design and marketing consultants. The University of Michigan contract outlined these obligations as follows:

> NIKE shall continue its efforts to produce high quality Products through consultation with coaches and staff of successful athletic programs such as UNIVERSITY and whose full cooperation is important to NIKE, as such individuals have knowledge that can be useful in the research, development and production of NIKE products, and is of the essence of this Agreement. Upon request by NIKE, UNIVERSITY shall request designated Coaches and Staff to provide NIKE with written or oral reports concerning the NIKE Products supplied to each through NIKE's product development and testing program. (University of Michigan 2001, 13)

The blurring of roles between universities and their corporate partners is also enabled by the growing role played by Nike and Adidas in the recruitment of coaches and athletes, particularly men's basketball players. Wetzel and Yaeger (2000) describe how corporations now sponsor middle and high school boys' basketball teams and camps, in addition to university, professional, and national teams. By running these camps, corporations are able to build links to the top high school players in the country, and by providing shoes to players on summer teams and to the schools in which they are enrolled, they develop a direct connection to youth in neighborhoods across the country (Zimbalist 2001).

These relationships are also thought to help in college recruitment efforts, of both athletes and coaches. While ASU wanted a Nike full-program contract to entice better athletes, they also, in 1997, tried to lure Utah basketball coach Rick Majerus to coach the men's team. Majerus, however, was about to sign another contract with Reebok that paid him approximately $500,000 in addition to his salary. According to various media reports, Majerus eventually withdrew from the running because ASU could not match what the coach made with Reebok and because at that time ASU thought it was one the verge of becoming a "Nike school," a move that would compromise Majerus's obligations to Reebok if he were to transfer (Dougherty 1998; Gates 1997). It could be argued, then, that corporations are recruiting coaches and athletes on behalf of universities, recruiting *their* coaches and athletes to what are becoming *their* schools.

Disparagement Clauses

Three of eight contracts include a disparagement clause that bans criticism of corporate partners by members of the university community. The ASU clause reads, "University shall not, during the Contract Term and for a period of two years following the termination or expiration of this Agreement, disparage the adidas brand name, adidas products, or adidas" (Arizona State University 1999, 9). In his discussion of disparagement clauses, Zimbalist (2001) describes how the University of Wisconsin–Madison's 1996 agreement with Reebok met with opposition when members of the campus community discovered the inclusion of a clause that read, "University will take all reasonable steps necessary to address any remarks by any University employee, agent or representative, including a coach, that disparages Reebok" (University of Wisconsin–Madison 1996, 144). Campus members found the clause particularly troubling in light of the international controversy about athletics apparel companies' overseas labor practices: Would the clause mean that someone who was opposed to the use of sweatshop labor be prevented from expressing his or her views? In this case, Reebok agreed to remove the clause, but disparagement continues to be forbidden in some contracts.

The inclusion of clauses requiring corporations to meet university anti-sweatshop/human-rights policy codes is testament to the success of antisweatshop campaigners at campuses across the United States, although how their clauses are enforced varies considerably. Four of eight contracts included such a clause. The University of Michigan and University of Arizona contracts require the use of an independent monitor to determine whether Nike is in breach of the universities' labor standards policies. In the case of the University of Arizona, however, the university and the corporation select the "independent monitor," and no budget is outlined for funding the monitor's work. The time limit for Nike to rectify a breach is set at thirty days, but this can be extended if the situation is impossible to fix within that time. The main limit of the clause, however, is that the university is under no obligation to terminate the contract should violations be found, a reality that has been amply illustrated by the university's weak response to violations brought to its attention by Students against Sweatshops.

In 2007 and 2008, controversy continued to arise across university campuses over the effectiveness of these clauses and the refusal of university administrations to challenge their corporate partners. At the University of California–Berkeley, students engaged in protests against Adidas for threatening to reduce production at an Indonesian factory where workers attempted to form a union, and at the University of Wisconsin–Madison they put pressure on the university administration to drop its agreement with Adidas after a factory in El Salvador subcontracted to produce Adidas university apparel refused to pay about \$825,000 in back pay and severance to workers after the factory closed (Kroll 2007). In the latter case, the university has begun to solicit donations from alumni to repay the workers and requested that Adidas let the university monitor its factories, but it has not responded to the company's violation of the code of conduct. Factory workers and their student allies have thus succeeded in drawing huge amounts of attention to the exploitative practices of apparel companies and a degree of accountability that would have been unimaginable when full-program contracts and brand-name athleisure wear first emerged. But maintaining these contracts and the licensing agreements that allow Adidas and Nike to use university logos remains the top priority of university administrators in spite of persistent public outcry, a certain testament to the priorities of the corporate university.

Conclusion

In the corporate university, students are (captive) consumers delivered by universities to corporations like Nike and Adidas, but potential and existing students, student-athletes, and coaches are also consumers delivered by corporations to universities. In this way, all-school contracts exemplify the increasingly porous boundaries between the function and workings of public universities and the functions and workings of the private sector. In some cases, all-school contracts bring considerable revenue to university athletics departments; in other cases, the fiscal benefits are less pronounced. But in either case, universities are engaging in activities that do nothing to enhance their educational function and much to contribute to the increasingly commercial and branded environment in which education is pursued. Most problematically, networks of actors located both within and outside the university who create and manage full-program contracts seek to deny the multiple meanings of visual symbols in order to protect their exchange value and in so doing exercise strategies at odds with academic freedom and the free flow of ideas.

Crucially, however, this management process is never complete, because full-program contracts help intensify the meaning and "value" invested in brands and thus enable further struggle among those who seek to reduce global inequalities and the increasing privatization of human existence. As Rosemary Coombe argues, "To the extent that specific legal infrastructures create particular forms of signifying power, they also enable, provoke, or invite particular forms of resistance or alternative appropriations" (1999, 262). The Nike swoosh has been successfully appropriated by antisweatshop activists and incorporated into campaigns aimed at drawing attention to the conditions of workers who produce Nike products. In one example, an image of a smiley face accompanied by the caption "happy worker" sits alongside a frowning face in which the Nike swoosh is substituted for the mouth and accompanied by the caption "Nike worker." Thus, as manufacturing has moved offshore and corporations have devoted their energies to image rather than product, distinct logos have become the most valuable assets they own as well as the most valuable assets available to activists who seek to undo the exploitative and culture-cannibalizing practices of the corporations and their university partners.

NOTES

1. Vaccaro was fired by Nike in 1991 and later went on to do similar work for both Adidas and Reebok.

2. The University of Louisville's contract ran from 1998 until 2003, when it was renewed for another five years. The University of Wisconsin–Madison's agreement ran until 2006, when it was renewed for another five years. The University of Kentucky's contract ran until 2002, when it was renewed for another five years. The first University of Michigan contract lasted seven years and was renewed for another seven, until 2008, when the school switched to Adidas. Texas A&M University's first contract ran until 2002, when it was renewed for another five years; in 2007, the school also switched to Adidas.

REFERENCES

Arizona State University. 1999. *Arizona Board of Regents on Behalf of the Arizona State University and Adidas Promotional Retail Operations, Inc. Sponsorship Agreement.* Available from Arizona State University, Tempe.

Benjamin, M. 2000. "Toil and Trouble: Student Activism in the Fight against Sweatshops." In *Campus, Inc.: Corporate Power in the Ivory Tower*, ed. G. White and F. Hauck, 237–252. New York: Prometheus Books.

Carty, J. 2007. "Bill Martin Talks Adidas, Part 1." *Ann Arbor (MI) News*, July 22. Available at http://blog.mlive.com/jim_carty/2007/07/bill_martin_talks_Adidas_part.html.

Chomsky, N. 1998. *Profit over People: Neoliberalism and Global Order.* New York: Seven Stories Press.

Comaroff, J., and J. Comaroff. 2000. *Millennial Capitalism and the Culture of Neoliberalism.* Durham, NC: Duke University Press.

Coombe, R. 1999. "Sports Trademarks and Somatic Politics: Locating the Law in a Critical Cultural Studies." In *Sportcult*, ed. R. Martin and T. Miller, 262–288. Minneapolis: University of Minnesota Press.

Dougherty, J. 1998. "ASU Plays Footsie with Nike." *Phoenix New Times*, March 12. Available at http://www.phoenixnewtimes.com/1998-03-12/news/asu-plays-footsie-with-nike/.

Duderstadt, J. 2000. *Intercollegiate Athletics and the American University: A University President's Perspective.* Ann Arbor: University of Michigan Press.

Duggan, L. 2003. *The Twilight of Equality? Neoliberalism, Cultural Politics, and the Attack on Democracy.* Boston: Beacon Press.

Ewen, S. 2001. *Captains of Consciousness: Advertising and the Social Roots of the Consumer Culture.* New York: Basic Books.

Frank, T. 1997. *The Conquest of Cool.* Chicago: University of Chicago Press.

Gates, C. 1997. "Did Reebok Deal Make Majerus a Shoe-In for U.?" *Deseret News* (Salt Lake City, UT), October 2. Available at http://www.deseretnews.com/article/586458/Did-Reebok-deal-make-Majerus-a-shoe-in-for-U.html.

Giroux, H. 2007. *The University in Chains: Confronting the Military-Industrial-Academic Complex.* Boulder, CO: Paradigm.

Goldman, R., and S. Papson. 1996. *Sign Wars: The Cluttered Landscape of Advertising.* New York: Guilford Press.

Hanley, L. 2001. "Conference Roundtable." *Found Object* 10:103.

Herbert, I. 2005. "Selling Their Soles: the Commercialization of College Sports." *Michigan Daily*, September 21. Available at http://www.michigandaily.com/content/selling-their-soles-commercialization-college-sports?page=0,0.

King, S., and S. Slaughter. 2004. "Sports 'R' Us: Contracts, Trademarks and Logos." In *Academic Capitalism and the New Economy: Markets, State, and Higher Education*, ed. S. Slaughter and G. Rhoades, 256–278. Baltimore: Johns Hopkins University Press.

Klein, N. 2002. *No Logo*. New York: Picador.

Kniffin, K. 2000. "The Goods at Their Worst: Campus Procurement in the Global Pillage." In *Campus, Inc.: Corporate Power in the Ivory Tower*, ed. G. White and F. Hauck, 36–50. New York: Prometheus Books.

Kroll, A. 2007. "Adidas under Fire at Wisc., Berkeley: Athletic Department Signed Contract with Adidas in June." *Michigan Daily*, October 18. Available at http://www.michigan daily.com/content/adidas-under-fire-wisc-berkeley.

Nelson, C., and M. Bérubé. 1995. *Higher Education under Fire: Politics, Economics, and the Crisis of the Humanities*. New York: Routledge.

Nelson, C., and S. Watt. 1999. *Academic Keywords: A Devil's Dictionary for Higher Education*. New York: Routledge.

Ohmann, R. 2003. *The Politics of Knowledge: The Corporatization of the University, the Professions, and Print Culture*. Middletown, CT: Wesleyan University Press.

Rose, N. 1999. *Powers of Freedom: Reframing Political Thought*. Cambridge, UK: Cambridge University Press.

Rovell, D. 2007. "Michigan Goes Adidas as Nike Runs Out on Big Blue." CNBC, July 11. Available at http://www.cnbc.com/id/19710056/.

Sack, A., and E. Staurowsky. 1998. *College Athletes for Hire: The Evolution and Legacy of the NCAA's Amateur Myth*. Westport, CT: Praeger.

Sage, G. 1999. "Justice Do It! The Nike Transnational Advocacy Network: Organization, Collective Actions, and Outcomes." *Sociology of Sport Journal* 16:206–235.

Savan, L. 1994. *The Sponsored Life: Ads, TV, and American Culture*. Philadelphia: Temple University Press.

Shaw, R. 1999. *Reclaiming America: Nike, Clean Air, and the New National Activism*. Berkeley: University of California Press.

Shulman, J., and W. Bowen. 2001. *The Game of Life: College Sports and Educational Values*. Princeton, NJ: Princeton University Press.

Slater, J., and C. Lloyd. 2004. "It's Gotta Be the Shoes: Exploring the Effects of Relationships of Nike and Reebok Sponsorship on Two College Athletic Programs." In *Sport Marketing and the Psychology of Marketing Communication*, ed. L. R. Kahle and C. Riley, 191–210. Mahwah, NJ: Erlbaum.

Slaughter, S., and G. Rhoades. 2004. *Academic Capitalism and the New Economy: Markets, State, and Higher Education*. Baltimore: Johns Hopkins University Press.

Sperber, M. 1990. *College Sports, Inc.: The Athletic Department vs. the University*. New York: Holt.

———. 2001. *Beer and Circus: How Big-Time College Sports Is Crippling Undergraduate Education*. New York: Holt.

Texas A&M University. 1997. *Texas A&M University and Nike USA, Inc. Texas A&M University Multi-Sport Agreement*. Available from Texas A&M University, College Station.

Thelin, J. 1994. *Games Colleges Play: Scandal and Reform in Intercollegiate Athletics*. Baltimore: Johns Hopkins University Press.

Thelin, J., and L. Wiseman. 1989. *The Old College Try: Balancing Academics and Athletics in Higher Education*. Washington, DC: George Washington University, School of Education and Human Development.

Twitchell, J. 1996. *Adcult USA: The Triumph of Advertising in American Culture*. New York: Columbia University Press.

U.S. Air Force Academy Athletic Association. 2002. *Air Force Academy Athletic Association Partnership Agreement Contract. No. F05611-02-H-0399 between the United States Air Force Academy Athletic Association and Nike USA, Inc.* Available from the U.S. Air Force Academy, Colorado Springs, CO.

University of Arizona. 1998. *Sponsorship Agreement between Nike Inc. and the Arizona Board of Regents Contracting Solely for and on Behalf of the University of Arizona.* Available from the University of Arizona, Tucson.

University of Kentucky. 1997. *University of Kentucky and Nike USA, Inc. University of Kentucky All Sport Product Supply Agreement.* Available from the University of Kentucky, Lexington

———. 2001. *University of Kentucky and Nike USA, Inc. University of Kentucky All Sport Product Supply Agreement.* Available from the University of Kentucky, Lexington.

University of Louisville Athletic Association. 1998. *Team Agreement between Adidas Promotional Retail Operations, Inc. and Oregon Corporation (Adidas) and University of Louisville Athletic Association.* Available from University of Louisville, Louisville, KY.

University of Michigan. 1994. *Regents of the University of Michigan and Nike USA, Inc. University of Michigan Multi-Sport Agreement.* Available from the University of Michigan, Ann Arbor.

———. 2001. *Regents of the University of Michigan and Nike USA, Inc. University of Michigan Multi-Sport Agreement.* Available from the University of Michigan, Ann Arbor.

University of Wisconsin–Madison. 2001. *Adidas Promotional Retail Operations, Inc. and the Board of Regents of the University Wisconsin System on Behalf of the University of Wisconsin–Madison Division Intercollegiate Athletics Sponsorship Agreement.* Available from the University of Wisconsin–Madison.

Washburn, J. 2005. *University, Inc.: The Corporate Corruption of American Higher Education.* New York: Basic Books.

Wetzel, D., and D. Yaeger. 2000. *Sole Influence: Basketball, Corporate Greed, and the Corruption of America's Youth.* New York: Warner Books.

White, G., and F. Hauck, eds. 2000. *Campus, Inc.: Corporate Power in the Ivory Tower.* New York: Prometheus Books.

Zimbalist, A. 2001. *Unpaid Professionals: Commercialism and Conflict in Big-Time College Sports.* Princeton, NJ: Princeton University Press.

6

Growth and Nature

Reflections on Sport, Carbon Neutrality,
and Ecological Modernization

BRIAN WILSON

t is becoming commonplace for sport organizations and sport-related corporations to develop and publicize their efforts to operate in more sustainable and environmentally friendly ways. These efforts include creating or upgrading sport venues in ways that reduce environmental impacts, running spectator events while remaining sensitive to concerns about carbon emissions and the recycling of trash, and producing athletic goods and apparel from more sustainable materials.

Views on these emerging "corporate environmentalist" and "sustainable-development" movements vary. On one hand, a wealth of research outlines the potential benefits of more sustainable practices—both for the environment and for businesses aiming to succeed in a marketplace that is increasingly requiring sensitivity to the environmental concerns of consumers (Poncelet 2004). Underlying many of these measures is a belief that economic growth and progress on environmental issues are compatible and can be mutually reinforcing.

On the other hand, some social critics argue that corporate environmentalist practices in particular—referring to industry-driven voluntary "eco-guidelines" and activities intended to promote sustainability—are in many cases hypocritical attempts by businesses to postpone or prevent efforts by government to regulate their industry (Gibson 1999). Implicated in this critique are governments that support deregulation and reregulation practices that leave environmental issues to be addressed through market-related mechanisms and through the work of nongovernmental partners/monitors. The main issue here is that environmental standards imposed by external regulators (e.g., about the use of toxic materials in apparel production or the use of chemicals on golf courses) are likely stricter than those that are "self-imposed" by businesses themselves. If we assume that stricter standards impact the profits of sport-related industries, then it would make good business sense for organizations/

corporations to embrace and publicize *voluntary* corporate environmentalist efforts (Hoffman 2001). It would also seem likely that some businesses would market their pro-environment attitudes without fully embracing eco-friendly practices, what some authors term "greenwashing" (see Lubbers 2002).

Building from a critical assessment of these various and distinct perspectives, I argue in this chapter that responses to concerns about problems associated with, for example, pollution and climate change—responses that are based on the premise that progress on environmental issues should be fueled by continued economic growth—are often ambiguous and easily adopted in ways that prioritize economic concerns over environmental ones. In making this argument I describe and critically assess the interrelated "ecological modernization" (EM) and "sustainable-development" approaches to environmental problems that are commonly adopted by industry and government, discuss concerns about overreliance on scientific advancements and industry-driven "research and development" as solutions to environmental problems, and consider how a more nuanced understanding of power relations should inspire important questions about the environmental practices/promotions of sport-related industries. I also locate these various developments in a historical moment when widespread "neoliberal" policies underlie and drive the decisions made by government about environmental issues. This sociopolitical context is crucial for thinking through not only the characteristics of a theory like ecological modernization (and its relationship with free-market ideologies) but also reasons why an approach like EM is commonly presented as the *only* reasonable response to environmental problems.

In the final section of the chapter, I examine recent claims of "carbon neutrality" by promoters of major sport events as a way of reflecting on the tensions and contradictions underlying industry-driven practices that are motivated by the assumption that progress on environmental issues and economic growth is compatible and mutually reinforcing. As background for this discussion, I begin with a brief overview of key issues of sport and the environment and introduce the concepts *ecological modernization* and *sustainable development*.

Sport, the Environment, and a "Light Green" Response

With the 1994 publication of *Greening Our Games*, David Chernushenko introduced many sport scholars and managers to issues about the impacts of sport on the environment. The book was groundbreaking at the time for identifying environmental issues that are now central considerations for many sport scholars and practitioners. For example, Chernushenko describes the following:

- The impacts of water sports like canoeing and paddling on rivers and lakes that are sometimes modified to improve conditions for competition and training—modifications that have been known, for example, to reduce wetland area (thus reducing breeding area for birds, fish, and insects)

- Ecological problems associated with alpine skiing, including pollution derived from cars driving to resorts, wildlife disruption, soil erosion, and destruction of natural vegetation (see Clifford 2002; Stoddart 2008)
- Issues of the destruction of habitat and forests to create golf courses and the use of scarce water resources and hazardous pesticides to maintain grasses on courses (Wheeler and Nauright 2006)
- The negative environmental legacy of major sport events related to, for example, the construction of facilities that were underused or scrapped following "one-off" events, and the creation of waste and pollution by spectators traveling to and from international events and local venues

Chernushenko's (1994, 30) accompanying discussion of the "impact of a degraded environment of sport" on athletes effectively foreshadowed concerns about pollution in Beijing during the 2008 Olympic summer games (Michaelis 2007). He goes on to insightfully outline preliminary links between commercialization, globalization, and environmental degradation, describing how major sport event organizers, sporting goods manufacturers, and professional sport franchises and leagues have an ecological footprint that "is often big and deep" because these organizers/companies "employ thousands, purchase and consume resources, produce millions of consumer products, use energy and water, generate solid and liquid waste, develop land and operate fleets of vehicles" (Chernushenko, van der Kamp, and Stubbs 2001, 6).

Also included in Chernushenko's writings is a set of recommendations for those interested in running environmentally, socially, and economically responsible sport-related organizations. A key tenet of Chernushenko's approach is that "responsible sport is good business," a view that underlies his argument that running sport events in environmentally friendly ways is becoming essential business practice in light of emerging concerns about environmental impacts, and that it does not have to be overly expensive. He uses several examples to demonstrate this argument, including a description of the 1999 Pan Am Games (under the heading "Pan Am Games Cashes In on the Environment") that includes monetary estimates of donations that were made to the games' environment program by government and business partners/sponsors (Chernushenko, van der Kamp, and Stubbs 2001, 96).

Chernushenko's appeal to the business values of event organizers, sponsors, and managers left him open to critique from critical sociologists like Helen Lenskyj. Lenskyj's view is that Chernushenko, in adopting a liberal approach to environmental issues that is at the base of his appeal to the financial interests of his readers, is both limited and in some ways contradictory (1998, 342). That is, while Chernushenko deserves credit for making important initial steps in the movement against "environmental destruction through sport," his approach positions the environment as an economic resource to be either used or (in this case) preserved as a way of continuing to support economic growth.

Underlying Lenskyj's argument is the suggestion that businesses driven to adopt pro-environment practices because of profit motives are more likely to "greenwash" their environmental image—a point supported by several scholars and environmentalists (see Lubbers 2002) and one that I discuss later in this chapter. According to Lenskyj, the perspective advocated by Chernushenko differs markedly from the "dark green" or "ecocentric" view of the natural environment as "having intrinsic worth" (Lenskyj 1998, 342). The dark green position also implies that existing political/economic systems "are to be challenged when they pose a threat to the environment" (Lenskyj 1998, 342).

Ecological Modernization

By contrasting the "light green" or "ecological modernist" perspective with the "dark green" or ecocentric perspectives commonly promoted by environmentalists and social critics, Lenskyj begins to identify some of the main (and conflicting) perspectives within contemporary environmental sociology. The EM perspective that underlies the views and practices of many corporate environmentalists is based on the assumption that existing industrialization processes can be altered in ways that will make production and consumption "cleaner" and more sustainable. That is, supporters of this approach see economic development and progress on environmental issues to be compatible. Those supporting this view tend to emphasize that eco-efficient business is ultimately more cost effective when expenditures associated with waste reduction, energy use, and litigation/fines (e.g., related to the use of hazardous chemicals) are accounted for—along with the usually emphasized "improved public image" benefit that can lead to sponsorships and loyal customers/staff (Dryzek 2005). If new eco-efficient products are developed and the technologies/products patented and sold, then this is also considered good for business.

It is important to note here that although "ecological modernization" will be the term used and explored throughout this chapter, the concept has much in common with "sustainable development." Sustainable development, which is defined as "the form that economic activity would take if we were to be able to meet the material needs of human society without further harming the planet" (Chernushenko, van der Kamp, and Stubbs 2001, 10), has been described as the "'central story line' of the policy discourse of ecological modernization" (Gibbs 2000, 11, drawing on Hajer 1995). Others scholars, like Dryzek (2005) and Gibbs (2000), take some issue with this depiction, suggesting that strands of EM offer a more rigorous and well-developed theoretical foundation for guiding policy decisions and environmental practice. Either way, and as might be expected, critiques of "sustainable development" as a concept commonly adopted/distorted to promote sustained *economic* development (at the expense of the environment) are akin to criticisms frequently aimed at EM.

With this background, the EM perspective—as an analytic approach—is founded on the assumption that industrial societies progress to the point where new technologies enable the development of more ecologically sensitive "superindustrial" processes, and that various pressures for efficiency require industry to move in this direction (Huber 1985). This presumption about societal development and evolution at least implicitly guides recommendations for governments attempting to intermingle economic and environment progress, and to rouse industry-NGO-consumer relationships that will push these developments. The belief that industry can create new technologies to support these changes is central to this perspective. Coca-Cola's development of more energy-efficient coolers that used hydrocarbon (HC) cooling systems (as opposed to apparently more environmentally damaging hydrofluorocarbons [HFCs]) in response to criticisms from Greenpeace before the 2000 Sydney Olympics—and their promise to heighten their research and development on refrigeration technologies—is commonly cited by EM advocates because it "fits" the theory so well. That is, NGOs and consumers effectively influenced a corporation's decision to develop new technologies that make "business as usual" (i.e., selling cola) more environmentally friendly.

Versions of Ecological Modernization and Their Critics

Hannigan (2006) and others offer powerful critiques of various aspects of ecological modernization. A primary concern is that the theory offers little insight into power relations that surround and underlie interactions between business, government, activists, citizens, and others. For example, abuses of power imbalances within partnerships between corporations and especially activists are commonly shown in studies describing "stakeholder" relationships (e.g., Kearins and Pavlovich 2002). Put another way, and as McCarthy and Prudham (2004) point out, the perspective does not inform thinking about the actual capacity of NGO-monitored corporate participation in markets to address/redress environmental problems (280). The theory also says little about the extent to which corporate leaders are actually motivated to pursue technological solutions at the pace required to address pressing environmental concerns. Other commentators suggest that as long as profit is the primary goal of corporate-driven environmental work, the *appearance* of environmental friendliness will be prioritized over its practice (Lubbers 2002). Again, without sensitivity to power relations in capitalist societies, these fundamental issues will continue to be overlooked. For readers of this book, it will be unsurprising that authors like McCarthy and Prudham observe that the "green capitalism" that will apparently arise from corporate cultural shifts and direct citizen pressure "is suspiciously coterminous with the self-regulation and neo-corporatism characteristic of neoliberalism more broadly" (McCarthy and Prudham 2004, 280).

Still other critics argue that there is no reason to believe that technological advances will be able to adequately respond to ongoing environmental problems (a compelling argument when we consider that many environmental problems are a result of technological developments). As Homer-Dixon (2000) suggests, there is an increasing "ingenuity gap" between the creation/emergence of (environmental) problems and our ability to deal with them.

It is important to note here, however, that, some of these critiques are most applicable to a strand of EM theory known as *"weak" ecological modernization* (Gibbs 2000). The strand refers to a particular philosophical/policy commitment to sustained economic growth alongside the development of new technologies for addressing environmental issues; decision making about the environment driven by scientific, political, and corporate elites; and the use of the preceding principles to guide, sustain, and advance the global economic advantage of "developed" countries (Gibbs 2000, 13, drawing on Christoff 1996). "Strong" versions of the theory, while still based on the idea that continual economic growth and new technologies can drive eco-centered change in industrial societies, point also to the need for a "value reorientation" within the institutional economic structures of society, which is driven by education about environmental issues; more participatory, open, and democratic decision making; and a concern with "international dimensions of the environment and development" (Gibbs 2000, 13). In fact, the "strong" version of the theory is based on a more reflexive understanding of ecological modernity, "whereby political and economic development proceed on the basis of critical self-awareness involving public scrutiny and democratic control"—a contrast to the "weak" form, which is described as being "a lifeline for capitalist economies threatened by ecological crisis" (Gibbs 2000, 12).[1]

Differences between "strong" and "weak" versions of EM are certainly relevant when it comes to devising and attempting to implement social change in the environment and in determining the relationship between ecological modernization and neoliberal approaches to governance. That is, weak forms of ecological modernization tend to be optimistic about market-driven neoliberal approaches, while stronger versions could be viewed as a moderate response to problems associated with market-driven approaches. This does not change the fact that neither version of the theory adequately accounts for issues of power. For example, although proponents of "strong" ecological modernization are optimistic about change that is more democratic and participatory, the model does not aid an understanding of why many corporations have been shown historically to be reluctant/hostile collaborators with other environmental stakeholders and to greenwash their image (in lieu of making changes in industrial practices) (Harvey 1996). This also does not offer a framework for thinking through why EM is in many cases seen by industry and many governments as the *only* reasonable guide for environmental change, with other potentially progressive approaches being marginalized (Dryzek 2005). As pertinently, neither strand adequately accounts for the possibility that there may be environmentally based limits to economic growth.

Neoliberalism and Ecological Modernization

Still, the distinction between the stronger and weaker version of EM is significant when it comes to examining the environmental practices of sport-related organizations/corporations, and especially the sociopolitical context within which these practices take place. Put simply, strong ecological theory is not akin to an "open markets" approach to dealing with environmental problems that has been associated with neoliberal forms of governance. Arthur Mol, an advocate for ecological modernist approaches to environmental problems, makes this point clearly in his suggestion:

> Economy-mediated environmental innovations and transformations as they are developing now are significant and a major step, but they are far from sufficient. Economic mechanisms, institutions and dynamics will always first follow economic logics and rationalities, which implies they will always fall short in fully articulating environmental interests and pushing environmental reforms, if they are not constantly paralleled and propelled by environmental institutions and environmental movements. Neo-liberals who would have us believe that we can leave the environment to the economic institutions and actors are wrong. Besides, since economic interests are distributed unequally, any environmental reform brought about by economic players will display similar inequalities, making the results sometimes ambivalent. (2002, 103–104)

Mol's point is an important one because it implicitly highlights the distinction between stronger versions of EM—which see a role for government regulation that is not overly influenced by the desires of industry elite—and market-driven approaches to environmental concerns. While I agree that neoliberal governance should not be equated with an ecological modernist strategy generally speaking, this does not change the fact that *when neoliberal reformists speak of environmental change, aspects of weak ecological modernist discourse are commonly and selectively adopted.* For example, the pursuit of scientific innovation to address environmental problems (a central tenet of ecological modernist thinking) is well aligned with neoliberal thinking and can be easily adopted by market-driven thinkers who deemphasize the government regulation measures recommended by strong EM proponents.

In a related way, the neoliberal and EM commitment to sustained economic growth as part of the "solution" to environmental problems is similarly susceptible to manipulation by believers in a deregulated open market system or, as many analysts of neoliberal environmentalism note, a "reregulated" system in which governments are structured to selectively intervene and regulate in ways that are especially enabling for corporate environmentalists (Bakker 2004). The pursuit of the best solutions to environmental problems through participation in a global marketplace is palatable from an ecological modernist perspective and a fundamental part of neoliberal-influenced approaches to governance. Similarly, the commodification of both "nature" and environmental impacts (e.g., in the development of carbon credits that can count against carbon emissions at sport events) is a central feature of neoliberal discourse and something that ecological modernization discourse is either ambivalent to or implicitly supportive of in its commitment to the linking of economic growth and progress on environmental issues.

The key point here is not to suggest that neoliberalism and ecological modernization are the same. They are not the same, as ecological modernization supporters are clear to point out through their critiques of neoliberalism. The main argument is that existing research and theory that describe how power inequalities are maintained and reinforced would offer a foundation from which to explain why EM responses to environmental problems—which, in theory, are about balancing economic growth and progress on environmental issues— would likely be manipulated in ways that ultimately favor economic growth.

The Treadmill of Production and
Weak Ecological Modernization

Motivated by just this issue, several authors within environmental sociology have devised neo-Marxist-inspired critiques of societies in which economic growth is prioritized over environmental issues and sustainability. One of these commentators is Allan Schnaiberg (1980; see also Schnaiberg and Gould 2000), who is best known for developing the "treadmill of production" concept. The treadmill metaphor emerges from Schnaiberg's observation that environmental damage is the result of a self-reinforcing mechanism, in which the policies that support economic growth (and environmental damage) are continually revised to encourage more economic growth. That is, the response to resource shortages is always the pursuit of new areas to exploit, not the reduction of consumption or modification of lifestyles. The treadmill argument is founded on long-standing critiques of consumer culture that speak to the myriad ways that consumer demand is created and reinforced in order to meet the underlying goal of a hypercapitalist culture—economic growth. The model is based on the idea that consumer cultures implicitly support an ambivalent view of the ecological impacts of this growth.

The actions of governments in their dual role as an initiator of economic growth and a regulator of environment-affecting activity are intriguing in this context because, of course, these actions will ultimately be guided by the governmental priorities—priorities that, in a neoliberal era, would favor market-driven activity (Hannigan 2006). Hannigan speaks to this issue in his suggestion that economic growth remains the priority for many governments, although efforts are made to appease (environmentalist) others:

> Governments often engage in a process of "environmental managerialism" in which they attempt to legislate a limited degree of protection sufficient to deflect criticism [e.g., about environmental concerns] but not significant enough to derail the engine of economic growth. By enacting environmental policies that are complex, ambiguous and open to exploitation by the forces of production and accumulations the state reaffirms its commitments to strategies for promoting economic development. (2006, 21)

Also pertinent here are the interrelationships between government, business, and some NGOs in generating consent for the policies that privilege growth-driven solutions to environmental problems. In this context, approaches like EM may be privileged as part of a political strategy that is, as Davidson and MacKendrick argue, based on the

> concealment of tensions and contradictions regarding a given political issue [e.g., about the best approach for tackling climate change], while giving the impression of goal achievement. Such symbolic practices utilized in official policy discourse could become quite powerful, particularly if they are able to exclude ideas that economic development and environmental protection are in serious tension. (2004, 50)

The Practice and Discourse of Ecological Modernization in Sport

With this background, I discuss some instances and ways that sport organizations and corporations have adopted ecological modernist discourse and practices in doing and publicizing their environmental work—and identify instances where the types of "tensions and contradictions" referred to by Davidson and MacKendrick (2004) appear to be concealed. In particular, I focus on the case of "carbon neutral" sport events to demonstrate ways that EM discourse appears to have guided environment-related efforts and to identify "blind spots" and contradictions in the practice and promotion of carbon neutrality.

My intent in discussing the topic in this manner is certainly not to diminish the efforts of those working to improve environmental conditions who are guided by strong ecological modernist principles. The goal is simply to highlight ways that these pro-environment efforts can be distorted, and to suggest that alternative possibilities for dealing with environmental issues cannot inform an evolving dialogue about "solutions" when they are marginalized. For example, approaches to dealing with environmental problems that are not based on principles that underlie the smooth workings of a consumption-oriented culture are rarely considered—which is why the "treadmill of production" approach and other critical perspectives are so crucial in guiding reflections/analyses on environmental work. Put another way, advocates for ecological modernization who are frustrated by greenwashing practices of many industries and the selective and problematic adoption of ecological modernization principles benefit greatly from critical analyses that are informed by theories designed to explain relations of power.

Sport, Carbon Neutrality, and the "Offset Credit"

It is becoming routine for sport organizations to promote their goal of running "carbon-neutral" mega-events. The list of well known/publicized examples of this includes the 2006 Winter Olympics in Turin, Italy; the FIFA 2006 World Cup in Germany; the 2007 Super Bowl in Miami; and the 2006 Commonwealth

Games in Melbourne, Australia. What this means is that event organizers implement a variety of initiatives to reduce emissions associated with, for example, travel to events (air and ground), waste through disposable materials, and electricity use. Initiatives may include the following:

- The use of renewable energy technologies (e.g., solar energy panels were used in Dolphin Stadium at the 2007 Super Bowl in Miami)
- Featuring bottle-recycling stations throughout event venues
- Trash reduction strategies, including sorting stations and education about waste reduction for event attendees
- Encouraging the use of energy-efficient transportation (e.g., a hydrogen-powered bus was provided for media transport at the 2006 World Cup, and the event's spectators were encouraged to access venues using buses and bicycles; at the 2007 Indy 500, all cars ran on 100 percent fuel-grade ethanol, an emission-friendly form of fuel)

(Davidson 2007)

A crucial final step for event organizers intent on running "carbon neutral" events is the purchase of "carbon offset" credits. Purchasing a credit is akin to making a contribution to a carbon-reducing initiative (e.g., a renewable energy project). These projects are often located in developing countries because many of these countries do not have carbon emission targets as determined within the Kyoto Protocol—a criterion for projects that receive "carbon offset" approval from Green Standard (a widely recognized certification system). It is also relevant, of course, that funding offset projects is much less expensive in developing countries. Examples of offset projects funded through the FIFA 2006 World Cup offset program are described in the following excerpt taken from a press release by the United Nations Environment Programme (UNEP):

The Organizers [of the World Cup] . . . purchased 500,000 Euros-worth of carbon offsets in India where 900 farmers and their families in Tamil Nadu are getting biogas cooking fuel from cow dung instead of using fuel wood or fossil fuels. Offsets also came from investments in South Africa with financing from FIFA, Deutsche Telecom and PlasticsEurope in a sewage gas project in Sebokeng Township near Johannesburg and a sawdust-fuelled fruit drying furnace in Letaba, northern South Africa. These offsets saved an estimated 100,000 tonnes of carbon dioxide entering the global atmosphere. Christian Hockfeld of the Oeko Institute said: "That means that at the end we over-compensated the additional emissions in Germany by 8,000 tonnes. It means that the Green Goal actually went further than we had planned by also compensating for the estimated 5,100 tonnes as a result of international travel by teams and officials." (United Nations Environment Programme 2006)

To determine the number of credits that need to be purchased, event organizers work with independent experts who verify the carbon emissions of an event (e.g., Super Bowl organizers worked with Oak Ridge National Laboratory, a facility of the U.S. Department of Energy located in Tennessee [see Davidson 2007]).

It would be fair to suggest that these offset programs are becoming a standard for major sport events, as both an environmental practice and a marketing tool. While sport organizations feature their environmental-related successes in promotional material aimed at green consumers, a *Forbes* article on the "greening" of the Super Bowl would suggest that positive media coverage also accompanies claims of "carbon neutrality" (Davidson 2007). Such benefits would be predicted by Chernushenko and other ecological modernists, who argued that "going green" is good for business. Carbon offsetting is becoming so entrenched in strategy for addressing environmental problems that a 2007 UNEP report that evaluated the progress of the Beijing Olympic Games on environmental issues—a report that was largely positive in its assessment of the work that has been done to date—was critical of the Beijing Organizing Committee for the Olympic Games (BOCOG) for excluding carbon offsetting as an eco-friendly practice:

> Concerns [that UNEP has about the work of BOCOG on environmental issues] include a missed opportunity in terms of offsetting greenhouse games. The Torino Winter Olympics of 2006 offset additional carbon dioxide through funding environmentally friendly energy projects in developing countries. The Green Goal initiative of the FIFA World Cup adopted similar measures to cover greenhouse gases that could not be easily reduced at home. Eric Falt, UNEP Director of Communications and responsible for the organization's sports and environment programme, said carbon offsetting is "increasingly a feature of high-profile events and is an initiative being adopted by a growing number of sports organizations and private sector entities. It is not too late for BOCOG to opening declare a commitment on climate change and offsetting." (United Nations Environment Programme 2007)

Too Good to Be Green?

Underemphasized or unsaid in many reports about the environmental successes and strategies of sport event organizers is the ongoing controversy about the practice of carbon offsetting. Even for those who generally support market-driven responses to societal concerns, it is acknowledged that carbon offsetting is virtually impossible to implement in a fully standardized manner. For example, it is extremely difficult to determine whether a project that is being funded through a carbon offset program would have taken place if the offset donation were not available, as Gillenwater and colleagues explain:

> There is no correct technique for determining additionality [the term that refers to the ability of a project to "add" an emission offset that would not

have taken place otherwise] because it involves the evaluation of counterfactual circumstances. No test for additionality can provide certainty about what would have happened otherwise. The challenge is akin to statistical hypothesis testing. Adopt tests that are too stringent and one risks disqualifying many truly additional projects, thus restricting offset supplies and increasing their prices. (2007)

A related problem is that offset programs, as they stand, do not have a standardized system for regulation (Gillenwater et al. 2007). While the World Wildlife Fund (WWF) and several other NGOs support the "Gold Standard" certification program that offers the most stringent criteria for determining eligible credits, there are various other programs—and it is still debatable whether any of these programs are capable of assessing something as intangible as "additionality" or the relationship between carbon emissions at mega-events and carbon offset through environmental projects. In fact, at least some of those sympathetic to market-driven approaches (like Gillenwater et al. 2007) admit that "mandatory government policy must be our primary approach to dealing with climate change and the GHG [greenhouse gas] emissions that cause it," although support remains for the use of voluntary compliance measures while guidelines are being developed.

Others point out that when carbon credits are sold "up front" for projects that have not yet been completed, it is possible that the project will not be completed at all—and will not fulfill the promise of emission savings (meaning that the "claimed" carbon offset never takes place). Still others point to the difficulties experienced by those hired to calculate the carbon emissions of mega-events, who try to distinguish between "avoidable" and "unavoidable" emissions. For example, a report prepared by the Öko-Institut in Berlin that described environment-related projects for the World Cup 2006 indicated that "92,000 tonnes of unavoidable greenhouse gas emissions that were brought about by the 2006 FIFA World Cup in Germany will be more than offset by three climate protection projects" (Stahl, Hochfeld, and Schmied 2006, 93). An emissions-trading expert from the same organization was referred to in an article by Schiermeier (2006) in the journal *Nature* that problematized carbon offsetting. The article reads:

> It's almost impossible for big companies and events to decide which activities to include and where to draw the line between necessary and avoidable emissions, says Martin Cames, an emissions-trading expert with the Öko-Institut in Berlin. This means that extra emissions are often underestimated. For example, the Öko-Institut worked out the carbon footprint of the World Cup for FIFA, but simplified the calculation by counting only the extra flights caused by the event. (Schiermeier 2006, 976)

Schiermeier goes on to point out that afforestation and reforestation projects, which are commonly used for offsets, are problematic because "there is no guarantee that a forest will be permanent . . . [and] when trees die, they release all the CO_2 they absorbed during their lives" (2006, 977). For this reason, those applying "Gold Standard" certification principles will not certify these projects—although other certification programs continue to include them.

Reflections on Sport, Carbon Offsetting, and Ecological Modernization

Although leaders and participants in the movement for "carbon neutral" sport events may not recognize themselves as "ecological modernists," their practices and discourses are in many ways consistent with the views underlying the EM perspective. At a minimum, the practices used by event organizers—such as carbon offsetting and the creation/adoption of new technologies that enhance energy efficiency—are based on the assumptions that economic growth and progress on environment-related issues are compatible and that new technologies can be relied on to aid a transition toward more sustainable sport. As noted earlier, these are central tenets of the EM perspective, in both its strong and weak forms.

Other characteristics of the "carbon neutral" movement are akin to either a weak variety of EM or, in other instances, a more blatant mode of "market environmentalism." Consider, for example, the unstandardized, ambiguous regulatory system that is now in place regarding carbon offsetting. Researchers like Schnaiberg and Gould (2000) would rightly point out that this system is ripe for exploitation as part of the treadmill of production that prioritizes economic profit over environmental issues. Scholars like Dryzek, Hajer, and Davidson and MacKendrick, who study ways that discourses are used to promote the interests of certain groups by presenting particular versions of reality, would likely point to the assertive claims made by sport organizations about achieving "carbon neutrality" as a form of greenwashing. That is, with clear, assertive, and unequivocal claims that link eco-friendliness and offsetting through press releases and mass media coverage, the ambiguous evidence and the problematic assumptions underlying carbon offsetting fall away, and carbon offsetting becomes an unquestioned, commonsense approach to dealing with environmental destruction.

That said, it would be unfair to suggest that the hegemony of carbon offsetting and other market-driven approaches to dealing with sport-related environmental problems is in any way "complete." A variety of critical commentators have questioned the assumptions underlying these eco-strategies (Lohmann 2005; Monbiot 2006; Thornes and Randalls 2007), and environmental groups like Friends of the Earth commonly question these strategies. Still, if the UNEP's report on the Beijing Olympics and the widespread acceptance that carbon offsetting receives in positive coverage of "carbon-neutral" sport events is any indication, it would be naïve to think that the promotion and implementation of this practice is not central to the greenwashing efforts of at least some sport organizations.

Exposing Ecological Modernization

Also exposed in the discussion of carbon offsetting are the myriad ways that assumptions underlying "strong" and "weak" versions of ecological modernism are problematic and, in turn, why responses to sport-related environmental problems that are overly reliant on ecological modernist solutions are problematic. For example, the faith in technology that is fundamental to EM's premise that "economic growth" and "progress on environmental issues" are compatible is brought into question by those who critique existing procedures for balancing carbon emissions against offset projects. While offsetting advocates may argue that it is "just a matter of time" before a standardized and effective system is devised, this does not alleviate the contradiction that exists between an environmental problem (e.g., climate change) that requires a timely solution and a paradigm that is based on the unpredictable ability of researchers to arrive at this solution in a timely fashion. This is what Homer-Dixon (2000) refers to in his description of an "ingenuity gap" that emerges in societies that are overly focused on scientific "progress." Robertson extends this argument in his suggestion that in a neoliberal (meaning, in this case, market-driven) approaches to nature, "there is no room for a view of science as a shifting and constructed set of knowledges" (2004, 118).

It would also seem that the carbon offset projects themselves that take place in developing countries could be subject to the same sorts of critiques that are aimed at some "sport for development" programs (e.g., little regard for local cultures, inadequate self-assessment tools, underdeveloped exit strategy [see Giulianotti 2004]). These problems take on particular significance because of claims made by sustainable-development advocates who are intent on creating solutions that jointly address development-related social and environmental issues. There is also a well-developed critique of partnerships between NGOs, government, and corporations in sport-related contexts and elsewhere that would seem to undermine the optimistic view of collaboration offered by some ecological modernists. For example, Kearins and Pavlovich's (2002) study of the role played by stakeholders in the "greening" of the Sydney Games described the undesirable compromises that are sometimes made by environmental groups who are less powerful members of collaborations. Beder (2002) offers a more incisive critique in her outline of ways that the NGO Greenpeace has lost much credibility because of the group's moderate, passive, and/or hypocritical stances on issues like "the disposal of toxic waste in landfill" in their work with the Sydney Organizing Committee for the Olympic Games (SOCOG).

Abstractions, Fictitious Commodities, and the Promethean Response

Among the most troubling aspects of a discourse about the environment that is almost exclusively EM-inspired is, quite simply, the unquestioned positioning of "nature" as something that is, by right, owned and manipulated by humans. Marxist-inspired authors have described this as the "inscription of capital on

nature, [an inscription that is] . . . mediated by an array of representation practices, including narratives of science and commodification" (Robertson 2000,
464, drawing on Smith 1990).

Several issues here are especially pertinent to the "carbon offsetting and
sport" case and can be drawn out with the help of Marxist-related theory on the
environment. First, carbon offsetting around mega sport events, even if well
regulated (which it currently is not), can be understood as a form of "abstrac-
tion" in the Marxist sense. That is, by measuring and documenting the level
of emissions associated with, for example, the destruction of trees to build a
highway to an event venue, the distinctiveness of the tree (and the air that will
be impacted by increased traffic and fewer trees) in the context within which
it exists (e.g., Vancouver or Beijing) is lost—*even if more trees are planted in
another location*. In this way, the carbon emission of a tree that is to be destroyed is severed/abstracted from "the messy uniqueness of the physical site
in which it exists" (Robertson 2000, 473). The destroyed tree or polluted air is
further abstracted when the carbon emission measure that is associated with it
is considered to be "equivalent to"—in terms of purchasable carbon credits—
emission-saving efforts in another part of the world (see Castree 2003).

Dryzek (2005) refers to the discourse that underlies this approach to environmental issues as the Promethean discourse.[2] A central assumption that
permeates Promethean thinking is that "the Earth"/nature—which is considered to be inert and passive—is a resource to be exploited for human use. A
related assumption is that human beings are inherently competitive and that
this competition, if channeled correctly, leads to "innovative means for overcoming emerging scarcities" (Dryzek 2005, 58). It is not a stretch to see how
Promethean discourse pervades and is taken for granted within arguments that
underpin EM and neoliberal thinking.

What is missing from EM discourse is any recognition of the *interrelationships* (i.e., the nonbinary relationships) that societies and individuals have with
"nature." Responding to this shortcoming, theorist Bruno Latour (1993, 1999)
has come to prominence because of his insightful and provocative descriptions
of ways that humans and nature's nonhuman "actants" are *co-creators/co-con-
structors* of the world's environments (and that all environments are products of
the social and biophysical). Stoddart (2008), in his study of eco-politics, skiing,
and the environment, describes (drawing on Latour) person-nature "collectives"
on ski hills and identifies interrelationships between skiers, snow, mountains,
and animals. Emphasized in his account is the agency of nonhumans in the
form of avalanches, weather, and "good and bad" snow conditions. Drawing on
Donna Haraway's (2003) work, Stoddart also illustrates the role of animals as
"companion species" or "significant others" on ski hills, indicating how "beyond
the symbolic bears or caribou that are recruited into skiing discourse, there are
actual animals that share the skiing landscape . . . that may be negatively affected by human activity within that landscape" (Stoddart 2008, 108–109).

With this in mind, it would seem that greater emphasis on interrelationships between humans and nonhumans, and especially the agency of nonhu-

mans in this context, would sensitize analysts and policy makers to some of the problems with abstracting, commodifying, and modifying "nature." To articulate this point, Castree uses the example of genetically modified foods produced by transnational corporations like Monsanto, suggesting that "those foods and their ecosystemic outcomes can take on very powerful, unpredictable and lively agency with real consequences" (2002, 130). In this sense, and following the work of Polanyi, the positioning of nature as an abstracted "fictitious commodity" that cannot "be detached from the rest of life" takes on particular significance (1957, 72).

Conclusion

> Imagine a conversation between an economist and a geologist over the space-time horizon for optimal exploitation of a mineral resource. The former holds that the appropriate time horizon is set by the interest rate and market price, but the geologist, holding to a very different conception of time, argues that it is the obligation of every generation to leave behind an aliquot share of any resource to the next. There is no logical way to resolve the argument. It, too, is resolved by force. The dominant market institutions prevailing under capitalism fix time horizons by way of the interest rate and in almost all arenas of economic calculation (including the purchase of a house), that is the end of the story. (Harvey 1996, 229)

Harvey's scenario is helpful for demonstrating how an analysis of existing responses to environmental problems requires sensitivity to relations of power—something to which strict ecological modernization advocates are not sensitive. The underlying commitment to economic growth and unwavering faith in science that is integral to EM thinking would be less disconcerting if it were not *the* perspective that guides so many sport-related, corporate-driven responses to environmental problems. Reactions to vital issues like those raised about the environment require creative and multifaceted strategies informed by a variety of perspectives. When EM is the taken-for-granted guide to environmental practices such as carbon offsetting, then "utilitarian and fetishistic dispositions toward the biophysical world" become entrenched, as Heynan et al. (2004, 12) observe. The point of this chapter is that the good intentions and actions of sport managers/organizers who are guided by EM are at times undermined/distorted because the approach lacks a fundamental explanation of power relations.

It is here in particular that critical sociologists of sport have a crucial role to play. Although scholars like Lenskyj (1998, 2002), Beder (2002), Cantelon and Letters (2000), Maguire et al. (2002), Wheeler and Nauright (2006), Stoddart (2008), and those who published articles in the 2009 special issues of the *Journal of Sport and Social Issues* on sport and the environment have initiated research on environmental issues, much work is needed. On the one hand, attention must be paid to alternative approaches to addressing sport-related environmental concerns, including novel and effective forms of resistance, and strategies for impacting environmental policy. This includes identifying and highlighting eco-friendly subcultures and lifestyles within sporting worlds, as Wheaton (2008) has done in her research on the environmental pressure group Surfers against Sewage. On the other hand, studies are needed that continue to document and examine environmental politics in and around sport (e.g., Stolle-McAllister's 2004 study of the anti-golf movement in Mexico), with the goal of exposing myths that hinder creative/inclusive thinking about pro-environment social and political action. The hope is that these forms of research and critique will contribute to a more democratic debate about and response to one of the pressing issues of our time.

NOTES

1. In these respects, strong versions of EM are akin to Ulrich Beck's (1992) vision of a reflexive and modernizing "risk society." That is, Beck and strong ecological modernists like Mol (1995) share a belief that a society that has come to recognize the problems it has created through modernization and industrialization must, in turn, solve these problems through *more* modernization, industrialization (and science) (see Buttel 2000). As Buttel (2000) notes, though, Beck and strong ecological modernists differ markedly in their views on the contributions to be made by radical environmentalists and new social movement groups in the change process.

2. The Promethean response refers here to Greek mythology, in which the Titan Prometheus stole fire from the god Zeus, thus increasing the ability of humans to manipulate the Earth. According to Dryzek, "Prometheans have unlimited confidence in the ability of humans and their technologies to overcome any problems—including environmental problems" (2005, 51).

REFERENCES

Bakker, K. 2004. "Neoliberalizing Nature: Market Environmentalism in Water Supply in England and Wales." In *Neoliberal Environments: False Promises and Unnatural Consequences*, ed. N. Heynan, J. McCarthy, S. Prudham, and P. Robbins, 101–113. New York: Routledge.
Beck, U. 1992. *Risk Society*. Beverly Hills, CA: Sage.
Beder, S. 2002. *Global Spin: The Corporate Assault on Environmentalism*. White River Junction, VT: Chelsea Green.
Buttel, F. 2000. "Ecological Modernization as Social Theory." *Geoforum* 31 (1): 57–65.
Cantelon, H., and M. Letters. 2000. "The Making of the IOC Policy as the Third Dimension of the Olympic Movement." *International Review for the Sociology of Sport* 35 (3): 249–308.
Castree, N. 2002. "False Antitheses: Marxism, Nature and Actor-Networks." *Antipode* 34 (1): 119–148.
———. 2003. "Commodifying What Nature?" *Progress in Human Geography* 27 (3): 273–297.
Chernushenko, D. 1994. *Greening Our Games: Running Sports Events and Facilities That Won't Cost the Earth*. Ottawa, Canada: Centurion.
Chernushenko, D., A. van der Kamp, and D. Stubbs. 2001. *Sustainable Sport Management: Running an Environmentally, Socially and Economically Responsible Organization*. Nairobi, Kenya: United Nations Environment Programme.
Christoff, P. 1996. "Ecological Modernisation, Ecological Modernities." *Environmental Politics* 5 (3): 476–500.

Clifford, H. 2002. *Downhill Slide: Why the Corporate Ski Industry Is Bad for Skiing, Ski Towns, and the Environment*. San Francisco: Sierra Club Books.

Davidson, A. 2007. "Greening the Super Bowl." *Forbes*, January 19. Available at http://www.forbes.com/2007/01/19/super-bowl-green-sports-biz-cz_ad_0119green.html.

Davidson, D., and N. MacKendrick. 2004. "All Dressed Up with Nowhere to Go: The Discourse of Ecological Modernization in Alberta, Canada." *Canadian Review of Sociology and Anthropology* 41 (1): 49–65.

Dryzek, J. 2005. *The Politics of the Earth: Environmental Discourse*. New York: Oxford University Press.

Gibbs, D. 2000. "Ecological Modernisation, Regional Economic Development and Regional Development Agencies." *Geoforum* 31 (1): 9–19.

Gibson, R. 1999. "Questions about a Gift Horse." In *Voluntary Initiatives and the New Politics of Corporate Greening*, ed. R. Gibson, 3–12. Peterborough, Canada: Broadview Press.

Gillenwater, M., D. Broekhoff, M. Trexler, J. Hyman, and R. Fowler. 2007. "Policing the Voluntary Carbon Market: Voluntary Greenhouse-Gas Emission Offset Markets Are in Need of Government Oversight." *Nature Reports Climate Change*, October 11. Available at http://www.nature.com/climate/2007/0711/full/climate.2007.58.html.

Giulianotti, R. 2004. "Human Rights, Globalization and Sentimental Education: The Case of Sport." *Sport in Society* 7 (3): 355–369.

Hajer, M. 1995. *The Politics of Environmental Discourse*. New York: Oxford University Press.

Hannigan, J. 2006. *Environmental Sociology*, 2nd ed. New York: Routledge.

Haraway, D. 2003. *The Companion Species Manifesto: Dogs, People, and Significant Otherness*. Chicago: Prickly Paradigm.

Harvey, D. 1996. *Justice, Nature and the Ecology of Difference*. Oxford: Blackwell.

Heynan, N., J. McCarthy, S. Prudham, and P. Robbins. 2004. "Introduction: False promises." In *Neoliberal Environments: False Promises and Unnatural Consequences*, ed. N. Heynan, J. McCarthy, S. Prudham, and P. Robbins, 1–21. New York: Routledge.

Hoffman, A. 2001. *From Heresy to Dogma: An Institutional History of Corporate Environmentalism*. Stanford, CA: Stanford University Press.

Homer-Dixon, T. 2000. *The Ingenuity Gap: Can We Solve the Problems of the Future?* New York: Knopf.

Huber, J. 1985. *Die Regenbogengesellschaft: Ökologie und Sozialpolitik* (The Rainbow Society: Ecology and Social Policy). Frankfurt am Main, Germany: Fischer.

Kearins, K., and K. Pavlovich. 2002. "The Role of Stakeholders in Sydney's Green Games." *Corporate Social Responsibility and Environmental Management* 9:157–169.

Latour, B. 1993. *We Have Never Been Modern*, trans. C. Porter. Cambridge, MA: Harvard University Press.

———. 1999. *Pandora's Hope*. Cambridge, MA: Harvard University Press.

Lenskyj, H. 1998. "Sport and Corporate Environmentalism: The Case of the Sydney 2000 Olympics." *International Review for the Sociology of Sport* 33 (4): 341–354.

———. 2002. *The Best Olympics Ever: Social Impacts of Sydney 2000*. Albany: State University of New York Press.

Lohmann, L. 2005. "Marketing and Making Carbon Dumps: Commodification, Calculation and Counterfactuals in Climate Change Mitigation." *Science as Culture* 14 (3): 203–235.

Lubbers, E., ed. 2002. *Battling Big Business: Countering Greenwash, Infiltration and Other Forms of Corporate Bullying*. Monroe, ME: Common Courage Books.

Maguire, J., G. Jarvie, L. Mansfield, and J. Bradley. 2002. *Sport Worlds: A Sociological Perspective*. Champaign, IL: Human Kinetics.

McCarthy, J., and S. Prudham. 2004. "Neoliberal Nature and the Nature of Neoliberalism." *Geoforum* 35 (3): 275–283.

Michaelis, V. 2007. "Beijing's Pollution Could Be Athletes' Toughest Foe." *USA Today*, November 25. Available at http://www.usatoday.com/sports/olympics/2007-10-24-beijing-pollution_N.htm.

Mol, A. 1995. *The Refinement of Production*. Utrecht, Netherlands: Van Arkel.

———. 2002. "Ecological Modernization and the Global Economy." *Global Environmental Politics* 2 (2): 92–115.

Monbiot, G. 2006. "Paying for Our Sins." *The Guardian*, October 18. Available at http://www.guardian.co.uk/environment/2006/oct/18/green.guardiansocietysupplement.

Polanyi, K., 1957. *The Great Transformation*. Boston: Beacon Press.

Poncelet, E. 2004. *Partnering for the Environment: Multistakeholder Collaboration in a Changing World*. Toronto: Rowman and Littlefield.

Robertson, M. 2000. "No Net Loss: Wetland Restoration and the Incomplete Capitalization of Nature." *Antipode* 32 (4): 463–493.

———. 2004. "The Neoliberalization of Ecosystem Services: Wetland Mitigation Banking and the Problem of Measurement." In *Neoliberal Environments: False Promises and Unnatural Consequences*, ed. N. Heynan, J. McCarthy, S. Prudham, and P. Robbins, 114–125. New York: Routledge.

Schiermeier, Q. 2006. "Climate Credits." *Nature* 444 (7122): 976–977.

Schnaiberg, A. 1980. *The Environment: From Surplus to Scarcity*. New York: Oxford University Press.

Schnaiberg, A., and K. Gould. 2000. *Environment and Society: The Enduring Conflict*. West Caldwell, NJ: Blackburn Press.

Smith, N. 1990. *Uneven Development: Nature, Capital and the Production of Space*. Cambridge, MA: Blackwell.

Stahl, H., C. Hochfeld, and M. Schmied. 2006. *Green Goal: Legacy Report*. Frankfurt, Germany: Organizing Committee 2006 World Cup.

Stoddart, M. 2008. "Making Meaning Out of Mountains: Skiing, the Environment and Eco-Politics." Doctoral dissertation, University of British Columbia.

Stolle-McAllister, J. 2004. "Contingent Hybridity: The Cultural Politics of Tepoztlán's Anti-Golf Movement." *Identities: Global Studies in Culture and Power* 11 (2): 195–213.

Thornes, J., and S. Randalls. 2007. "Commodifying the Atmosphere: 'Pennies from Heaven'?" *Geografiska Annaler* 89 (4): 273–285.

United Nations Environment Programme. 2006. "Greening World Cup Tournament 2006." Press release, December 1. Available at http://www.unep.org/Documents.Multilingual/Default.asp?DocumentID=496&ArticleID=5446&l=en.

———. 2007. "Greening of 2008 Beijing Games Impressive Says UN Environment Programme Report." Press release, October 25. Available at http://www.unep.org/Documents.Multilingual/Default.asp?DocumentID=519&ArticleID=5687&l=en.

Wheaton, B. 2008. "From the Pavement to the Beach: Politics and Identity in 'Surfers against Sewage.'" In *Tribal Play: Subcultural Journeys through Sport*. Vol. 4 of *Research in the Sociology of Sport*, ed. M. Atkinson and K. Young, 113–134. Bingley, UK: Emerald Group.

Wheeler, K., and J. Nauright. 2006. "A Global Perspective on the Environmental Impact of Golf." *Sport in Society* 9 (3): 427–443.

7

The Uncanny of Olympic Time

Michael Phelps and the End of Neoliberalism

GRANT FARRED

The logic is obvious, simple even. In sport, nothing is impossible.

In 2008, much like any other year, that was the signal cry of successful athletes. But, unlike any other year in sports, 2008 was the year of inarticulable triumph—the athlete reduced to the excessively loaded cryptic phrase in one instance and what can be described only as intensity beyond language in another.

First, and memorably (the image is seared into our heads, courtesy of ESPN's persistent replays), there was the Boston Celtics' Kevin Garnett, newly recruited during the off-season from the hapless Minnesota Timberwolves, shouting—literally—to the rafters, sounding like an exhausted but triumphant revivalist preacher, "Nothing is impossible!" So Garnett yelled to the world, his eyes hooded, covered by his trembling fingers, on the brink of tears. Garnett's voice was breaking, a disturbing admixture of barely suppressed sobs, enthusiasm, and an unidentifiable mania. Or maybe it was just relief, or, more likely, disbelief for Garnett, having just won a National Basketball Association championship with the Boston Celtics that must have seemed so distant just a year before, when he was toiling for naught in the Twin Cities. During Garnett's "outburst," he seemed to be unable to contain himself; it was not exactly fury, or repressed anger, but something too proximate to both of those emotions for (spectatorial) comfort, the madness that is always at the core of the ecstatic a little too obvious to the viewer. What could be more disturbing, or mesmerizing, than to hear Kevin Garnett shouting, "Nothing is impossible! Nothing is impossible!"

Second, and more memorably, there was Michael Phelps in Beijing, at the Water Cube, at the climax of the men's 400-meter freestyle relay: "going crazy . . . I had no words. I had only screams" (Phelps 2008, 2). When America beat the favored French relay team in a historically close race at the 2008 Olympics, "no words" were necessary. With that victory in the 400-meter relay, with the veteran Jason Lezak overcoming the world 100-meter freestyle record holder Alain Bernard, the impossible Olympic dream—Phelps's quest to win an unprecedented eight gold medals—was alive. In sport, we can now be fairly sure, ecstasy is its own "crazy" language.

Ecstasy is its own discursive reward, Kevin Garnett might say, because it gives voice—as he so singularly did—to the triumph over "impossibility." There is, however, something particular about Michael Phelps's successful quest, his ability to have made the previously impossible possible: to win eight gold medals at a single Olympic Games. Garnett was right. Phelps's singularity derives, of course, entirely from his historic accomplishment, thereby erasing the achievement of fellow U.S. swimmer Mark Spitz from the record books. In 1972, at the Munich Olympic Games, Spitz won seven golds. Spitz was also the first to win six gold medals at a single Games, a feat that often goes unremarked on. In Beijing, Phelps went one better.

However, there is something strangely ambivalent—that admixture of acknowledgment and denial, giving credence to the past and insisting on the present as its own event—in Phelps's declaration: "I never set out to be the second Mark Spitz. I only wanted to be the first Michael Phelps" (Phelps 2008, 3). This is not quite the invocation of that old sport's truism "Second is nothing," or its more denunciatory articulation, "Second is for losers," but a more entangled thinking of the record-breaking athlete's place in Olympic history: the contemporary feat is always foreshadowed by its half-spoken, partly refused predecessor—"Mark Spitz," in this case, and the number of his medals.

Without the predecessor, there can be, so to speak, no history—no record to break. To be the "first" (Michael Phelps, in this case) is also, of course, to understand the historic feat of the self in its full contingency—the first is, even if only for a moment, always "second" because even as it surpasses the "first," it is working against the unarguable reality of the history it is trying to eradicate, the history it is trying to assign to history—that is, to write Spitz's secondariness into history. When Phelps, Garnett-like, proclaims that "nothing is unattainable" and that "there are no limits," then the "history of secondariness," that which went before, is clearly audible in his articulation. That "secondariness" can be figured, simultaneously, as both Spitz and Phelps himself because in order to become the first eight-gold-medal winner, he had to surpass the historic mark set of seven set by Spitz (Phelps 2008, 113, 6). And, as is the case with all records (which, in sports logic, are made only to be broken), there is a certain anxiety about it: when will the new record be made historic, obsolete, by the athlete of the future? To be the "first" is always to anticipate the arrival of the moment of secondariness—or, more precisely perhaps, of "secondness." All because, as Garnett's manic moment reminds us, "Nothing is impossible." Nine gold medals in London come 2012, anyone?

What renders Phelps distinct from Garnett, this chapter argues, is not (just) that they participate in different sports. This distinction is, for Phelps, no small matter. The stature of basketball is, of course, well in excess of that of swimming in the United States, an imbalance that Phelps hopes his record gold medal tally in Beijing will help redress. "My biggest dream," Phelps insists with a kind of philanthropic zeal that peppers his autobiography, *No Limits: The Will to Succeed* (which is organized into eight chapters, one for each of Phelps's gold medals in Beijing), is "to elevate swimming's place in the American sports landscape . . . to make it an every-year sport instead of a once-every-four-years sport" (Phelps 2008, 3). Instead, Phelps's singularity derives from the ways in which he, and the "ethic of competition" to which he subscribes, reveals an insight into the complex intersection between sport and the discourse of neoliberalism.

Neoliberalism is understood here as a mode of socioeconomic being founded on the premise that only the free market can produce the kind of competition that enables individuals in all walks of life to achieve their full potential—individuals released from all unnecessary constraints imposed by the state, the Keynesian welfare state in particular. Of course, the logic of all sport, especially professional sport, coincides with the competitive thrust of neoliberalism. If all barriers are removed, then the dynamic subject can flourish fully (neoliberalism's critique is leveled against the kind of state regulation that characterized the postwar Keynesian state and inhibited, because of the pact among the state, capital, and organized labor, the growth of the entrepreneurial individual in society). Winning eight gold medals proves, as it were, that nothing is impossible. This reading of Michael Phelps in relationship to neoliberalism is not an arbitrary reading but a deeply historical one, especially as it pertains to the provocative, historical phantasm that is Mark Spitz. Phelps's "predecessor" is the present-absent body that resonates through the intervening decades of Olympic time, the event of "seven" (gold medals) that hung over subsequent Games as the mark of "ultimate" accomplishment.

According to David Harvey, the most convincing historian of neoliberalism, this economic modality can be traced to 1973 with the overthrow of the socialist government of Salvador Allende in Chile by the CIA-backed Pinochet (coincidentally, on September 11). If, broadly conceived, the 1972 Games in Munich mark the last time the Olympics took place under the auspices of the welfare state, then there is something uncannily appropriate and "cyclical" about Spitz's record being broken by Phelps in 2008. In this cyclical reading, what Spitz's record precipitated—the neoliberalism (soon) to come—came full circle by the time of Beijing. Barely weeks after Phelps set his record, neoliberalism—as it knew itself, as it was known to the world—collapsed. By September–October 2008, with hedge funds about to collapse, the banking system teetering under the weight of bad loans, and the federal monetary insurance agency requiring massive government bailouts, neoliberalism seems to have run its course. In its own surprising, way, the road from Spitz to Phelps, from seven to eight, tells the story of the Olympic Games and the age of neoliberalism.

There is, of course, nothing precise about this coincidence except the strange power of the sport-economic uncanny. The year 1972 saw not only a Munich (West Germany, as it was then known) Games full of Olympic history and violence but also the turn to the metaphor of athletics as lubricant in global politics. The Munich Olympics saw Spitz, an American Jew, win his seven golds and then be hastily escorted from the Games after the attack on the Olympic village in Munich. (Spitz was evacuated from Munich when eleven athletes and officials from Israel's Olympic team were kidnapped and later killed by Palestinians. Olympic officials were concerned that Spitz, because of his Jewish heritage, might be threatened by the same group. Fortunately for Spitz, he had already finished his events. In politics, there were Kissinger, Nixon, Mao, and Zhou and their "opening of China," facilitated by the "Ping-Pong diplomacy" of 1971 when an American table tennis team (composed of nine players, four officials, and two spouses) played a series of exhibition matches in China in April 1971. The key match was between the American Glenn Cowan and the three-time Chinese world champion Zhuang Zedong. This cultural encounter, worked at behind the scenes by Kissinger and Zhou before the principals took center stage, produced a thawing in Sino-U.S. relations, so much so that in February 1972 the historic meeting between Nixon and Mao took place in Beijing.

Little wonder, then, given the pivotal role that Mark Spitz had played in the Munich Olympics, that the 2008 Games witnessed the most vibrant calling into public iteration the living ghost of Mark Spitz. It was also the year when, with the Olympic Games being held in Beijing, there was the event of Michael Phelps and the inexorable coming into being of China as a superpower. One doubts, somehow, that either Mao or Nixon, the key players in that long-ago game of political realpolitik (dramatized, of course, by no small amount of showmanship), imagined that this is what would happen when they embarked on Ping-Pong diplomacy. How could we then not say that the historical account of neoliberalism, its rise and its incipient fall, was coterminous with the historic event of two ideologically laden Olympic Games?

How much, as C.L.R. James remarked in his book about cricket, *Beyond a Boundary* (1983), we have to learn from sport.[1] (One wonders what James, arch critic of Stalinist economic policy—he called it "state capitalism"—would have made of the Deng-derived economic practices of communist China. Or what Mao, who advocated "friendship first, competition second," would have made of this new intensity of contestation today in Beijing.) In recognizing the coterminous temporalities of the Spitz-to-Phelps record(s) and the era of neoliberal economics, we might indeed think of the uncanny veracity of Kevin Garnett's ecstasy: nothing is impossible, least of all the propensity of sport to mirror the political or to tell the story of major social trends. It is only by thinking the conjuncture of sport and capital that it becomes possible to critique Phelps's triumph through neoliberalism, with the condition, as this chapter demonstrates, that we engage how sport and the neoconservative proclivities—or fundament, some might say—of neoliberalism are bound up in each other.

However, what is most engaging about Phelps's achievements at the Beijing Olympics is that it can simultaneously be understood as indivisible from the capitalization of sport, as a critique of the failures of neoliberal capital and as a mode of athletic-economic being that is at once deeply implicated in the functioning of neoliberal capital and yet rooted, in profoundly ideological terms, in a white blue-collar industrial ethic. As much as their status as historic, record-holding, record-breaking Olympic gold medalists binds Phelps and Spitz together, it is the capitalization of sport that distinguishes them from each other. While Spitz competed only as an amateur (and retired at the tender age of twenty-two), Phelps was already a professional by his early teens. As if to underscore the uncanny connection, here too there is a link between the two men of Olympic history, albeit one that marks a division rather than a continuation. Spitz was declared a professional and barred from further participation as an amateur (or "shamateur," as some were known, given how the Soviet bloc competitors were in fact sponsored by the state, and athletes from other countries managed to be funded, while nominally holding "jobs," in order to prepare for the Olympic Games) when he modeled, for reimbursement, a Speedo bathing suit. Phelps might owe a gold medal or three to that selfsame company. Not only did Speedo guarantee Phelps $1 million if he won eight gold medals, but it also created—just in time for Beijing—the controversial, body-hugging, space-age one-piece LZR racer. By Phelps's own admission, the LZR improved his performance. Speedo's endorsement and others enabled Phelps to skip college (Spitz went to the University of Indiana; Phelps trained with the rival Big Ten conference University of Michigan team but was not eligible to represent the Wolverines because of his professional status) and concentrate on preparation for the Olympics. His professional status gave Phelps the resources to focus on the events he would participate in during the Beijing Olympics after he competed, as a teenager in Sydney (2000) and Athens (2004). As Phelps says, "Not accomplishing my goals in Sydney had driven me for all the months in between. I had always known how badly it hurt to lose, how much I hated it" (Phelps, 2008, 80).

Neoconservatism and the Single Mother

US neoconservatives favour corporate power, private enterprise, and the restoration of class power. Neoconservatism is therefore entirely consistent with the neoliberal agenda of elite governance, mistrust of democracy, and the maintenance of market freedoms. (Harvey 2005, 82)

Unleashing of the full force—the "potential," its supporters will say—of neoliberal capital is, as Harvey insists, is only part of what U.S. neoconservatives truly want. For U.S. neoconservatives, free-market capitalism by itself would mean considerably less if it were not girded in, and working (mainly, if not solely) in the interests of, American nationalist supremacy. Recalibrating Harvey, then, we might say that what U.S. neoconservatives want more than anything is permanent, uninterrupted, American hegemony. They want American power to be unbridled and unchallenged. "United States rules!" is the true desire—and also the exclamatory construction of this unbridled Americanism—that the neoconservatives (and more than a few constituencies to the left of them) are never afraid to express.

In this sense, Michael Phelps is, unapologetically, an American of the more fervent patriotic variety: "As I listened to the anthem, playing for me, for my country, my eyes grew moist" (Phelps 2008, 26). However, in Phelps's resonant pride (his autobiography is awash with this kind of pro-American sentiment), there are also, saliently, for the purposes of a critique of neoliberalism, traces of an American voice—an America, if you will—beset by uncertainty: "I felt profound humility at learning how I had become a source of inspiration for so many back home, everyone who said I offered renewed proof that America and Americans could still take on the world with courage and grit, who declared that the virtues so many Americans hold so dear—hard work, character, commitment to family, team, country—could still triumph" (Phelps 2008, 4).

What emerges from Phelps's "commitment to family, team, country" is, for this reason, more than simply a glaringly obvious anxiety—"America and Americans could *still* take on the world," America "could *still* triumph" (Phelps 2008, 4; emphasis added). In Phelps's articulation there is the revealing of a nation not only on the defensive but at once in recovery and under threat. It is uncertain, however, as to precisely what America is in "recovery" from: The defeat in the 400-meter free relay at the previous (2004) Olympics by the South Africans and the Dutch? The concern that American "virtues"—"hard work, character"—were in decline? What is more certain is that America is a nation living in fear of losing its dominance—more specifically, a nation concerned about how its dominance is being threatened by the host of the 2008 Games, China. Phelps demonstrates what Stuart Hall, in his critique of Margaret Thatcher's "authoritarian populism," calls a "wall of virulent and gut patriotism" that "feeds off the disappointed hopes of the present and the deep and unrequited traces of the past" (Hall 1982, 6–7).

For his part, Phelps embraces fully his role as the embodiment of American resurgence—in fact, literally the physical body responsible for the resurgence—since it is he, and he alone (that is the implication, anyway) who can assume this task. "I offered renewed proof": America is, in 2008, a nation that once again, after doubt and failure, must prove its dominance—through "courage and grit," the negation of the "disappointed hopes of the present." It is dependent, furthermore, on its singular articulation: not so much, in this instance, an American exceptionalism as its other, equally recognizable formulation, the exceptional individual. Phelps represents himself as the Olympic athlete (the bearer of a "gut patriotism") who, through exemplary, record-breaking, history-making performance, can restore the nation to its "rightful" place: the exceptional, hegemonic United States.

Raised by a single mother, Phelps was the youngest child surrounded by two athletically gifted (talented, competitive swimmers) and confident sisters; his invocation of "family values" is burnished by a genuine conviction: "I also saw firsthand, watching my mother, what family values and work ethic truly meant" (Phelps 2008, 135). His is, for this reason, an appealing iteration of the neoconservative dedication to the nation because it emphasizes commitment to and recognizes the leadership emerging from within the most fundamental social unit: the family in which Debbie Phelps represents the hardworking single mother from a rural background (a mill town in western Maryland), who rises to the position of school principal without the support of a husband (a state trooper, from a similar class background)—the mother who sees the triumph of her youngest, her son, to the exceptionalism that is his unprecedented Olympic glory. There is in Phelps a real identification with the single-mother family. He admires one of his teammates in the 2008 400-meter relay, Cullen Jones, because Jones, "in a family sense, is somewhat like me. He's very close to his mother. In his case, his dad died of lung cancer when Cullen was sixteen" (Phelps 2008, 58).

There is, of course, nothing inherently neoconservative about commitment to family except that in Phelps's case the Debbie-led household is championed as the reason for America's potential reemergence as hegemonic. Debbie Phelps's values remind the world (and, presumably, America itself) of the nation's aptitude for "hard work," "grit," and "character." In the discourse of the successful athlete, the family directly, unlike the nation (which is more removed and symbolic), plays a critical and calculable role. (When Debbie Phelps is identified by a security guard in a mall parking lot as the "seven-medal mama," she does not "miss a beat" as she responds, "Eight" [Phelps 2008, 228].) The athletic family is either the social unit to be celebrated, à la Phelps (and countless others because it contributes, unfailingly, to the athlete's chances for success), or it must be "overcome" (that is, the disadvantages of class or race or dysfunctionality are hurdles that must be negotiated in order for the athlete to achieve his or her goals). In Phelps both of these options are in play: as a child he was diagnosed with attention deficit disorder (ADD) (a condition he beat, in large measure because of his willpower), and his is a supportive, intensely motivated primary collective. Debbie Phelps instilled in her children the recognition that they had to "have goals, drive, and determination. We would work for whatever we were going to get. We were going to strive for excellence, and to reach excellence you have to work at it and for it" (Phelps 2008, 22).

However, it is in this way that Phelps's triumph, in coinciding with the crisis in neoliberal capital, offers itself as a critique of neoliberalism's failures. With its determination to enable freedom without responsibility, its refusal to demand "hard work," its propensity for making possible con artists such as Bernie Madoff, and its deregulatory impulses (as a consequence of which the financial industry, banks, hedge fund managers, and insurance brokers such as AIG produced a disaster that may, when all is said and done, exceed that of the Great Depression), neoliberalism's ethos is decidedly at odds with the values of the Phelps household.

Phelps's relationship to neoliberalism is, especially in his autobiography, directly implicated in that particularly familiar enunciation of neoconservatism. (*No Limits* is, like all other works in this genre, personality and event-driven and strategically organized around the subject's triumphs and, secondarily, the disasters that, of course, serve only to fuel the "redemption" that is success.) Phelps demonstrates, in largely unremarked on (and therefore all the more revealing) terms, the ambivalences of the neoconservative-neoliberal conjuncture. Phelps's rise to glory is grounded in American exceptionalism and supplemented by those key ideological components of neoliberalism, utter loyalty to and pride in the nation, "family values," and what can only be loosely described as the postindustrial Puritan work ethic that is not, as we discuss later, a feature of late neoliberalism. "That work ethic, and that sense of teamwork, was always in our home. All of that went into the pool with me, from a very early stage" (Phelps 2008, 23) is how Phelps describes the relationship between his athletic goals and labor in a household run by women—Phelps's mother, Debbie, and his sisters, Whitney and Hilary (a potential Olympic swimmer whose career was curtailed by a back injury). These three women, led by Debbie, were the major influences his life after his father, Fred, moved out when Michael was seven years old. Phelps is cryptic, but not bitter, in his description of the estrangement of father from son: "My father moved out of the house when I was seven. As time went on, we spent less and less time together. Eventually, I stopped trying to include him in my activities and he, in turn, stopped trying to involve himself in mine" (Phelps 2008, 23).

Phelps's rise to success is, therefore, not simply the account of a talented athlete but a tribute to and consequence of the values instilled from an early age, father or no father, by his mother. Without labor, no reward, that was the Debbie Phelps lesson: "Things were going to get done in our house, and done a certain way . . . Homework was going to get done. Clothes were going to get picked up off the floor" (Phelps 2008, 23).

Such was the goal orientation in the Phelps household that there was no room for teenage experimentation (with another sport) or any allowance for the usual social needs of an adolescent (of the community of friends, of friendship through community):

> My freshman year in high school, I wanted to fit in with my football-playing friends.
>   Let's talk about this, Michael, my mom said.
>   Where is football likely to take your friends? Will they make the varsity team? . . . Play in the pros?
>   I doubt any of them is going to play in the NFL, I said.
>   Okay, she said. Now what can you do with swimming?
>   I did not play football. (Phelps 2008, 72)

There could be, in the Debbie Phelps–Bob Bowman plan (Bowman was Phelps's coach, who has the distinct honor of being the only coach the swimmer has ever had), no athletic desire outside swimming. Adolescent desire was foreclosed ("I did not play football"), and so that pleasure had no place in the prodigy's life, or it must all have been sublimated into the demands of swimming—as a young boy and a teenager, twice-a-day practices, four hours morning and afternoon; swimming meets; international competitions; the Sydney Olympics at age fifteen. In this singular, some might say perverse logic, it is precisely because there are "no limits" that there can be only one goal.

The calculus of future prospect and reward—mortgaging adolescence for Olympic medals in Sydney, Athens, and Beijing—produces itself as an intense form of delayed gratification. More disconcertingly, it is given the sheen of adolescent agency: "I had to make the decision myself. Did I love swimming enough to push me to be the very best I could be?" (Phelps 2008, 73). Again and again, be it the desire for peer group friendship through playing high school football or golf or just the impulse to go sledding in winter, the logic of sacrifice and focus prevails without any sense on young Michael's part that something valuable—irreplaceable, the time of adolescence—is being lost. One is reminded, in reflecting on the antisocial logic of cost-benefit (youth versus Olympic gold) analysis in the Phelps-Bowman camp, of Maggie Thatcher's brassy pronouncement: "There is no such thing as society, only individuals." That Phelps would, when living on his own for the first time in Ann Arbor, Michigan (in training for the Beijing Games), commit a DUI (driving under the influence) offense and, after the 2008 Olympics, be caught on YouTube smoking a bong with other college students in South Carolina, seems—because of the extreme regimentation of his life—like a "reckless" effort to make some type of claim on a "compromised" (not yet entirely lost) youth. Because of the bong incident, Phelps lost his Wheaties sponsorship, an endorsement reserved for icons of American sport. One wonders, however, if these acts (driving under the influence, smoking marijuana), typical among college-age kids, are merely the cost of repressed desire. Is this what happens when you cannot, or, more correctly, are effectively not allowed to, play football or golf or go sledding with your friends as an adolescent? Is this what happens when you win eight gold medals? Is this when, in the aftermath of the event, you recognize the cost of history?

There is, however, a larger contradiction in Phelps. He is blue-collar industrial in his work ethic and laissez-faire in his capacity to simultaneously reject the social (adolescent friends) and embrace it (on the Olympic swim team, even though he is competing against these same guys in the pool). For this reason, Phelps's commitment to the "macro-social," to coin an awkward phrase, is reminiscent of the instrumentality of neoliberalism—the insistence on "free markets," "government accountability," "transparency" and "democracy" in third world states has nothing to do with improving the living conditions of sovereign states in Africa or Asia but everything to do with opening up new and profitable markets for multinational U.S. and European corporations. However, this is not to suggest that Phelps is cynical about his teammates but rather to understand them—his friendships with the likes of Jason Lezak and Cullen and his ability to say that "Lochte is a good friend of mine, one of my best friends in swimming"—as located at the exact conjuncture where the social does not need to be forsworn: in relation to, in the moments before or after, nongoal activities (which have taken or are about to take place) (Phelps 2008, 35).

Phelps's success is, for these reasons, not simply attributable to capitalization (the decline of the amateur and the rise of the professional, the era of Spitz finally erased by the triumph of Phelps). Rather, capitalization, neoliberalism, and a Puritan structure of work and individual (and collective) responsibility combine to produce and ensure the success of the massively skilled athlete through an almost masochistic discipline and capacity for self-sacrifice. In Phelps's case this network of ideological forces is not complicated only by the (benign) "failure" of the suburban white nuclear family ("benign" because the family unit itself suffers no real adverse effects from the absence of the father) and the replacement of the father by what can only be termed the über-male figure: Bob Bowman, coach, father substitute, friend, mentor, and disciplinarian. The absolute submission to the ethic of athletic labor makes Phelps an odd fit with the lack of fiscal and managerial discipline that led to the undoing of neoliberalism—it would be difficult to use a term other than *discipline* (with its almost Benthamite overtones), considering how entirely Phelps commits himself to the training regime, from well before his teenage years, that allows him to succeed so spectacularly. There is in Phelps's inordinate capacity for self-sacrifice (the willingness to forgo the usual pleasures of adolescence, to train for long periods of time, to give up on experimenting with other sports, as his peers appeared to do with a joie de vivre that can come only from participating in sport without professional expectation—no possibility of an NFL career)—a single-mindedness that is, as we have seen, not only impressive but also over-determined.

In her critique of John Rawls's importance to contemporary liberal thought, Chantal Mouffe (2005) offers an insight into Phelps's work ethic. Commenting on the status of Rawls's *A Theory of Justice*, Mouffe writes that the "'deontological' or 'rights based' paradigm has put an end to the incontestable supremacy of utilitarianism in Anglo-Saxon theoretical reflection, and all criticism must come to grips with what is considered its most advanced elaboration" (25). There is, of course, simultaneously nothing and everything that is "utilitarian" about swimming miles, doing endless laps at altered speeds, in the same pool day after day. Winning gold medals does have real "utility" in that victory translates into capital—from the "real" money accrued through endorsements to the celebratory status that comes with Olympic victory—a different kind of capital, of course. However, Phelps's aptitude for labor—his enjoyment of "working" for his medals—suggests a mode of thinking that has a great deal in common with the "blue-collar area of western Maryland" where his parents grew up (Phelps 2008, 22). Debbie Phelps is the daughter of a carpenter; Michael's maternal grandfather was a miner. It is in identifying these "ontologies" in Phelps, that we might say, in a misappropriation of Hall, that there is indeed something of "use," not just a malevolent patriotism to be retrieved, to lay claim to, in those "unrequited traces" of Phelps's western Maryland "past."

As Bowman repeatedly told his charge, a mantra that Phelps took on board completely, "One thing that's common to all successful people: They make a habit of doing things that unsuccessful people didn't like to do" (Phelps 2008,

108). What Bowman is advocating, and Phelps did (in those innumerable training sessions), is not, of course, labor for its own sake but a neo-Puritanical (might we say neoliberal?) revisioning of the "utilitarian": the subject's ability to understand that pure labor, that thing that "unsuccessful people didn't like to do," is what distinguishes the multiple Olympian from his competitors—the ability to find, to recognize the value of "doing those things." "Those things" cannot be properly named because "success," "Olympic champion," and "gold medal record holder" are only what is or might be publicly appended to them. In the pool, in those moments of Bowman-Phelps labor, they are nothing but industrial labor, the body at work, the body working for itself, working for a moment that extends far beyond itself, labor for, in that precise moment, its own sake: the honor that the carpenter might find in work, the miner's pride in his work ethic. This is not how Phelps describes it, but his liminal recollection—in paying tribute to his mother's ability to have raised her own three children—of his western Maryland roots suggest an unexpected, unremarked-on immersion in a labor practice that is purely industrial. Michael Phelps, we might suggest to Mouffe, "redeems" a certain value for the "ethic of utilitarianism" in the age of a failing neoliberalism.

Race, Sonic Immersion, and Singularity

Like Michael Phelps, Cullen Jones is also exceptional, but for a different reason. Cullen is singular because he was the only African American on the 2008 U.S. swim team. (And only the third in the history of U.S. swimming, after Anthony Ervin and Maritza Correia.) Phelps's regard for Jones, however, highlights another complexity—it is not quite a contradiction but resonant with enough tension and a sense of oppositionality to be troubling—in Phelps. In a critical sense, of course, Jones is nothing like the eight-gold-medal winner—the condition of growing up African American as the son of a widowed mother in New York City is nothing like growing up the son of a divorced white mother in the sedate suburbs of Maryland. And yet Phelps is, like many of his white contemporaries, representative of the second or third generation of suburban youth who are deeply immersed in hip-hop culture. (If, that is, one dates the popularity of hip-hop culture for white suburban youth to the late 1980s, with a group such as, say, Public Enemy, and Spike Lee's movie *Do The Right Thing* and the concomitant birth of "New Jack" cinema.) For his part, the African American Jones hardly comes across as a fan of hard-core hip-hop. (For his part, however, Phelps is keen to establish, shall we say, his street cred, and so there are moments, discordant but not disingenuous, to be sure, where he lapses into the hip-hop vernacular with a "for real" and a whimsical "back in the day.")

As is well known, Phelps's favorite rapper is Lil' Wayne (Dwayne Michael Carter, Jr.). Before every Olympic race, Phelps played Lil' Wayne's "I'm Me" on his iPod. The lyrics are X-rated, undeniably misogynistic ("Niggas is bitches, bitches; I think they full of estrogen"; "I'm a mothafuckin' cash money millionaire"), and yet nonetheless in tune with Phelps's single-mindedness. Phelps's accomplishment translates easily into Lil' Wayne's soundscape since, in athletic terms, winning eight gold medals at a single Olympic Games really is "un-fuck-in'-believable." More importantly, the insistence of "I'm Me" on the rapper's singularity (and individuality)—"Yes, I'm the best, and no, I ain't positive, I'm definite / I know the game like I'm reffing it"—is consistent with Phelps's out-look: "Because I believe in myself, because I reach for my goals" (Phelps 2008, 112). There is not only a lyrical and ideological intensity to "I'm Me" but also a profound sense of the ontological; what draws Phelps to Lil' Wayne is not simply the braggadocio of the rapper but the shared self-knowledge: a hip-hop artist's "I'm the best" is, after all, nothing more than an Olympic gold medal swimmer's "I believe in myself." As Phelps admits, "The lyrics to 'I'm me' are definitely not G-rated. But that's not, for me, the point. When I hear Lil' Wayne do that song, I hear him saying, I'm my own individual, and that's me" (Phelps 2008, 49). There is in that insistently (and grammatically poorly) constructed phrase, "I'm my own individual," a moment of veracity and overidentification: "I'm me." The expletives, and they are plentiful indeed, are of no consequence because the point is to inhabit an intense singularity: "I'm my own individual."

However, this is also the point of divergence: Phelps's drive is not only for individual gain, though there is a significant measure of that (more, in fact, than the genre of the autobiography and Phelps's faux modesty in *No Limits* will allow), but also for nationally inflected glory. Lil' Wayne, on the other hand, is much more unambiguous. The rapper is in the game, which he knows as well as those who officiate it ("like I'm reffing it"), only for his own gain and self-aggrandizement: "I'm a mothafucking cash money millionaire / I know that ain't fair, but I don't care." There is in Lil' Wayne's unreconstructed desire for wealth, glory, and the right to infinite disregard what is for Phelps utter-able only as the loaded, cryptic "I'm me." Lil' Wayne is, in hip-hop speak, "for real." Not for the profane artist is the pretense of individual modesty, public respectability, or commitment to nation. Lil' Wayne is, in broad psychoanalytic terms, the id to Phelps's ego: Lil' Wayne will not repress any of his libidinal desires—not his desire for "cash" or for fame; he will neither concede his right to misogynistic expression nor refrain from using the N-word. Lil' Wayne does not even pretend to be about the team. He is for himself, and his "cash money millionaire" self, alone. "I'm Me" is the closest Phelps gets, can allow himself to get, to his own excessively competitive id; it is for Lil' Wayne never anything less than pure id.

By tapping his own repressed id on his iPod, Michael Phelps was able to make Lil' Wayne the voice—the soundtrack, if you will—of his own uncon-scious. Lil' Wayne said what Phelps could not, dare not. It is, of course, an old trope in American discourse: the black helpmeet who enables, in a kind of bil-dungsroman, the white protagonist, from the title character of Harriet Beecher Stowe's famous novel to the 2000 movie *Bagger Vance* to the buddy-movie genre (for example, Danny Glover, the cop with the stable family, partnered with the risk-taking single white guy, Mel Gibson, in the *Lethal Weapon* franchise), to recognize and fulfill his own potential. It is either the black sidekick or the subjugated black who enables the white protagonist to uncover his or her aptitude for moral goodness (Uncle Tom) or capacity for athletic success (Bagger Vance caddying for Rannulph Junuh) or something approaching emotional stability or maturity (*Lethal Weapon*). No wonder Phelps turned to Lil' Wayne before every race: Lil' Wayne got him pumped up by saying exactly the things that Phelps not only believed but also aspired to. Lil' Wayne's public articulation was Phelps's private credo.

However, as much as Cullen Jones strikes a sympathetic chord of self-identification with Phelps (by virtue of sharing the experience of being raised by a single mother), as much as Lil' Wayne functions as Phelps's (publicly inaudible) voice, the presence of (the silent) black articulation or the exceptional (in terms of U.S. swimming, anyway) black body also resonates with another silence. It is the unnerving silence of the city in which Phelps trained from his preteen years, the city that feted him as its champion; it is nevertheless the city that lies beyond the swimmer's purview. He is, at least in genealogical terms (and as it pertains to his propensity for "industrial labor"), closer to (his roots in) western Maryland than he is to the city of Baltimore, an overwhelmingly black city (by recent counts, Baltimore is at least 60 percent African American). He is not necessarily closer to the work ethic of the now deindustrialized white western part of the state but certainly closer than he is to the deindustrialized inner city that is invisible in Phelps's imaginative cartography of the United States—a city, we should say, whose postindustrial devastation has had disastrous consequences for Baltimore's majority black population. Swimming in the suburbs of northern Baltimore, where the neighborhood landscape's verdant, meandering streets and its charming public ponds and undulating (if small) parks owe much to the vision of Frederick Olmsted, who also designed Central Park, Phelps is in no way connected to the devastation that is south Baltimore, where Lil' Wayne's "niggas" might be found—at the very least, where the "niggas" who inspired the massively successful HBO series *The Wire* are sure to be encountered.

That Baltimore, if not Baltimore itself, is kept in Tom Waits's hauntingly melodic theme song for *The Wire*, "Way Down in the Hole." The "hole" that is the black absence in Phelps's engagement with African American culture, the "hole" of his unconscious in which Phelps "buries" any discussion about race and relation to the place that is Baltimore. No wonder. *The Wire*, with its unrelenting critique of Baltimore's corrupt politicians (white ethnics as well as African Americans), the rampant drug trade, the hopelessly inadequate and inefficient health care system, the roguish police department, the unethical newspaper journalists, the wholly inept justice system and, last but not least, the criminally negligent education system, does not register in Phelps's consciousness because it would demand an interrogation of the effects of neoliberalism of which he is incapable. Lil' Wayne blocked out more than simply the noise of the Water Cube's crowds or Phelps's competitors. Lil' Wayne is displaced from his "real," disarticulated from places such as Baltimore.

As much as the black voice functioned as his id, the white athlete was still in supreme command of his own superego. That explains why Phelps's immersion in Lil' Wayne did not open him up to the nearby violence or socio-economic devastation to which Lil' Wayne's community of "niggas" were—and continue to be—subjected. Instead, and here Phelps is true to the Thatcher-ite ethic of the individual, the Olympic swimmer could experience Lil' Wayne only instrumentally: as a direct address to him, as a form of athletic motivation. Phelps hears Lil' Wayne as a call to attention: to focus on the task ahead. Nothing concentrates the white Olympic athlete's mind like an African American countryman's hip-hop anthem. Nothing says "I'm me" or "I'm better and bold" quite like eight Olympic gold medals. Can "bling" ever get more "real" than eight gold medals won, not made, like so many products in the neoliberal world today, in China?

Michael Phelps is, in this way, an odd product of the neoliberal era in Olympic swimming. He is the beneficiary of deregulation, the child prodigy who overcomes ADD and adapts his inherited blue-collar work ethic of western Maryland to the opportunities offered by white suburbia. Most importantly, he is the face of extreme individuality that is able to make itself ideologically tenable as the representative of a nation's resurgence. Phelps can, we realize, speak the language of representation only ambivalently. While he insists, in the terms of contemporary cool, on the inalienable right to be silent (or to retreat into internal, iPod-facilitated singularity), he also wants to refashion Thatcher's dialectic. It is not, for Phelps, that there is no such thing as society. It is, rather, that society is only, if in deeply cathected ways, the by-product of unrepresentable individuals. "I'm my own individual" is the ideal mantra for the hyper-self-aware subject of an expiring neoliberalism. "I'm my own individual" is not just Lil' Wayne's signature way of saying, "Nothing is impossible."

Including the ironies of history.

The China that Nixon, Kissinger, Mao, and Zhou opened up with "Ping-Pong diplomacy" had little to do with the China where Phelps won his historic gold medals. Today, however, China is one of the few countries where industrial labor (while being, with its sweatshops and its exploitative work practices, by no means an ethical practice) still obtains as enough of a threat to the rule of the Communist Party. However, the ideology of neoliberalism in contemporary China is not dissimilar to the kind of work ethic to which Phelps has subjected himself for years. There is, then, something suggestive if not appropriate about Phelps making history in a place where (exploited, underpaid) industrial labor and neoliberalism are mutually constitutive of each other. This is not exactly analogous to the relationship of western Maryland to the North Baltimore Aquatic Club, but China is one of the few places in the world where only labor—not of the Phelps variety, but labor nonetheless—makes everything possible. In declaring himself a proud American, in praising "hard work . . . commitment to family, team, country," Phelps might as well have been lauding the "values" of his hosts.

Moreover, as the economic collapse of 2008 showed, only the Chinese, because of their industrial base, could continue to practice neoliberalism in any recognizable form. Michael Phelps's highly individualized triumph, no matter his proclamations of love for team, we might suggest, was the last hurrah for neoliberalism American-style. As David Harvey argues, much as neoliberalism began as an "experiment" somewhere other than the metropole—Chile, to be precise—so it would, it now seems clear, reach its apogee outside the West too. While Phelps was reclaiming his "lost" adolescence in South Carolina, neoliberalism turned its eyes back to China, and so soon after the Olympics too. Have Nixon and Kissinger's historic recognition of the Middle Kingdom as the "new frontier" of global politics been transformed, less than four decades later, into the forlorn hope that Asia's industrial labor could save the neoliberal project? Or has that prospect been smashed out of the realm of possibility like the authoritative Zhuang Zedong return of a Glenn Cowan serve?

NOTE

1. James writes, famously, "Cricket had plunged me into politics long before I was aware of it. When I did turn to politics I did not have too much to learn" (1983, 61).

REFERENCES

Hall, S. 1982. "The Empire Strikes Back." *New Socialist* 6:5–7.

———. 1988. *The Hard Road to Renewal: Thatcherism and the Crisis of the Left.* New York: Verso.

Harvey, D. 2005. *A Brief History of Neoliberalism.* New York: Oxford University Press.

James, C.L.R. 1983. *Beyond a Boundary.* New York: Pantheon Books.

Mouffe, C. 2005. *The Return of the Political.* New York: Verso.

Phelps, M., with A. Abrahamson. 2008. *No Limits: The Will to Succeed.* New York: Simon and Schuster.

II

Government, Governance,
and the Cultural Geographies
of Neoliberalism

8

The Governance of the
Neoliberal Sporting City

MICHAEL L. SILK

DAVID L. ANDREWS

The axioms and anxieties associated with the perceived decline of the North American city (particularly that within the U.S. context) became a defining feature of the cultural politics of the 1970s and 1980s. Nevertheless, the once pervasive disavowal of the very idea, let alone the experience, of the contemporary city has been conclusively arrested by a perceptible economic and emotional (re)turn to North America's urban landscapes. Certainly, today's vibrant city spaces bear little resemblance to the dystopic urban environments that dominated public perceptions and experiences of the American city less than a generation ago. Wrought by broader shifts from industrial to postindustrial orders (Harvey 1989), and attendant transformations in the dominant mode of economic (re)production and regulation (see, e.g., Gottdiener 2000; MacLeod, Raco, and Ward 2003), cities (as understood to be the confluence of particular social, cultural, economic, and political forces and spatial arrangements associated with the instantiation of modernity/the modern) have become preoccupied with the reconstitution of urban space—or more accurately, select parcels of urban America—into multifaceted environments designed for the purpose of encouraging consumption-oriented capital accumulation (Friedman, Andrews, and Silk 2004; Zukin 1991). The presence of, in various permutations, shopping malls, themed restaurants and bars, entertainment-oriented museum and gallery installations, gentrified housing developments, conference complexes, waterfront pleasure places, and professional sport mega-complexes has, at least partially, precipitated the advancement of a new epoch in the material (re)formation of the American urban landscape. High-profile redevelopment zones within cities such as Baltimore, Cleveland, Memphis, Chicago, Los Angeles, and Seattle (see, e.g., Bockmeyer 2000; Davis 1990; Friedman, Andrews, and Silk 2004; Gibson 2003; Harvey 2000; Silk 2004, 2007; Silk and Andrews 2008; Soja 1989) are the primary vehicles through which the culture of the city in general, and that of specific cities in particular, has been symbolically (re)defined in more positive terms to both internal and external constituencies alike. The subsequent rush to instantiate "spectacular urban space" (Harvey 2001, 92) can thus be seen as a response to ever more intensifying interplace competition, waged on the terrain of what have become increasingly domineering logics of flexible, diversified capital accumulation, and through which new urban economies based on tourism, entertainment, and culture (Gottdiener 2000; Judd and Simpson 2003; Savitch and Kantor 2003) have come to the fore.

As with any spectacular edifice, the newly anointed American city of the late capitalist moment (Jameson 1991) bears forth some uncomfortable truths, particularly if one dares to venture behind the seductive, corporate, commercially inspired veil of urban regeneration. Rather than wholesale structural reformation and redistribution—which may actually begin to ameliorate the social divisions and injustices that characterize, for many, the lived experience of the North American city—the entrepreneurial form of development adopted by many city overseers (and we use the term pointedly) has lacked ambition in the geographic (both physical and human) scale of its regenerative ambitions—something that has necessarily limited its scope for enacting meaningful social change. Instead, a form of American urban apartheid has been instantiated through constellations of public-private development partnerships (Judd and Simpson 2003) that commandeer disused, neglected, or redundant urban tracts and transform them into "islands of affluence . . . sharply differentiated from the surrounding urban landscape" (Judd 1999, 53). Given such spatially concentrated practices of regenerative investment, urban neglect and disrepair of both built environments and human experiences are evident on the fringes of, and certainly proliferate the farther one ventures from, the phantasmagorical—to borrow from Benjamin (2002)—zones of inner urban commercial investment and revitalization within America's remodeled cityscapes. Regardless of the propaganda espoused by inveterately sanguine—or perhaps delusional—chambers of commerce, most American cities presently incorporate multiple, and starkly divergent, narratives, populations, and experiences (Walks 2001). Put simply, there exists an uneasy juxtaposition between those served by the city as "capital space" (Harvey 2001) and those either servile to or shunned by its overdetermining consumerist logics. Thus, within the newly entrepreneurial city, urban populations and indeed spaces become bifurcated between the generative affluent and the degenerative poor, the private consumer and the public recipient, the civic stimulant and the civic detriment, and the socially valorized and the socially pathologized.

Within "capital space," the *sanctioned* public sphere (and its constitutive populace) is rendered visible through the preservation, management, and sustenance of the boundary between the *bodies proper* that fulfill the "obligations" of participatory democratic citizenship (through appropriate rates and acts of consumption) and those constitutive socially, morally, and economically pathologized "*outsiders*." Like Dostoevsky's (1968) déclassé civil servants in *Crime and Punishment* (see Merrifield 2000), these outsiders become positioned as an invisible source of life that protects the constitution of the consuming polis by rendering it visible and thereby distinguishing it from those who do not *properly belong* to it (Butler 1993; Zylinska 2004). Within this theoretical sketch, we intend to illuminate the neoliberal context of the multidiscursive (political, economic, social, juridical, and architectural) constitution of new urban glamour zones and associated populations, the brutalizing injustices resulting from the advancement of profoundly divisive social geographies (incorporating interdependent social and spatial dimensions) within today's city spaces (MacLeod 2002), and the processes and practices of social governance through which both valorized and pathologized urban bodies are made visible, regulated, and managed, as they contribute toward materializing the differentiated (and indeed differentiating) new urban landscape. In essence, this chapter offers a theoretical account of the various narratives underpinning the discursive constitution of belonging and difference, the categories of inclusion and exclusion, in the construction and management of a powerful symbolic space of representation (Soja 2000).

Actually Existing Spaces of Neoliberalism: City Space

"Where did this idea come from that everybody deserves free education, free medical care, free whatever? It comes from Moscow, from Russia. It comes straight out of the pit of hell" (Debbie Riddle, Texas state representative, quoted in Giroux 2004, 206). Riddle's astounding statement is emblematic of a pervasive populist political ideology and praxis graphically explicated within Giroux's (2000, 2001, 2003a, 2003b, 2004) reappropriation of the poststructrualist leitmotif pertaining to the *death of the social*. In Giroux's (2001) terms, the morbidity of the social sphere can be evidenced from the hegemony of neoliberal cynicism toward all things public and collective, the corollary of which has been the rise of a virulent contempt for the notion of social welfare provision; an equally pernicious and questioning attitude toward those who are its recipients; and an individualizing culture of surveillance, accountability, and resentment. Of course, this palpable shift in the political landscape—what Stuart Hall (1983) referred to as the "Great Moving Right Show"—emerged from particular sociostructural conditions. Specifically, the political landscape became profoundly altered in response to intensifying conditions of local/global recession, the related decline of mass-manufacturing economies and industries, and the precipitated crisis of Keynesian welfarism. Thus, coming to the fore in the late 1970s and early 1980s after a considerable incubation period, within most Western democracies an alternative political philosophy was strategically advanced, prefigured on the need to dismantle the basic institutional components of the postwar social welfare consensus, and mobilize policies intended to extend market discipline, competition, and commodification throughout society (Brenner and Theodore 2002a, 2002b; Hobbs et al. 2000; Jessop 2002). This ideologically and economically based form of political revisionism provoked an "epochal shift" away from the supposed "social mentality" proclivities underpinning the role of the state (Rose 1999): a shift that saw the state relieved of its powers of obligation to answer for all society's needs for order, health, security, and productivity. For Rose, this involved a "double movement of autonomization and responsibilitization [in which] [p]opulations once under the tutelage of the social state are to be made responsible for their destiny and for that of society as a whole. Politics is to be returned to society itself, but no longer in a social form: in the form of individual morality, organizational responsibility, and ethical community" (1999, 1400).

The emergent and active period of "roll-out neoliberalism," predicated on the technocratic embedding of routines of neoliberal governance, the extension of neoliberal institutions, and the erosion of pockets of political and institutional resistance, has meant that particular attention needs to be directed toward the "purposeful construction and consolidation of neoliberalized state forms, modes of governance, and regulatory relations" (Peck and Tickell 2002, 384). For Brenner and Theodore (2002a, 351), this has meant a systematic geography of the "actually existing spaces of neoliberalism": a reconceptualization of how the destructive and creative moments of neoliberalism have been mobilized through distinctly geographical strategies, within the major institutional arenas in which capital accumulation and regulation occurs. The worldwide ascendancy of neoliberalism in the early 1980s was closely intertwined with a pervasive rescaling of capital-labor relations, intercapitalist competition, financial and monetary regulation, state power, the international configuration, and uneven development throughout the world economy (Brenner and Theodore 2002a). Subsequently, the loosening or dismantling of the various institutional constraints on marketization; the logics of competitiveness; commodification; the hyperexploitation of workers; the deconstruction of labor unions and social welfare programs; and the discretionary power of private capital, processes of deregulation, liberalization, and state retrenchment (or more accurately, reorganization) became manifest in an alarming range of spaces, institutions, and policies (Brenner and Theodore 2002a, 2002b; Peck and Tickell 2002). However, and following Brenner and Theodore (2002a), as the primacy of the national became undermined in each of these areas, "actually existing neoliberalism" is occurring with particular intensity, and is particularly pronounced, at the urban scale. That is, within major cities and city-regions, a brutalizing neoliberal sensibility has become both exteriorized and interiorized through a range of measures, including the imposition of new fiscal constraints and budgetary measures on cities (because of the retrenchment of national welfare state regimes and national intergovernmental systems), the spread of neoliberal fundamentals into urban policy regimes (deregulation, privatization, liberalization, and enhanced fiscal austerity), the reconfiguration (both material and symbolic) of the city as an arena for market-oriented growth and elite consumption practices (place marketing, enterprise and empowerment zones, local tax abatements, urban development corporations, public-private partnerships, and property-redevelopment schemes), and the mobilization of new strategies of social control and surveillance designed to more effectively police the spectacular cityscape (Brenner and Theodore 2002a, 2002b).

Despite the neoliberal reformation of the contemporary city, the "politics, institutional dynamics, and socio-spatial effects have been rarely theorized explicitly at the urban scale . . . the complex spatialities have yet to be examined and theorized systematically" (Brenner and Theodore 2002b, 343). Thus, much historically grounded empirical, theoretical, and political work remains to be done in order to decode and ultimately dismantle the everyday violence of neoliberalism: the "utopia of unlimited exploitation" (Bourdieu 1998, quoted in Brenner and Theodore 2002b, 345). This is despite recognition not only that neoliberalism affects cities but also that cities have become key institutional arenas in and through which neoliberalism is itself evolving, a space which has become inscribed with new forms of social exclusion, injustice, and disempowerment (Brenner and Theodore 2002b). In this way, transformations within cities are not just the result of the uneven hand of capitalism, and local complexities are neither neutral nor innocent with respect to the practices of domination and control; rather, urban design and city planning embody, implicitly or explicitly, power/knowledge relations—plans are never neutral tools of spatial ordering and the imagination and different forms of representation seep subtly, and at times more visibly, into the rhetoric of governmental practice. Indeed, as Harvey (1989) suggests, place development and urban entrepreneurialism, waterfront revitalization, the serial reproduction of cultural spectacles, privatized forms of local governance—the logics of capitalist spatial development within the powerful disciplinary effects of interurban competition—offer, if not naturalize, the lowest common denominator of social responsibility and welfare provision.

The Cultural Politics of Sterile City Space: Spaces of Sporting Consumption

In contrast to the national orientation of the Fordist-Keynesian political-economic order, localities are now back on the agenda across the political spectrum—cities have become strategically crucial geographic arenas in which a variety of neoliberal initiatives have been instantiated (Brenner and Theodore 2002a, 2002b). The breaking down of the national bargain, the rolling back of the Keynesian welfare state, the emergence of post-Fordist patterns of production and consumption (e.g., MacLeod, Raco, and Ward 2003; Walks 2001), along with the problems of deindustrialization, a falling tax base because of suburban flight, and the associated concentration of impoverished residents in inner areas (Brenner and Theodore 2002a; Goodwin 1993), has meant that—faithfully evoking the political hegemony of neoliberal ideologies and policies—urban governments have sought to (re)capitalize on the economic landscapes of their cities (MacLeod 2002). Engaging in a competitive process of cultural economic restructuring to reposition and represent themselves as the service centers for the financial services, for information and communication services central to the network society, and as spaces of consumption (Gottdiener 2000; Mac-Leod, Raco, and Ward 2003; Sassen 2001; Whitson and Macintosh 1996), by the early 1990s, formerly industrial cities had begun to revive their fortunes on the basis of corporate-oriented downtown strategies and new economies based on tourism, entertainment, leisure, sport, and culture (Cohen 1999; Gottdiener 2000; Judd and Simpson 2003). While they may belie the mid-twentieth-century processes of suburbanization and the perception of the inner city as unsafe areas of unchecked blight, racial strife, criminality, and deviance (Friedman, Andrews, and Silk 2004; Hannigan 1998; Judd 1999; Savitch and Kantor 2003), these spectacular spaces of consumption—predicated on shopping malls, themed restaurants, bars, theme parks, mega-complexes for professional sport franchises, gentrified housing, conference complexes, waterfront pleasure domes, and the attraction of a "cultural class" (Florida 2002; Gottdiener 2000; MacLeod, Raco, and Ward 2003; Silk 2007)—are part of the efforts to attract middle-class, suburban consumers back into downtown areas and promote (no matter how false) an image of the city as an acknowledged cog—a necessary destination, if you will—within the "global circuits of (tourist) promotion" (Whitson and Macintosh 1996).

Within these processes, a greater importance becomes attached to promoting the positive, unique, and differential amenity and service attributes of a city inasmuch as the entire urban core is looked on as a recreational environment and as a tourism resource (Jansen-Verbeke 1989). This "symbolic commodification of place" (Whitson and Macintosh 1996) is based on the manufacturing and promotion of a positive brand identity for a city, designed to appeal to and attract tourists and surburbanites and maintain the residence of "desired populations" in gentrified downtown cores. This of course gives an enhanced role to those in the culture industries who produce the range of symbolic goods and experiences of "culture" within the contemporary city.

As such, specially designed, sanitized, entertainment districts concentrated in small areas have emerged, physically bounded spaces that cordon off and cosset the desired visitor while simultaneously warding off the threatening "native" (Fainstein and Gladstone 1999; Friedman, Andrews, and Silk 2004; Harvey 2001; Silk 2010). Despite a growing skepticism, these "tourist bubbles" (Judd 1999, 53) are often predicated on convention facilities and sporting investment (Judd and Simpson 2003) that are argued to have the potential to generate significant economic activity, promote the brand image of a city, function as a locus of community affect and identity, and reproduce the concept of a spatially constructed (imagined) unity (Rowe and McGuirk 1999). International sport, major events, franchises, new stadiums, and other sporting experiences have thus become one of the most powerful and effective vehicles for the showcasing of place and for the creation of a "destination image" (Whitson and Macintosh 1996). In essence, then, the city is adopting an increasingly spatialized function and taking on a somewhat surreal identity. As Wilcox and Andrews (2003) propose, the previously decaying remnants of the industrial city are renovated into branded consumption spaces for (suburban) tourists. Investment in sports appears crucial—for a city to legitimately claim a position on the world stage, in addition to a significant role in transnational (financial and communication) business, a city must become a significant "place" in the global sports market-place (Wilcox and Andrews 2003). This can be achieved through the building of spectacular facilities—sporting monumentalities to consumption (such as the FedEx Forum in Memphis, Camden Yards in Baltimore, Sports City in Dubai, or the Marylebone Cricket Club (MCC) branded cricket villages in India)—or through the hosting of a sporting mega-event (such as a Formula One race, a Commonwealth Games, an Olympics, a leg of the America's Cup, or a rugby World Cup). Indeed, with sporting events having arguably eclipsed other forms of mega-event, they have thus assumed increased significance in global city promotion and urban renewal strategies (Chalkey and Essex 1999).

The emergence of sterile and replicable cityscapes predicated on spectacular spaces of (sporting) consumption stresses the aesthetics of place over all other considerations (Mitchell 2001). However, while the renaissance of these tenderly *managed* landscapes may have done much to resuscitate the (symbolic and economic) value of many city centers, help to define a city among potential visitors, and repair the "pockmarks" of a dilapidated and obsolete urban core (MacLeod, Raco, and Ward 2003), important questions remain about the relevance and, indeed, the morality of such spaces for the wider urban citizenry, in particular when considering the constitutively linked sadistic criminalization of urban poverty, the war against welfare, and the erosion of social justice that accompanies the commercial spectacularization of city space (Harvey 2000; MacLeod 2002). As MacLeod proposes, this is not least given that "the fragile maintenance of space is ever more intricately dependent on a costly system of surveillance—performed through a blend of architectural design, CCTV, private security, and a range of legal remedies—seemingly designed to inculcate 'acceptable' patterns of behavior commensurate with the free flow of commerce and the new urban aesthetics" (2002, 605). Indeed, as Coleman and Sim (2000) point out, place-marketing strategizing often invokes discourses of safety and security with the intent of reimagining locations as safe places to do business.

There has thus been a stretching of the neoliberal policy repertoire in which urban governance has moved more, rather than less, into line with the naked requirements of capital accumulation (Harvey 1989, 15). Thus, to secure the extension, maintenance, reproduction, and indeed the management of the consequences of "market rule" (Peck 2003, 224), the cultural politics of the contemporary city embraces a range of extramarket forms of governance and regulation: the selective appropriation of community and nonmarket metrics, the incorporation of local-governance and partnership-based modes of policy development in areas such as urban regeneration and social welfare, the mobilization of "little platoons" in the shape of voluntary associations in the service of neoliberal goals, and the evolution of invasive, neopaternalist modes of interventions, discourses and techniques in areas such as penal and workfare policy (Peck and Tickell 2002). Ironically, while neoliberalism aspired to create a utopia of free markets liberated from all forms of state interference, it has actually entailed a dramatic intensification of coercive, disciplinary forms of state intervention in order to impose market rule on all aspects of social life (Brenner and Theodore 2002a; MacLeod 2002). These mutations have meant that neoliberalism is no longer narrowly concerned with the mobilization and extension of markets (and market logics), but increasingly with "the political foregrounding of new modes of 'social' and penal policy making, concerned specifically with the aggressive regulation, disciplining, and containment of those marginalized or dispossessed by the neo-liberalization of the 1980s" (Peck and Tickell 2002, 389).

The Control of Control: Governing Interdictory City Space

"In the punitive city, the postmodern city, the revanchist city, diversity is no longer maintained by protecting and struggling to expand the rights of the most disadvantaged, but by pushing the disadvantaged out, making it clear that, *as broken windows rather than people, they simply have no right* to the city" (Mitchell 2001, 71; emphasis added). For Mitchell (2001), the "postjustice" city is one of the most active sites of neoliberalized, authoritarian statecraft: a new urban policy configuration based on social and racial containment, the purification of public spaces, the subsidization of the elite consumption, the privatization of social reproduction, the normalization of economic insecurity, and the specter of preemptive crime control (Peck 2003). This is not necessarily less government, but *different* government (Peck 2003)—a contextual embeddedness of neoliberalism that has stressed the recriminalization of poverty, the normalization of contingent work, and its active enforcement through welfare retrenchment, workfare programming, and active employment policies—strategies to reproduce regimes of precarious work and mobilize the poor for work readiness—that discipline, incarcerate, intervene, and increase social surveillance of those outside market discipline (Peck and Tickell 2002). For Soja, borrowing from Foucault, urban space has become "a collection of carceral cities, an archipelago of normalized enclosures and fortified spaces that both voluntarily and involuntarily barricade individuals and communities in visible and not-so-visible urban islands, overseen by restructured forms of public power and private authority" (2000, 299). These geographies of fortification, based on physical and institutional barriers, cosseted private worlds that share little in common with adjacent neighborhoods, are, of course, bolstered by the securitization of degenerate communities and curfew orders that restrict the movement of particular groups to ensure the "success," safety, and visitor-friendly aspects of urban environments (MacLeod, Raco, and Ward 2003). Peck (2003) extends Soja, suggesting that it is possible to talk of emergent processes of carceralization in which the prison system is understood as an epicentral institution of neoliberalized times (around two-thirds of all African American men in their twenties in the deindustrialized cities of the northeastern United

States are in prison, on parole, or on probation). This recent explosion in incarceration (see Peck 2003; Wacquant 2001) can be seen as part of the brutal reregulation of the urban poor (which becomes even more pronounced and gendered when considering employment marginalization and "workfare") and points to the systemic inequalities of neoliberal capitalism and society that seemingly deracializes what is a racialized order (Peck 2003; Wacquant 2001). Yet it is beyond the boundaries of the prison that the "intensity of the state's involvement seems to be increasing, as rising moral panics around 'law and order', urban unrest, immigration and homelessness and 'welfare dependency' license new forms of microsocial intervention, social-service delivery, the regulation of immigration, urban programming, crime control and job markets" (Peck 2003, 227). In this way, the state is able to play a profoundly active role in the remaking of class relations (which is often played out in racial terms; see, for example, Goldberg's [2008] discussion of racial neoliberalism) yet, in true neoliberal fashion, routinely subordinates such roles and experiences to the overdetermining logic of the *market* (Peck 2003).

To fully understand these geographies of fortification requires consideration of the broader rationalities and technologies of governance pertaining to the "conduct of conduct" that have been mobilized and instrumentalized in the name of good citizenship, public order, and the control or elimination of criminality, delinquency, and antisocial conduct (Rose 2000). In this sense, the processes of carceralization extend beyond the institutional borders of the penal system and are powerfully enacted and produced within the discourses, architectures, and management of what Flusty (2001) has termed "interdictory spaces." These banal, normalized, and naturalized spaces (gated communities, shopping malls, publicly subsidized corporate plazas) are designed to systematically exclude those adjudged to be threatening or unsuitable to the contemporary urban environment. Such disciplinary neoliberalism points toward consideration of pseudo-carceral spaces and raises profound questions over the security-obsessed architectures of the contemporary city and the authoritarian legal measures and policing tactics MacLeod (2002; see also MacLeod and Ward 2002) designed to regulate the spatial practices of the displaced urban poor.

For Flusty (2001, 658), interdictory spaces are barricaded streets, privately administered plazas, police helicopter overflights, and traffic lights festooned with panning, tilting, and zooming video cameras. Such urban disamenities have in turn, for Flusty (2001), aggregated to form paranoid-built typologies— gated residential "luxury laagers," for instance—where clusters of expensive single-family homes are surrounded by security fortifications, shopping malls equipped with video observation cameras, palisaded parking lots, and police substations. These newly fortified topographies are underpinned by a strict demarcation of public and private space—streets are privately owned and their upkeep is the responsibility of home and shop owners. As space is reconfigured in the name of security, new conceptions of "criminogenic spaces" and new strategies of situational crime control have taken shape, reconfiguring the work of security agencies and the police. City space is thus increasingly constituted around, within, and through the multifarious constituents of the security-industrial complex (Rose 2000)—embodied discourses constructed to render problems (people) thinkable and hence governable. In this way, specific populations are quite literally subjected to (they become the objects of) particular forms of governance in a way that operationalizes and institutionalizes particular sociospatial political agendas (MacLeod, Raco, and Ward 2003; Rose 1999). There has thus been a convergence and transformation of programs, strategies, and techniques for the conduct of conduct, the "rationalities and technologies underpinning a whole variety of more or less rationalized and calculated interventions that have attempted to govern the existence and experience of contemporary human beings and to act on human conduct to direct it to certain ends" (Rose 2000, 322). These initiatives stress the problems (people) deemed *appropriate* to be governed, the sites within which these problems come to be defined, the diversity of authorities that have been involved in the attempts to address them, and the technical devices that aspire to produce certain outcomes in the conduct of the governed devices that are, in many respects, far removed from the political apparatus as traditionally conceived (Rose 2000). As Peck and Tickell eloquently surmise:

> New technologies of government are being designed and rolled out, new discourses of "reform" are being constructed (often around new policy objectives such as "welfare dependency"), new institutions and modes of delivery are being fashioned, and new social subjectivities are being fostered. In complex simultaneity, these social and penal policy incursions represent both the advancement of the neoliberal project—of extending and bolstering market logics, *socializing individualized subjects, and disciplining the noncompliant*—and a recognition of sorts that earlier manifestations of this project, rooted in dogmatic deregulation and marketization, clearly had serious limitations and contradictions. (2002, 390; emphasis added)

Allied with the turn toward place promotion and sporting spaces of consumption, these discourses have meant that "degenerate" places and peoples are discursively constructed as urban problems to be addressed by specific policy measures, the imposition of tightly authoritarian regulatory technologies, and the promotion of entrepreneurial values within target populations (MacLeod, Raco, and Ward 2003). Codes of conduct that explicitly aim to regulate behavior in the downtown areas of major cities have become commonplace—a process that points to how political discourses play a critical role in shaping the new urbanism (MacLeod, Raco, and Ward 2003). As a result, certain people and places become pathologically labeled as the threatening or undeserving "other" whose behavior needs disciplining, often through new strategies of zero tolerance policing that "are operationalized through new technologies of secur(itis)ing space, designed to regulate subjects who are deemed to be threatening 'others' who may unsettle the image and disrupt the perceived safety of places" (MacLeod, Raco, and Ward 2003, 1665). This is an urban politics based on the "social construction of suspicion" (Norris and Armstrong 1998, 10), the construction of a politics of inclusionary respectability and exclusionary otherness, and promulgated by a private sector playing an increasingly central role in constructing definitions of risk and danger in the city and who should be targeted to avoid these risks and dangers (Coleman and Sim 2000).[1] The management and mobilization of closed-circuit television (CCTV), community safety orders, and curfews, accompanied by the design of secure architecture and public space, prevents, regiments, and polices the gathering and movement of *certain* bodies in space under the guise of maintaining a "rationalized" if not "paramilitarized urban landscape" (Davis 1990). Such management routinely takes place without so-called political liability, as the new urban policy is prefigured on governmentalities that punctuate various modes of policing, and disciplinary social policies vis-à-vis the labor and housing markets, security focused architecture, and technologies (MacLeod, Raco, and Ward 2003; Raco 2003).

In short, the mode of regulation associated with the corporate entertainment city points to an intensified social and spatial control of leisure spaces via formal mechanisms such as increased surveillance and door security staff, restrictive bylaws and design of the built environment, and attempts to literally sanitize through style (Chatterton and Hollands 2002; Christopherson 1994; Soja 2000). It is in the regenerated city, with its not-so-subtle lessons for proper conduct in public space—its reemphasis on spectacle, consumption, sport, and leisure—that neoliberal governance has successfully sustained economic polarization, as well as having assumed a greater role in *managing* its social consequences through the deployment of authoritative categories that discursively constitute the *other* (Coleman and Sim 2000). Thus, Flusty (2001) proposes that interdictory space is far from democratically distributed—it is commonly designed, built, and administered by those affluent enough to do so, but it is done with the wants and sensibilities of the similarly affluent consumer in mind. Centered on Los Angeles, Flusty's (2001) work suggests that interdictory space maintains itself through the exclusion of others, and that these interdicted spaces and precincts redefine the remainder, indeed the majority, of Los Angeles's diverse community landscape as "other," thereby working to exclude that otherness. In this way, interdictory space is selectively exclusionary space: space in which the other is reconstituted as pathologically degenerate and is welcomed only on condition that behavior is *appropriate* and *regulated*. Of course, "what constitutes appropriate behavior in interdicted spaces is rigidly defined and strenuously enforced by management—in short, difference is fine, as long as it is surrendered at the gate" (Flusty 2001, 659).

Conclusion

The corollary, then, to the spectacular spaces of sporting consumption that dominate urban cores is the bifurcation of the urban social formations, characterized by the extension of the penal code, the deinstitutionalization of the prison-industrial complex, and the widespread dissemination of a rhetoric of fear. In this way, those who are different, those who threaten the "normative universality" of the urban core, are increasingly subject to measures that will secure the extension, maintenance, reproduction, and management of the consequences of market rule (Peck 2003)—that is, any "tactical appropriation" (Certeau 1984) of space through the rhetoric and performativity of walking is governed and regulated (who walks, when, and where) when articulated with the social formation (Grossberg 1992; Morris 2004; Silk 2010). Access to consumption space is thus guarded, under electronic surveillance, private security policing, and other technologies of surveillance that eviscerate or expel those who have no legitimate—that is, consumer-oriented—reason to be there (Rose 2000). In essence, these arrangements speak to the destruction of the liberal city, a situation in which inhabitants are no longer entitled to basic civil liberties, social services, and political rights. The working class–industrial city is thus recast through a (re)emphasis on urban disorder, disdain and suspicion, dangerous classes, and economic decline that creates a concomitant moment of new and discriminatory forms of surveillance and social control, new policies to combat social exclusion by reinserting individuals into the labor market, the mobilization of zero-tolerance policing and entrepreneurial discourses, and representations on the need for revitalization, reinvestment, and rejuvenation (Brenner and Theodore 2002a; Kearns and Paddison 2000). These degraded borderlands of the contemporary Western city, the naturalized or banal interdictory (Flusty 2001) city spaces of capitalism, thus form the heart of what Giroux (2003a) termed the insufferable climate of increased repression and exploitation in which youth and communities of color become collateral damage in the war against justice, freedom, citizenship, and participatory democracy itself.

However, and rather than prophesize some cataclysmic abyss, spaces of neoliberalism, as MacLeod (2002) argued, are negotiated, enacted, performed, lived in and lived through, contested, and representative. In spite of increased commodification, public space is "always in a process of being shaped, re-shaped, and challenged by the spatial practices of various groups and individuals whose identities and actions undermine the homogeneity of contemporary cities" (McCann 1999, 168, quoted in MacLeod 2002). Doreen Massey (1999, 160, cited in MacLeod and Ward 2002), for example, has suggested that despite the numerical dominance and confidence of street police and private guards and their attempts to erase the traces of others, other stories still live on that emerge in other places and at other times (see, for example, L'Aoustet and Griffet's [2004] account of youthful serendipity in Marseille's Borely Park, or Simpson's [2000] tale of the performance of youthful difference, designed to shock and anger middle-class sensibilities, at the Blue Chair music store in Ybor City). To counter the repressive cultural politics of urban glamour zones, and indeed to avoid representing such spaces purely as the apex of neoliberal utopias (MacLeod and Ward 2002), we need multiple, pejorative stories. To do so, and to accompany, compliment, extend, and challenge urban theorizing (such as this chapter), we need to address the complexities and unevenness—the local differences (Massey 2000), peculiarities, and relationships within and between cities (as some chapters in this volume do). That is, as academics committed to a critical pedagogy (see, e.g., Darder and Miron 2006; Giroux 2005; Giroux and Giroux 2006; Harvey 2007) and an urban insurgency, we need to resist, transgress, and oppose, unshackle the padlocks of purified urban sites (and scholarly work that reifies such spaces) and thereby challenge the official, market-oriented, growth-machine representations of urban space (MacLeod 2002). The chapters in Part II of this volume are one such effort.

NOTE

1. While our argument in this chapter is centered primarily on the North American city, we should mention the recent anxieties over "hoodies" in the United Kingdom. Banned from schools and shopping centers such as Bluewater, youth apparel such as hooded tops (hoodies) and baseball caps have been under increasing fire from a government intent on the discipline and control of "feral youth."

REFERENCES

Benjamin, W. 2002. *The Arcades Project*, trans. H. Eiland and K. Kevin McLaughlin. Cambridge, MA: Belknap Press.

Bockmeyer, J. 2000. "A Culture of Distrust: The Impact of Local Political Culture on Participation in the Detroit EZ." *Urban Studies* 37 (13): 2417–2440.

Brenner, N., and N. Theodore. 2002a. "Cities and the Geographies of 'Actually Existing Neoliberalism.'" *Antipode* 34 (3): 349–379.

——— 2002b. "Preface: From the New Localism to the Spaces of Neoliberalism." *Antipode* 34 (3): 341–347.

Butler, J. 1993. *Gender Trouble: Feminism and the Subversion of Identity*. New York: Routledge.

Certeau, Michel de. 1984. *The Practice of Everyday Life*, trans. S. F. Rendall. Berkeley: University of California Press.

Chalkey, B., and S. Essex. 1999. "Urban Development through Hosting International Events: A History of the Olympic Games." *Planning Perspectives* 14:369–394.

Chatterton, P., and R. Hollands. 2002. "Theorising Urban Playscapes: Producing, Regulating and Consuming Youthful Nightlife City Spaces." *Urban Studies* 39 (1): 95–116.

Christopherson, S. 1994. "The Fortress City: Privatized Spaces, Consumer Citizenship." In *Post-Fordism: A Reader*, ed. A. Amin, 409–482. London: Blackwell.

Cohen, P. 1999. "In Visible Cities: Urban Regeneration and Place-Building in the Era of Multicultural Capitalism." *Communal/Plural* 7 (1): 9–28.

Coleman, R., and J. Sim. 2000. "'You'll Never Walk Alone': CCTV Surveillance, Order and Neo-liberal Rule in Liverpool City Centre." *British Journal of Sociology* 51 (4): 623–639.

Dardor, A., and L. Miron. 2006. "Critical Pedagogy in a Time of Uncertainty." *Cultural Studies ↔ Critical Methodologies* 6 (1): 5–20.

Davis, M. 1990. *City of Quartz: Excavating the Future in Los Angeles*. New York: Verso.

Dostoevsky, F. 1968. *Crime and Punishment*. New York: Washington Square Press.

Fainstein, S., and D. Gladstone. 1999. "Evaluating Urban Tourism." In *The Tourist City*, ed. S. Fainstein and D. Judd, 21–34. New Haven, CT: Yale University Press.

Florida, R. 2002. *The Rise of the Creative Class*. New York: Basic Books.

Flusty, S. 2001. "The Banality of Interdiction: Surveillance, Control and the Displacement of Diversity." *International Journal of Urban and Regional Research* 25 (3): 658–664.

Friedman, M., D. Andrews, and M. Silk. 2004. "Sport and the Façade of Redevelopment in the Post-Industrial City." *Sociology of Sport Journal* 21 (2): 119–139.

Gibson, T. 2003. "The Trope of the Organic City: Discourses of Decay and Rebirth in Downtown Seattle." *Space and Culture* 6 (4): 429–448.

Giroux, H. 2000. *Impure Acts: The Practical Politics of Cultural Studies.* New York: Routledge.

———. 2001. "Cultural Studies as Performative Politics." *Cultural Studies ↔ Critical Methodologies* 1 (1): 5–23.

———. 2003a. *The Abandoned Generation: Democracy beyond the Culture of Fear.* New York: Palgrave.

———. 2003b. *Public Spaces, Private Lives: Democracy beyond 9/11.* Lanham, MD: Rowman and Littlefield.

———. 2004. "War Talk, the Death of the Social, and the Disappearing Children: Remembering the Other War." *Cultural Studies ↔ Critical Methodologies* 4 (2): 206–211.

———. 2005. *The Terror of Neoliberalism.* New York: Palgrave.

Giroux, H., and S. Giroux. 2006. "Challenging Neoliberalism's New World Order: The Promise of Critical Pedagogy." *Cultural Studies ↔ Critical Methodologies* 6 (1): 21–32.

Goldberg, D. T. 2008. *The Threat of Race: Reflections on Racial Neoliberalism.* Oxford: Wiley-Blackwell.

Goodwin, M. 1993. "The City as Commodity: The Contested Spaces of Urban Development." In *Selling Places: The City as Cultural Capital, Past and Present*, ed. G. Kearns and C. Philo, 145–162. Oxford: Pergamon.

Gottdiener, M. 2000. "Lefebvre and the Bias of Academic Urbanism: What Can We Learn from the New Urban Analysis?" *City* 4:93–100.

Grossberg, L. 1992. *We Gotta Get Out of This Place: Popular Conservatism and Postmodern Culture.* New York: Routledge.

Hall, S. 1983. "The Great Moving Right Show." In *The Politics of Thatcherism*, ed. S. Hall and M. Jacques, 19–39. London: Lawrence and Wishart.

Hannigan, J. 1998. *Fantasy City: Pleasure and Profit in the Postmodern Metropolis.* London: Routledge.

Harvey, D. 1989. *The Condition of Postmodernity: An Enquiry into the Origins of Cultural Change.* Cambridge, MA: Wiley-Blackwell.

———. 2000. *Spaces of Hope.* Boulder: University of Colorado Press.

———. 2001. *Spaces of Capital: Towards a Critical Geography.* London: Routledge.

———. 2007. "Neoliberalism and the City." *Studies in Social Justice* 1 (1): 2–13.

Hobbs, D., S. Lister, P. Hadfield, S. Winslow, and S. Hall. 2000. "Receiving Shadows: Governance and Liminality in the Night-Time Economy." *British Journal of Sociology* 51 (4): 701–717.

Jameson, F. 1991. *Postmodernism, or, the Cultural Logic of Late Capitalism.* Durham, NC: Duke University Press.

Jansen-Verbeke, M. 1989. "Inner Cities and Urban Tourism in the Netherlands: New Challenges for Local Authorities." In *Leisure and Urban Processes: Critical Studies of Leisure Policy in Western European Cities*, ed. P. Bramham, I. Henrey, H. Mommas, and H. Van Der Poel, 213–253. London: Routledge.

Jessop, B. 2002. "Liberalism, Neoliberalism, and Urban Governance: A State-Theoretical Perspective." *Antipode* 34 (3): 452–472.

Judd, D. 1999. "Constructing the Tourist Bubble." In *The Tourist City*, ed. S. Fainstein and D. Judd, 35–53. New Haven, CT: Yale University Press.

Judd, D., and D. Simpson. 2003. "Reconstructing the Local State: The Role of External Constituencies in Building Urban Tourism." *American Behavioral Scientist* 46 (8): 1056–1069.

Kearns, A., and R. Paddison. 2000. "New Challenges for Urban Governance." *Urban Studies* 37 (5–6): 845–850.

L'Aoustet, O., and J. Griffet. 2004. "Youth Experience and Socialization in Marseille's Borely Park." *Space and Culture* 7 (2): 173–187.

MacLeod, G. 2002. "From Urban Entrepreneurialism to a 'Revanchist City'? On the Spatial Injustices of Glasgow's Renaissance." *Antipode* 34 (3): 602–624.

MacLeod, G., and K. Ward. 2002. "Spaces of Utopia and Dystopia: Landscaping the Contemporary City." *Geografiska Annaler* 84B (3–4): 153–170.

MacLeod, G., M. Raco, and K. Ward. 2003. "Negotiating the Contemporary City: Introduction." *Urban Studies* 40 (9): 1655–1671.

Massey, D. 2000. "Understanding Cities." *City* 4:135–144.

Merrifield, A. 2000. "The Dialectics of Dystopia: Disorder and Zero Tolerance in the City." *International Journal of Urban and Regional Research* 24 (2): 473–489.

Mitchell, D. 2001. "Postmodern Geographical Praxis? Postmodern Impulse and the War against Homeless People in the 'Postjustice' City." In *Postmodern Geography: Theory and Praxis*, ed. C. Minca, 57–92. Oxford: Blackwell.

Morris, B. 2004. "What We Talk about When We Talk about 'Walking in the City.'" *Cultural Studies* 18 (5): 675–697.

Norris, C., and G. Armstrong. 1998. "Introduction: Power and Vision." In *Surveillance, Closed Circuit Television and Social Control*, ed. C. Norris, J. Moran, and G. Armstrong, 3–18. Aldershot, UK: Ashgate.

Peck, J. 2003. "Geography and Public Policy: Mapping the Penal State." *Progress in Human Geography* 27 (2): 222–232.

Peck, J., and A. Tickell. 2002. "Neoliberalizing Space." *Antipode* 34 (3): 380–404.

Raco, M. 2003. "Remarking Place and Securitising Space: Urban Regeneration and the Strategies, Tactics and Practices of Policing in the UK." *Urban Studies* 40 (9): 1869–1887.

Rose, N. 1999. "Community, Citizenship, and the Third Way." *American Behavioral Scientist* 43 (9): 1395–1411.

———. 2000. "Government and Control." *British Journal of Criminology* 40:321–339.

Rowe, D., and P. McGuirk. 1999. "Drunk for Three Weeks: Sporting Success and the City Image." *International Review for the Sociology of Sport* 34:125–142.

Sassen, S. 2001. *The Global City: New York, London, Tokyo*, 2nd ed. Princeton, NJ: Princeton University Press.

Savitch, H., and P. Kantor. 2003. "Urban Strategies for a Global Era: A Cross-National Comparison." *American Behavioral Scientist* 46 (8): 1002–1033.

Silk, M. 2004. "A Tale of Two Cities: The Social Reproduction of Sterile Sporting Space." *Journal of Sport and Social Issues* 28 (4): 349–378.

———. 2007. "Come Downtown and Play." *Leisure Studies* 26 (3): 253–277.

———. 2010. "Postcards from Pigtown." *Cultural Studies* ↔ *Critical Methodologies* 10 (2): 143–156.

Silk, M., and D. Andrews. 2008. "Managing Memphis: Governance and Regulation in Sterile Spaces of Play." *Social Identities* 14 (3): 395–414.

Simpson, T. 2000. "Streets, Sidewalks, Stores and Stories: Narrative and the Uses of Urban Space." *Journal of Contemporary Ethnography* 29 (6): 682–716.

Soja, E. 1989. *Postmodern Geographies: The Reassertion of Space in Critical Social Theory.* London: Verso.

———. 2000. *Postmetropolis: Critical Studies of Cities and Regions.* Oxford: Blackwell.

Wacquant, L. 2001. "Deadly Symbiosis: When Ghetto and Prison Meet and Mesh." In *Mass Imprisonment in the United States*, ed. D. Garland, 82–120. London: Sage.

Walks, R. 2001. "The Social Ecology of the Post-Fordist/Global City? Economic Restructuring and Socio-Spatial Polarisation in the Toronto Urban Region." *Urban Studies* 38 (3): 407–447.

Whitson, D., and D. Macintosh. 1996. "The Global Circus: International Sport, Tourism and the Marketing of Cities." *Journal of Sport and Social Issues* 20:239–257.

Wilcox, R., and D. Andrews. 2003. "Sport in the City: Cultural, Economic and Political Portraits." In *Sporting Dystopias: The Making and Meanings of Urban Sport Cultures*, ed. R. Wilcox, D. Andrews, R. Pitter, and R. Irwin, 1–16. New York: State University of New York Press.

Zukin, S. 1991. *Landscapes of Power: From Detroit to Disney.* Berkeley: University of California Press.

Zylinska, J. 2004. "The Universal Acts: Judith Butler and the Biopolitics of Immigration." *Cultural Studies* 18 (4): 523–537.

9

Governing Play

Moral Geographies, Healthification, and Neoliberal Urban Imaginaries

CAROLINE FUSCO

What is it "to govern in an advanced liberal way" (N. Rose 1996, 53)? For some time now, I have been interested in questions of space and how bodies are governed, (dis)located, and (dis)placed. In a study of locker rooms (Fusco 2003), I concluded that ideologies of regimes of "healthification" (Fusco 2006) pervade fitness spaces. *Healthification* is a term that I have coined to describe how the continuous deployment of a broad range of specialized strategies and technologies, expertise, and techniques (e.g., policy and educational initiatives, architectural arrangements, urban planning, measures of public order, health and safety regulations, self and other observations) produce "healthified" spaces and subjectivities. Healthified space is a "spatial practice" (Lefebvre 1991), and it demonstrates institutional commitments and individuals' responsibility for the consumption of regimes of healthification.[1] The concept of healthification was inspired by several authors' analyses of health under neoliberalism. According to scholars, neoliberal regimes of health demonstrate commitments to healthism (Crawford 1980; Lupton 1995), because they "encourage" individuals to take responsibility for their own health and well-being and/or the health of others through cultures of philanthropy (King 2006), as well as the consumption of privatized health services and products of health and wellness (Herrick 2011; Ingham 1985; Lupton 1995; Petersen and Bunton 1997; Petersen and Lupton 1996; Wheatley 2005). Drawing from these ideas about the effects of neoliberalism's healthist discourses, I am concerned about how neoliberalism impacts on the production of physical activity and health spaces.

According to urban sociologists, "place matters" (Fitzpatrick and LaGory 2003), and it is, therefore, important that the intersections of neoliberalism, health, and the material conditions of space and place be addressed. I take up these concerns to examine how healthification and govern*mentality*[2] produce conceptions of space, spatial practices, and experiences of (lived) space for young people in particular urban spaces.[3] We know that young people are targets for neoliberalism's healthist discourses (Wright and Harwood 2009; MacNeill 2006; Reid-Boyd 2006; Varpalotai and Singleton 2006) and that many youth in Western societies have taken up dominant constructions of health (Beausoleil and Rail 2006). Indeed, evidence illustrates that the discourses of risk and epidemic, so prevalent in health discourses, have produced representations of the "(un)healthy child" in a manner that aligns with the political rationalities of late modernity and neoliberalism (McDermott 2007). What is less known with respect to healthism and neoliberalism is how the increasingly relevant issue of locale is for "young people's entry into citizenship in terms of competency, participation and responsibility" (Hall, Coffey, and Williamson 1999, 502).

Neoliberalism and the (Un)Healthy Subject

"The regulation of conduct becomes a matter of each individual's desire to govern their own conduct freely in the service of the maximization of a version of their happiness and fulfillment that they take to be their own, but such a lifestyle maximization entails a relation to authority in the very moment as it pronounces itself to be the outcome of free choice" (N. Rose 1996, 58–59). Neoliberalism has been defined in many ways (see Barry, Osborne, and Rose 1996; Chomsky 1999; Dean 1999; Giroux 2004; Harvey 2005; Miller and Rose 2008; N. Rose 1996, 1999). For the purpose of this chapter, I understand neoliberalism as a set of policies, practices, and regimes that seek to extend the market economy (of health) into areas of the community, which have been previously organized and governed in other ways (Bargh 2007). Neoliberalism's economic thinking diffuses the notion of enterprise throughout society as its general organizing principle, with an emphasis on choice, commodity form, and the manageralism of identity (Lather 2007). This results in the "capitalization of life" (Gordon 1991, 44) or what Navarro has referred to as "capitalism without borders" (2007, 1). Neoliberalism seeks to extend the spaces in which a certain kind of economic freedom might be practiced in the form of personal autonomy, enterprise, and choice: it desires to "govern at a distance" (N. Rose 1996, 43).

Discourses such as individualism, consumerism, citizenship, personal responsibility, accountability, and individual choice are essential for the operation of the complex apparatus of health and therapeutics that have been assembled in the name of neoliberalism (Miller and Rose 2008; N. Rose 1996). Yet neoliberalism's adherence to "the virtues of the market-oriented society have produced higher income inequality and lower social cohesion and, presumably, either lowered health status or a health status which is not as it might otherwise been" (Coburn 2000, 137). Indeed, "rising inequality of different types of capital—cultural, economic, environmental, social, and political—between as well as within nations are frequently cited as tangible indicators of the imprint of neoliberalization" (England and Ward 2007, 2). Yet these increases in inequality, which take place through restructuring and destruction of public social services, are jettisoned from the public imaginary because of the concomitant rise in discourses of self-regulation and risk management (Castel 1991; Lupton 1999). These latter discourses invite individuals to engage in self-governance and risk management where their health is concerned (Petersen 1997; Wheatley 2005). Healthism and bodyism, combined with enterprise and rationality, form the nexus of health promotion strategies in new public health under neoliberalism (Petersen 1997). The self that is privileged and normalized is the entrepreneurial self, one who is willing to take action to improve his or her health status (Lupton 1995; N. Rose 2007). Those who do not participate are deemed to be personal and social failures, morally weak, and are deemed to have "a reprobate attitude toward the body" (Ingham 1985, 48). Youth, of course, are not exempted from these neoliberal health discourses.

Neoliberalism, Youth, and Moral Geographies

"The soul of the young citizen has become the object of government through expertise" (N. Rose 1989, 134). Since the eighteenth century, concerns about public health have been intimately connected to the control of urban environments (see Armstrong 1993; Foucault 1980; Herrick 2011). Health experts have used surveillance, analysis, intervention and modification to create a biopolitical order that controlled and monitored where and how bodies moved, worked, and played (Armstrong 1995; England and Ward 2007; Foucault 1980). Children and their families have not been immune to these kinds of (urban) management. Indeed, an emphasis on a biopolitics of population (Foucault 1978; Kontopodis 2011; Peters 2007; N. Rose 2007) means that family life and the organization of family health, sexuality, education, and space have been under great scrutiny with the advent of both modernity and now neoliberalism. Consequently, attention has been paid to the institutional spaces that children and youth inhabit, such as homes, schools, and parks, and the disciplinary and spatial technologies operating in these spaces ensure an adherence to normative behaviors (Dillabough and Kennelly 2010; Foucault 1978; Kirk 1998). Historically, young people's behaviors and occupations of space have been of great concern to adults, and young people's presence in public and private spaces has generated much uneasiness in modern times (Aitken 2001; Dillabough and Kennelly 2010).

Sport and physical activity have always been depicted as solutions to the "problem" of youth and urban spaces (Fusco 2007; Gagen 2000). So it is not surprising that in North America and many other industrialized countries, health discourses of childhood inactivity and obesity, which have woven their way into peoples' consciousnesses (McDermott 2007), point to the production of sports and physical activity spaces for youth as the antidote (Active Healthy Kids Canada 2011; Canadian Fitness and Lifestyle Research Institute 2011). There has been a sustained critique of the "obesity epidemic" and the deployment of these discourses for youth consumption (Evans, Davis, and Wright 2004; Gard and Wright 2005; Kirk 2006; McDermott 2007; Smith, Green, and Roberts 2004; Wright and Harwood 2009; Singleton and Varpalotai 2006). Moreover, scholars have demonstrated that sport and physical activity spaces are highly normalized, regulated, and disciplined (see Bale 1994; Eichberg 1993; Fusco 2005, 2006; Van Ingen 2003; Vertinsky 2004a, 2004b; Vertinsky and Bale 2004, Vertinsky and McKay 2004). Yet we have not fully grasped how neoliberalist discourses of youth's physical (in)activity produce, and are produced by, space. If, as cultural geographers have suggested, youth's spaces are produced through hegemonic power relations (Aitken 2001; Dillabough and Kennelly 2010; Philo and Smith 2003; Skelton and Valentine 1998; Valentine 1996), corporatization (Borden 2003; Holloway and Valentine 2000; McKendrick 1999a, 1999b), policing and moralizing (Aitken 2001; Valentine 1996), and increasingly "militarization" (Giroux 2004; Gallagher and Fusco 2006), then the interrogation of youth geographies of health in neoliberal times remains salient.

Findings: Neoliberal Urban Imaginaries

"Neoliberal globalization as material practice and as a hegemonic discourse is yet another in a long line of attempts to tame the spatial" (Massey 2005, 99). As noted previously, neoliberal ways of governing seek to impose a kind of moral normativity on individuals in order to shape and guide their choices, within the context of expert discourses, promises, dire warnings, and threats of intervention, organized increasingly around a proliferation of norms, normativities, and risk (N. Rose 1996; Herrick 2011). I have been interested in how this impacts on the spatialization of youth's health.[4] If (adult) urban spaces are increasingly imagined in terms of neoliberal ideologies (Boudreau, Keil, and Young 2009), health and active living discourses (Silk and Andrews 2006), and consumerism (Herrick 2011), then how is space conceived in such a way that may incite youth to become engaged civic participants in the new public health? In order to answer this question, methodologically, I adopt a microgenealogical of space to examine the "techne" of neoliberal government (Dean 1999) and to investigate what discourses and practices direct, with a certain degree of deliberation, the "conduct of conduct" (Dean 1999) of youth health spaces. A microgenealogical approach "encourages an attention to the humble, the mundane, the little shifts in our ways of thinking and understanding, the small contingent struggles, tensions and negotiations that give rise to something new and unexpected" (N. Rose 1999, 11). This methodology derives its analysis from Foucault's "analytics of government," which is concerned with how different forms of truths are produced in social, political, and cultural practices. Specifically here, I draw from Richardson and Jensen's (2003) "cultural sociology of space"' by paying attention to how spatialities and their symbolic meanings are "constructed" in policies pertaining to youth, health, and education. That is, I interrogate how space and place are articulated, conceived, represented, and imagined in government urban health and education initiatives, and how these may be symbolically linked to youth's health and the future health of the city and nation. G. Rose suggests that "particular imagined spatialities are constitutive of specific subjectivities" (1995, 335). Moreover, Gulson suggests that the "notion of 'neoliberal spatial technologies,' a bricolage of neoliberalism, governmentality and relational space" are apparent in inner-city educational policies and "constitute particular students as possible neoliberal educational subjects" (2007, 179). Consequently, I am driven to ask: What does youth space, conceived through neoliberal health agendas, look like and what kind of youth subjectivities do neoliberalist spatial agendas fantasize and seek to produce?

In Canada, there has been a proliferation of federal, provincial, and municipal government policies and media communications directed toward youth, health, and physical activity. In Ontario, the most populated province in Canada, municipal and provincial governments have actively promoted youth's health in the last five years through programs (e.g., "Daily Physical Activity in Schools Initiative," "Healthy Schools Initiative," "Pause to Play," "It's Not Going to Kill You," "ReActivate TO!" and "Our Common Grounds") and places (e.g., the Nike Malvern Sports Complex). This range of programs with catchy titles and the subsequent places through which to realize them demonstrate that neoliberal interests can be dispersed through the social body through practices that misleadingly appear to be outside the realms of government or consumer capitalism (King 2006, xi). Moreover, the programs and the places they imagine and represent seem to align with the "taming of space," which is a neoliberal priority, according to Massey (2005).

Overwhelmingly, it appears that neoliberalist representations of space promise salvation to youth by placing an emphasis on youth's futures. This is not a surprising episteme of government, since "the neoliberal model does not purport so much to describe the world as it is, but the world as it should be" (Clarke 2005, 58). Governing in "advanced" liberal societies requires a multiplication of regulatory instances (Dean 1999; N. Rose 1996) and the management and organization of space in order to provide neoliberalism with multiple sites for the application of power; provision of spaces for youth then makes it possible to govern youth and their health practices in an "advanced" liberal way (N. Rose 1996). In Toronto, Canada, many "neoliberal" invitations have been "offered" to youth to enhance their health, and these inevitably entail some kind of *re*imagining of space. First, adults (parents, to be precise) are asked to fulfill their (parental) civic duties by investing in healthified spaces on behalf of (their) youth. "Our Common Grounds," a city of Toronto publication, states, "Our Strategic Plan calls for lifelong activity because it's what we must all do to stay healthy until the end. It calls for a focus on the development of children and youth because we know they are our future and they are not sufficiently active to maintain their health" (2004, 33). Adult stakeholders (parents, community groups, teachers, guardians, police, and politicians) are asked to facilitate and realize *their* youth's potential through an imagined (and common) community (Anderson 1991) and to work at producing involved, responsible, and caring youth citizens. There is an emphasis on accountability, active participation, and investment in (our) youth's futures. "Our Common Grounds" continues:

> We need to offer youth inclusion into something larger than themselves. We need to eliminate barriers that feel like exclusion. We need to offer welcoming alternatives to gangs, which youth sometimes join to protect themselves from unsafe streets. (2004, 27)

Here the space of the "common" (people) is constituted as degenerative, and it is a space that must be changed or else there will be dire consequences. Such conceptions may seek to open up spaces of decision making and action for youth, as they are encouraged to "bring the future into the present" (N. Rose 1996) by making the right choices among the possibilities offered to them.

While adults are asked to envision a healthy future for youths, the city, and the province (and aging adults), youths are also incited to take it upon themselves to find salvation in the spaces of sports and physical activity. The Pause to Play website, an Ontario Ministry of Health Promotion initiative that contains not only many images of happy, active youths in a variety of sports spaces but also links to fitness information, interactive tools, and posters, implores youths, "Sports are a great way to be active. Choose a sport. There are lots to go around" (Ontario Ministry of Health Promotion 2012a).

> When you can dribble in public and not get lectured by grown-ups, it's got to be a good thing. . . . Forget television. Ignore your parents' pleas to watch the news. If they try to stop you from playing b-ball, use an excuse like "It's helping me learn about fair play, self-confidence and teamwork. And you want me to stay in shape, don't you?" Works every time. (Ontario Ministry of Health Promotion 2012b)

Here, youth are assumed to have an interest in producing themselves as healthy citizens and in take charge of their own health destinies. These destinies, of course, can be realized if youth literally (ex)change places and move themselves from the screen to the park. Ironically, the child is depicted as the one who resists parents' pleas to stay indoors, which is contrary to popular representations of parents imploring their children to "go outside and play." If children choose to go outside, there is a whole world waiting for them to discover it. Another municipal report, "ReActivate TO!" continued to promise youth that the world outside their house is a safe place for their future:

> Parks & Recreation is committed to supporting the development of happy, healthy children and youth. From wide open green spaces, playgrounds and water play areas to organized sports, pre-school and after school programs and camps for all ages, abilities and interests, to leadership development, recreation employment preparation and other programs specific to

the needs of today's youth, Parks & Recreation makes Toronto a great place to grow up. ("ReActivate TO!" 2004)

According to theorists, achieving well-being in neoliberal times depends on the subject being dutiful and governable (Lupton 1995; Miller and Rose 2008; N. Rose 2007), and it requires "living human beings who can act" (Dean 1999, 13–14). Here, youth are asked to be agents and entrepreneurs on behalf of their own health. This demonstrates the convergence of "questions of government, politics and administration to the space of bodies, lives, selves and persons" (Dean 1999, 12). Not surprisingly, this kind of governance requires that youth spaces be subjected to the neoliberal audit culture that sets targets and performance indicators for health and well-being, through quantitative checklists of environmental needs and assessments (Osborne 1997).[5] Seemingly benevolent discourses about play and physical activity, wide-open spaces, safety, and organization, then, can be connected to neoliberalist conceptions of health and wellness in the city. In this kind of neoliberal political economy, space and youth are to be taken charge of.

Neoliberal discourses promise youth reactivation, regeneration, and salvation from *all* the risks that they could confront in urban areas—crime, sedentary behavior, degenerating urban spaces, and so on. But these promises can be realized only through youth's participation, which presupposes "the primary freedom of those who are governed entailed in the capacities of acting and thinking" (Dean 1999, 15). A previous Ontario government campaign, "It's Not Going to Kill You," openly chastised young people for their lack of involvement in physical activity. The website's home page showed a young girl opening her school locker and becoming so terrified at the sight of a soccer ball falling out that she runs away screaming. The text read, "It's not going to kill you to get some exercise. But you could die younger if you don't." The website, which was managed by the Ontario Ministry of Health Promotion, was devoted to motivating tweens and young teens in Ontario to live more physically active lives and make healthier food choices. In its own words, the program was

all about getting active, eating right, and getting and staying healthy.
   Did you know that there are gazillions of activities out there that build muscles and get your heart pumping? Even a trip to the mall counts as exercise. That's right. All it takes is a couple of laps around the shopping plaza and you've taken the first step towards fitness. Check out this site and see how you can 'Get Movin'. (Leisure Information Network, n.d.)

These kinds of statements align well with neoliberal agendas as they extol the virtues of young people becoming the agents of their own health and spatial destinies. The irresponsible youth, of course, is the one who runs away and is frightened of physical activity and sports. The responsible youth is the one who takes up one of the "gazillion choices" made available to him or her. Both Pause to Play and It's Not Going to Kill You appear to champion a new relationship between the self-regulating youth citizen and expert discourses about exercise, thus enabling a merging of expertise and knowledge about physical activity with youth's projects of self-mastery and life enhancement (N. Rose 1996).

The "participatory imperative" (Petersen and Lupton 1996, 147) that is pervasive in all these government documents, policies, and websites evokes the fantasy of an active, healthy, and committed youth citizen. Indeed, through the linking of health to youth's everyday consumption and especially to popular representations of space and exercise (i.e., "it's not gonna kill you"), "it has become possible to actualize this notion of the actively responsible individual because of the development of a new apparatus that integrates subjects into a moral nexus of identifications and allegiances in the very processes in which they appear to act out their most personal choices" (N. Rose 1996, 57–58). In this nexus of identifications, ambiguity is squeezed out of public space (Giroux 2004), while govern*mentality* is cemented in youth's desire to belong to an active and health culture in the school and in the city.

Boyz in the Hood to New Civichood

> We have lately seen the violence that results when youth in despair are left without programs or help for the future, when their energies go unchanneled. Violent crime goes up: young men and women die or waste themselves in jail. We can't just let these things happen—if for no other reason than we won't be able to afford the billions it will cost to take care of this inactive echo. They will be prone to chronic diseases early on in life. When they become elderly, if they become elderly, they will be hobbled by fractures brought on by osteoporosis, by heart disease, hypertension, and stroke. It's not in the common interest to let the future take care of itself. We have to turn the river of the city's youth in a new direction. But first we have to understand where it is flowing. . . . We believe that by making youth our priority in all aspects of Parks and Recreation's responsibilities, by calling on them to steward our parks and ravines, to help plant trees and native species, to lead environmental programs, by offering opportunities for them to work for the City and to acquire the kinds of skills they want, the river will turn in the right direction. ("Our Common Grounds" 2004, 27)

Since the early 1990s there has been increasing moral panic about youth gun crime, violence, bullying in schools, and youth obesity and sedentary lifestyles in North America. Consequently, the policy documents that I examined about youth, health, and city space appeared to point toward the dangers of "deviant" youth, risky behaviors, and the concomitant discourse of saving youth from themselves. Revitalized parks spaces are imagined to be the answer for youth who want to "turn their lives around" because "whatever it costs to support their acquisition of skills will be cheaper than failing to involve them in parks and recreation" ("Our Common Grounds" 2004, 28). According to "Our Common Grounds," it costs CAN$100,000 to keep one young offender in jail for a year. For the same budget, Parks and Recreation could offer an alternative future and training for a lifelong commitment to health (2004, 28). The use of the language of economy provokes youth to think and act in fiscally responsible ways and to "take charge of (their) life" (Foucault 1978).[6] While they are consuming city spaces, individual youth are asked to practice a "new prudentialism" (Dean 1999) in which they are obliged to simultaneously adopt a calculative and "prudent" personal relationship to risk and danger (Bunton 1997) and recognize the health choices and opportunities that are afforded to them. New prudentialism requires that youth consume all the spaces that are being conceived of on their behalf but that they do so in productive rather than wasteful ways. The Nike Malvern Sports Complex in Toronto is a space that is perceived as being free from risk and that youths are encouraged to consume.

> How do you improve the health of a community? It starts with 50,000 donated running shoes. . . . [President of Nike Canada:] "We want to thank all of the Toronto residents who make this new Nike Malvern Sports Complex a reality. . . . Over the past decade, we've seen a positive impact of Nike Grind facilities in communities around the world and we are proud that we are able to bring that experience to Canada." In addition to Nike's $500,000 donation to build the Nike Malvern Sports complex, Nike Canada today donated an additional $50,000 in athletic equipment for the community. (CNW Group 2006, 1)

The Nike Malvern Sports Complex has been a joint initiative between the Toronto Catholic District School Board, the City of Toronto, and Nike Canada. This sports complex, which has been conceived of as a space for youth to engage in physical activity, is situated in one of Toronto's most marginalized communities. This space is juxtaposed with the unhealthy, immoral, "defiled," and degenerate spaces in the neighborhood, which are the usual representations of Malvern's urban environment. While it is not necessarily problematic to offer these kinds of opportunities to Malvern's youth, I pose a counternarrative, one that opposes Nike's capitalist, consumption, and corporate practices that I believe end up reinscribing local and global spatialized oppressions (see Fusco 2007). The valorization of such spaces, I have argued, renders the power relations that underpin youth's geographies invisible. First, the violent geographies of marginalization (Gregory and Pred 2007) that are an everyday reality for the mostly racialized, urban youth who play here are not adequately addressed. Second, the celebratory nature of Nike's commitment to Malvern ignores the structural and systemic oppressions, persecutions, and violent acts that have been perpetrated in Nike's name (see Cole and Hribar 1995; Cooky and McDonald 2005). These oppressions and persecutions, which are enacted in *specific places* (e.g., urban areas, offshore markets, sports stadiums, and media representations), remain the absent-present of the Malvern space. Indeed, the racialized and working-poor youth (mostly boys and young men) who are encouraged to consume this space are (unknowingly) implicated in what feminist geographer Doreen Massey (1997) has called a "progressive sense of place." This space is one that is not circumscribed by the local but rather extends to the power that ebbs and flows from complex (racialized, gendered, and sexualized) global connections. The production of a space like the Nike Malvern Sports Complex has repercussions both for the health of Toronto's youth and for the youth and adults who are exploited by neoliberal economic restructuring and global markets (see Navarro 2007). As a neoliberal spatial practice, the Nike Malvern Sports Complex "embodies" local and global sociopolitical and economic relations because it is fully implicated in a set of 'power geometries' (Massey 1994) that position different social groups and different individuals in distinct ways in relation to local flows and connections. The Nike Malvern Sports Complex may be said, then, to have an illiberal agenda (Dean 1999; N. Rose 1996): it fails to fully address how the racialized and classed bodies of that space and other (global) spaces are subjected to poor living conditions, collapsing infrastructure, and heavy police profiling (Goldberg 1993; Ray and Rose 2000).

But, as Duggan (2003) astutely points out, neoliberalism cleverly organizes itself in terms of socioeconomic class, race, gender, and sexuality as well as other social categories in ways that actively obscure the connections between these categories of organization and the political economy (or spaces) in which they are embedded. With respect to Malvern, neoliberalist agendas also align well with the discourses of crime and fear. When the Nike Malvern Sports Complex opened, Toronto's mayor David Miller's lament for the lack of "real" facilities for youth in the city exemplifies the linkages between risk, fear, and hope. "'There are a lot of studies that show if you get to young people early and give them real opportunities and hope, they can break out of it,' Miller said, referring to the neighbourhood troubled by gangs and violence. 'The sad thing in Toronto is, we don't have the kinds of facilities we need'" (Christie 2006, S3). The Nike Malvern Sports Complex demonstrates that hegemonic conceptions of space are intricately connected to prescriptions about *how to live* in the city. However, despite the neoliberal and neoconservative underpinnings of such beliefs and the concomitant exercise of government, it is difficult for a critical scholar to critique the provision of such spaces. King argues, in the case of philanthropy and the breast cancer movement, that tools such as cause-related marketing, the production of benevolent citizens, and corporatization of disease "rely on and gain their legitimacy through the good intentions of citizens [and] they are particularly resistant to critique or dissent" (2006, 124). The Nike Malvern Complex may fulfill its neoliberal agenda because it offers the marginalized youth who play there a chance to be seen as active individuals both in the fabrication of their own existence (N. Rose 1996) and in the production of their own civichood. Those who choose the "other Malvern life" need to be worked on so that they can aspire to a future of engagement with the Nike (health) program.

Those "excluded" from the benefits of a life of choice and self-fulfillment are no longer merely the passive support of a set of social determinations: they are people whose self-responsibility and self-fulfilling aspirations have been deformed by the dependency culture. . . . And, it thus follows, that they are to be assisted . . . through their engagement in a whole array of programmes for their ethical reconstruction as active citizens . . . programmes of empowerment to enable them to assume their rightful place as the self-actualizing and demanding subjects of an "advanced" liberal democracy. (N. Rose 1996, 59–60)

Nike's global domination has paved the way for the production of Malvern youth and their spaces to fulfill neoliberal agendas. While there has been a sustained critique of Nike's economic injustices in physical cultural studies of sport, the neoliberal spatial footprint is so pervasive that it hardly appears to require critical and analytical examination. On the surface, it seems heretical to criticize spaces such as the Nike Malvern Sports Complex. Can we blame the mayor for his plea to build more facilities that will keep Toronto citizens safe? In the immediate and myopic view, it could be argued that Toronto citizens will not really care about the child laborer who makes Nike shoes in the Philippines for twenty cents a day, especially if one more "hoop dream" prevents one less bullet being discharged in Toronto. Consequently, the mayor and others like him, in their appeals to hegemonic views of health, safety, and well-being, are allowed to ignore the utter devastation of children (and adults) elsewhere around the globe. And in the moment of the spatial consumption (of the Nike Malvern Complex), the disconnection is complete. We can feel good about a space such as this because neoliberal technologies of healthification and citizenship, established over and over again, are so persuasive that neoliberalist destructive agendas in local and global contexts no longer seem to matter. Is there a continued need for an analysis of physical cultural spaces in a neoliberal era? Or is it too late to make such critiques matter when neoliberalism is already so paved into our consciousness?

Conclusion

We must reengage with youth, listen to them, make programs that entice them, train them to lead, and hire them—so they will become healthy, productive adults. ("Our Common Grounds" 2004, 8)

Childhood is the most intensively governed sector of personal existence . . . linked in thought and practice to the destiny of the nation. (N. Rose 1989, 121)

This brief analysis of excerpts from government policy and website documents demonstrates that neoliberal urban imaginaries and moral geographies of healthification are centered on life, health, and well-being. In the context of the omnipresent backdrop of risk and degenerating urban landscapes, health-ified living spaces, policies, and initiatives are technologies that seek to manage youth's conduct through their choice of reimagining themselves as a consumers and citizens of the (active) city. Indeed, as Gulson argues, "Neoliberal spatial technologies" provide conditions of possibility, or conditions of "recruitment," for neoliberal educational subjectivities to be "conceived and constituted" (2007, 184). Neoliberal spatial discourses of healthification appear to make new kinds of social life and social space in the city available to youth, and these spaces are conceived and perceived as emancipatory and transcendent spaces: healthified space is ready for projects of self-actualization, agency, and personal empowerment.

Children and youth do deserve spaces to play and a time for justice (Ait-ken 2001). However, while spatial practices of healthification may be lauded as opportunities for salvation and projects of self-actualization, they must also be regarded as part of a wider neoliberal and even neoconservative strategy to protect and defend hegemonic, normative, and economic interests. Discur-sive tropes of choice, good citizenship, morality, and self-responsibility render invisible the larger spatial contexts of young people's lives in which poverty, sexism, heterosexism, racism, adult violence, exclusion, and global exploita-tion are pervasive (see Dillabough and Kennelly 2010). These contexts of mar-ginality are conveniently forgotten when the discourses of healthification are prevalent. Also forgotten are the increasing govern*mentalities* regulations, surveillances, and overmanagement of youth's lives. Obviously, neoliberal ide-ologies will impact on youth in different ways and in different local and global spaces, but we must remain attentive to how a war is being waged on youth in North America and how youth are disappearing in the age of market funda-mentalism (Giroux 2004).

Neoliberalist desires to contain and "conduct the conduct" of youth's bod-ies, moralities, and citizenship may be destabilized by the freedoms required by neoliberalism (Massey 1994, 2005). We know from cultural geographers that spaces are not fixed, but are in a constant state of transition as a result of continuous, dialectical struggles of power, agency, negotiation, appropriation, and resistance (Cahill 2000; Childress 2004; Malone 2002). It is incumbent on physical cultural studies researchers, then, to intensify their (spatial) analyses of neoliberalisms' agendas and to investigate how individuals take up, chal-lenge, and/or refuse current descriptive and prescriptive policies and spatial initiatives designed for their consumption, and to offer alternatives to coun-ter neoliberalism's pervasive spatial imprint (MacEwan 2005; Sinha 2005). A spatial analysis may deepen still further the critique of neoliberalism and may be able to articulate an alternative ethics and pedagogy of subjectivity that is as compelling as the rationality of the market and the valorization of choice (N. Rose 1996). Continuing to read neoliberalism geographically (Massey 2005) is necessary to interrogate how youth, and others in their lives, are in-cited to produce spaces in which to practice their (physical activity) freedoms in "advanced" liberal societies.

NOTES

1. Spatial practice is the material expression of social and power relations in space (Lefebvre 1991). The organization of a locker room or a park is a spatial practice.

2. I understand governmentality in the Foucauldian sense, in which government is inextricably bound up with the activity of thought and the emergence of a distinctly new form of thinking about and exercising power in certain societies (Dean 1999; N. Rose 1999).

3. Representations of space are conceptual abstractions that inform configurations of spatial practices, for example, architectural drawings. Finally, lived space is space appropriated by the imagination or experienced in the everyday (see Lefebvre 1991).

4. Spatialization is the way in which social life literally takes place (Gregory 1994).

5. The Daily Physical Activity in Schools Initiative "encourages" principals and teachers to continuously auditing school spaces. The ANGELO (Analysis Grid for Environments Linked to Obesity) framework is "a conceptual model designed to help communities identify obesity-promoting environments and set priorities for action" (Ontario Ministry of Health and Long-Term Care 2004, 46).

6. I believe that new public health discourses are differently spatialized in the city. I am suggesting that the panic about obesity is about the health, well-being, and future generation of the white, middle-class leaders of the nation, which may produce a different set of priorities, programs, and spatial practices for these youth. Escalating panic about youth crime and constructions of "at-risk" youth are spatialized differently and may call on urban spaces, policy, and planning to direct racialized and working-poor youth away from a "probable" life of crime and toward a more "productive life."

REFERENCES

Active Healthy Kids Canada. 2011. "2011 Report Card Overview." Available at http://www .activehealthykids.ca/ReportCard/2011ReportCardOverview.aspx.

Aitken, S. 2001. Geographies of Young People: the Morally Contested Spaces of Identity. London: Routledge.

Anderson, B. 1991. Imagined Communities: Reflections on the Origins and Spread of Nationalism. London: Verso.

Armstrong, D. 1993. "Public Health Space and the Fabrication of Identity." Sociology 27:393–404.

———. 1995. "The Rise of Surveillance Medicine." Sociology of Health and Illness 17:393–404.

Bale, J. 1994. Landscapes of Modern Sport. London: Leicester University Press.

Bargh, M. 2007. Resistance: An Indigenous Response to Neoliberalism. Wellington, New Zealand: HUIA.

Barry, A., T. Osborne, and N. Rose. 1996. Foucault and Political Reason: Liberalism, Neoliberalism and Rationalities of Government. Chicago: University of Chicago Press.

Beausoleil, N., and G. Rail. 2006. "Youth Narratives on Learning about Health and Fitness." Paper presented at the Canadian Association for Women's Studies in Education, York University, Toronto, May 31.

Borden, I. 2003. Skateboarding, Space and the City: Architecture and the Body. London: Berg.

Boudreau, J.-A., R. Keil, and D. Young. 2009. Changing Toronto: Governing Urban Neoliberalism. Toronto: University of Toronto Press.

Bunton, R. 1997. "Popular Health, Advanced Liberalism and Good Housekeeping Magazine." In Foucault, Health and Medicine, ed. A. Petersen and R. Bunton, 223–248. New York: Routledge.

Cahill, C. 2000. "Street Literacy: Urban Teenagers' Strategies for Negotiating Their Neighbourhood." *Journal of Youth Studies* 3:251–277.

Canadian Fitness and Lifestyle Research Institute. 2011. "Bulletin 02: Physical Activity Levels of Canadian Children and Youth." February 18. Available at http://72.10.49.94/node/101.

Castel, R. 1991. "From Dangerousness to Risk." In *The Foucault Effect: Studies in Governmentality*, ed. G. Burchell, C. Gordon, and P. Miller, 281–297. London: Harvester Wheatsheaf.

Childress, H. 2004. "Teenagers, Territory and the Appropriation of Space." *Childhood* 11:195–205.

Chomsky, N. 1999. *Profit over People: Neoliberalism and Global Order.* New York: Seven Stories Press.

Christie, J. 2006. "Malvern Complex Aimed at Youth." *Globe and Mail*, May 18, S3.

Clarke, S. 2005. "The Neoliberal Theory of Society." In *Neoliberalism: A Critical Reader*, ed. A. Saad-Filho and D. Johnston, 50–59. London: Pluto Press.

CNW Group. 2006. "Nike Canada Creates and Then Opens Half Million Dollar Athletic Complex Made from Recycled Running Shoes." May 17. Available at http://business.highbeam.com/1758/article-1G1-145907217/nike-canada-creates-and-then-opens-half-million-dollar.

Coburn, D. 2000. "Income Inequality, Social Cohesion and the Health Status of Populations: The Role of Neoliberalism." *Social Science and Medicine* 51:135–146.

Cole, C., and A. Hribar. 1995. "Celebrity Feminism: Nike Style Post-Fordism, Transcendence, and Consumer Power." *Sociology of Sport Journal* 12:347–369.

Cooky, C., and M. McDonald. 2005. "'If You Let Me Play': Young Girls' Inside-Other Narratives of Sport." *Sociology of Sport Journal* 22:158–177.

Crawford, R. 1980. "Healthism and the Medicalisation of Everyday Life." *International Journal of Health Services* 19:365–388.

Dean, M. 1999. *Governmentality: Power and Rule in Modern Society.* London: Sage.

Dillabough, J.-A., and J. Kennelly. 2010. *Lost Youth in the Global City: Class, Culture and the Urban Imaginary.* New York: Routledge.

Duggan, L. 2003. *The Twilight of Equality? Neoliberalism, Cultural Politics, and the Attack on Democracy.* Boston: Beacon Press.

Eichberg, H. 1993. "New Spatial Configurations of Sport? Experiences from Danish Alternative Planning." *International Review for the Sociology of Sport* 28:245–261.

England, K., and K. Ward, eds. 2007. *Neoliberalization: States, Networks, Peoples.* Malden, MA: Blackwell.

Evans, J., B. Davis, and J. Wright. 2004. *Body Knowledge and Control: Studies in the Sociology of Physical Education and Health.* New York: Routledge.

Fitzpatrick, K., and M. LaGory. 2003. "'Placing' Health in Urban Sociology: Cities as Mosaics of Risk and Protection." *City and Community* 2 (1): 33–46.

Foucault, M. 1978. *The History of Sexuality*, vol. 1. New York: Random House.

———. 1980. *Power/Knowledge: Selected Interviews and Other Writings, 1972–1977*, trans. C. Gordon. New York: Pantheon Books.

Fusco, C. 2003. "'There Are a Lot of Eyes on This Space!' The (Re)Production of Subjectivities in Cultures of Work and Working Out: A Postmodern, Intertextual, and Spatial Ethnography." Dissertation, Graduate Department of Community Health, University of Toronto.

———. 2005. "Cultural Landscapes of Purification: Sports Spaces and Discourses of Whiteness." *Sociology of Sport Journal* 22 (3): 283–310.

———. 2006. "Inscribing Healthification: Governance, Risk, Surveillance and the Subjects and Spaces of Fitness and Health." *Journal of Health and Place* 12 (1): 65–78.

———. 2007. "Healthification and the Promises of Urban Space: A Textual Analysis of Representations of Place, Activity, Youth (PLAY-ing) in the City." *International Review for the Sociology of Sport* 42 (1): 43–63.

Gagen, E. 2000. "Playing the Part: Performing Gender in America's Playgrounds." In *Children's Geographies: Playing, Living, Learning,* ed. S. Holloway and G. Valentine, 213–229. London: Routledge.

Gallagher, K., and C. Fusco. 2006. "I.D.ology and the Technologies of Public (School) Space: An Ethnographic Inquiry into the Neo-liberal Tactics of Social (Re)production." *Journal of Ethnography and Education* 1 (3): 301–318.

Gard, M., and J. Wright. 2005. *The Obesity Epidemic: Science, Morality, and Ideology.* New York: Routledge.

Giroux, H. 2004. *The Terror of Neoliberalism: Authoritarianism and the Eclipse of Democracy.* Boulder, CO: Paradigm.

Goldberg, D. 1993. *Racist Culture.* London: Blackwell.

Gordon, C. 1991. "Governmental Rationality: An Introduction." In *The Foucault Effect: Studies in Governmentality,* ed. G. Burchell, C. Gordon, and P. Miller, 1–51. London: Harvester Wheatsheaf.

Gregory, D. 1994. *Geographical Imaginations.* Cambridge, MA: Blackwell.

Gregory, D., and A. Pred, eds. 2007. *Violent Geographies: Fear, Terror, and Political Violence.* New York: Routledge.

Gulson, K. 2007. "'Neoliberal Spatial Technologies': On the Practices of Educational Policy Change." *Critical Studies in Education* 48 (2): 179–195.

Hall, T., A. Coffey, and H. Williamson. 1999. "Self, Space and Place: Youth Identities and Citizenship." *British Journal of Sociology of Education* 20:501–513.

Harvey, D. 2005. *A Brief History of Neoliberalism.* Oxford: Oxford University Press.

Herrick, C. 2011. *Governing Health and Consumption: Sensible Citizens, Behaviour and the City.* Bristol, UK: Policy Press.

Holloway, S., and G. Valentine, eds. 2000. *Children's Geographies: Playing, Living, Learning.* London: Routledge.

Ingham, A. 1985. "From Public Issue to Private Trouble: Well-Being and the Fiscal Crisis of the State." *Sociology of Sport Journal* 2:43–55.

King, S. 2006. *Pink Ribbons, Inc.: Breast Cancer and the Politics of Philanthropy.* Minneapolis: University of Minnesota Press.

Kirk, D. 1998. *Schooling Bodies. School Practice and Public Discourse, 1880–1950.* London: Leicester University Press.

———. 2006. "The 'Obesity Crisis' and School Physical Education." *Sport, Education and Society* 11 (2): 121–133.

Kontopodis, M. 2011. "Biomedicine, Psychology and the Kindergarten: Children at Risk and Emerging Knowledge Practices." *Sport, Education and Society* 1:1–19.

Lather, P. 2007. *Getting Lost: Feminist Efforts toward a Double(d) Science.* New York: State University of New York Press.

Lefebvre, H. 1991. *The Production of Space,* trans. D. Nicholson-Smith. Oxford: Blackwell.

Leisure Information Network. n.d. "notgonnakillyou.ca." Available at http://lin.ca/resource-details/8867.

Lupton, D. 1995. *The Imperative of Public Health: Public Health and the Regulated Body.* London: Sage.

———. 1999. *Risk.* London: Routledge.

MacEwan, A. 2005. "Neoliberalism and Democracy: Market Power versus Democratic Power." In *Neoliberalism: A Critical Reader*, ed. A. Saad-Filho and D. Johnston, 170–176. London: Pluto Press.

MacNeill, M. 2006. "Healthy Bodies, Healthy Minds and Risky Relations in Knowledge Engagement." Paper presented at the Canadian Association for Women's Studies in Education, York University, Toronto, May 31.

Malone, K. 2002. "Street Life: Youth, Culture and Competing Uses of Public Space." *Environment and Urbanization* 14:157–168.

Massey, D. 1994. *Space, Place and Gender.* Minneapolis: University of Minnesota Press.

———. 1997. "A Global Sense of Place." In *Reading Human Geography: The Poetics and Politics of Inquiry*, ed. T. Barnes and D. Gregory, 315–323. London: Arnold.

———. 2005. *For Space.* London: Sage.

McDermott, L. 2007. "A Governmental Analysis of Children 'at Risk' in a World of Physical Inactivity and Obesity Epidemics." *Sociology of Sport Journal* 24 (3): 302–324.

McKendrick, J. 1999a. "Not Just a Playground: Rethinking Children's Place in the Built Environment." *Built Environment* 25 (1): 75–78.

———. 1999b. "Playgrounds in the Built Environment." *Built Environment* 24 (4): 1–6.

Miller, P., and N. Rose. 2008. *Governing the Present: Administering Economic, Social and Personal Life.* Cambridge, UK: Polity Press.

Navarro, V. 2007. *Neoliberalism, Globalization and Inequalities: Consequences for Health and Quality of Life.* Amityville, NY: Baywood.

Ontario Ministry of Health and Long-Term Care. 2004. *Healthy Weights, Healthy Lives: 2004 Chief Medical Officer of Health Report.* Available at http://www.health.gov.on.ca/english/public/pub/ministry_reports/cmoh04_report/cmoh_04.html.

Ontario Ministry of Health Promotion. 2012a. "Pause to Play." March 21. Available at http://www.mhp.gov.on.ca/en/youth/p2p/index.asp.

———. 2012b. "Get Active: Basketball." March 21. Available at http://www.mhp.gov.on.ca/en/youth/p2p/get-active/basketball.asp.

Osborne, T. 1997. "Of Health and Statecraft." In *Foucault, Health and Medicine*, ed. A. Petersen and R. Bunton, 173–188. New York: Routledge.

"Our Common Grounds." 2004. Toronto Parks and Recreation Strategic Plan. Available at http://publiccommons.ca/public/uploads/OurCommonGrounds_cl002.pdf.

Peters, M. 2007. "Foucault, Biopolitics and the Birth of Neoliberalism." *Critical Studies in Education* 48 (2): 165–178.

Petersen, A. 1997. "Risk, Governance and the New Public Health." In *Foucault, Health and Medicine*, ed. A. Petersen and R. Bunton, 189–206. New York: Routledge.

Petersen, A., and R. Bunton. 1997. *Foucault, Health and Medicine.* New York: Routledge.

Petersen, A., and D. Lupton. 1996. *The New Public Health: Health and Self in the Age of Risk.* London: Sage.

Philo, C., and F. Smith. 2003. "Guest Editorial: Political Geographies of Children and Young People." *Space and Polity* 7:99–115.

Ray, B., and D. Rose. 2000. "Cities of the Everyday: Socio-Spatial Perspectives on Gender, Difference, and Diversity." In *Canadian Cities in Transition: The Twenty-First Century*, ed. T. Bunting and P. Filion, 402–424. Don Mills, Canada: Oxford University Press.

"ReActivate TO!" 2004. Toronto Parks and Recreation. Available at http://www.toronto.ca/civic-engagement/2004/reactivate-to-may.htm.

Reid-Boyd, E. 2006. "Writing on the Body as Health Education for Girls." Paper presented at the Canadian Association for Women's Studies in Education, York University, Toronto, May 31.

Richardson, T., and O. Jensen. 2003. "Linking Discourse and Space: Towards a Cultural Sociology of Space in Analyzing Spatial Policy Discourses." *Urban Studies* 40 (1): 7–22.

Rose, G. 1995. "Making Space for the Female Subject of Feminism: the Spatial Subversions of Holzer, Kruger and Sherman." In *Mapping the Subject: Geographies of Cultural Transformation*, ed. S. Pile and N. Thrift, 332–354. London: Routledge.

Rose, N. 1989. *Governing the Soul: The Shaping of the Private Self.* London: Routledge.

———. 1996. "Governing 'Advanced' Liberal Democracies." In *Foucault and Political Reason: Liberalism, Neo-liberalism and Rationalities of Government*, ed. A. Barry, T. Osborne, and N. Rose, 37–64. Chicago: University of Chicago Press.

———. 1999. *Powers of Freedom: Reframing Political Thought.* Cambridge: Cambridge University Press.

———. 2007. "Molecular Biopolitics, Somatic Ethics and the Spirit of Biocapital." *Social Theory and Health* 5 (1): 3–29.

Silk, M., and D. Andrews. 2006. "The Fittest City in America." *Journal of Sport and Social Issues* 30 (3): 315–327.

Singleton, E., and A. Varpalotai. 2006, *Stones in the Sneaker: Active Theory for Secondary School Physical and Health Educators.* London: Althouse Press.

Sinha, S. 2005. "Neoliberalism and Civil Society: Project and Possibilities." In *Neoliberalism: A Critical Reader*, ed. A. Saad-Filho and D. Johnston, 163–172. London: Pluto Press.

Skelton, T., and G. Valentine. 1998. *Cool Places: Geographies of Youth Cultures.* London: Routledge.

Smith, A., K. Green, and K. Roberts. 2004. "Sports Participation and the Obesity Health Crisis." *International Review for the Sociology of Sport* 39 (4): 457–464.

Valentine, G. 1996. "Angels and Devils: Moral Landscapes of Childhood." *Environment and Planning D: Society and Space* 14:581–599.

Van Ingen, C. 2003. "Geographies of Gender, Sexuality and Race: Reframing the Focus on Space in Sport Sociology." *International Review for the Sociology of Sport* 38:201–216.

Varpalotai, A., and E. Singleton. 2006. "'How to be healthy': Girls and Health Education—Past, Present and Future." Paper presented at the Canadian Association for Women's Studies in Education, York University, Toronto, May 31.

Vertinsky, P. 2004a. "Locating a 'Sense of Place': Space, Place and Gender in the Gymnasium." In *Sites of Sport: Space, Place, Experience*, ed. P. Vertinsky and J. Bale, 8–24. London: Routledge.

———. 2004b. "'Power Geometries': Disciplining the Gendered Body in the Spaces of the War Memorial Gym." In *Disciplining Bodies in the Gymnasium: Memory, Monument, Modernism*, ed. P. Vertinsky and S. McKay, 48–73. London: Routledge.

Vertinsky, P., and J. Bale. 2004. *Sites of Sport: Space, Place, Experience.* London: Routledge.

Vertinsky, P., and S. McKay. 2004. *Disciplining Bodies in the Gymnasium: Memory, Monument, Modernism.* London: Routledge.

Wheatley, E. 2005. "Disciplining Bodies at Risk: Cardiac Rehabilitation and the Medicalization of Fitness." *Journal of Sport and Social Issues* 29:198–221.

Wright, J., and V. Harwood, eds. 2009. *Biopolitics and the Obesity "Epidemic": Governing Bodies.* New York: Routledge.

10

Neoliberal Redevelopment, Sport Infrastructure, and the Militarization of U.S. Urban Terrain

KIMBERLY S. SCHIMMEL

As Brenner and Theodore (2002b) have stated, cities are "strategically crucial geographic arenas" (2) in which to analyze neoliberal initiatives in all their variations because cities have become "central to the continuation and reproduction of neoliberalism itself during the last two decades" (28). In ideological terms, neoliberalism is a theory of "creative" political-economic practices that assumes that human well-being is best advanced if capitalist market forces are "unleashed" from their regulatory moorings. The role of the state, therefore, is reduced to activities that support the basic institutional requirements of a liberal market order characterized by private property rights, individual liberty, and free trade. However, while maximal entrepreneurial freedoms, unfettered by state interference, are the "utopia" to which neoliberalism aspires, there is a deep disjuncture between the neoliberal ideological project and its everyday political practices. For a variety of reasons, the state has been far from passive in "actually existing neoliberalism" (Brenner and Theodore 2002a) than its ideological tenants posit (see also Harvey 2005). In fact, the "grim alignment" (Giroux 2004, 45) of the state with corporate power, transnational corporations, and military force is one of the hallmarks of neoliberalism. This and other disjunctures between neoliberal doctrine and reality are among its most essential features (see Brenner and Theodore 2002b; Harvey 2006). Peck and Tickell argue that the creatively destructive capacity of neoliberalism to evolve and mutate according to local institutional (re)forms and path-dependencies means that neoliberalism, "like globalization[,] should be understood as a process, not an end-state" (2002, 383).

Portions of this chapter were previously published in K. Schimmel, "Deep Play: Sports Mega-Events and Urban Social Conditions in the USA," in *Sports Mega-Events: Social Scientific Analysis of a Global Phenomenon*, ed. J. Horne and W. Manzenreiter, 160–174 (Oxford: Blackwell/*Sociological Review*, 2006).

Framed by theoretical perspectives in urban political economy, this chapter focuses on the development of infrastructures necessary to host large sporting events, set against broader neoliberalizing trends and geopolitical transformations, whereby contemporary cities have become "the battlegrounds on which global powers and stubbornly local meanings and identities meet" (Graham 2004b, 8). I address both the escalating economic expenditures devoted to major sport infrastructure and the intensifying militarization of urban space where "security" has become the justification for measures that contribute to downgrading the quality of life for urban residents. Sport and sport-related infrastructure development is powerfully bonded to the material, cultural, and discursive representations of urban space. Themed cultural landscapes and aggressive marketing and promotion of a city's image have been the hallmarks of urban design in the United States since the late 1980s. However, in the post-9/11 era, the physical planning of cities, the control of urban space, and management of urban residents and visitors is being reshaped by a far-reaching "homeland security" agenda. At the intersection of all of these trends stands sport: reconstituting large areas of urban space for stadium and area construction, connecting city image creation to professional sport franchise location and hosting championship games, and the increasing normalization of military doctrine and tactics in an attempt to control urban populations and "secure" sporting events.

Urban Competition and Sport-Related Capital Investment

Transformations in the U.S. urban landscape in the post–World War II period are well known. Decreasing traditional private capital investment in inner cities combined with white middle-class population outmigration to suburbs resulted in weakened tax and commercial retail bases. A period of capitalist economic restructuring and social adjustment, which began in the 1980s and continues today, resulted in a shift away from mass-production industries. This shift generated a series of crises and conflicts, including (among others) rising unemployment, increasing polarization between socially excluded groups and the middle class, and deleterious environmental conditions (Jewson and MacGregor 1997). The parallel decline of the central city and the development of its suburban rings are well documented in the academic literature. However, uneven development and the devalued property of the central city sets the stage for the movement of capital in a "fixed built environment as new opportunities for value arise from the ashes of the devalued" (Weber 2002, 523). As Weber explains, the policies and practices of urban redevelopment have become increasingly neoliberalized. State-sponsored tax increment financing districts and business improvement districts (for example) are used for large-scale downtown redevelopment and gentrifying neighborhoods. Neoliberal governance of urban redevelopment often seeks to alter the sign value of devalued businesses and places and is an important component in the contemporary processes of spatialized capital accumulation (Weber 2002). In the United States, these political-economic efforts are enacted at the local state level.

U.S. cities are heavily dependent on locally generated taxes to provide social services (such as fire and police protection, education, infrastructure maintenance, and library construction). This differs from many European contexts (see, Jessop, Peck, and Tickell 1999; Smith 1988) where there exists a more unitary and centralized urban finance structure. In the United States—the "capital of capitalism" (see Kantor 2010)—fierce competition for capital investment and jobs produces winner and loser cities (and sections of a city) and glaring social inequalities. Some social critics have concluded that this local dependency means that the United States has no national urban policy. But in fact it does. As urban studies theorist Harvey Molotch notes, "The US urban policy is to create structures and ideologies that intensify competition among cities in what they will provide to urban investors" (Molotch 1993, 35). This system of finance compels localities to maintain the revenue base by enticing mobile capital and supporting investment that increases the market value of real property, a point made quite explicitly by the federal government. After eliminating all policies designed to aid distressed cities, the Reagan administration's first *National Urban Policy Report of 1982* (U.S. Department of Housing and Urban Development 1982, 14) stated that state and local governments have primary responsibility for urban health, and hence they would "find it is in their best interest to concentrate on increasing their attractiveness to potential investors, residents, and visitors" (see also Judd 2002; Leitner 1990). This U.S. "Doctrine of Home Rule" means that cities must handle "their own" problems (Molotch 1993, 34) and establishes a social dependency on private investment. The result can now be seen in the hegemony of growth politics, the use of public subsidies to entice private investment (including sport), and the manipulation and regulation of urban land, one of the few autonomous realms of local-level governance (Molotch 1993; Schimmel 2002; Zukin 1991).

Since the 1980s, cities have been involved in a competition with each other so fierce that Haider (1992) refers to it as "place war." City governments, shifting away from managerial functions and into entrepreneurial roles (see Harvey 1989; Hill 1983) provide a wide array of public subsidies including tax abatements, low-interest loans, direct grants, revenue bonds, and land allocation in attempt to stimulate development. In addition, cities engage in various strategies designed to represent themselves positively in the new geographies of late capitalism or post-Fordism (Short 1999). The more decentralized governmental system of the United States, in comparison to much of Europe, allows for more local-level urban boosterism. There are no limits on the amount U.S. cities can spend on place advertising, in contrast to Britain, for example, where local officials operate within severe restrictions. Part of this place promotion advertises a city's "good business climate" in an attempt to obtain or retain fixed investment. However, reimagining is especially intensified through competition for circulating capital, such as retirees, tourists, conventions, and some sporting events, which can be thought of as "footloose consumption" not bound to a specific locale (Short 1999, 39, 42). As Peck and Tickell stress, "Clearly this regime of interurban competition was not simply a product of neoliberalism, nor can it be reduced entirely to its logic" (2002, 394). However, the "naturalization of neoliberalism" (Harvey 2006) was accomplished as an ideological project in parallel with these transurban strategies and has been crucial to "reinforcing, extending, and normalizing them" (Peck and Tickell 2002, 394). Some hope for a new national urban policy emerged in the 2008 presidential campaign when a major portion of the Obama-Biden platform included a new focus on urban issues, arguing that cities "need a partner in the White House" (Obama 2008) and for a shift to more regionalism in economic affairs. Less than one month after his inauguration, Obama established the White House Office of Urban Affairs. Placed under the president, the agency is intended to coordinate federal policy for cities and to develop a coherent strategy for metropolitan America. As of this writing, however, no new urban policies have been enacted.

Here we turn our attention to sport. Sport has been linked to the dominant discourse of urban growth and regeneration in ways that are as powerful as they are problematic. These linkages are both material and symbolic and involve both fixed and circulating capital. The material dimension includes the reconstitution of urban space and the use of public funds for the purpose of sport-related infrastructure development and megaprojects such as stadiums. Stadium construction is often necessary both to retain existing major professional sport franchises (amid franchise owners' threats of relocation) and to obtain expansion franchises or entice existing ones to move in. It is also necessary in order to host tourist related sport mega-events, including the National Football League (NFL) Super Bowl championship game (discussed shortly). The public's return on investment in major sport development is touted to include numerous material benefits, including employment growth and revenue creation, that solve urban problems and thereby benefit all residents.

Almost two decades of social science research refutes the claims made by local-level growth advocates about the supposed benefits to the "city as a whole" of sport megaproject development. Nevertheless, public investment in major sport facility construction continues apace. A national survey reported by Judd, Winter, Barnes, and Stern (2003) revealed that two-thirds of the U.S. central cities that responded to the survey had built or were undertaking to build sports stadiums. Expressed in 2003 dollars, the aggregate cost of sport facilities in which U.S. major-level football, baseball, basketball, and hockey franchises play was $23.8 billion. The public sector's share of that amount was approximately $15.2 billion, which represented 64 percent of the total (Crompton 2004).

Funding mechanisms for major sport facility construction have changed over time. However, as Crompton points out, even though the proportion of the cost contributed by the public is now lower, because of the enormous price tags of new facilities, the total dollar amount of that lower percentage remains relatively unchanged. Speaking to the role that stadium construction plays in cities' attempts to capture tourism-related revenues, Perry (2003, 27) states that cities are often willing to "sacrifice material logic for [the] symbolic identity" that comes from hosting major sport. Perry's position is shared by numerous of his colleagues in tourism studies (see Hall 2006), reinforced by sport economists, and echoed by sport studies and urban studies scholars. Current levels of public finance investment in sport megaprojects in the United States are fundamentally economically irrational. Furthermore, we should not assume that the investment of public capital assures the construction of an urban public space. There is a difference between public and "publicness" (see Akkar 2005; Roberts 2008). The "publicness" of urban terrain can be manipulated by, among other things, urban planning and the privatization and marketing of quasi-public spaces. Cities and the people who live in them are ranked and sorted.

Urban Hierarchies: Places, Projects, People

By the mid-1990s, U.S. downtowns were transformed into "packaged landscapes" (Boyer 1993) designed to represent themselves as exciting, clean, and safe places to work and play. New corporate towers and luxury apartments alongside bars, restaurants, festival marketplaces, and shopping malls aimed to develop urban cores into sites that would serve both business professionals and middle-class residents and attract visitors. Fueled by a culture of consumption, the postindustrial city was symbolically projected as "spectacularized urban space" (Harvey 1989) competing for tourism revenues and fixed capital investment from corporate, government, and retail sectors. The corporate/entertainment mix was copied by cities all over the United States and resulted in a remarkably standardized template for economic revitalization (Friedan and Sagalyn 1990).

In recent years, the commodification and marketing of culture (arts, theater, fashion, music, and history or "heritage") has moved to the forefront of the urban regeneration industry (Zukin 1995). But as Salmon (2001) points out, while projects developed according to this strategy emphasize local distinction and the virtues of "localism" (see also Goss 1996), they also advance some localities over others. The result is paradoxical in that "cities across the nation are pursuing virtually identical strategies that are premised on the notion that each locality is culturally unique" (Salmon 2001, 111). These strategies are ultimately destructive in that they heighten the competition between local areas for capital investment and place local tax bases under further strain. Thus, an urban status hierarchical structure emerges, and as Judd cautions, "just as some cities failed to become successful sites of production in the industrial age, in the next few years as some will fail to succeed as sites of consumption . . . abject total failure is possible" (2002, 296). The imperatives of U.S. urban policy leave the "public entrepreneurs" of "failure" cities feeling as if they have little choice but to invest more deeply in the competition. Cities, therefore, are turned into accomplices in their own subordination through zero-sum competition and also by the seeming absence of "realistic" local alternatives (Peck and Tickell 2002, 393.)

Within this context of "creeping urban homogeneity" (Friedman, Andrews, and Silk 2004), local governments and urban residents in the United States have spent, since 1990, more than $10 billion to subsidize major sport facilities (see also Kaplan 2003). As anchors of broader redevelopment schemes, massive sport stadiums are the featured set pieces (replacing the ubiquitous festival malls of the 1980s) cities use in an attempt to differentiate themselves from one another (Austrian and Rosentraub 2002; Bale 1994; Hannigan 1998; Turner and Rosentraub 2002). In the late 1990s there were approximately 113 major sport franchises in the United States (Perry 2003), each requiring a stadium or area—in some cases franchises of different sports share a "home" facility in a city. With so many stadiums dotting the urban landscape across the United States, it is logical to ask how stadiums "differentiate" one city from another. First, there are more cities that desire to host a major league sport franchise than there are franchises available. Thus, hosting a major-league team means a city can represent itself as a "major-league city" vis-à-vis other cities of lesser status. Second, because of these conditions of artificial scarcity in major league sport, franchise owners can move to more desirable locations. Therefore, cities engage in a veritable "arms race" to build more massive and modern (and profitable to owners) stadiums, thereby holding (or attracting) franchises in an increasingly high-stakes gamble in which fewer cities can compete. Third, at the top of the hierarchy are the superstructures located in "favorable" urban locations that meet the requirements for successful bids to host sports mega-events.

The most prestigious domestic, major sports event in the United States is the NFL championship game, called the "Super Bowl," which rotates around U.S. cities. The Super Bowl is unlike the championship series in major-league basketball, baseball, and hockey, in which games are located in the cities of the teams that qualify. Rather, Super Bowl sites are "awarded" to cities after a competitive bidding process. Football stadiums are now developed based on not only franchise owners' demands regarding profit and control but also the NFL's increasingly security-focused requirements for hosting a Super Bowl (Schimmel 2011). These requirements reach beyond the confines of the stadium itself and onto the urban places the NFL considers to be Super Bowl worthy. For example, according to the bid specifications from 2000 made public by the city of San Diego (quoted in Alesia 2004), the NFL requires the following:

- The stadium must seat at least 70,000.
- The city must have at least 24,500 "quality" hotel rooms within a twenty-mile radius.
- The city must provide free utilities and give over control of stadium-owned parking to the NFL.
- The city must provide staffing at 300 percent above the normal levels for sell-out events at the stadium.
- The city must be able to provide 600,000 square feet of space for the "NFL Experience," a temporary interactive theme park.

Occupying a position on the top of the urban status hierarchy of major sport cities requires massive infrastructure development, massive funding, and massive ideological support, especially if the public is called on to foot the bill, which it almost always is. In addition to the economic impact studies and supposed material benefits that are promised, major sport development schemes almost always appeal to a sense of solidarity based on territory and a sense of community. Local political elites assert that hosting major sport provides a focus point for "us all to rally around," generates a sense of pride, and symbolizes "us" as a "major league" or "world class" city. According to this mantra, sport stadiums and major sport teams are "community assets" that enhance our quality of life. For example, in a study commissioned by the Indianapolis Colts franchise of the NFL, titled *The Value of the Indianapolis Colts to Indiana Residents and Their Willingness to Pay for a New Stadium*, the researchers concluded:

> The excitement generated by sports and the attention it attracts have been the factors that have made teams *valued community assets* inexorably associated with cities and their fans. . . . For more than 2000 years, this excitement and identity have made sports an important part of social life in virtually every society. . . . Further, [Indiana's major sports teams] . . . help to define Indiana's image and attract visitors and economic activity to the state. (Rosentraub and Swindell 2005; emphasis added)

Such hyperbole and flawed historical perspective is common in reports commissioned by major sport teams. Indianapolis, it should be noted, has built a $900 million stadium and convention center, replacing the one it built in the 1980s to anchor downtown development and lure the NFL's Colts away from Baltimore (see Hudnut 1995; Rosentraub 2003; Schimmel 2001, 2009).

When we consider the notion that major sport teams and events are "community assets," we should be mindful of the hypermobility of capital and the fixed-placeness of the communities it exploits. In other words, capital is mobile; cities are not. In brutal contrast to the "imagineering" accomplished by civic elites and city boosters regarding mega sport stadiums, we may recall the images of New Orleans residents crowding into the Superdome during the 2005 Hurricane Katrina evacuation. The Superdome was built with taxpayer money on the assertion it would "be a benefit to the community as a whole[,] displacing no one and providing such spin-off effects as more tourist money, [as well as] greater tax money generated by tourism" (Smith and Keller 1983, 135). In 2005, ticket prices to attend an event in the Superdome averaged $90, season passes to watch the football team were $1,300, and luxury box rental was $109,000 (http://www.neworleanssaints.com). Most of the 25,000 community residents who entered it as a so-called Shelter of Last Resort during the hurricane were probably first-time visitors. Media coverage of Hurricane Katrina showed us urban life in New Orleans outside the "tourist bubble" (Judd 1999) and reminded us that business and culture industry elites are "most conspicuously beyond the reach of ordinary folks, of the 'natives' tied fast to the ground" (Bauman 2001, 56; see also Smith and Ingham 2003). Under neoliberalism, argues Giroux (2005), the category of "waste" now includes not just material goods, but also human beings. Populations who are no longer economically productive or possess "no positive cultural capital or social role are increasingly viewed as an unwarranted burden to neoliberal society and left unprotected" (Giroux 2005, 27).

Part safe space, part spectacle (Perry 2003), the new urban landscape had to be carved out of the remnants of the industrial past and tourists cordoned off from the harsh realities of existence for "mobility frozen" (Ingham and Mc-Donald 2003) urban residents. "Islands of affluence" (Judd 1999) hide the over-all decline of the postindustrial city, reducing it to a "simulacrum" (Boyer 1993) and a distorted representation of the real thing (see also Friedman, Andrews, and Silk 2004). Revitalized spaces within "revanchist" cities (MacLeod 2002), with newly developed cultural attractions, walled off from the presumed dangerous places (and people), are created to solve urban image and social control problems. These spaces are defended by measures that solidify the relationships with capital, making them "secure" for capital investment. Railroads, highways, and bridges are used to establish rigid zones of demarcation between the "good" and the "bad" parts of a city. Buildings and other barricading structures can serve the same purpose. Atrium malls, convention centers, and domed stadiums were once thought to provide near-perfect enclosures for protection against the sordid aspects of local urban life. But space can also be reclaimed through intensive policing and surveillance. Throughout the 1990s, as amenity infrastructure development and tourist zones became much larger, policing tactics extended into ever further reaches of U.S. cities (Davis 1992; Judd 2003).

Militarizing Sport Terrain/Militarizing the City

As global violence telescopes within and through local places, so now physical, social, and psychological barriers are being constructed and enacted. In the wake of 9/11, and other catastrophic terrorist attacks in the last few years, the design of buildings, the management of traffic, the physical planning of cities, migration policy, or the design of social policies for ethnically diverse cities and neighborhoods, are being brought within the widening umbrella of "national security." (Graham 2004b, 11)

At the present historical moment, new relationships are emerging—and established ones are intensifying—between sport culture and the U.S. geopolitical agenda and between sport events and the militarization of urban civil society. The link between major sports events and the ideological construction of support for the George W. Bush administration's "war on terror" (a phrase subsequently decommissioned by the Obama administration) has been taken up by a number of sport studies scholars. For example, extending what Giroux (2003, ix) has identified as the "on-going militarization of visual culture," King (2008) examines the ways in which major sport leagues incorporated Bush administration policy, both through marketing strategies and through spectacles and displays at sport events. King goes further to show how, simultaneously, the "sportification" of political life was intensified through the Bush administration's association with major U.S. sport. McDonald (2005) explores mediated contextualizing of major sport in the days immediately following 9/11, as do Silk and Falcous (2005), who focus on media representations of Super Bowl XXXVI and the 2002 Salt Lake City Winter Games. In addition, Atkinson and Young (2005) provide a broad analysis of political violence and the Olympic Games, which includes a detailed case study of the 2002 Salt Lake City Games and the relationship between terrorism, political ideology, and sport as presented via the mass media.

Less explored, however, are relationships between major sport events and the transformed and transforming urban terrain on with they occur (see Silk 2004). For my purposes here, this includes the ways in which U.S. military doctrine and "homeland security" concerns are shaping the urban landscape, including major sport infrastructure, and the lives and experiences of people who live in, work in, and visit urban areas. Confronting the rhetoric that attracting major sport will benefit the "city as a whole" is the reality that the urban spaces in which they are held are being transformed from "civil to militarized environments, in support of transnational hegemonic actors" (Warren 2004, 216), and that major sport structures and events are being used to intensify and accelerate that transformation. It is important to stress, following Graham and his colleagues (2004a), that many "changes" in the U.S. urban milieu are a continuation of trends already underway before September 11, 2001, some of which have been highlighted in this chapter, but reinforced and aggravated by concerns over terrorism.

The prognosis regarding the impact of the war on terrorism on urban life in U.S. cities, and especially inner cities, is not an optimistic one. Peter Marcuse (2004) details a number of these predictions, and although he does not include a discussion regarding major sport/sport infrastructure, the implications are not difficult to conjecture. Among his predictions is increasing "citadelization" of construction for major businesses and affluent residents and intensified "barricading" strategies, further restricting movement and use of public space, and separating sections of the city from each other. Increasing public funds will be diverted from social welfare programs into security and surveillance and control mechanisms. The results, summarizes Marcuse, will be a "continual downgrading of the quality of life in US cities . . . particularly for members of darker-skinned groups" (2004, 264).

Stadium developments, as ever symbolizing a city's urban status and late-capitalist regeneration "success," are now in addition positioned as "terrorist targets."[1] The urban spaces in which major sport events occur are increasingly viewed as terrain on which military tactics and weaponry are necessary to protect capital investments, control crowds, and prevent and respond to terrorist attacks. Thus, many citizens accept the increasing militarization of sport facilities and events as a natural part of contemporary urban life. U.S. military doctrine now serves as a guide to "protect" an increasing array of sport events, both domestically and globally (Warren 2004, 225).

As Warren (2004) explains, widely accepted and currently accelerating strategies for carrying out urban military missions were first detailed in the

U.S. Army's 1979 Field Manual titled *Military Operations on Urbanized Terrain* (MOUT) (U.S. Department of the Army 1979). Until the 1990s it was assumed that MOUT doctrine would be primarily applied outside the United States and other industrialized nations. However, a number of events in the 1990s, including racial violence in Los Angeles (1992) and the bombings of the World Trade Center (1993), the Murrah Federal Building in Oklahoma City (1995), and the Olympic Summer Games in Atlanta (1996) resulted in "Homeland Defense" becoming a recurrent theme in U.S. military writing (Warren 2004, 218). By 2000, the MOUT doctrine contained well-established and broadly agreed-upon strategies for carrying out both domestic and overseas operations. Drawing from information compiled by Glenn, Steeb, and Matsumura (2001), Warren (2004, 218; emphasis in original) summarizes MOUT doctrinal strategies, some of which are as follows:

- *Intelligence, surveillance*, and *reconnaissance enhancement* include the development of technologies to prevent . . . elements of the built environment from obscuring the location of adversaries. . . .
- *Denial of access* strategies are designed to prevent entry into urban areas. . . .
- *Nodal operations* have the goal of selecting key spatial nodes within a city, rather than the whole metropolitan area to be directly controlled. . . .
- *Non-combatant control* is intended to influence civilian "attitudes and behaviors" to benefit the military. . . .
- *Selective dominance* involves the ability to control areas without physically occupying them.

The 2002 Salt Lake City Winter Olympic Games, the first Olympics to be designated as a "National Special Security Event," were an opportunity to display U.S. military dominance to a global audience (see Atkinson and Young 2005). The White House issued numerous press releases assuring U.S. citizens that they and the Games would be protected through the investment of more than $300 million in "security" measures, which included 4,500 military personnel; the resources of numerous federal, state, and local government agencies; a no-fly zone over all Olympic venues and within a forty-five-mile radius of the city; portable x-ray equipment; biometric scanners; traffic barricades; surveillance cameras; armed soldiers at airport terminals; fighter jets; and Black Hawk helicopters. In addition, the President's Press Office reported that the Salt Lake City Games were also the first Winter Olympics to "subject all visitors at all venues to metal detectors (nearly 1000 of them)." Planning for the security of the 2002 Games began well before 9/11 but was enormously enhanced afterward, even as the George W. Bush administration declared, "We will show the world we can safeguard the Olympic ideal without sacrificing our American ideals—openness, mobility, and economic opportunity in the process" (Office of the Press Secretary 2002).

The George W. Bush administration's policies and procedures—much of which has now been turned into the policy of the U.S. Department of Homeland Security—extend to numerous U.S. domestic sport events. In July 2004, the Department of Homeland Security hosted a "Security Forum for Sports Executives," including a full-day seminar in which sport officials and security personnel were instructed about Homeland Security capabilities and responsibilities (Forest 2006). The "best practices" that were encouraged by the federal government included installing surveillance cameras and other detection and monitoring equipment, increasing perimeter patrols, and establishing restricted areas of access. And still, nine years after 9/11, the federal government constantly reminds us of the lurking danger of another attack and that stadiums are a prime target.

By far the most intensive incursion of MOUT doctrine and related security measures into U.S. domestic sport occurs in the National Football League and especially the Super Bowl championship game. In fact, in the post-9/11 era, a particular journalistic focus in the lead-up to "Super Bowl Sunday" is the escalation of security measures over time. News reports describe the security buildup at each successive Super Bowl since 2001 as the "largest," or "biggest," or "most technologically advanced yet." The National Football League's "anti-terrorism" policies and procedures have recently been awarded the Department of Homeland Security's highest reliability rating, winning it exemption from lawsuits if terrorists attack a site they are protecting (as reported in Frank 2009). Beginning in 2006, the NFL ordered "patdown" body searches of all fans entering all stadiums where the teams play throughout the entire football season. Since most NFL stadiums are publicly owned and maintained, the cost of extra security is often passed on to taxpayers. The Stadium Authority in Jacksonville, Florida, has pursued (failed) legal action against the NFL in an attempt to reclaim the cost of extra security since 9/11, including the cost of the patdowns that the authority said costs $7,500 per game. In addition, a Jacksonville season ticket holder sued the NFL (and lost), claiming that the patdowns violated his constitutional rights (Varian 2009).

These actions may be seen as relatively mild forms of resistance, however, against a league that controls the Super Bowl, whose security procedures have federally protected status. They are especially mild when one considers the security measures put in place in 2005 when Jacksonville hosted Super Bowl XXXIX. Local government and police leveraged the extra security demands of hosting the game to "expand their capabilities" of surveillance into Jacksonville's downtown. Their plan illustrates the trend in convergence between state and commercial surveillance described by Lyon (2004, 2001). For an initial cost of $1.7 million, the city contracted private security firm GTSI and its InteGuard Alliance partners, who had previously worked with the Pentagon, to install approximately one hundred virtual private network (VPN) encrypted video cameras throughout the stadium and the city. Initially deployed for the game, the system was designed to "expand," stay "for decades," and go "beyond the Super Bowl for other needs" (McEachern Gibbs 2005).

Super Bowl XL, between the Pittsburgh Steelers and Seattle Seahawks, was held at Ford Field stadium in February 2006 in Detroit, Michigan. It was the first Super Bowl to be located close to an international border—half a mile from Canada. It also became one of the largest security operations in U.S. history, according to media accounts. The United States asked Canadian officials to restrict private plane travel in Canadian airspace near the stadium. A thirty-nautical-mile no-fly zone, barring planes from flying lower than 18,000 feet throughout the game, was in operation around the stadium. The Federal Bureau of Investigation (FBI) and Detroit police were assisted by fifty federal, state, and local law enforcement agencies, following eighteen months of preparation. The obsessive concern with "security" permeated the usual pre–Super Bowl media hype and game preparation, as it was reported that, for example, "SWAT teams—aided by digital maps covering every inch of Ford Field" would "be ready at a moment's notice" (NewsEdge Corporation 2006).

Writing in 1983, Richard Hill described Detroit as a city that could no longer compete for development within the institutional rules of the game, absent national and regional planning and coordination. Nearly thirty years ago, Hill (1983, 116) asked, "What is to be done to save Detroit?" Currently Detroit's image is an enduring symbol of post-Fordist urban decline. Less than a month before 2006 Super Bowl XL was played on Detroit's Ford Field, the Ford Motor Company announced plans to eliminate 25,000–30,000 jobs, constituting 20 percent of its workforce, and shut fourteen factories in North America over the next six years. Nevertheless, city officials insisted that the Super Bowl would give the city a chance to "polish its image" and "showcase its improvements to visitors" (Haugh 2006; Saraceno 2006). Can there be any better example than Super Bowl XL in Detroit (and elsewhere) to observe the complex connections between major sport and the landscapes of neoliberalizing urbanism? In the post-9/11 era, it is still asserted that we are "privileged" Super Bowl host communities and football fans, even as we are surveilled, digitally scanned, corralled, barricaded, and patted down.

Conclusion

This chapter highlights the connection between the development of infrastructures necessary to host large sporting events and broader neoliberalizing trends and social conditions in U.S. society. U.S. urban change, and the role that major sport plays in it, is both a consequence and component of a complex political-economic environment driven by interurban competition for status enhancement and capital accumulation. Here—in a society fixated on being number one—winners emerge and losers are left to take a "status bloodbath" (to borrow Clifford Geertz's 1973 use of Erving Goffman's term). I have underscored the state's role in contributing huge sums of public money to urban megaprojects that further erode its ability to provide for urban social services.

Within this larger context of neoliberal finance-led, state-sponsored urban redevelopment, stadiums often exist in close proximity to citizens who cannot afford the price of admission and who disproportionately bear the burden of increased taxation. Moreover, breakdowns in barriers to free trade and the free flow of capital are now accompanied by an increasing fortification of barriers between urban spaces and disruption of the flow of people throughout what Mitchell (2001) has termed the "postjustice city." Nowhere are these trends more evident than in the case of major-league stadium developments and sports mega-events that they house. Hosting major sports events in the United States sorts cities and citizens into hierarchal ranks, enabling a collective experience for some, but excluding most. In the redeveloped postindustrial U.S. city, professional sport is high among the consumption-based strategies that distinguish "prestige communities" (Ingham and McDonald 2003) from all the rest. Infrastructural investments and status-differentiated cultural power are reinforced and defended by state-sponsored surveillance and control tactics in an escalating militarization of urban civil society and accepted by many U.S. citizens as an inevitable fact of life in post-9/11 America.

NOTE

1. For an analysis of the emerging discourses of stadium and event security at the 2000–2010 Super Bowl game, see Schimmel 2011. For an analysis of the intersections between the NFL's security practices and the U.S. Department of Homeland Security's counterterrorism agenda, see Schimmel, forthcoming.

REFERENCES

Akkar, M. 2005. "The Changing Publicness of Contemporary Public Space: A Case Study at Grey's Monument Area, Newcastle upon Tyne." *Urban Design International* 10:95–113.

Alesia, M. 2004. "I Believe We'll Get One." IndyStar.com, December 21. Available at http://www2.indystar.com/articles/8/203740-4858-009.html/.

Atkinson, M., and K. Young. 2005. "Political Violence, Terrorism, and Security at the Olympic Games." In *Global Olympics: Historical and Sociological Studies of the Modern Games*, ed. K. Young and K. Wamsley, 269–294. London: Elsevier.

Austrian, Z., and M. Rosentraub. 2002. "Cities, Sports and Economic Change: A Retrospective." *Journal of Urban Affairs* 24 (5): 549–563.

Bale, J. 1994. *Landscapes of Modern Sport*. London: Leicester University Press.

Bauman, Z. 2001. *Community: Seeking Safety in an Insecure World*. Malden, MA: Blackwell.

Boyer, C. 1993. "The City of Illusion: New York's Public Places." In *The Restless Urban Landscape*, ed. P. Knox, 111–126. Englewood Cliffs, NJ: Prentice Hall.

Brenner, N., and N. Theodore, eds. 2002a. "Cities and the Geographies of 'Actually Existing Neoliberalism.'" In *Space of Neoliberalism: Urban Restructuring in North American and Western Europe*, ed. N. Brenner and N. Theodore, 2–32. Oxford: Blackwell.

———, eds. 2002b. *Space of Neoliberalism: Urban Restructuring in North American and Western Europe*. Oxford: Blackwell.

Crompton, J. 2004. "Beyond Economic Impact: An Alternative Rationale for Public Subsidy of Major League Sport Facilities." *Journal of Sport Management* 18:40–58.

Davis, M. 1992. "Fortress Los Angeles: The Militarization of Urban Space." In *Variations on a Theme Park: The New American City and the End of Public Space*, ed. M. Sorkin, 154–180. New York: Hill and Wang.

Forest, J.J.F. 2006. *Homeland Security: Protecting America's Targets*. Westport, CT: Praeger Security International.

Frank, T. 2009. "NFL Exempt from Terrorism Lawsuits." *USA Today*, March 10. Available at http://www.usatoday.com/news/nation/2009-03-09-safety-act_N.htm/.

Friedan, B., and L. Sagalyn. 1990. *Downtown, Inc.: How America Builds Cities.* Cambridge, MA: MIT Press.

Friedman, M., D. Andrews, and M. Silk. 2004. "Sport and the Façade of Redevelopment in the Post-Industrial City." *Sociology of Sport Journal* 21 (2): 119–139.

Geertz, C. 1973. "Deep Play: Notes on the Balinese Cockfight." In *The Interpretation of Cultures*, 412–453. New York: Basic Books.

Giroux, H. 2003. *Public Spaces, Private Lives: Democracy beyond 9/11.* Lanham, MD: Rowman and Littlefield.

———. 2004. *The Terror of Neoliberalism: Authoritarianism and the Eclipse of Democracy.* Boulder, CO: Paradigm.

———. 2005. *Stormy Weather: Katrina and the Politics of Disposability.* London: Paradigm.

Glenn, R., R. Steeb, and J. Matsumura. 2001. *Corralling the Trojan Horse: A Proposal for Improving U.S. Operations Preparedness in the Period 2000–2025.* Santa Monica, CA: RAND Arroyo Center.

Goss, J. 1996. "Disquiet on the Waterfront: Reflections on Nostalgia and Utopia in the Urban Archetypes of Festival Marketplaces." *Urban Geography* 17:221–247.

Graham, S., ed. 2004a. *Cities, War and Terrorism: Towards an Urban Geopolitics.* Oxford: Blackwell.

———, ed. 2004b. "Introduction: Cities, Warfare, and States of Emergency." In *Cities, War and Terrorism: Towards an Urban Geopolitics*, ed. S. Graham, 1–26. Oxford: Blackwell.

Haider, D. 1992. "Place Wars: New Realities of the 1990s." *Economic Development Quarterly* 6:588–601.

Hall, C. M. 2006. "Urban Entrepreneurship, Corporate Interests and Sports Mega-Events: The Thin Policies of Competitiveness within the Hard Outcomes of Neoliberalism." In *Sports Mega-Events: Social Scientific Analyses of a Global Phenomenon*, ed. J. Horne and W. Manzenreiter, 59–70. Oxford: Oxford University Press.

Hannigan, J. 1998. *Fantasy City: Pleasure and Profit in the Postmodern Metropolis.* London: Routledge.

Harvey, D. 1989. *The Condition of Postmodernity: An Inquiry into the Origins of Cultural Change.* Oxford: Blackwell.

———. 2005. *A Brief History of Neoliberalism.* Oxford: Oxford University Press.

———. 2006. "Neoliberalism as Creative Destruction." *Geografiska Annaler* 88B (2): 145–158.

Haugh, D. 2006. "Super Bowl Hosts Polishing Image: Much-Maligned Detroit Hopes the Game Will Showcase Its Improvements to Visitors." *Chicago Tribune*, January 3. Available at http://articles.chicagotribune.com/2006-01-03/news/0601030247_1_super-bowl-xl-bears-detroit.

Hill, R. 1983. "Crisis in the Motor City: The Politics of Economic Development in Detroit." In *Restructuring the City: The Political Economy of Urban Development*, ed. S. S. Fainstein, N. I. Fainstein, R. C. Hill, D. Judd, and M. P. Smith, 80–125. London: Longman.

Hudnut, W. 1995. *The Hudnut Years in Indianapolis, 1976–1991.* Bloomington: Indiana University Press.

Ingham, A., and M. McDonald. 2003. "Sport and Community/Communitas." In *Sporting Dystopias: The Making and Meanings of Urban Sport Cultures*, ed. R. Wilcox, D. L. Andrews, R. Pitter, and R. L. Irwin, 17–33. Albany: State University of New York Press.

Jessop, B., J. Peck, and A. Tickell. 1999. "Economic Crisis, State Restructuring, and Urban Politics." In *The Urban Growth Machine: Critical Perspectives Two Decades Later*, ed. A. Jones and D. Wilson, 141–162. Albany: State University of New York Press.

Jewson, N., and S. MacGregor, eds. 1997. *Transforming Cities: Contested Governance and New Spatial Divisions.* New York: Routledge.

Judd, D. 1999. "Constructing the Tourist Bubble." In *The Tourist City*, ed. S. Fainstein and D. Judd, 35–53. New Haven, CT: Yale University Press.

———. 2002. "Promoting Tourism in U.S. Cities. In *Readings in Urban Theory*, ed. S. Fainstein and S. Campbell, 278–299. Oxford: Blackwell.

———. 2003. "Building the Tourist City: Editor's Introduction." In *The Infrastructure of Play: Building the Tourist City*, ed. D. Judd, 3–16. Armonk, NY: Sharpe.

Judd, D., W. Winter, W. R. Barnes, and E. Stern. 2003. "Tourism and Entertainment as Local Economic Development: A National Survey." In *The Infrastructure of Play: Building the Tourist City*, ed. D. Judd, 50–76. Armonk, NY: Sharpe.

Kantor, P. 2010. "City Futures: Politics, Economic Crisis, and the American Model of Urban Development." *Urban Research and Practice* 3 (1): 1–11.

Kaplan, D. 2003. "Forecast: Venue Financing Tougher in '03." *Street and Smith's SportsBusiness Journal* 5 (37): 1, 25.

King, S. 2008. "Offensive Lines: Sport-State Synergy in an Era of Perpetual War." *Cultural Studies ↔ Critical Methodologies* 8 (4): 527–539.

Leitner, H. 1990. "Cities in Pursuit of Economic Growth." *Political-Economic Quarterly* 9 (2): 146–170.

Lyon, D. 2001. *Surveillance Society: Monitoring Everyday Life.* Buckingham, UK: Open University Press.

———. 2004. "Technology vs. 'Terrorism': Circuits of City Surveillance since September 11, 2001." In *Cities, War and Terrorism: Towards an Urban Geopolitics*, ed. S. Graham, 297–311. Oxford: Blackwell.

MacLeod, G. 2002. "From Urban Entrepreneurialism to a 'Revanchist City'? On the Spatial Injustices of Glasgow's Renaissance." *Antipode* 34 (3): 602–624.

Marcuse, P. 2004. "The 'War on Terrorism' and Life in Cities after September 11, 2001." In *Cities, War and Terrorism: Towards an Urban Geopolitics*, ed. S. Graham, 263–275. Oxford: Blackwell.

McDonald, M. 2005. "Imagining Benevolence, Masculinity and the Nation: Tragedy, Sport and the Transnational Marketplace." In *Sport and Corporate Nationalisms*, ed. M. Silk, D. Andrews, and C. Cole, 127–141. New York: Berg.

McEachern Gibbs, C. 2005. "Security Scores at Super Bowl." *CRN*, January 18. Available at http://www.crn.com/news/security/57700788/security-scores-at-super-bowl.htm;jsessionid=mz3xCQfP6XQ0DhC35PuryQ**.ecappj01.

Mitchell, D. 2001. "Postmodern Geographical Praxis? The Postmodern Impulse and the War against Homelessness in the Post-Justice City." In *Postmodern Geography: Theory and Praxis*, ed. C. Minca, 57–92. Oxford: Blackwell.

Molotch, H. 1993. "The Political Economy of Growth Machines." *Journal of Urban Affairs* 15:29–53.

NewsEdge Corporation. 2006. "Supersizing Bowl Security for Super Bowl XL." *Detroit News*, January 13. Available at http://www.securityinfowatch.com/press_release/10592801/supersizing-bowl-security-for-super-bowl-xl/.

Obama, B. 2008. "Remarks to the U.S. Conference of Mayors in Miami, Florida." American Presidency Project, June 21. Available at http://www.presidency.ucsb.edu/ws/index.php?pid=77555#axzz1s2iETuMc/.

Office of the Press Secretary, U.S. Department of Homeland Security. 2002. "Preparing for the World: Homeland Security and Winter Olympics." January 10. Available at http://georgewbush-whitehouse.archives.gov/news/releases/2002/01/20020110-7.html/.

Peck, J., and A. Tickell. 2002. "Neoliberalizing Space." *Antipode* 34 (3): 380–404.

Perry, D. 2003. "Urban Tourism and the Privatizing Discourses of Public Infrastructure." In *The Infrastructure of Play: Building the Tourist City*, ed. D. Judd, 19–49. Armonk, NY: Sharpe.

Roberts, J. M. 2008. "Public Spaces of Dissent." *Sociology Compass 2* (10): 1–21.

Rosentraub, M. 2003. "Indianapolis: A Sports Strategy, and the Redefinition of Downtown Redevelopment." In *The Infrastructure of Play: Building the Tourist City*, ed. D. Judd, 104–124. Armonk, NY: Sharpe.

Rosentraub, M., and D. Swindell. 2005. "The Value of the Indianapolis Colts to Indiana Residents and Their Willingness to Pay for a New Stadium." Available at http://images .ibsys.com/2005/0331/4335591.pdf/.

Salmon, S. 2001. "Imagineering the Inner City? Landscapes of Pleasure and the Commodification of Cultural Spectacle in the Postmodern City." In *Popular Culture: Production and Consumption*, ed. C. L. Harrington and D. Bielby, 106–119. Malden, MA: Blackwell.

Saraceno, J. 2006. "To Help Its Troubled Image, Detroit Puts on Sunday Best." *USA Today*, January 29. Available at http://www.usatoday.com/sports/columnist/saraceno/2006-01-29-saraceno-detroit_x.htm.

Schimmel, K. 2001. "Sport Matters. Urban Regime Theory and Urban Regeneration in the Late-Capitalist Era." In *Sport in the City: the Role of Sport in Economic and Social Regeneration*, ed. C. Gratton and I. Henry, 259–277. London: Routledge.

———. 2002. "The Political Economy of Place: Urban and Sport Studies Perspectives." In *Theory, Sport and Society*, ed. J. Maguire and K. Young, 335–351. Oxford: Elsevier.

———. 2009. "Political Economy: Sport and Urban Development." In *Sociology of Sport and Social Theory*, ed. E. Smith, 55–66. Champaign, IL: Human Kinetics Press.

———. 2011. "From 'Violence-Complacent' to 'Terrorist-Ready': Post 9/11 Framing of the US Super Bowl." *Urban Studies* 48 (15): 3277–3292.

———. Forthcoming. "Protecting the NFL/Militarizing the Homeland: Citizen Soldiers and Urban Resilience in Post-9/11 America." *International Review for the Sociology of Sport*.

Short, J. 1999. "Urban Imagineers: Boosterism and the Representation of Cities." In *The Urban Growth Machine: Critical Perspectives Two Decades Later*, ed. A. Jones and D. Wilson, 27–54. Albany: State University of New York Press.

Silk, M. L. 2004. "A Tale of Two Cities: The Social Production of Sterile Sporting Space." *Journal of Sport and Social Issues* 28 (4): 349–378.

Silk, M. L., and Falcous, M. 2005. "One Day in September/a Week in February: Mobilizing American (Sporting) Nationalisms." *Sociology of Sport Journal* 22:447–471.

Smith, J., and A. Ingham. 2003. "On the Waterfront: Retrospectives on the Relations between Sport and Community." *Sociology of Sport Journal* 20 (4): 252–275.

Smith, M. 1988. *City, State, and Market: The Political Economy of Urban Society*. New York: Blackwell.

Smith, M., and M. Keller. 1983. "Managed Growth and the Politics of Uneven Development in New Orleans." In *Restructuring the City: The Political Economy of Urban Development*, ed. S. S. Fainstein, N. I. Fainstein, R. C. Hill, D. Judd, and M. P. Smith, 126–166. London: Longman.

Turner, R., and M. Rosentraub. 2002. "Tourism, Sports and the Centrality of Cities." *Journal of Urban Affairs* 24 (5): 487–492.

U.S. Department of Housing and Urban Development. 1982. *The President's National Urban Policy Report*. Washington, DC: U.S. Government Printing Office.

U.S. Department of the Army. 1979. *Military Operations on Urbanized Terrain FM 90-10*. Washington, DC: U.S. Government Printing Office.

Varian, B. 2009. "Fans Can Expect to Be Frisked." *New York Times*, January 22, 1B.

Warren, R. 2004. "City Streets—The War Zones of Globalization: Democracy and Military Operations on Urban Terrain in the Early Twenty-First Century." In *Cities, War and Terrorism: Towards an Urban Geopolitics*, ed. S. Graham, 214–230. Oxford: Blackwell.

Weber, R. 2002. "Extracting Value from the City: Neoliberalism and Urban Redevelopment." *Antipode* 34 (3): 519–540.

Zukin, S. 1991. *Landscapes of Power: From Detroit to Disney*. Berkeley: University of California Press.

———. 1995. *The Cultures of Cities*. Cambridge, MA: Blackwell.

11

Economies of Surf

Evolution, Territorialism, and
the Erosion of Localism

LESLIE HEYWOOD
MARK MONTGOMERY

M uch research in sport studies has taken a uniformly negative view of economic globalization and its undergirding philosophy of neoliberalism, seeing it as the inculcation of a conservative agenda that has had a negative impact on sports, undermined traditional communities and team loyalties, and created a star system that exaggerates the competitive individualism already endemic in many sites (Andrews 2001; Bale and Cronin 2003; Maguire 1999; Miller et al. 1999, 2001). In the words of Miller and colleagues, "to many critics, sport's manifest nationalism has masked dependency, as indigenous sports were displaced by those of the colonizers—the process of competition, ranking, and nationalism inscribing a deep structure of Western culture" (Miller et al. 1999, 23). Although the sport of surfing exhibited precisely these patterns with the appropriation of the "hang loose" Hawaiian surf style by Anglos who developed a much more competitive style in California and Australia, surfing has also been interpreted as a form of colonial resistance. Moreover, surfing in its Polynesian origins itself exhibited a dominance hierarchy that privileged royalty and men and was expressed through the different kinds of surfboards individuals were allowed to ride and who was given first access to waves, a hierarchy that resembles forms of localism today (Walker 2008; Kampion 2003; Ford and Brown 2006). We discuss how recent forms of economic globalization and its attendant neoliberal attitudes have affected the omnipresent phenomenon of localism in the sport of surfing, and how localism has been historically shaped by evolution, culture, and life stage (Pritchard, Quacquarelli, and Saunders 2004; Waitt and Warren 2008).

Globalization, Neoliberalism, and Changing Surfing Localisms

Although these terms are sometimes used interchangeably, neoliberalism marks a particular stance toward globalization, that of the so-called Washington consensus, and is a set of assumptions that is used to shape policy (Gray 1988; Held and McGrew 2003). John Gray articulates what is often, from a neoliberal perspective, supposed to be characteristic of globalization: the idea that "democratic capitalism will soon be accepted throughout the world. A global free market will become a reality. The manifold economic cultures and systems that the world has always contained will be redundant. They will be merged into a single universal free market" (Gray 1988, 2). Therefore the neoliberalism of the Washington consensus advocates, in the words of David Held and Anthony McGrew, "deregulation, privatization, structural adjustment programs, and limited government" (Held and McGrew 2003, 5)—which means a reduction in public spending on social services and public goods of all kinds, including roads, bridges, and even fire departments, as well as a reduction in government controls pertaining to the environment and safety on the job. In the neoliberal view, the free market will solve all, and individual responsibility for one's own condition is paramount. Recent protest movements such as the Occupy movement, which started in New York as an occupation of the Wall Street financial district, have spread throughout the United States and around the developed world, call neoliberalism into question, point to the structural inequality associated with the "1 percent," and hold the financial services sector responsible for the financial crisis of the late 2000s. While neoliberalism seems to no longer be functioning as a seamless ideology the way it did at the end of the twentieth century, it nonetheless had an impact on all sectors of human interaction, including sport, and articulated itself within surfing culture in particular ways.

Researchers have begun to note the impact of neoliberalism on "localist" traditions in surfing, and the term *localism*, with its specific meanings in surf culture, needs explanation. Many researchers have addressed the phenomenon of localism (Preston-Whyte 2002; Evers 2007, 2008; Booth 2003). Its occurrence is so pervasive that, according to Ford and Brown, "on a popular level, the whole matter of surfing's inherent scarcity, that is, questions of crowding, regulation, and jockeying for position within the lineup, is so basic to contemporary surfing that it is practically taken for granted" (Ford and Brown 2006, 78). Clifton Evers, an Australian researcher and surfer who has published widely on the subject, defines localism as "a process of dominating a territory and imposing its cultural laws on others." Localism tends to be characterized by an insider, "'us vs. them' culture . . . in which the 'them' is never as good or right as we are. Surfers have a long tradition of spray-painting 'Locals Only' on footpaths and rock walls to let people know that particular beaches and pieces of turf are 'theirs'" (Evers 2008, 412).

In the localist view, who counts as local? The usual definition tends to be anyone who has surfed a particular break for a long period of time and has "paid his dues" by undergoing a apprenticeship-like period in which the established hierarchy of surfers based on skill and seniority teaches the newcomer the way of the break—how the waves tend to act in what conditions and therefore how one should conduct oneself so that everyone is safe. But this is a mixed, exclusionary legacy, because the opportunity to become part of the group of "mates" that tends to make up the hierarchy often explicitly excludes women, nonwhites, anyone who does not vehemently identify as heterosexual, and anyone who does not demonstrate the "right" surfing style.

As Gordon Waitt writes of his research subjects, "Men surfing body boards were described by shortboard surfers as 'failed men.' . . . [T]hrough processes of domination, subordination, institutional authorisation and complicity, particular styles of masculinity become hegemonic in the surf, having power through defining what is naturalised as 'normal' attributes of being male (Waitt and Warren 2008, 356). Waitt and Warren's research further reveals the ways such masculinities can be predicated on both exclusion and domination:

> Surfing a shortboard is a significant means of ideologically promoting conventional ideas of a white-settler Australian masculinity. Enforcement of these conservative norms is most recently illustrated through the enhanced notoriety of the Braboys, a group of men who take their name from Maroubra, Sydney, and who assert their claims of ownership over the surf-breaks of this suburb. The masculinity performed by the Braboys is imitated through language, ritualized tattooing, physical domination of surf-breaks, aggression, sexism, racism and homophobia. (Waitt and Warren 2008, 354)

A recent documentary called *Bra Boys* (2007), narrated by Russell Crowe and written and directed by Bra Boys members, became the highest-grossing non-IMAX documentary in Australia and shows that these traditional localist behaviors are often normalized.

Recent changes in this form of localism are directly related to globalization and the neoliberal values associated with some forms of that globalization. A number of sport researchers who focus on surfing have found that, in the last decade, traditional patterns of localism at surf breaks have been disrupted by an influx of new surfers who do not respect traditional authority and who demonstrate what might be called a neoliberal ideology. In Southern California, "the local social order gave precedence to seniority and surfing skill and endowed a sense of belonging and esteem to group members . . . the traditional order, valuing seniority and skill, is being eclipsed by a new order, which values competitiveness and individual gratification" (Daskalos 2007, 158). In the Australian context, Clifton Evers writes that "hierarchies at surf spots are increasingly being challenged as surfing becomes more popular" (Evers 2008, 412). The advent of new technologies, which have made boards easier to ride, wetsuits more effective, and surf conditions easier to track and anticipate through websites, have expanded the base of people who actively surf. The same attitude of entitlement that characterizes consumer culture—"I bought and paid for it, therefore I deserve it"—seems to extend itself into the idea of access to the waves for new surfers.

For instance, one of Daskalos's research subjects, who considers himself a "local" at his Encinitas, California, break, exhorts him:

Tell those friggin' kooks [novice surfers] that I don't care who they are on land. When you come out to surf my waves you better show me respect. You better show respect to all the guys that have been surfing here for years, ten years, fifteen years for Christ's sake. I don't give a shit if you're CEO of WidgetCom! It doesn't matter! It happens . . . you know, we'll be out there [surfing] and some yuppie who just dropped a grand on a new Joel Tudor board will drive up in his shiny SUV and see us out there. He'll paddle out and think he's going to catch our waves. Fuck him, who's he to surf our waves? He doesn't have the right to even be there. He may think he does but he doesn't. (Daskalos 2007, 162)

Here the local surfer articulates two competing ideologies, two different claims to the wave: one based on experience and seniority, the other based on current purchasing power. From the locals' perspective, prestige on land—purchasing power, prestigious job—does not equal prestige in the water, which is based on skill level and time spent surfing the particular break.[1] Presumably, from the new surfer's perspective, he's bought the right equipment and in doing so has the right to participate in the sport, and the same prestige that enables him to buy the equipment in the first place should be conferred and indicated by that equipment. Daskalos reports what his research subjects articulate as the "'fuck it, I'm going!' mentality of the newcomers as surfers . . . a competitive, individualistic mindset of the crowd . . . similar to the mindset found on the freeways in the area . . . and a complete disregard for the enjoyment and, most important, the safety of others" (Daskalos 2007, 165). In the locals' perspective, it is crucial that newcomers obey the so-called law of surf, which is universal and dictates who gets a given wave and where he should get it, a code designed for safety (Nazer 2004). In addition, each newcomer has to "pay his dues" of respect to those who have been there and demonstrate skill in the sport.

The kind of localism Daskalos discusses in relation to shortboard surfing is replicated in the most recent explosion of big-wave surfing in the 1990s. Laird Hamilton, Dave Kalama, and other Hawaiian big-wave riders who used tow-in technology to conquer fifty- or even hundred-foot waves created a media frenzy, and big-wave surfing became the new ideal standard in some contexts. As with shortboard surfing, the explosion of participants in big-wave riding triggered traditional localist attitudes in the surfers who had been there first. For instance, members of Laird Hamilton's crew were quoted in *Sports Illustrated* saying, "A lot of these new guys don't understand the pecking order . . . how the hand-me-down from the first guys who surfed Waimea to where Laird's at now has been an interesting and respectful evolution. There are gonna be some tombstones on the beach if they think they can pay their money and go around the experience part of it. . . . This is the sport of kings. It is not the sport of bozos" (Casey 2006, 66).

While globalization in a neoliberal key has had a negative impact on traditional localisms that rely on distinctions between "kings" and "bozos" and is beginning to displace them, the surfer traditions that were established in the twentieth century were themselves based on the appropriation and displacement of the Hawaiian and local Polynesian cultures where surfing had its origins. Furthermore, the Polynesian traditions were themselves based on exclusion and hierarchy and made much the same distinctions. As Drew Kampion writes, "The use of long, narrow *olo* surfboards (fashioned from *wiliwili* wood) was reserved for the hereditary chiefly *ali'i*, who also claimed exclusive use of certain surf spots. Violators of this *kapu* could be put to death in unpleasant ways" (Kampion 2003, 34). Surfing localism therefore has a long and not exclusively Western tradition that often takes the form of exclusionary practices based on race, gender, sexuality, and surfing style. The most recent form of globalization and its attendant neoliberal assumptions disrupts an exclusionary "tradition" that is firmly entrenched, and this form of globalization is the only thing that has managed to challenge it—demonstrating, in the view of those who find dominance hierarchies based on in-groups and out-groups problematic—what might be formulated as a positive aspect of recent globalization. In traditional surfer localisms, including that of the Polynesians, the "us" group is established and a hierarchy maintained regarding access to waves. In the neoliberal approach, there is no "us," and the "them" is everyone else who is trying to compete for waves. We argue that the patterns of exclusion demonstrated by both "old school" surfer locals and the "fuck it" new surfer neoliberals are illuminated when examined in the context of an evolutionary approach to stigmatization, an approach that helps explain "localist" behavior in a way other approaches cannot.

Research Approach and Method

The research methods incorporated in this study were drawn from a theoretical base in evolutionary biology and ethnographic research in sport studies. Since our focus was to assess the impact of globalization and one of its attendant philosophies on the sport of surfing in relation to its cultural traditions of localism, a detailed literature review and five semistructured interviews by telephone with white male surfers in their thirties and forties, primarily in the northern California area, were our main methods of new-data collection.

Two of the interviewees are prominent surf journalists. One is a famous longboarder in the classic style who was featured in *Endless Summer II*, one of the core surf culture movies. One is a longtime participatory surfer who is a filmmaker, and another is a participant who grew up waterskiing in Louisiana and fell in love with surfing through magazines and television. Like a growing number of recent surfers, he got involved in the sport in the last fifteen years, learning to surf as an adult. With the exception of the latter, all have been surfing regularly for seventeen to thirty-eight years. The interviewees ranged from thirty-three to forty-six years of age. In terms of our own positioning, one of us, a male who is a longtime surfer of the same demographic, conducted the interviews, and therefore had immediate credibility within this community. The small size of our sample makes our findings preliminary, but these findings resonate with the research of Waitt and Warren (2008) in a way that adds credence.

Evolutionary biology provided a "deep historical" perspective on these findings perhaps best articulated by historian Daniel Smail: "The large human brain evolved over the past 1.7 million years to allow individuals to negotiate the escalating complexities posed by human social living. . . . [M]any of the things we do are shaped by behavioral predispositions, moods, emotions, and feelings that have a deep evolutionary history. These body states are . . . physiological entities, characteristically located in specific parts of the brain and put there by natural selection . . . but . . . behaviors that are shaped by predispositions and emotions are often plastic, not hardwired. Basic social emotions are almost certainly universal . . . but they do different things in different historical cultures" (Smail 2008, 113–114). This perspective helped us understand surfing localism as a global phenomenon demonstrating shifts in response to the contemporary context of globalization. Localism read in terms of evolved cognitive forms in the brain that are plastic (pliable) while retaining deep historical tendencies helps make sense of the current manifestation of mixed, ambivalent behaviors reported by many researchers.

Evolutionary Perspectives on Stigmatization in Group Formation

Although the evolutionary approach is commonplace in many disciplines, disciplines within the social sciences with a cultural constructivist bent have tended to dismiss evolutionary theory, often without reading it, as "essentialist." The fear that seems to be operational here, as David Buss points out, is that evolutionary theory claims that "human behavior is genetically determined" and that "if it's evolutionary, we can't change it" (Buss 2008, 18). "Much of the resistance to applying evolutionary theory to the understanding of human behavior," Buss writes, "stems from the misconception that evolutionary theory implies genetic determinism. Contrary to this misunderstanding, evolutionary theory in fact represents a truly interactionist framework. Human behavior cannot occur without two ingredients: (1) evolved adaptations and (2) environmental input that triggers the development and activation of these adaptations" (2008, 18). Changes in a given environment can prevent the activation of mechanisms, or change the mechanisms themselves. Tellingly, the etymology of "evolution" is concerned with change, not stasis.

In an influential article, anthropologist Robert Kurzban and psychologist Mark R. Leary (2001) seek an ultimate explanation for competitiveness between groups and the processes of social exclusion used to define groups. In evolutionary biology, the distinction between ultimate mechanisms (those that refer to mechanisms evolved in relation to selection pressures faced by a species during its evolutionary history) and proximate mechanisms (the specialized functional mechanisms that evolved to solve issues related to these pressures within the organism's environment) is fundamental. On the level of ultimate explanation, Kurzban and Leary discuss the mechanisms evolved to solve the problem of human sociality and to place limits on it, and "propose that human adaptations for sociality include cognitive mechanisms that cause people to be selective in their social interactions" (Kurzban and Leary 2001, 189). Humans have specific adaptations for various forms of sociality, including the one most relevant here, within-group cooperation for between-group conflict and competition.[2] Kurzban and Leary argue that the phenomenon of stigmatization derives from several different factors, including coalitional exploitation—that is, "a suite of adaptations designed to cause one to exclude individuals from reaping the benefits of membership in one's group, particularly if it is a locally dominant one, and to exploit excluded individuals" (Kurzban and Leary 2001, 192). Coalitional exploitation and other mechanisms developed, in this view, because

> in order for sociality to be functional, there must be "brakes" on sociality. An organism that chose to socialize . . . with every other creature it encountered would be . . . at a selective disadvantage. We should expect therefore that natural selection would fashion constraints and limits on sociality that cause one to direct one's social efforts in productive ways. We suggest that these brakes, a result of the necessity to be discriminating in one's selection of partners for particular kinds of social interactions, might play an important role in generating the stigma phenomenon. (Kurzban and Leary 2001, 192)

Kurzban's and Leary's hypothesis is that in evolutionary human history, three forms of social exclusion evolved in order to confer survival advantage in relation to the need for social contact and the reciprocal need to limit it. They argue that these selected cognitive mechanisms take the form of (1) disgust toward and avoidance of others who may be carriers of disease or parasites, (2) exclusion of those who seem unable to reciprocate socially or who display low social capital, and (3) disregard for and exploitation of groups outside one's own, particularly in response to competition for resources. As we discuss in detail in the research findings section, group exclusion in surfing localism would appear to be particularly relevant to last form, which is associated with coalitional exploitation, given that in conditions of overcrowding, waves are seen as a limited resource. This perspective helps to explain what may otherwise seem like the inexplicable behavior of fighting over a wave: "research on group processes consistently shows that considering oneself as a member of a particular group leads to discriminatory, competitive, and, in extreme cases, violent behavior toward the members of other groups" (Kurzban and Leary 2001, 195). Behaviors displayed in surfing localism become more intelligible in this sense.

Research Findings and Applications

The compelling research that has been done on localism thus far demonstrates an ambivalence—localism provides a sense of safety, belonging, and affirmation for those who practice it but excludes others on what might be construed as objectionable grounds such as race, gender, or sexuality, as well as a morally and legally questionable assertion of ownership of public space (Evers 2008; Nazer 2004). This ambivalence in the research becomes more intelligible *as* ambivalence, however, if one looks at the phenomenon of localism in evolutionary terms—that is, from the perspective of an adaptationism that interprets current human behaviors as products of evolved cognitive forms in the brain that developed to process information in particular ways. Current research on surfing, particularly that of Evers and Waitt (Evers 2007, 2008; Waitt 2008), provides a vivid cultural history of localism, but there is also an evolutionary history that informs but does not replace or trump that cultural history. It is one form of historicity that interacts with others to present a more complete picture than would an analysis based on any single perspective. Both evolutionary and cultural histories are important, as they intricately shape each other. In our interpretation of our interview data and of the research of others, we suggest that an evolutionary framework can help explain the contradictions and ambivalence toward in-group and out-group behavior found in many sporting sites, in this case, the site of localism in surfing.

An insider to the sport, Evers writes particularly eloquently on the phenomenon of localism, the group loyalties it engenders, and the identities it sustains:

> The surf sessions, afternoons at the pub, fights, and so on that my mates and I experience as a "local crew" are collaborative. They're a mixed assortment of touch, smell, sight, sound, and taste that spill all over each other. A sensual economy of masculinity is built that ties us together, and teaches us how to behave in situations. We share interest, excitement, enjoyment, fear, shame, pride, anger. When we surf we experience varying combinations of these feelings that keep us coming back for more, but so does the sharing of these feelings with each other. It reaches the point where it's as if my mate's blood is the same as mine. The brotherly love that you feel is physical—as long as the touching stays in the "right" places. Homophobia is rife in the surfing culture. (2007, 4)

Two seemingly contradictory sensibilities are expressed here—the love and respect for his "mates," a deep, embodied understanding of how athletic practices and group culture and sensual economy constitute his very physiology, identity, behavior, and feelings, and a sense that these practices and culture perform in exclusionary ways that to some extent divide him from himself and create complicated, conflicted awareness and feelings. "My mate's blood is the same as mine," except that "sameness" is based on an attitude, homophobia, Evers does not seem to share.

An evolutionary perspective can help account for this kind of contradictory sensibility in a way that some other perspectives cannot. Ambivalence is a key term in Kurzban and Leary's formulations: "Stigmatization often involves considerable ambivalence on the part of the stigmatizer. This ambivalence may arise when people hold competing values, such as when one's egalitarian belief that all people are equal conflicts with one's negative attitudes toward members of a particular group. Our analysis raises the possibility that this ambivalence occurs because of two competing adaptations" (Kurzban and Leary 2001, 202). In the sense expressed by Evers, the two competing adaptations would be the adaptation for affiliation, and the adaptation designed to limit it. He is strongly affiliated with his mates, but the exclusionary practices that help sustain or even constitute that affiliation create a conflict. A group cannot include everyone, and the particular form that exclusion takes here—the stigmatization of homosexuals who are not seen as "real men"—is disturbing to the group loyalty that constitutes Evers's identity as a surfer who belongs to a particular place, affiliated with a particular group of people. The plasticity associated with neural mechanisms related to affiliation and conflict is of key importance, because, as Kurzban and Leary state, "although evolution is likely to fashion mechanisms that are specifically suited to solving a particular problem, various systems operate in the same organism, requiring the simultaneous activation and deactivation of systems in dynamic fashion" (2001, 201). Such simultaneous activation and deactivation can help explain Evers's deep simultaneous sense of belonging and alienation, a frisson or cognitive dissonance that leads him to reflect further.

In addition to providing an explanation of plasticity and variability, Kurzban and Leary provide insight into continuity, into how frameworks of affiliation also become frameworks for exclusion: "We should expect human beings to be designed to desire to become part of particular groups and value membership in them. Furthermore, by virtue of membership in a particular group, especially one that is in a dominant position and able to exploit other individuals, one should be motivated to exclude other individuals from joining one's group, thereby limiting the number of individuals among whom resources need to be divided" (2001, 195). Keep in mind that to be able to surf in the first place, conditions need to be just right and are dependent on particular weather in particular seasons, which means that a given break is not surfable for much of the year.

Since the surf is increasingly a limited resource, particularly at breaks where the conditions are good for surfing in popular ways such as big-wave riding, Kurzban and Leary's formulations seem directly pertinent to the form of localism in regard to which Evers is particularly eloquent. His eloquence helps us understand how those group loyalties function to engender exclusionary behaviors that can result in violence when threatened:

> This bonding makes me feel strong, comfortable and in command. My mates and I will share morning toast, borrow wax on rocky headlands, talk of waves and sit together in the surf. Surfers form a sensory relationship with the local weather patterns, sea-floors, jetties and rock walls. . . . Knowing how to ride "with" a wave at a particular spot is a clear marker that you're a local and works as a way to signal ownership of a space in an

increasingly crowded surfing world. The environment and how it works becomes so ingrained that a local should be able to tell the different surf seasons by the way their body feels. We bond with the geographical turf, and we will band together to fight dodgy development approvals, sewage outfalls, and anyone else who wants a piece of it. (Evers 2007, 4–5)

The way Evers writes is itself sensual, embodied, and evocative, providing a unique perspective into why people would act in exclusionary, violent ways that on the surface may seem inexplicable. These are people who belong to a place and to each other, whose very being is intertwined with the sport and the particular place they practice it. Here Evers articulates the modalities of localism in a positive sense that is absent from sensationalized media portrayals that represent surfers as street gangs. It reflects a sense of belonging and community often absent in the decentralized, globalized world of compressed time and space and global flows of people and goods that work to erode just this sense of belonging.

However, demonstrating precisely the ambivalence related to the simultaneous activation and deactivation of competing adaptive forms, Evers is also eloquent about the price of that belonging: "Of course, if you step out of line localism dictates that you should be mocked, abused or even beaten up. Violence is used as an instrument of power to shape the ways that we see, and thereby come to know, certain things. I got used to this violent process while growing up in the surfing culture. The cruelty acts as a test" (Evers 2007, 6). The reasons why someone would endure violence as the price of belonging, and accept the kind of bodily and subjective interpellation that dictates their behavior and the way they come to process information, is made further intelligible if considered in the light of competing adaptations for sociality.

This framework helps make sense of some of the ambivalence Evers expresses, localism in both its positive and negative functions. The plastic dimensions of such a framework, moreover, is reflected in our own research on a thirty-something male surfer cohort, especially when it is considered next to Waitt and Warren's research on a twenty-something male surfer cohort. Read together, the research suggests that the behaviors associated with localism may be part of a stage in the life course and not determinative of surfers' behaviors throughout that course—especially when the surfing conditions have been modified by globalization and neoliberalism in the specific ways discussed previously in this chapter.

Localism and Life Course

Waitt (2008) and Waitt and Warren (2008) focus on surfing primarily in relation to gender and reflect on the role of localism in the production of masculinities. In doing so, they provide a revision to the so-called hegemonic masculinity thesis (Connell 1995):

> Rather than just assuming that the gender inequalities found in the Australian surf are preconfigured by the relationships of power of patriarchal masculinity . . . we demonstrate that what is important in doing masculinity for many young men who surf together is how they feel and present themselves as capable and "in control." We argue that men who surf together validate and develop an emotional history of their masculinity as surfers through becoming "locals," and bonding practices including praising and shaming. (Waitt and Warren 2008, 354)

As in Evers's work, Waitt's and Warren's work describes both the plasticity of mechanisms related to sociality and in-group/out-group formations and the continuity of the mechanisms that seem to structure these formations such as those related to stigmatization and shame. While their emphasis is on plasticity, both plasticity and continuity are visible simultaneously in their accounts of the ways gender scripts are produced in relation to localism: "Capacities always exist to reconfigure masculinity in the surf. Each time a surfer enters the ocean they begin a complex process of negotiation through their bodies to configure and stabilise their subjectivity through making connections with the surf conditions and people. This relies upon a sensual economy of masculinity, the nods, pats and looks that transfer respect, pride, shame and disgust" (Waitt and Warren 2008, 360). This passage points to the way evolved mechanisms interact with the current environment to produce particular behaviors, and Waitt's and Warren's emphasis on both the stability of these behaviors and how these behaviors change is explicable in these terms. More simply put, as a quote from one of Waitt's research subjects illustrates, surfers often see themselves and their group formations and treatment of out-groups in naturalized terms: "Locals get umm, [pause]. They sorta like [pause], get very narky at people that you know that come from other beaches. [pause] It is like a spider in a web, and you've got another spider that comes in the web [pause]. They're very territorial. You know what I mean?" (Waitt 2008, 86). Localism is a way of negotiating territory that in turn shapes the production of masculinity in the surfers who practice it. Although its particular form is continually renegotiated and plastic, the mechanisms for distinction that contribute to this negotiation, always themselves evolving and responding to their environments, have a deep history.

Our interviews reflect continuity with the patterns of localism expressed here and provide some insight into a different demographic of male surfers than do Waitt and Warren's. The specific style of surfing they describe as constituting the surfing identities of this demographic centers on "killing" the waves—that is, surfing in an aggressive style (Waitt 2008)—and always competing for those waves in the lineup. While they focus on the younger demographic of twenty-something men, our subjects were all older than thirty and demonstrate perspectives that suggest that the "struggle" with the waves and with other surfers outside one's own group may change somewhat in later years. One subject, an ex–pro surfer who still works in the industry, describes a shift in his emphasis when surfing:

> And without even really thinking about it, I drove to the beach. I didn't even care about surfing well. I went out on my longest board and just rode four waves, and I kind of felt balanced again. That's when I like it. When it [surfing] can still be this thing that I can do at times like that and it sort of filters a lot of stuff out. When the surf is good, it's still a big deal for me to try and go out and surf really well, and that gets really frustrating cause I don't do it as often as I used to. But there is still a social aspect too. I still want to be friendly in the water and talk with friends about surfing. (Warshaw 2006)

This description evokes all the patterns we have seen this far—a hierarchy in which riding shortboards is seen as more difficult and "manly," and in which surfing performance and the evaluations of that performance is linked to riding them. In this context, "talking to friends about surfing" while in the water helps construct surfing as an activity done in a group while performing for and being confirmed by that group. As Waitt and Warren put it, "how the young men in this study come to know, feel and perform like men at these breaks, we have argued, is shaped by their strong commitment to caring for each other, their sense of ownership over a break and a surfing identity fashioned by big-wave riding" (Waitt and Warren 2008, 364). Our interviewee speaks almost wistfully about participating in just such practices here, and indicates how differently he sometimes surfs now. "Not even caring about surfing well," he chooses his "longest board" rather than a shortboard and pursues the activity by himself. He performs the kind of immersive activity associated with "soul" rather than competitive surfing, and does so to "feel balanced" and "filter stuff out" rather than to confirm his place in the lineup. A tone of nostalgia for competitive surfing—and an insistence that he still does it, that the immersive surfing is not *all* he does—creeps into his description with "when the surf is good" (meaning good wind and swell directions), "it's still a big deal to get out there and surf really well." "Surfing well" is placed in a context of judgment and is connected to "the social aspect" of "being friendly in the water." His surfing has changed, but he wants to emphasize that he still does it the old way, the way described by Waitt and Warren, the way of the young.

His ambivalence becomes more explicit in his next statement: "The older I get, the more important [*checks himself here, measuring his words in what appears to be an effort to phrase this right*]—the more important that it is to me to just get in the water and connect [to it] and disconnect [from what he wants to 'filter out'], the greater trouble I have when there's anyone else in the water, especially when it's crowded 'cause I don't want to have to do a turn that's going to impress somebody else." Other people in the water, especially crowds, means having to surf the way he used to, to surf to "impress." He no longer wants to surf that way:

I don't want to have to hassle or hustle for waves anymore. I still can in a pinch, but it's harder and harder for me to get in that mode. There are a lot of times when I just forget the board and just go out and bodysurf—just pull into some close-out tubes bodysurfing. That seems to me to be almost the most direct way for me to get a huge benefit cause there's no pressure to perform, there's no board that's going to hit me, there's no one looking. I don't care if I do it well or not. It's just quick connection into that energy I'm looking for when I surf. (Warshaw 2006)

"Getting into the mode" that Waitt and Warren describe as characterizing their young surfing cohort is "harder and harder" for this forty-something, and he even is willing to bodysurf just to get in the water, an activity that is lower in the surfing hierarchy than shortboarding or longboarding. He has given up group membership and the performance that sustains it, opting instead for "a quick connection into that energy I'm looking for," rather than having to "hassle or hustle for waves" and perform for others. He furthermore defines this in relation to crowds: "I don't go out anywhere anymore when it's really crowded. Occasionally, if the waves are really good, I can put on that hat and get aggressive, and I can get waves. But it's not as good of a feeling to get it that way. I do it less and less. It's not as important to me" (Warshaw 2006).

Another respondent articulated a similar perspective: "There are two types of surfing for me. There's performance surfing where I'm in a situation where the surf is really good, everybody's watching, cameras are on the beach. And then there are the surf sessions that are just for me. The latter are the sessions that are becoming more common for me, where I'm just out there to play, not perform" (Weaver 2006). As with the first subject, the surfer finds himself in the localist modality of performing for a particular crew of men, or even a general crowd, less and less.

Another interview subject articulated both the patterns related to group formation and localism and his desire to no longer participate:

The top dogs, who are making their living by getting exposure, have set the tone. They have to get waves. They have to continually prove themselves. They have to take what they see as theirs to take. That's just part of the deal, and that's what the kids learn. . . . And once you do earn your spot in the lineup, you have to maintain it. And it's much more difficult than ever to maintain. It's done through pretty raw aggression—dog eat dog—truly. . . . I don't surf a lot of my old breaks because they're too crowded with aggressive locals. I still get waves, but I have to go out and mix it up, and it gets tense, and I don't enjoy that. (Bingham 2006)

Furthering this line of argument, where older surfers seem to gravitate away from the performance behaviors associated with localism, one of our interviewees surfs only in the solitary, noncompetitive, immersive style. He sees the experience of surfing in this manner as a *departure* from evolutionary struggle, and from activities related to "productivity": "So much of biological life is about competition, beating yourself, others, preserving your family unit, fighting against others, trying to get yours. All these things, so much of what one does on Earth, is productive in one way or another. I guess there's something about surfing that seems to me to be an expression of some element of pure delight with the world in which we find ourselves that is very special and unusual to me" (Duane 2006). This respondent never surfs in a group of locals and does not participate in the in-group/out-group rituals. Performing for crowds, competing for waves, sustaining their places in the lineup as part of the local group, all characteristics of the twenty-something surfers Waitt and Warren profiled, are all activities these thirty- and forty-somethings have lost interest in, suggesting that localism and the practices associated with it may be linked to life stage. In addition, these attitudes may also be linked to globalization, neoliberalism, and all its attendant effects of advanced technologies that enable older surfers—who often have conflicts related to family and work responsibilities—to be able to check surf conditions on the web rather than driving around for hours looking for a good spot. Improved technologies related to boards and wetsuits may also help compensate for diminished physical capabilities, allowing older surfers to surf much further into their life course.

Conclusion

As much as they have been critiqued for good reasons, globalization and neoliberalism have an ambivalent legacy. The increasing proximity of various races, ethnicities, and cultures because of diaspora and migration, which have brought significant changes to "local" contexts, has affected the specific instance of surfing localisms in ways that some may interpret as positive. Patterns that exclude women and anyone who is not traditionally "masculine" or is nonwhite have been a significant part of surfing localisms in the United States and Australia, and a global justice perspective that would question these practices has been facilitated to some extent by recent globalization patterns and the proximity to "others" they necessitate.

Similarly, for all its problems, localism can also be seen to serve a positive function related to care and safety. From an evolutionary perspective, localism is the manifestation of evolved forms for the production of sociality, and sociality is always based on some form of exclusion. As the work of Evers (2006, 2007, 2008), Waitt (2008), and Waitt and Warren (2008) has shown, localism serves as an important bonding mechanism and source of meaning for those who practice it, and those who are excluded from it often form their own groups, as in the groups of women who surf together (Comer 2010). Furthermore, our research suggests that localism is to some extent a behavior related to life stage, and older surfers may not want to "have to hustle and hassle for waves anymore."

From an evolutionary perspective, the exclusive behaviors associated with localism may be seen as an evolutionary hangover effect, the residue of evolved cognitive forms that shaped the behavior of our ancestors, but have not adjusted quickly enough to be effective in the current environment. The residual existence of these cognitive forms should not be taken as support for an argument that they therefore cannot change and the behavior produced by them should be tolerated but rather that, if we are aware of their function and effect on behavior, we may better be able to influence these historical cognitive tendencies to be more effective in the current context. Group bonding mechanisms evolved from earlier periods and continue to evolve, and the way neoliberalism, with its emphasis on the individual, has served to activate patterns generated by these mechanisms and change the behaviors developed in relation to them provides insight into deep history, as well as providing the certainty that these mechanisms will continue to change and evolve. Recent economic developments such as the crisis within the financial sector, growing unemployment, and ecological problems associated with decentralization, economies of scale, and long supply chains suggest a possible return to forms of local production and provide an even greater need for analysis of small group dynamics as localism gains prominence as an economic model. An evolutionary approach to behaviors like localism in surfing—forms of which are arguably replicated with differences in virtually every sport—adds a valuable dimension to the research models implemented in sport studies thus far. The field is wide open for such research.

NOTES

1. While there has been quite a bit of fieldwork on the perspective of the locals (Evers, Daskalos, Waitt), I have yet to turn up any fieldwork on the perspective of consumers who are newer to surfing except that done on women's surf camps in Krista Comer's *Surfing the New World Order* (2010). Comer's is a nuanced and careful reading of all the complications of this perspective and is the definitive book on the cultural implications and manifestations of women's surfing.

2. The domain-specific module theory that Kurzban and Leary rely on here is explained in more detail in Cosmides and Tooby 1994. See also Barkow, Cosmides, and Tooby 1992. For a general introduction to evolutionary psychology, see Buss 2008 and Dunbar, Barrett, and Lycett 2007. For an accessible overview of all things evolution, see Wilson 2007.

REFERENCES

Andrews, D. L. 2001. *Michael Jordan, Inc.* Albany: State University of New York Press.

Bale, J., and M. Cronin, eds. 2003. *Sport and Postcolonialism.* London: Berg.

Barkow, J., L. Cosmides, and J. Tooby, eds. 1992. *The Adapted Mind.* New York: Oxford University Press.

Bingham, C. 2006. Interview by the author. Santa Cruz, CA, May 8 and 10.

Booth, D. 2003. "Expression Sessions: Surfing, Style, and Prestige." In *To the Extreme: Alternative Sports, Inside and Out,* ed. R. E. Rhinehart and S. Syndor, 315–336. Albany: State University of New York Press.

Bra Boys. 2007. Directed by Sunny Abberton. Los Angeles: Berkela Films.

Buss, D. 2008. *Evolutionary Psychology: The New Science of the Mind.* Boston: Pearson Education.

Casey, S. 2006. "The Jaws Paradigm." *Sports Illustrated* 105, no. 5 (August 7): 64–70.

Comer, K. 2010. *Surfing the New World Order.* Durham, NC: Duke University Press.

Connell, R. W. 1995. *Masculinities.* Cambridge, UK: Polity Press.

Cosmides, L., and J. Tooby. 1994. "Origins of Domain Specificity: The Evolution of Functional Organization." In *Mapping the Mind: Domain Specificity in Cognition and Culture,* ed. L. Hirschfield and S. Gelman, 85–116. New York: Cambridge University Press.

Daskalos, C. 2007. "Locals Only! The Impact of Modernity on a Local Surfing Context." *Sociological Perspectives* 50 (1): 155–173.

Duane, D. 2006. Phone interview by the author. May 24.

Dunbar, R., L. Barrett, and J. Lycett. 2007. *Evolutionary Psychology: Human Behavior, Evolution, and the Mind.* Oxford: Oneworld Press.

Evers, C. 2006. "How to Surf." *Journal of Sport and Social Issues,* 30 (3): 229–243.

———. 2007. "Locals Only!" In *Everyday Multiculturalism Conference Proceedings,* ed. S. Velayutham and A. Wise, 1–7. Sydney: Centre for Research on Social Inclusion, Macquarie University.

———. 2008. "The Cronulla Race Riots: Safety Maps on an Australian Beach." *South Atlantic Quarterly* (Spring): 411–429.

Ford, N., and D. Brown. 2006. *Surfing and Social Theory: Experience, Embodiment, and the Narrative of the Dream Glide.* Abingdon, UK: Routledge.

Gray, J. 1988. *False Dawn: The Delusions of Global Capitalism.* New York: New Press.

Held, D., and A. McGrew. 2003. "The Great Globalization Debate." In *The Global Transformations Reader,* ed. D. Held and A. McGrew, 1–50. Cambridge, UK: Polity Press.

Kampion, D. 2003. *Stoked: A History of Surf Culture.* Salt Lake City, UT: Gibbs Smith.

Kurzban, R., and M. Leary. 2001. "Evolutionary Origins of Stigmatization: The Functions of Social Exclusion." *Psychological Bulletin* 127 (2): 187–208.

Maguire, J. 1999. *Global Sport: Identities, Societies, Civilizations.* Cambridge, UK: Polity Press.

Miller, T., G. Lawrence, D. Rowe, and J. McKay. 1999. "Modifying the Sign: Sport and Globalization." *Social Text 60* 17 (3): 15–33.

———. 2001. *Globalization and Sport: Playing the World.* Thousand Oaks, CA: Sage.

Nazer, D. 2004. "The Tragicomedy of the Surfer's Commons." *Deakin Law Review* 9 (2): 655–713.

Preston-Whyte, R. 2002. "Constructions of Surfing Space at Durban, South Africa." *Tourism Geographies* 4 (3): 307–328.

Pritchard, C., N. Quacquarelli, and C. Saunders. 2004. "Women in Surfing: Changing Equalities over a Life Course." Available at http://www.liv.ac.uk/geography/under graduate/fieldclasses/santacruz/SCRS2004/2004PDFs/Pritchard_et_al.pdf, 69–72.

Waitt, G. 2008. "'Killing Waves': Surfing, Space, and Gender." *Social and Cultural Geography* 9 (1): 75–94.

Waitt, G., and A. Warren. 2008. "'Talking Shit over a Brew after a Good Session with Your Mates': Surfing, Space, and Masculinity." *Australian Geographer* 39 (3): 353–365.

Walker, I. 2008. "Hui Nalu, Beachboys, and the Surfing Border-lands of Hawaii." *Contemporary Pacific* 20 (1): 89–113.

Warshaw, M. 2006. Phone interview by the author, May 11.

Weaver, R. 2006. Phone interview by the author, May 15.

Wilson, D. S. 2007. *Evolution for Everyone: How Darwin's Theory Can Change the Way We Think about Our Lives.* New York: Delacorte Press.

12

Free Running

Post-sport Liminality in a Neoliberal World

MICHAEL ATKINSON

(Pre)Script

Brian Pronger's (2004) call for "post-sport" physical cultures deeply critiqued the logic and practices of mainstream power and performance sports cultures. It equally drew attention to how modern sport is an exogenously determined social terrain, shaped more by educational logics, market capitalist discourses, military doctrines, scientific philosophies, and state health agendas than organic, moral, erotic, and humanistic uses of sport. In the modern(ist) sport lacunae, cultural ethics of consumption, competition, and rational body perfection indeed reign supreme in physical athletic practice over ideologies of freedom and ecstasy.

A post-sport physical culture is, by contrast, one that subverts modernist ideologies and practices outright, and is one in which corporeal dichotomies between sacred and profane bodies are smashed through subaltern and autonomous forms of athletic movement. Whereas traditional sports practices contain, discipline, and enframe physical bodies as resources to be deployed toward the attainment of competitive and performative sport outcomes, post-sport practices eschew such physical culture. Post-sports are at once moral, reflexive, community-oriented, green, spiritual, anarchic, and potentially Eros-filled physical cultural practices. They often simulate or mimic mainstream sports forms and techniques of play (e.g., swimming, running, cycling)—what Wheaton (2004) describes as the "residual" elements of modernist sport—but their individual or collective engagement bears little similarity. Post-sport is a connected set of sinewy athletic practices that are decisively anticommercial, cooperative over competitive, rejectionist of advanced material technology, socially inclusionary rather than hierarchical, process-oriented, holistic, and internally differentiated in their orientation and engagement. A post-sport physical culture values human spiritual, physical and emotional realization through athleticism beyond kinesiological boundaries.

Few have written about or explored what an existential sociology of post-sport might look like or how it might be theorized (Atkinson 2009). This owes largely to the fact that most sociocultural researchers have relatively ignored or discounted the empirical presence or social relevance of post-sport physical cultures. A narrative about the post-sport, physical cultural practice of free running is thus offered in this chapter. Free running is (or can be) an urban, guerrilla, and anarcho-corporeal brand of athleticism that imbibes and rearranges traditional sports forms including running, gymnastics, and martial arts. Free runners, often referred to as *traceurs*, move individually or in crews through city as if its architecture had been assembled as their sprawling jungle gym. Traceurs filter through the city streets in flamboyant, precarious, artistic, physically draining, and fluid streams. As a post-sport, free running often eschews the traditionally disciplined and governmental physical culture of mainstream sport, while offering an athletic modality of life predicated on the exploration of *ecstasis* (Heidegger [1954] 1977) and "limit experiences" (Foucault 1961). Free running intentionally excavates one's inner energies, desires, and forms of *puissance* (Pronger 2004) typically suppressed or inhibited in mainstream sports cultures. Free running may, using Pronger's (2004) terms, attempt to "de-eclipse" the cultural limits and rhizomatic boundaries of modernist sport.

Situating Free Running

The philosophical roots of free running as a physical cultural practice date back more than one hundred years. The late modern manifestation of free running is a particular offshoot of a style of training called "Hébertism." Hébertism emerged in the early twentieth century through the athletic philosophies and practices of French naval officer George Hébert.

A lifelong advocate of exploring intense physical training as a means of developing personal virtue, Hébert was particularly impressed by the physical development and body-environmental oneness of indigenous peoples he encountered across the African continent. While tutoring at the College of Rheims, Hébert innovated a path-breaking physical cultural lifestyle reflective of the indigenous cultural training regimens he encountered, which he dubbed the "Natural Method." Hébert's Natural Method typically placed practitioners in a wooded setting, wherein they would be instructed to run a course ranging from five to ten kilometers. Practitioners were simply told to run through the woods, over bushes, and through streams; climb up and down trees; and traverse fields. Students were also instructed, at particular time or distance points, to lift fallen logs, carry and throw heavy stones, or even hang from trees. Hébert believed that by challenging his students to practice basic human muscular-skeletal movements in "uncontrolled" settings, they would develop qualities of strength and speed toward being able to walk, run, jump, climb, balance, throw, lift, defend themselves, and swim in practically any geographic landscape. In a liminal and energetic sense, the Natural Method demanded that one possesses sufficient energy, willpower, courage, coolness, and *fermeté* to conquer any physical or mental obstacle. In a moral sense, by experiencing a variety of mental and emotional states (e.g., fear, doubt, anxiety, aggression, resolve, courage, and exhaustion) during training, one cultivated a self-assurance that would lead to inner peace.

Hébert became the earliest proponent of what the French call the *parcours* (obstacle course) method of training. The contemporary subcultural moniker "Parkour" (the first French term to be used in reference to urban free running) clearly derives from Hébert's use of the term *parcours(e)* and the French military term *parcours du combattant*. Hébert's Natural Method of training had a special impact on French military training in the 1960s. Among the French soldiers exposed to the Natural Method was Raymond Belle. After his tour of duty in Vietnam, Belle taught his son David the principles of the Natural Method. The younger Belle had participated in martial arts and gymnastics as a young teen and immediately took to the method. After moving to the Parisian suburb of Lisses, David Belle further explored the rigors and benefits of the Natural Method with his friend Sébastien Foucan. By age fifteen, Belle and Foucan developed their own suburban style of the Natural Method, which they termed "Parkour." Belle and Foucan gathered followers across Europe through the 1990s. By the end of the decade, Parkour became a global movement.

In the summer of 2005, I met and first started collecting data on two groups of free runners in Toronto and Hamilton, Canada. I launched the project by "hanging around" with a core group of four traceurs in an eastern borough of Toronto, and eight in a west-end suburb of Hamilton. While teaching an undergraduate course in Hamilton, Ontario, I first encountered a traceur who invited me to watch a training session involving thirteen traceurs in Toronto. Between July 2005 and December 2006, I found myself fully immersed in the local Hamilton crew, investigating the meaning of free running for the young men in the crew on a firsthand, participatory basis. A free runner in the crew invited me to travel with him to a training jam in Toronto, where I met six of his friends from two separate crews. During this time as well, I traveled to Toronto on almost a weekly basis to train in the city with them. Between 2005 and 2006, I interviewed more than thirty-two traceurs from these local crews to investigate their social constructions of the activity.

The general ethos among those observed and interviewed reflected stereotypical resistance subculture attitudes toward mainstream sport. Traceurs expressed disdain for highly organized, scripted, contained, authoritarian, competitive, and consumer-based sports experiences. They preferred free, creative and liminal forms of athletic movement. Among those with whom I interacted, free running is a method of personal exploration through movement, a do-it-yourself form of urban gymnastics, and a rejection of traditional ways of seeing and training a body. In terms of their "playing field," the traceurs described a need to poach and reinscribe local city space for their own purposes, and to use their natural environment to meet their own physical, emotional, and psychological needs. Most described free running as a way of life and an ideology permeating all of their thoughts and actions. In this chapter, I unpack a series of their ideologies and practices as typical, or at least representative of, a post-sport.

Post-sport Contexts

In order to make *sociological* sense of free running, one must appreciate the diffuse social, political, economic, and technological contexts in which free running is situated. In particular, free running has developed at a time when social and cultural boundary crossing proliferates. Boundary crossing is a hallmark of late modernism. Late modern arguments about the relationship between cultural fragmentation and boundary crossings are almost universally encapsulated by, in either subtle or overt ways, Jameson's (1991) and Lyotard's (1979) analysis of the "death" of Western institutional meta-narratives (i.e., as discourses that create and help reinforce social boundaries). From Jameson (1991) and Lyotard (1979), cultural studies theorists have drawn attention to how the fragmentation of work and the economy, education, religion, health and medicine, the arts, the media, and other institutional spheres produces a zeitgeist of distrust for any culturally overarching truth claim. Cultural meta-narratives such as belief in government, science, God, patriarchy or other totalizing frames erode in conditions of late modernity. The power to "know" and to produce "reality" is far more public than private and institutional. The splintering of cultural knowledge production, representation, and dissemination into a billion pieces leads to a looseness of (cultural) meaning in late modern, neoliberal social spaces.

Anderson's (1991) historiography of the emergence of imagined communities succinctly captures the ways in which symbolic representations of spatially recontextualized "We" cultural boundaries are tactically formed by actors in highly fragmented postindustrial nations to (at least attempt to) create ontological/cultural order and meaning. Wilson and Atkinson's (2005) examination of the Rave and Straightedge online communities in North America, for example, illustrates how groups of politically disenfranchised and alienated middle-class youth may actually never come into embodied, face-to-face interaction with one another. Yet participants understand members' biographies, lived experiences, and practiced lifestyles as communally bound. Virtual boundary lines provide meaning in the practitioners' everyday lives by creating common bonds and systems of representation with "others like me, out there." Chaney (1994) argues that the global (re)formation of culture as instances of local networking and bricolage increasingly produces a condition in societies of differentiation and boundary mixing (see also Maguire 1999).

Logics of neoliberalism, (mass) market consumption and reflexive representation extolled in Western nations further destabilize notions of dominant or authentic cultural identity in any space (Andrews 2006; Giddens 1991;

Hannerz 1996). As groups are mix-and-match cultural objects, images, and practices as part of "doing" unfettered reflexive identity, established-outsider cultural practices bounded in (definitive) space and time are replaced by the practice of situated representation and the aesthetics of everyday life. Spivak (1993) argues that the decentering of dominant cultural identities and exploration of polymorphous or "subaltern" cultures allows for a vast array of representational practices to be deployed within institutional landscapes.

From the preceding perspectives, and others not included, cultural life may be nothing short of the simulacra or "screened-out" society Baudrillard (1995) outlines. Muggleton (2000) describes the contemporary cultural milieu in Western nations as a "supermarket" of commodity and ideological style, where identities are not anchored in stable cultural images and systems of practice, but attached to transitory, fleeting, and polysemic texts, languages, and images. Straw (1991) describes the cultural movement toward reflexive identity construction and boundary disruption as a sociogenesis into "taste culture" lifestyles. In a world perhaps oversaturated by global commodities and cultural flows, one must thus question whether stable, intersubjective understandings of culture—as a system of problem solving, meaning making, and collective representation—are possible (Lash 1999).

Given, then, late modern expansion and the normativity of boundary crossings within neoliberal cityscapes, new doors have been opened for the exploration of nonmainstream sports forms, identities, and physical cultural practices. The destabilization of modernist boundaries ushered into popular culture through neoliberal fragmentation has paved the way for an eclipsing of traditional modernist physical practices including sport. Thus, questions about the "real," about one's inner desire, and of personal/collective essences within sport and elsewhere are unintentionally encouraged. If anything, late modern, neoliberalist life in Western contexts like the United States and Canada are fertile social spaces for exploring existential truth, desire, authenticity, and purpose through athletics.

The late modern emergence of free running as a physical practice is therefore contextualized in this chapter as dialogical with late modern, neoliberalist cultural trends and trajectories in countries like Canada. This chapter is broadly concerned with how neoliberalist ideologies and trends toward widespread cultural boundary crossing and the deregulation of modernist modalities of identification have become catalysts for the social exploration of post-sport physical practices like free running. The contemporary neoliberalist emphases on the destabilization of tradition, risk assessment, mix-and-matching, do-it-yourself health work, and hyperreflexive self-work have ironically and unintentionally created a social field for the free runner.

Free Running and Late Modern Liminality

Traceurs engage existential questions about the self in late modern social life through the post-sport, free-running lifestyles. Principally, they ask whether new sensibilities regarding the nature of existence and one's essence are to be learned through ascetically grounded forms of athleticism. They venture into free running and explore what multiple truths lie beneath the culturally, institutionally discursive framed self; in doing so, they describe a collective desire to tap knowledge of the existing body that precedes and cannot be wholly assembled through extant late modern discourses. Free running is a biopedagogical project designed to release what traceurs believe to be a life force, spirit, and desire underpinning all human existence, accessible to them only when the boundaries of their own selves are destabilized and crossed. Zen Buddhist scholars, as with other Chinese Buddhists, refer to such a force as the *qi* of life. In the Upanishads, Hindu philosophers refer similarly to the *prana*, or the vital, life-sustaining force of living beings and energy in natural processes of the universe. Pronger (2004) describes a similar life force as the essential *puissance* of the free, desiring body and spirit.

Traceurs in Toronto argued that in order to tap *prana*, and to explore aspects of the human condition in late modernity, the social self needs to be disassembled through innovative physical cultural practice, and a veritable emptiness created. Here, their practices curiously resemble a late modern, neoliberalesque, and secular brand of religious *self-mortification*. The painful and exhaustive ritual of free running reminds practitioners how physical and emotional (read ascetic) suffering can be a vehicle for self-discovery. Le Breton (2000), like Lyng (1990) has documented how members of the Western middle classes increasingly seek out symbolic death experiences in high-risk adventure sports. By using intense forms of physical training and movement involving risk, anxiety, pain, and injury, traceurs destabilize the socially ascribed self to which they have been heretofore attached and, they believe, limited by in everyday life. Their sense of athletic play is remarkable in this respect, as they search for alternative aesthetics, pleasures, and biopedagogies of truth through via self-detachment in seemingly "playful" physical cultural practices like free running.

Roger Caillois (1967) might argue that traceurs' quest to experience *qi*, *prana*, or puissance through self-mortification is a form of *ilinx*, a type of play that (through the overloading of the senses during action) produces physical and cognitive vertigo that people find exhilarating. *Ilinx* contexts are "based on the pursuit of vertigo and which consist of an attempt to momentarily destroy the stability of [self] perception and inflict a kind of voluptuous panic upon an otherwise lucid [culturally framed] mind. In all cases, it is a question of surrendering to a kind of spasm, seizure, or shock which destroys reality with sovereign brusqueness" (Caillois 1967, 23).

Caillois's (1967) notions of *ilinx* were refined and extended through conceptualizations of the "limit experience." The limit experience, principally emerging from the writing of Georges Bataille (1943) and Michel Foucault (1961), is a demandingly visceral and sensual event that dislodges the subject and decentralizes identity. The emotionally and physically intense limit experience pushes one's concrete sense of subjectivity to the margins, as it exposes and eclipses the cultural limits and parameters of the "possible" in one's mind. According to Fromm (1973), the limit seeker carries a deep-seated frustration with heavily circumscribed modalities of late modern life—to the extent that a desire to ritually annihilate the socially dominated and confined self (which, of course, enframes one's learned sense of the possible) stirs and is mobilized through self-sadistic activities. In *America*, Baudrillard describes the limit experience of the runner who hurtles forward in agony as a means of self-escape, and as an emblem of postmodern isolation:

> Decidedly, joggers are the true Latter Day Saints and the protagonists of an easy-does-it Apocalypse. Nothing evokes the end of the world more than a man running straight ahead on a beach, swathed in the sounds of his Walkman, cocooned in the solitary sacrifice of his energy, indifferent even to catastrophes since he expects destruction to come only as the fruit of his own efforts, from exhausting the energy of a body that has in his own eyes become useless. Primitives, when in despair, would commit suicide by swimming out to sea until they could swim no longer. The jogger commits suicide by running up and down the beach. His eyes are wild, saliva drips from his mouth. Do not stop him. He will either hit you or simply carry on dancing around in front of you like a man possessed. (1998, 118)

For Baudrillard and others, the limit experience is categorized by a stark measure of liminality, an immersion into a gray zone of self-identification where one encounters possibilities of the self unbound by traditionally modern sensibilities.

Liminality is, then, the space between the fore and the after of free running, a region of existentialism wherein a traceur becomes. The liminal free-running state is characterized by ambiguity, openness, and indeterminacy through action, as the sport is unshackled from the constraints of modernist sport participation and identity confirmation, but it is also produced within a broader social environment that, both intentionally and unintentionally, now encourages boundary crossing. One's sense of identity dissolves to some extent, bringing about disorientation in liminal boundary crossing oeuvres. Liminality is a period of transition where normal limits to thought, self-understanding, and behavior are relaxed—a situation that can lead to new perspectives. But as traceurs describe, the liminality of free running helps a person become something new, but something that at the same time the person always was in an inner, existential sense.

Over the course of time, I learned that free-running post-sport lifestyles are anchored by the pursuit of liminality (qua boundary crossing as self-exploration). As such, traceurs may coalescence around this pursuit as a form of collective cultural identification. Wheaton's (2004) classification of lifestyle sports smacks of the description of post-sport (in many respects) given in this chapter, especially regarding the idea that emergent liminal/lifestyle/post-sports cultures value a sense of *communitas* (Turner 1967) forged by common goals and signifying practices. During liminal free running, normally accepted social boundary differences between the participants, such as gender, race, social class, and physical ability are deemphasized or ignored. A social ethic of *communitas* emerges based on common humanity and equality rather than recognized hierarchy (so common in modernist sports cultures that exacerbate rather than dismantle rigid hierarchies of social identity). It is the physical exploration of collective liminality in a neoliberal society that binds traceurs together.

In sum, then, the liminal free-running state is characterized by ambiguity, openness, and indeterminacy. One's sense of grounded self-identity dissolves to some extent in a free-running "jam," bringing about a kind of vertigo or disorientation (voluptuous panic) for the traceur. Free running is practiced by particular traceurs as a liminal venture of self-annihilation on the one hand, and engagement of puissance on the other, in neoliberal city space. As traceurs seize tightly scripted city spaces as the context of *ilinx*, the streets and outer façades of the urban environment become part of the space between identities, roles, and status sets of free runners.

The Existential Free Runner

The so-called founding fathers of free running, Belle and Foucan, described the ultimate goal of practice as an exploration of a new way, mode, or sensibility toward urban living. Their free-running "way" was one chiefly resistant to the lethargy, physical atrophy, hyperindividualism, alienation, and unfettered consumption they perceived to be rife in the French middle classes. Belle and Foucan ostensibly believed that the late modern capitalist orientation of French (sub)urban life instilled great suffering, distress, anxiety, and physical malaise among youth cultures; in other words, it did not encourage youth to reflexively explore the puissance of an existential self. Resultantly, their free-running method of physical training extolled the need to explore the parameters of one's mind, body, and spirit (i.e., essence) with one's immediate environment through spectacular and risky forms of athletic movement. Engaging the urban environment as a traceur became a method of detaching from materialist modes of living and finding inner peace through liminal communion with the environment. In this respect, Toorock (2005) argued that Belle and Foucan found influence in their construction of the free-running "way" in Chinese Taoist doctrines (which, in the case of Belle, were through martial arts training as a youth).

At the bedrock of "original" free-running philosophy lies an emphasis on using spectacular forms of running and gymnastic movement to engage intense self-introspection and awareness. For the traceurs with whom I interacted, undertaking the practice of free running is almost uniformly a tool for fostering critical self-analysis. The individual deliberately thrusts himself or herself into physically demanding, exhilarating, and anxiety-producing contexts of athleticism in order to confront the barriers of one's personal abilities, limits, beliefs, and thoughts. By pushing their own limits, or undertaking edgework, traceurs seek to explore the nature of their own will, desires, and wants, which move them to act. The essence of one's true nature, they feel, is masked and perverted by socially created wants and desires in late modern, neoliberal cultures. It is further "polluted" by the denaturalized state of their urban living conditions. Steven (age twenty-one) said, "A good jam is one when I go to the limits of my body and mind and find out who I am, what makes me tick. It's the moment when you can get seriously injured when you come face to face with what is, and what's not, important in life." Owen added, "Being on the edge made me learn who I am at my core. When I look into myself, and confront my humanity, I realize what makes me function. It's when my body and mind are punished that I learn about me. In the middle of a run, when nothing else in the world matters and I'm tired, I realize how controlled and forced the rest of my life is . . . so a monkey vault or cat leap is not agony or pain to me. It's the rest of my life and what's in my head every day that makes me hurt." By placing oneself in patterned contexts of suffering (physical, mental, emotional, and sometimes social), seasoned traceurs reflect on what creates suffering in their lives. Ultimately, a free-running session or collective "jam" becomes a liminal medium for letting go of socially instilled conscious thoughts and worries and becoming simply at one with the present, a hallmark feature of post-sport physical culture.

Albert Schopenhauer's (1903) conceptualization of the human will in *The World as Will and Idea* helps deconstruct traceurs' interests in examining the parameters of their suffering through urban athletic edgework. With clear affinities to Buddhist thought on life as suffering (*Dukkha*), Schopenhauer argues that most lived experience is replete with suffering. Indeed, neoliberalist risk and self-responsibility discourses point to the myriad sources of suffering the late modern citizen encounters in everyday life. But for Schopenhauer (1903), suffering is created by motivations of the human will (*Die Welle*) and the actor's pursuit of the will's fickle desires. Human will motivates both the construction of the external world as a sea of potential targets of self-gratification, and self-utilitarian lines of corresponding action within it. By and large, what one desires, or seeks to avoid, relates not to what the inner existential self requires, but rather what one learns to want or fear. Suffering emerges when the will encourages the pursuit of desires, or to avoid fear, with unchecked urgency, force, energy, and drive (Schopenhauer 1903).

Writing quite some time before sociological critiques of capitalist modernity, late modernity, or neoliberalism, Schopenhauer (1903) ostensibly predicted that Western cultures would become commodity-fetishized, alienated, and eventually fragmented along neoliberalist lines. He noted that the socially learned desires (will) to accumulate social power, material goods, and other forms of capital in the external world produce alienation and vast human suffering regardless of one's class, gender, ethnicity, or age. Since individual consumptive desires of the will are never fully satiated or fulfilled (only ever replaced) in market-oriented cultures, members whose wills are externally determined and referent to market logics are damned to suffer. We might add that in the context of physical sport culture, as long as one's participation is determined along modernist sport lines, one is never truly free to become a liminal athlete.

Akin to Schopenhauer (1903), Pascal ([1670] 1995) tells us in *Pensées* that any moment of desire satisfaction or fear removal is only a diversion from the will and thus from suffering. An instance of fleeting happiness created through, for example, the purchase of an object, the eating of a meal, a sexual conquest, or achieving victory in modernist sport allows for only a temporary cessation of suffering. Schopenhauer (1903) believed that as long as the will is calibrated externally by the wants and desires (re)presented to people within the tactile (and we might add now, neoliberal) world, suffering continues. Examples in the world of sport abound. Pronger (2004), for example, described in his critical assessment of modern health and fitness how technoscientific discourses (*pouvoir*) map themselves onto human desires to move and "be" (i.e., shaping the will to become fit and fitter), radically altering one's body powers (puissance). When one's desire to be healthy/thin and fear of disease/fat is molded externally by neoliberalist discourses, one will endlessly chase new diets, workout regimens, fitness classes, and other aids to be stronger, leaner, and young looking—goals without terminus or point of conclusion.

For Schopenhauer (1903), freedom from suffering occurs when one learns to shed the concerns of the culturally learned, habituated will through ascetic, liminal lifestyles. Schopenhauer (1903) believed that by practicing asceticism (what the ancient Greeks called *askesis*) and denying the socially referent will what it wants as a vehicle of liminality, one could encounter the existential nature of one's suffering. At the point of realization (i.e., the relationship between the will and suffering), traceurs often experience what Buddhists call the state of *Pranja-Paramita* (beyond all knowledge). Schopenhauer further argued that through the practice of self-mortification and denial, one achieves a truly pleasurable state of "no will, no representation, no world."

Strict renunciation of the cultural will's desires and fears is, for Schopenhauer (1903) the only path for truly freeing one from suffering. A twenty-four-year-old traceur named Sam said to me that "part of being Parkour [a free runner] is dedication and sacrifice to the [inner] way. It [Parkour] demands a pure mind and body. To achieve that, well, it's about giving up the need for anything else . . . [t]o lose yourself and just move." When the individual finds a way to turn inward and understand the essence of how desire, fear, and suffering are related to social conditioning and cultural edicts, he or she locates what Schopenhauer (1903) referred to as the "life drive" (or what has been referred to earlier as *qi*, puissance, or *prana*). Tom, age twenty-six, said, "Someone who's done this [free running] and is one with it feels a ray of light shooting out from your middle all the time. It's energy, you know, pure force. It's fucking art and ecstasy and rapture all at once."

Schopenhauer concluded his metaphysic by arguing that even ascetics are never freed entirely from the trappings of the will; in this sense, free runners will always live in a "liminoid" state. Through daily introspection, denial of external needs, and intense self-discipline via physically rigorous activity, the culturally imposed will can be largely tamed by free runners but never conquered. Jim said to me:

> I get up in the morning and do yoga for an hour and a half. Then I walk an hour to work . . . silent meditation at my desk for forty-five minutes and then I eat. . . . I walk back home, slip into my gear, and then out the door for a couple of hours of hard, sweat-pouring, body-pounding training. . . . I find my peace of mind by blocking out all else. There is a joy beyond words in being that strict, but it's never perfect, never complete or indestructible. You can't live in that bubble forever, and you find the world gets under your skin every day.

During training processes, traceurs like Jim first learn soft and fluid gymnastic movements—simple jumps, rolls, and running forms. As they progress, they experiment with more physically demanding acrobatics that require intense mind-body oneness and what they call a "present absence" (freedom from all external thoughts and influences). Physically demanding jumps, vaults, and run speeds make traceurs suffer in order to understand the nature of suffering. Traceurs use demanding styles of movement to learn how to "let go" physically and psychologically—to trust the mind and body to move and to simultaneously abandon one's social desires and fears. Highly risky tricks—which jeopardize the physical self—are initiated to remind one to let go of the willing, discursively determined social self. Joe (age twenty-six) said, "Giving your body to a move teaches you to submit to movement. To feel the body move as a body, and not as a mind in a body."

Traceurs devote hours of training weekly to practice, learn how to find comfort in uncomfortable sessions, and spartanly reject most other physical cultural practices in their lives. A traceur named Patrick told me that as one becomes a free-running apprentice, everything else in one's free time is abandoned and all needs and wants apart from free running are systematically removed. Patrick's submergence into the free-running lifestyle extracted him from many of the sources of suffering in his life:

> Doing it day in and day out, and shifting my mind to only Parkour moves, didn't allow drugs or sex, or video games or online shit, or whatever, rule my head. It also teaches you to not be concerned with how much someone else has or what they are doing and only worry about what you can control . . . oh yeah, and to take the time to stop and enjoy the beauty around you. How can I say this? It's like the body can be the most beautiful thing on Earth because of how it can move. That kind of nature is beautiful, not things you buy in a store.

Traceurs like Patrick encourage others to appreciate the aesthetic beauty of the "free-running body" and to avoid judging one another about the quality or skill of any one's technique; such is the nature of a post-sport physical culture. The point of free running is to quiet the mind and mute the will/desire by running, jumping, crawling, and vaulting in beautifully athletic manners. As such, focus on the liminal self, and not the performative abilities and status/identities of competing others, underpins one's practice. Such an ethos helps build a sense of cultural collectivity among traceurs and yet dismantle modernist status hierarchies between them. Free running is, then, a bizarre variant on the cultural current of reflexive individualism and neoliberalism so characteristic of late modernity ideology.

Practicing with a number of traceurs in training sessions helps them develop an appreciation of "the way." As social movement, esoteric lifestyle, or post-sport—whichever conceptual moniker we employ—free-running enthusiasts derive much social support among "the own" (Goffman 1963). Traceurs are careful to point out that as a social practice, however, free running should not involve the typical level of socially disintegrative and self-concerned competition or interpersonal bravado evidenced in most male-dominated sports cultures. Each should explore the prospects of free running at his or her own pace, step by step, leap by leap. Their collective emphasis is to help one another learn free-running techniques and facilitate a deeper understanding of "the way."

For traceurs, then, one begins to understand the spiritual and aesthetic essence of Parkour when rigorous movement becomes phenomenologically experienced as effortless and natural; part of this progression is based on learning to feel comfortable with voluptuous panic. The idea of liminally flowing through the city as a traceur is ultimately represented through the basic moves of free running. Moves such as the cat leap, monkey vault, and cat balance, as they suggest, involve mimicking animal movements that enable traceurs to travel over and between urban obstacles. These somewhat seemingly "unnatural" athletic movements (i.e., jumping from wall to wall, cascading off a three-story building onto the ground, or balancing on a ledge two hundred feet in the air) can appear aesthetically beautiful. The physical and aesthetic appreciation of free running by traceurs draws parallels in these ways to modern dance and movement cultures such as the Brazilian dance/martial art capoeira.

Traceurs often articulate that when one learns to let go of external desire through free running, one's body feels permanently different—flexible, energized, relaxed, and vital. In Pronger's (2004) terms, one has encountered one's own existential puissance. Traceurs compare the physical and mental state of free running to water flowing over rocks, not only because of the grace and the artistry of water's movement over rocks in a stream but also because flowing water seems to effortlessly pass across, under, over, or around any environmental obstacle it encounters. Traceurs correspondingly use the term "flow" to describe feelings of *ecstasis* (Heidegger [1954] 1977) during a particular jam. Flow is experienced when one is immersed in a free-running jam to such an extent that absolutely nothing else matters (no self, no mind), and one moves and reacts on relative "auto-pilot." Such is the phenomenological nature of liminal space. From Schopenhauer's (1903) philosophical position, when a traceur's body is no longer the subject or object of the will, one flows. The concept of flow was popularized by the Hungarian psychologist Csikszentmihalyi in his book *Beyond Boredom and Anxiety* (1975). Central to the attainment of flow for traceurs is the physical and psychological match between the demands of free running and the abilities one possesses to move as "water." The match promotes harmony of mind and body through movement and relaxed effort, and can produce a Zen-like, meditative state for traceurs.

During a Parkour flow experience, traceurs relinquish self-consciousness and doubt and become one with the activity. This engenders a biopsychological state in which the traceur is rewarded solely by movement and flight, and not by extrinsic (competitive) or will-oriented rewards as typically found in physical sport cultures. Christian (age twenty) said, "I had [free] run for almost ten miles one day before I even 'came to.' I was in it so heavy, soaking up the heat and the wind and listening to the air in my lungs go in and out. Better than any artificial high, yeah." Although athletes in mainstream sports often refer to flow experiences as being "in the zone," the flow experience that traceurs in Toronto describe seems to be highly coveted but rarely attained by elite-level athletes—perhaps because of a psychologically embedded focus on reward and recognition from others (see Wheaton 2004).

In the analysis of symbolic "death sports," le Breton (2000) argues that the burgeoning interest in flow experiences in natural and untamed environments (versus contained gymnasiums or sports facilities) is a sign of a diffuse late modern anxiety and isolation, leading young urbanites like traceurs to search for a new physical cultural way. Once the basic free-running edge techniques are habituated and flow is experienced on a quasi-regular basis, a traceur often articulates feeling as if he or she possesses a total connection with the prediscursive or socially determined self, movement, and the surrounding physical environment. Temporarily losing the desire to rationally control one's self, honing flow through free running, and developing a sense of connection with the urban landscape is articulated as something purely aesthetic. Traceurs believe that most people are motivated and moved by forces/wills beyond their control (i.e., market capitalism and neoliberal consumption), and their inabilities to move as present, minded agents manifest into personal feelings of inadequacy, fear, and alienation (i.e., suffering). By contrast, traceurs speak about feeling energetically invincible during a particular jam. Gerry (age twenty-seven) claimed, "The greatest power in life comes from being in a state of no power, where you have no concern for it. Parkour [free running] means being an empty vessel ready to move, not being a ball of worry about what you don't have." Their feelings of invincibility stem not from a competitive mastery over the self, others, or the environment (so typical in modernist sports cultures), but as a result of their abandoned desire to achieve competitive, consumption-based goals. Such a sense of being through free movement, what Pronger (2004) calls puissance and what Buddhists call mindlessness, liberates one from fears of personal failure and social impotence and creates an enduring feeling of ecstasy for a traceur.

Csikszentmihalyi (1975) suggests that during a flow experience the rational, other-oriented, and calculating self is relinquished. Like Hebért's woodland training method, a *parcours* session is designed to stimulate doubts, anxieties, wants, fears, and frustrations so that they may be eventually negated or removed from one's mind-set. In this respect, it is a liminal ritual par excellence. Jack (age twenty-one) told me, "It's the truest statement ever. The only way to get rid of fear is to love fear. The more scared I get, the less scared I become. I hardly worry about anything anymore." Free running is a autotelic activity in which flow is perceptively liberating for the individual. Traceurs switch off peripheral distractions and focus solely on movement, breathing, and the body's natural rhythms.

Discussion: After Separation, before Amalgamation

The free-running, post-sport enthusiasts discussed in this chapter articulate how the separation from traditional athletic physical practices may be underpinned by a collective desire to explore the parameters of the self through self-mortification or limit experiences. In many ways, the structural and cultural conditions of late modernity have thrust them onto the city streets, to engage their truth-seeking through free running. In this way, their preference for non-modernist sport experiences smacks of a neoliberal desire for sensuous self-reflexivity and realization, organic community-building, and enduring personal truth.

But clearly, free running is not approached with the same ideological framework for all participants and is a socially contested practice. Free running has not been able to escape the commercializing, incorporative trappings of late modern culture. The practice, especially in Western Europe, has undergone proliferation into popular culture and sportization over the course of the past decade. The physical culture of free running presently teeters on the edge of sporting amalgamation as free-running sport federations emerge, official workout kits are developed, and instruction classes within fitness centers develop.

In many ways free running itself is situated within a liminal space in most Western nations in which it is practiced. It is not a purely authentic post-sport physical culture in any romantic notion; nor has it been entirely, or crassly, co-opted into the pop cultural vacuum. Traceurs instruct, however, that the present is always a liminal zone, and such a focus on the present, emergent, and as-yet-undefined forces one to consider the arbitrariness of notions of the separated or amalgamated physical culture. Free running's symbolic value as a post-sport physical cultural practice is squarely rooted, I would argue, in its emphasis on the ludic, artistic, inclusionary, and boundary-transgressing aspects of athleticism. Traceurs' collective emphasis on the role of athletic activity for exploring the existence of the self within the social and physical environments of one's everyday life clearly challenges dominant constructions of sport, health and well-being. Further, their call to experience the ecstasies of being via intense physical activity is indeed a direct challenge to the modalities of life regulated more by anestheticizing market-consumptive logics and governmentally disciplining risk discourses than by personal will and inner desires. Although easily dismissed by outsiders as a hedonistic and fleeting youth neotribe in sport, free running may expose and rupture the core ideological elements underpinning modern and late modern sport and athletics.

REFERENCES

Anderson, B. 1991. *Imagined Communities: Reflections on the Origins and Spread of Nationalism.* London: Verso.

Andrews, D. 2006. *Sport-Commerce-Culture.* New York: Lang.

Atkinson, M. 2006. "Straightedge Bodies, Civilizing Processes." *Body and Society* 12:69–95.

———. 2009. "Parkour, Anarcho-Environmentalism and Poiesis." *Journal of Sport and Social Issues* 33:169–194.

Bataille, G. 1943. *Inner Experience.* Albany: State University of New York Press.

Baudrillard, J. 1995. *Simulation and Simulacra.* Ann Arbor: University of Michigan Press.

———. 1998. *America.* London: Verso.

Caillois, R. 1967. *Les Jeux et le Hommes.* Paris: Gallimard.

Chaney, D. 1994. *The Cultural Turn.* London: Routledge.

Csikszentmihalyi, M. 1975. *Beyond Boredom and Anxiety.* San Francisco: Jossey Bass.

Foucault, M. 1961. *Madness and Civilisation: A History of Insanity in the Age of Reason.* New York: Random House.

Fromm, E. 1973. *Anatomy of Human Destructiveness.* New York: Holt, Rinehart and Winston.

Giddens, A. 1991. *Modernity and Self-identity.* Cambridge, UK: Polity Press.

Goffman, E. 1963. *Stigma.* New York: Prentice Hall.

Hannerz, U. 1996. *Transnational Connections.* London: Routledge.

Heidegger, M. (1954) 1977. "The Question Concerning Technology." In *Martin Heidegger: Basic Writings*, ed. R. Krell, 99–124. New York: Harper and Row.

Jameson, F. 1991. *Postmodernism or the Logic of Late Capitalism.* London: Verso.

Lash, U. 1999. *Another Modernity: A Different Rationality.* Oxford, UK: Blackwell.

le Breton, D. 2000. "Playing Symbolically with Death in Extreme Sports." *Body and Society* 6:1–11.

Lyng, S. 1990. "Edgework: A Social Psychological Analysis of Voluntary Risk-Taking." *American Journal of Sociology* 4:851–886.

Lyotard, J.-F. 1979. *The Postmodern Condition.* Paris: Bourgois.

Maguire, J. 1999. *Global Sport: Identities, Societies, Civilizations.* Oxford: Polity Press.

Muggleton, D. 2000. *Inside Subculture: The Postmodern Meaning of Style.* Oxford: Berg.

Pascal, B. (1670) 1995. *Pensées.* New York: Penguin.

Pronger, B. 2004. *Body Fascism: Salvation in the Technology of Physical Fitness.* Toronto: University of Toronto Press.

Schopenhauer, A. 1903. *The World as Will and Idea.* New York: Macmillan.

Spivak, G. 1993. "Can the Subaltern Speak?" In *Colonial Discourse and Post-Colonial Theory: A Reader*, ed. P. Williams and L. Chrisman, 66–111. New York: Harvester Wheatsheaf.

Straw, W. 1991. "Systems of Articulation, Logics of Change: Communities and Scenes in Popular Music." *Cultural Studies* 35:368–388.

Toorock, M. 2005. "Parkour Philosophy." American Parkour, June 9.

Turner, V. 1967. *Betwixt and Between: The Liminal Period in Rites of Passage.* Ithaca, NY: Cornell University Press.

Wheaton, B. 2004. *Understanding Lifestyle Sport: Consumption, Identity and Difference.* London: Routledge.

Wilson, B., and M. Atkinson. 2005. "Rave and Straightedge, the Virtual and the Real: Exploring On-Line and Off-Line Experiences in Canadian Youth Subcultures." *Youth and Society* 36:276–311.

III

Consuming Pleasure

Citizenship, Subjectivities,
and "Popular" Sporting Pedagogies

13

Out-of-Bounds Plays

The Women's National Basketball Association and the Neoliberal Imaginings of Sexuality

MARY G. McDONALD

The public persona and marketing prowess of the Women's National Basketball Association (WNBA) offers an instructive site to investigate the articulation of sexuality discourses with neoliberal capitalism. Since the inaugural season in 1997, national advertising campaigns have attempted to build audiences and secure profits via feminist-inspired themes of empowerment and by promoting the league's players as concerned citizens and/or hardworking mothers (McDonald 2000). The advent of the 2008 WNBA campaign included a league-sponsored orientation program for first-year players, a third of which was devoted to fashion and makeup advice. Among seminars on nutrition, media, and finances, the incoming players were taught "how to arc their eyebrows, apply strokes of blush across their cheekbones and put on no-smudge eyeliner to receive the right attention off the court" (Ryan 2008, 1). This focus on appearance is not a new strategy; the 2006–2007 WNBA "Have You Seen Her" campaign "features top players on the court and off, looking sexy and glam" (Bailis 2008, para. 8). And since the league's inception, considerable media focus has been placed on such players as then Los Angeles Sparks player Lisa Leslie, who also worked as a professional model during her basketball career (McDonald 2002).

In an interview with the *Chicago Tribune*'s Shannon Ryan, then WNBA president Donna Orender (Laurel J. Richie replaced Orender as president in 2011) explained the seminar's focus on makeup and fashion tips as important for teaching each new player "how to be a professional" (Ryan 2008, 1). WNBA executive Renee Brown similarly reveals the league's interest in promoting the players' "womanhood" as "mothers, daughters, sisters, nieces and entrepreneurs." According to Brown, "You're a woman first. . . . You just happen to play sports. They enjoy dressing up and trying on outfits, where back in the day, everyone just wore sweats. . . . Call it what you want. We're just celebrating their womanhood" (quoted in Ryan 2008, 1).

Self-identified feminist bloggers on the Internet have been quick to decry WNBA management's narrow conceptualizations of womanhood as synonymous with appearance. Instead many insist such a focus is more about "adherence to conventional femininity" ("Recent Sports Articles" 2008, para. 6), which typically also conjures dominant assumptions about players' presumed "sexual availability to men" (Gwin 2008, para. 20). Blogger accounts additionally denounced the homophobia behind beauty-based and mother-centered WNBA marketing campaigns, insisting that such strategies are ways to "blush out" and "gloss over" the lesbian presence within the league's playing force and fan base (Bailis 2008). Such insights are consistent with Banet-Weiser's (1999) claims about earlier WNBA marketing campaigns, which focus on the leagues' wives and mothers. In marketing beauty, motherhood, and maternity, the league is attempting to "situate itself within a long and conflicted history about women and sport and has attempted to assuage sponsors and fans that their sport, although professional and athletic, was not overly masculine" or lesbian occupied (Banet-Weiser 1999, 404). That is, storylines focusing on family and beauty "attempt to deflect attention away from athletic, forceful female WNBA bodies while also imagining women's sport spaces as heterosexual spaces" (McDonald 2000, 38). WNBA marketing accounts thus help reaffirm heteronormativity via institutionalized practices that "legitimize and privilege heterosexuality and heterosexual relations as fundamental and 'natural' within society" (Cohen 1997, 440). This process in turn reifies notions of sexuality as static, stable identities rather than as fluid, contingent sets of practices embedded in power relations (Cohen 1997).

While heteronormative discourses continue to function as the "public face" of the league, closer scrutiny reveals another process at work within local WNBA communities: individual teams such as the Los Angeles Sparks and the Seattle Storm have used particular promotions and cross-marketing events to court lesbian fans. Such strategies also tap into broader niche marketing trends designed to secure the "pink dollar." Even the New York Liberty, who were once protested by "Lesbians for Liberty" via a "kiss-in" for not reaching out to lesbian fans (see McDonald 2008), are involved. The Liberty's marketing and outreach efforts now include gay and lesbian organizations, and the team has "worked with and recognized the New York LGBTQ Center and PFLAG, donated gear for fundraisers and sponsored an annual Human Rights campaign event" (Polen, Chauvin, and Warnock 2008, para. 16).

In this chapter I employ the strategy of contextual cultural studies to explore WNBA league and team marketing strategies. Such a theoretical and methodological approach recognizes that the WNBA, like all cultural forms, exists as "a concrete, historically produced, fractured totality made up of different types of social relations, practices and experiences" (Andrews 2002, 114). And while the WNBA generates a "relatively autonomous field of effects," such meanings and effects "are always overdetermined by the network of relations with which it is articulated" (Andrews 2002, 114). Constitutive of a diverse array of late capitalist sensibilities, the WNBA also exists as one element of the

National Basketball Association's (NBA's) highly mediated global presence as a "vehicle of multi-revenue stream capital accumulation" (Andrews 2006, 98). In this way, WNBA marketing campaigns articulate—that is, are linked to—intensified movements promoting entertainment and consumption. WNBA marketing narratives in turn emerge from a particular historical moment where neoliberal politics and policies continue to champion pro-business agendas, minimal state "interference," privatization, domesticity, and personal responsibility (Duggan 2003). The result of this confluence, as I demonstrate in this chapter, is that WNBA national and local team accounts promote a dominant cultural and economic agenda where questions of sexual citizenship are recast via the marketplace as private issues of individual choice. This use of contextual cultural studies to critically explicate and (re)contextualize particular late capitalist characteristics and WNBA marketing narratives thus further reveals that "neoliberalism in fact *has* a sexual politics, albeit a contradictory and contested sexual politics" (Duggan 2002, 177).

Normalizing and Integrating the (W)NBA Spectacle

Originally exclusively controlled by the NBA and mainly financed through corporate sponsorships, ticket sales, television rights, and licensing, the WNBA is the longest-standing U.S. professional team sport league for women. And even though by 2011 non-NBA owners controlled more than half (Connecticut Sun, Los Angeles Sparks, Seattle Storm, Tulsa Shock, Chicago Sky, and Atlanta Dream) of the twelve franchises, the league's inception and future prospects are inextricably tied to the NBA. This is the case even through the unsettling times of a contentious labor dispute and lockout initiated by the NBA owners before the 2011–2012 NBA season.

And while the NBA clearly possesses a more culturally visible and economically potent profile and thus continues to be cast as the WNBA's "financial angel and chief advocate" (Heath 2006), closer inspection reveals a symbiotic relationship in which the WNBA is one element of the NBA's global capitalist presence as a "multifaceted marketing and entertainment conglomerate" (Andrews 2006, 95). And there is additional evidence to suggest that despite contraction in the number of WNBA franchises and amid a post-2008 economic recession, this conglomerate's local and global reach is still quite considerable. For example, in the summer of 2008, then Baltimore mayor Sheila Dixon was approached by a group interested in starting a new franchise if the city agreed to build a new arena. At times various media accounts also report that the WNBA is considering San Francisco, Albuquerque, Denver, and Tennessee as possible locales for future growth (Klingaman 2008). Thanks to the negotiating power of the NBA, ABC and ESPN2 offered twenty-one U.S. national telecasts of WNBA games during the 2008 season, while an additional seventy games were shown on NBA TV, the league's own television network, further demonstrating the symbiotic relationship between the two entities. It is also worth mentioning that the WNBA's current and future economic prospects are not just limited to North America. During the 2008 season the WNBA featured games and programming in thirty-two different languages extending to 203 countries, while WNBA rosters were filled with twenty players from fifteen different countries ("Rosters Set" 2008).

In 2008, the NBA signed television contract agreements with several organizations in diverse locales, including Argentina, Bulgaria, Jamaica, Pan Africa, South Korea, and China, to televise WNBA games. The advent of the 2008 season additionally saw the first WNBA marketing partnership in China with Peak, a popular athletic shoe company ("WNBA and Peak" 2008). During the 2011 campaign, Boost Mobile served as a marquee marketing partner alongside several other notable sponsors: Adidas, American Express, Bacardi, BBVA, Coca-Cola, EA Sports, Gatorade, Hotel Indigo, Hewlett-Packard, Nike, Russell, Sanofi Aventis, Sanofi Pasteur, and Spaulding ("2011 WNBA Partners" 2011).

David Andrews's (2006) analysis of late capitalist principles that orient twenty-first-century sport and culture is particularly instructive for understanding the NBA-WNBA interrelationship and in making clear the conditions of its emergence. The NBA exists as part of late capitalist culture industries' intensified movement toward "the accumulation of capital via the manufacture of popular practices and pleasures for mass audiences" (Andrews 2006, 91). Part of this trend is the "Disneyization" of culture and economics, where the principles and philosophies of this famous corporation "are coming to dominate more and more sectors of American society as well as the rest of the world" (Bryman 1999, 26; Andrews 2006). One element of this process is the dedifferentiation of consumption, in which marketing practices and purchasing options "associated with different institutional spheres become interlocked with each other and increasingly difficult to distinguish" (Bryman 2003, 155). In the case of the NBA, films, videos, game broadcasts, and web content serve as "pivot points of cross-promotion through which the corporation markets its subsidiary—or perhaps more accurately, derivative—array of consumer products and experiences" (Andrews 2006, 93). Thus, whereas the Disney Corporation consists of blockbuster movies, theme parks, hotels, sport teams, and so forth, each of which promote the other, the NBA has similarly parlayed network and playoff game coverage and the enticement of athletic personas into its own universe of "20 divisions, including NBA Properties, NBA Entertainment, NBA International and NBA Ventures" (Andrews 2006, 95). The WNBA is one additional entity of this global creation, with the NBA serving as an "integrative fulcrum" of a "multifaceted consumer entertainment complex" (Andrews 2006, 97).

Nowhere is this interlocking sensibility more evident than on the NBA website (http://www.nba.com), which was accessible during the 2010 NBA Championship finals (June 7, 2010). At the top of each of the site's pages are links to related sites, including the WNBA, NBA Global (which features multilingual international sites for Brazil, Canada, China, France, Germany, Italy, Japan, Hong Kong, Taiwan, the United Kingdom, and the United States, as well as links with content in Spanish), the D-League (the NBA's developmental or "minor" league), and the NBA store, which sells merchandise and also offers connections to the WNBA store and the D-League store. Each of the respective stores—NBA, WNBA, and D-League—features a variety of items including team and league T-shirts, jerseys, hats, and videos. In this way, the league, "its teams and players can be experienced in multifarious commodified forms" (Andrews 2006, 100).

While the NBA, WNBA, Global, and D-League sites have individual content related to their particular entity, there is also, at times, considerable sharing of content, images, and links. For example, immediately before the 2008 Beijing Olympics, the NBA home page featured stories and images of the men's and women's U.S. Olympic basketball teams, composed entirely of NBA and WNBA players, as well as features about NBA and WNBA stars competing for other nations. Some of this content was additionally distributed on the WNBA and NBA Global sites. Video coverage of pre-Olympic games and behind-the-scenes action with the U.S. teams were offered on both the NBA and WNBA sites thanks to NBA TV broadband and such sponsors as Kia Motors and America Online.

Corporate advertising is integrated throughout all the websites with advertisements and special sponsorships. During the 2008 season, on the WNBA web page fans had the opportunity to receive updated information on the T-Mobile Race to the WNBA MVP award and the Hanes-G WNBA Rookie Report. WNBA corporate partners Spaulding, Russell athletic wear, and Craisins joined with the primary sponsor, Discover Card, to help enable the Home Court Challenge, in which nine- to fourteen-year-old participants register online and then physically compete in basketball skills competitions with the chance of winning $20 Discover cards and a new basketball court for the six participating cities. The Adidas I Design Contest, also featured on the NBA All-Access link, allows fans to design a WNBA shooting shirt, with the winning entries to be worn by WNBA teams on fan appreciation day. Several WNBA corporate partners also feature prominently on the NBA and Global website as Gatorade Winning Finishes allows fans to choose their favorite last-minute NBA plays. The Game Time Playbook with Lamisil features NBA flash animation and game footage, which documents on-court play.

Numerous other examples of the WNBA-NBA cross-promotional emphasis abound and are visible on the websites. For instance, more than ten current and former WNBA players made appearances at more than twenty-five different events during the 2010 NBA All-Star game festivities in Dallas, Texas. The San Antonio Silver Stars' Becky Hammon and Angel McCoughtry of the Atlanta Dream played in the celebrity all-star game held before the NBA all-star game. The Shooting Stars competition was won by a Texas team featuring current NBA Dallas Mavericks star Dirk Nowitzki, the WNBA's Hammon, and NBA legend Kenny Smith. During those 2010 festivities, several WNBA stars joined with NBA and NBA D-League players to conduct fitness clinics for more than 1,000 youth within the Dallas, Arlington, and Fort Worth areas. A similar philanthropic emphasis is evident throughout the year as both the WNBA and

NBA support community outreach via WNBA Cares and NBA Cares, with the WNBA sponsoring Read to Achieve programs designed to combat global illiteracy and featuring WNBA player appearances promoting literacy at NBA stores throughout the league. The Jr. WNBA/Jr. NBA programs are both designed to develop a lifelong love of basketball—and presumably to also cultivate future (W)NBA consumers—through a philosophy that emphasizes relationship building at school, home, and work; teamwork; and positive participation. Both junior programs promote local skills competitions and summer camps for youth.

Because of the rising number of independent owners, the WNBA and NBA also share marketing and promotional expertise via an NBA-sponsored team marketing business operations staff, which offers assistance to various WNBA franchises. As then WNBA president Orender explains, "We've created a kind of SWAT team that really specializes in analysis, on-site support, ticket sales, sponsorship sales, marketing, database management" (Steeg 2007, para. 24).

That the WNBA is a significant part of the NBA's interlocking and cross-promotional apparatus is further revealed by NBA commissioner David Stern's statement that the NBA has "a good strategic reason to support the WNBA, which is the growth of viewership and fans for basketball" (quoted in Heath 2006, E01). That is, the league's investment in the WNBA pays dividends in numerous ways beyond the bottom line, or, as Stern sees it, "The NBA support for the WNBA is a rounding error of our marketing expenses overall. And what we have is the premier women's sports league in the world. We view [the WNBA] as a serious investment in marketing to women" (quoted in "WNBA Teams" 2007). Stern also outlines additional benefits of the WNBA to the NBA in noting, "There's compelling logic . . . to have 20 dates [in an NBA arena] in the summertime, to have additional programming for your regional sports network and to have goodwill ambassadors in the community promoting the sport of basketball among boys and girls and fans of all ages" (quoted in Heath 2006, E01). According to Stern, "The WNBA is precisely within the strategic bull's-eye of whatever we do" (Heath 2006, E01).

This stated notion of the WNBA as strategic to the NBA's promotional aims lends further credibility to Andrews's (2006) analysis of the NBA as exemplifying movements within late capitalism. For example, Stern's characterization of the WNBA-NBA relationship is suggestive of Andrews's usage of Guy Debord's (1990) notion of an integrated spectacle. This means that the entertaining (W)NBA "intertextual economy of media productions" (Andrews 2006, 94) exists as both "capitalist product and production" (Andrews 2006, 93), which colonizes popular consciousness and orients broader understandings. Stated differently, the spectacle—as exemplified by the distribution of commodities and experiences by such multinational conglomerates as Disney and the NBA—"has spread itself to the point where it now permeates all reality" (Debord, quoted in Andrews 2006, 100) and "seeks to direct the consuming public toward an uncritical engagement with, and thereby perpetuation of, its own virtuosity" (Andrews 2006, 100).

While not always successful, attempts at maintaining this spectacular process require ongoing cultural work and emotional labor (Bryman 2003; Andrews 2006). In an effort to create emotionally salient identifications, the (W)NBA promotes a diverse array of basketball celebrities and common tropes routinely associated with everyday life, including "triumph and tragedy, falling and redemption, success and failure, and heroism and villainy" (Andrews 2006, 99).

Since the inception of the league, the (W)NBA marketing machine and a compliant media have mobilized images of beauty, liberal feminism, and idealized family life to advertise the league and its players (McDonald 2000). In this way, the WNBA is also analogous to Disney in advancing fantasies, happiness, and pleasures rooted in traditional gender ideologies, innocence, individualism, domesticity, and racial harmony. And yet, much like Disney, behind this innocence lies a multinational corporation whose narratives function in conservative and normalizing ways (McDonald 1996).

For example, Los Angeles Sparks teammates Lisa Leslie and Candace Parker, also known during the 2008 season as the "dunking divas" (at that time as the only two players to have then "dunked" a basketball during a WNBA game), were then two of the most visible players in the league (Leslie retired at the end of the 2009 season, while representations of Parker continue within this framing). Both were often represented as glamorous models and players negotiating the demands of basketball with traditional performances of femininity. Leslie has been quoted as saying, "My motto is: You don't have to look like the boys to play with the boys or play a 'boy sport.' I really embrace the fact that I'm feminine, that I am a woman, and I love that. But I also love the fact that I can go out there and beat a guy, and play hard and gain respect based on my physical ability" (quoted in "Lisa Leslie's a New Mom" 2009, para. 13). On the day she entered the league, Parker posed holding a Sparks uniform jersey with her fiancé, Sacramento Kings forward Sheldon Williams. The *Sacramento Bee* newspaper reported that Williams "could be seen kissing Parker just after she was selected by the Los Angeles Sparks" (Amick 2008, C7).

Late in her career as a new mother to daughter Lauren, Leslie was represented as balancing the demands of baby and basketball as she "joined the ranks of an estimated 25 million American women who juggle responsibilities at work and home" (Peter 2008, 21). Leslie is said to have once left a pregame warm-up routine to head to the stands to hold Lauren in an effort to quiet her down (Peter 2008). This is just the latest example of a touting of motherhood that has been a focus of the league from its inception. On Mother's Day 2008, the Minnesota Lynx issued a release on their web page, noting that "Mother's Day also has a little extra meaning for the Minnesota Lynx organization as one of our players, center Vanessa Hayden-Johnson, celebrates her first Mother's Day. Vanessa missed playing last season with the Lynx, but giving birth to her first child, daughter Zyon Brianna, on June 3, 2007, more than made up for the time away from basketball" ("Happy Mother's Day" 2008, para. 1). To commemorate Mother's Day in 2010, the WNBA web page featured an interview with former WNBA player and current San Antonio Silver Stars head coach

Sandy Brondello—then the mother of a three-year-old, with a second child expected in June—discussing the trials and tribulations of being a coach and mother in the WNBA (Brondello 2010). These and other portrayals are similar to the storyline of former WNBA star Susie McConnell Serio, who was represented by the league and the media as completely dedicated to the well-being and development of her four children (McDonald 2002).

The broader perceptions of the predominantly African American playing force and the league as "raceless" suggest that such images of traditional femininity, family bliss, and heteronormativity do not encourage critical engagement with the ways in which racialization operates in these representations (McDonald 2000). As I have argued elsewhere, images of idealized domesticity and femininity continue to circulate in the league, suggesting that WNBA marketing and media discourses help promote traditional gender beliefs and the nuclear family at a time when norms of whiteness and "family values" continue to be mobilized by conservatives to demonize the poor, especially poor women of color (McDonald 2002). Too frequently WNBA players are represented as moral, concerned, and dedicated to hearth and home and thus exemplify several conservative and normative imaginings while additionally implying that such bliss is a matter of personal choice, perseverance, and individual responsibility. In this way, WNBA representations function as the antithesis to stereotypical representations of poor women, especially poor single mothers of color who have been scapegoated by conservatives for all sort of social ills. Within the politics of representation and these attempts to project an idealized image of womanhood, WNBA accounts thus link to a powerful historically specific conservative project. In the quest for capital accumulation, this project also articulates "racialized notions of reproduction and racist discourses in the United States that serve to direct attention away from" racist and sexist social structures as well as pro-market, neoliberal policies, which continue to widen the gap between the rich and the poor while assaulting the welfare state (McDonald 2002, 389). Popular WNBA accounts thus join similar individualistic, idealized, and Disney-like representations that promote "family values," which in turn ideologically serve to demonize poor "black women, Latinas and recent immigrants as irresponsible mothers and in the case of single mothers, failed heterosexuals" (McDonald 2002, 389).

The Perfect Storm? Homonormativity and the WNBA

While the nuclear family, femininity, and beauty continue to be promoted as the "public face" of the WNBA, on the local level many teams have seemingly contradicted this heteronormative and homophobic focus by attempted to court lesbian fans. For example, the Los Angeles Sparks have hosted and attended events at a 12,000-member lesbian club in Los Angeles, GirlBar. Several franchises advertise in gay publications, and Atlanta Dream players reportedly marched in a gay pride parade in an effort to reach out to fans. Teams such as the Chicago Sky and Washington Mystics have sponsored events with the gay and lesbian Human Rights Campaign (HRC). A night with the New York Liberty, cosponsored by the HRC, is listed on the Greater New York HRC website, complete with details on how to purchase a game ticket. In 2008 the Seattle Storm reported securing a marketing arrangement with Olivia, a lesbian cruise line and resort company. In 2010 the Storm featured a promotional campaign on their team webpage offering discounted tickets to interested fans to help commemorate gay pride in Seattle.

These relationships suggest that just as the WNBA is enmeshed in the political and cultural economy of Disneyization, so too is it also part and parcel of late capitalist niche advertising trends that seemingly promote tolerance and espouse greater gay and lesbian visibility through the market. These are in turn part of the late capitalist push to create new consumers. "So at the same time that producers need national markets, they have also needed specialized markets and it is in this context that 'diversity' has been both a social value (however superficially) and an economic imperative" (Chasin 2000, 109). WNBA team marketing campaigns have thus emerged alongside such increasingly commercialized entities as gay and lesbian tourism, the globalization of Pride/ Mardi Gras/Gay Games mega-events, popular television shows such as *Queer Eye for the Straight Guy*, and the promotion of themed gay villages with trendy bars and restaurants (Bell and Binnie 2004). These images, spaces, and events are similarly rooted in a historical moment when neoliberal policies and politics championing the superiority of the free market have merged with sensibilities of tolerance to produce fresh strategies of profit maximization, which frequently mute elements of social movement concerns through an uncritical celebration of diversity (McDonald 2008; Chasin 2000). This means that given the rise of the consumer culture, increasingly sexual politics and civil rights "are recast as economic liberties" (Chasin 2000, xvii).

In this way, Olivia's slogan of the "feel free" is not about achieving the equality in difference, historically argued for within gay and civil rights movements, but rather represents a recasting of equity as available through the purchasing of products and experiences. This pursuit of entertainment, pleasure, and mainstream values has similarly influenced contemporary gay politics and gay rights organizations, which have shifted their focus from broader social criticism to the pursuit of "access to institutions of domestic privacy, the 'free market' and patriotism" (Duggan 2003, 179).

Thus while many may support then "out" lesbian and WNBA player Sheryl Swoopes's endorsement contract with Olivia, Samantha King (2009) argues that this arrangement between the player and the corporation is suggestive of this broader trend, or what Lisa Duggan (2002, 2003) refers to as the new homonormativity—that is, "a politics that does not contest dominant heteronormative assumptions but upholds and supports them while promoting the possibility of a demobilized gay constituency and a privatized, depoliticized gay culture anchored in domesticity and consumption" (Duggan 2002, 179). Indeed, despite notable challenges, including Swoopes's own narratives that work outside binary understandings of sexuality, popular storylines of Swoopes "coming out" in 2005 were most often framed via assumptions of homonormativity and whiteness. That is, initial accounts repeatedly positioned the visibility gained via an individual (celebrity athlete) coming out as key to overcoming homophobia in the WNBA and broader culture. While recognizing the symbolic power of visibility, King (2009) instead notes that such an exclusive political strategy does not automatically lead to the end of violence or the granting of political rights; nor does it acknowledge that white lesbians are differently positioned in relationship to lesbians of color. In other words, dominant narratives surrounding Swoopes, an African American, did not significantly shed light on the ways in which homophobia interacts with race and class relations beyond simplistic, stigmatizing, and homogenizing narratives of homophobia in the black community. Instead, many commentators repeatedly praised Swoopes's endorsement contract with Olivia as a sign of progress, noting, for example, that when tennis great Martina Navratilova came out in 1981 she lost numerous endorsement deals. Yet this narrative of progress and economic individualism does little to disrupt contemporary economic inequalities and instead serves to naturalize late capitalist relations and the attendant processes of Disneyization. In a similar way, the then sustained focus on Swoopes's monogamous relationship with partner Alicia Scott places the story firmly within normative, more culturally safe and thus more salable understandings of gay and lesbian relationships (King 2009). While this case allows us to investigate the workings of homonormativity more broadly, it should also be noted that in the summer of 2011 Swoopes subsequently announced her breakup with Scott and engagement to boyfriend Chris Unclesho, thus troubling conventional understandings of sexuality as fixed, although dominant narratives of this announcement were typically articulated with heteronormative frameworks.

While new narratives may be emerging with regard to Swoopes, similar sensibilities to the Olivia campaign are still at work among local WNBA team marketing campaigns. On the one hand, such campaigns help make lesbian bodies intelligible in a sporting site that continuously produces narratives of heteronormativity. And yet, on the other hand, they frequently do so in ways that cast lesbian concerns as commensurable with the market and domesticity. This is a notion consistent with broader neoliberal sensibilities seeking to privatize public concerns. And increasingly, national gay and civil rights organizations themselves have come to rely on corporate sponsorship and fundraising as ways to get their messages heard. This has certainly been the fate of the centrist HRC, which has actually bought hundreds of tickets to WNBA games as a method of both bringing more lesbians into the organization and using WNBA social events as fund-raising opportunities (Hetter 2001). One key effect of such a commercialized focus is that culturally palatable issues of equality, nondiscrimination, and access have come to the fore. Issues of difference and cultural transformation—once hallmarks of gay and lesbian and civil rights struggles—have faded into the background.

The complicated politics of capital and sexuality are vividly seen in representations of the Seattle Storm's many outreach and marketing efforts. Indeed, the "Storm has ads in gay and lesbian publications and a partnership with the Greater Seattle Business Association, the lesbian, gay, bisexual, transgender chamber of commerce. It hosts a Gay Pride Group Night and has invited the Seattle Gay and Lesbian Chorus to sing the national anthem" (Davila 2006, para. 18). In April 2008, the Storm teamed with Olivia, charters of the Seattle-based cruise line Holland America (with $4.7 million in annual sales), to form a multiyear partnership agreement. In the press release announcing the partnership, Olivia general manager Lisa Henderson explained:

> We are particularly excited about this relationship because of the tremendous brand of the Seattle Storm. . . . I've spent more than two decades working with some of the top consumer and technology companies in the world ranging from Nestle to MSN, and I am so impressed by the incredible fan and community support for the Storm. We have many customers who are loyal Storm fans and we anticipate our relationship with the Storm will bring us many new customers as well. ("Storm Cruises" 2008, para. 2)

The press release goes on to provide brief details about the nature of the relationship, noting that it "will include in-game entertainment, with emerging musical artists performing at Storm games during halftime and a trip giveaway on an Olivia Cruise line for two lucky Storm fans. Olivia will also promote their Olivia Fling™ four day party and play weekend packages built around Storm home games" ("Storm Cruises" 2008, para. 5).

These multiple and other cross-promotional marketing efforts have helped produce a diverse following of Storm fans and potential spaces from which to discuss broader cultural and economic politics. And yet, such efforts mirror neoliberal trends where entertainment and business interests reign. Just as with the broader WNBA league promotional campaigns, such an intimate connection with the market typically results in a depoliticized agenda so that the manifestations of heteronormativity—in its various guises across gender, race, class, and nation—are not challenged in any significant way, just as the strategies of late capitalism are naturalized (McDonald 2008). One additional but significant effect is the emergence of a new form of governance. That is, as political rights become confused with economic liberties, such as via WNBA team marketing strategies, the nation-state is increasingly "let off the hook" in addressing questions of full and inclusive sexual citizenship (Puar 2006). Stated differently, "the nation benefits from the liberalization of the market, one that acts to proffer placebo rights to LGBTIQ consumers who are hailed by capitalism but not by state legislators" (Puar 2006, 77).

Not-So-Final Thoughts: Imagining Other Possibilities

It is important to note that neoliberal capitalism is not a uniform project but is instead tied to local formations and histories (Duggan 2003). As this analysis suggests, the WNBA must be understood as embedded within the spectacle-producing promotional strategies of late capitalism via the NBA, and discourses that also advocate conservative sexual politics via the processes of heteronormativity and homonormativity. Reading the WNBA national and team marketing strategies side by side additionally reveals that binary understandings of heterosexuality and homosexuality are inadequate, as both performances are implicated in capital accumulation, and some heterosexuals and some gays and lesbians are more highly valued economically and culturally while others such as "the welfare queens, "punks," and "butches" are marginalized (Cohen 1997). In offering sanitized accounts, the WNBA narratives do little to challenge dominant neoliberal assumptions while bolstering a broader agenda of privatizing and the depoliticization of bodies and pleasures. One consequence of these confluences is that they focus attention away from subjugated knowledge and alternative ways of being.

Such an understanding encourages us all to rethink our relationship to commodified sports such the NBA/WNBA, for the pleasures that they potentially promote are enmeshed in inequitable social relations. In contrast to the (W)NBA's vision of social life are competing views, some of which may be helpful in mapping an ethical way forward. For example, those interested in social justice may consider advocating a perspective that recognizes the commodified, intersectional, and discursive character of power. Such a perspective recognizes multiple regulatory modalities beyond simple binary formulations such as heterosexual over gay and lesbian. It additionally recognizes that multiple economic and cultural "systems of oppression are in operation and these systems use institutionalized categories and identities to regulate and socialize" (Cohen 1997, 478). I hope that this discussion about the WNBA will generate further dialogue on alternative representations and ways of living beyond neoliberal imaginings of sexuality.

REFERENCES

Amick, S. 2008. "Kings Notes: Williams Stood by Parker on Her Big Day." *Sacramento Bee*, April 12, C7.

Andrews, D. L. 2002. "Coming to Terms with Cultural Studies." *Journal of Sport and Social Issues* 26 (1): 110–117.

———. 2006. "Disneyization, Debord and the Integrated NBA Spectacle." *Social Semiotics* 16 (1): 89–102.

Bailis, K. 2008. "Can't Make It Up: WNBA's Marketing Tool Is Makeup." *Keyboard Quarterbacks* blog on Newsday.com, May 6. Available at http://blogs.trb.com/sports/KBQB_blog/.

Banet-Weiser, S. 1999. "Hoop Dreams: Professional Basketball and the Politics of Race and Gender." *Journal of Sport and Social Issues* 34:403–420.

Bell, D., and J. Binnie. 2004. "Authenticating Queer Space: Citizenship, Urbanism and Governance." *Urban Studies* 41 (9): 1807–1820.

Brondello, S. 2010. "Sandy Brondello: Head Coach and Mom." WNBA, May 7. Available at http://www.wnba.com/features/from_playing_coaching_parentin_2010_05_06.html.

Bryman, A. 1999. "The Disneyization of Society." *Sociological Review* 47 (1): 25–47.

———. 2003. "McDonald's as a Disneyized Institution." *American Behavioral Scientist* 47 (2): 154–167.

Chasin, A. 2000. *Selling Out: The Gay and Lesbian Movement Goes to Market.* New York: Palgrave.

Cohen, C. J. 1997. "Punks, Bulldaggers, and Welfare Queens: The Radical Potential of Queer Politics." *GLQ* 3:437–465.

Davila, F. 2006. "Storm Is a Refuge: Lesbian Community Feels Accepted At WNBA Team's Games." *Seattle Times*, August 11. Available at http://community.seattletimes.nwsource.com/archive/?date=20060811&slug=storm11.

Debord, G. 1990. *Comments on the Society of the Spectacle.* London: Verso.

Duggan, L. 2002. "The New Homonormativity: The Sexual Politics of Neoliberalism." In *Materializing Democracy: Toward a Revitalized Cultural Politics,* ed. R. Castronovo and D. D. Nelson, 175–194. Durham, NC: Duke University Press.

———. 2003. *The Twilight of Equity? Neoliberalism, Cultural Politics and the Attack on Democracy.* Boston: Beacon Press.

Gwin, S. 2008. "The WNBA's New Marketing Strategy." *Silence Is Betrayal: A Feminist Blog,* May 12. Available at http://silence-is-betrayal.blogspot.com/2008/05/wnba-and-beauty.html.

"Happy Mother's Day from the Minnesota Lynx." 2008. WNBA, May 11. Available at http://www.wnba.com/lynx/news/happy_mothers_day_080511.html.

Heath, T. 2006. "A Matter of Value Instead of Profit: Despite Losses, WNBA Seen as Key to Sport's Growth." *Washington Post,* July 12, E01.

Hetter, K. 2001. "Playing for Keeps." *Curve* 11 (6). Available at http://backup.curvemag.com/Detailed/140.html.

King, S. 2009. "Homonormativity and the Politics of Race: Reading Sheryl Swoopes." *Journal of Lesbian Studies* 13 (3): 272–290.

Klingaman, M. 2008. "Opinions of City's WNBA Viability Vary." *Baltimore Sun,* July 12. Available at http://www.baltimoresun.com/sports/nba/bal-sp.wnba12jul12,0,1667102.story.

"Lisa Leslie's a New Mom." 2007. *Essence,* December 16. Available at http://www.essence.com/2007/07/27/lisa-leslies-a-new-mom/.

McDonald, M. G. 1996. "Michael Jordan's Family Values: Marketing, Meaning and Post-Reagan America." *Sociology of Sport Journal* 13 (4): 344–365.

———. 2000. "The Marketing of the WNBA and the Making of Post-Feminism." *International Review for the Sociology of Sport,* 35 (1): 35–48.

———. 2002. "Queering Whiteness: The Peculiar Case of the Women's National Basketball Association." *Sociological Perspectives (Special Issue on Gender and Sport)* 45 (4): 379–396.

———. 2008. "Rethinking Resistance: The Queer Play of Visibility Politics, the Women's National Basketball Association and Late Capitalism." *Leisure Studies* 27 (1): 77–93.

Peter, J. 2008. "Day in the Life of Lisa Leslie." Yahoo! Sports, July 21. Available at http://sports.yahoo.com/wnba/news?slug=jo-leslie072108&prov=yhoo&type=lgns.

Polen, T., K. Chauvin, and K. Warnock. 2008 "Give Me Liberty." *Go Magazine,* July 9. Available at http://www.gomag.com/article/give_me_liberty/.

Puar, J. 2006. "Mapping US Homonormativities." *Gender, Place and Culture* 13 (1): 67–88.

"Recent Sport Articles Remind Us That Female Athletes Are (Sexual and Maternal) Women First." 2008. *Don't Ya Wish Your Girlfriend Was Smart Like Me?* May 11. Available at http://smartlikeme.wordpress.com/?s=wnba.

"Rosters Set for 2008 WNBA Season." 2008. Our Sports Central, May 16. Available at http://www.oursportscentral.com/services/releases/?id=3641832.

Ryan, S. 2008. "WNBA Offers Advice to Rookies: Trying to Expand Fan Base by Marketing Its Players, the WNBA for the First Time Offers Rookies Lessons in Fashion and Makeup." *Chicago Tribune,* May 4, 1–2.

Steeg, J. L. 2007. "New Owners Stake Claim in Overhauling WNBA." *USA Today*, June 12. Available at http://www.usatoday.com/sports/basketball/wnba/2007-06-11-new-owners_N.htm.

"Storm Cruises into a New Season with Olivia Travel." 2008. Seattle Storm, April 10. Available at http://www.wnba.com/storm/news/olivia080410.html.

"2011 WNBA Partners." 2011. WNBA. Available at http://www.wnba.com/news/sponsors.html.

"WNBA and Peak Announce Marketing Partnership." 2008. WNBA, February 16. Available at http://www.wnba.com/features/peak_mccarvillebuescher_080216.html.

"WNBA Teams in a State of Flux: Comets' Transition Sign of Times in League, Where Attendance Is Down but Ratings Are Up." 2007. *Houston Chronicle*, January 19. Available at http://www.chron.com/disp/story.mpl/sports/bk/bkw/4482102.html.

14

Pedagogies of Fat

The Social Currency of Slenderness

JESSICA M. FRANCOMBE
MICHAEL L. SILK

The neoliberal reinvention of "welfare" that promotes choice, personal accountability, consumerism, and self-empowerment as ethics of citizenship while at the same time masking social forces (Ouellette and Hay 2008a, 2008b) that position people into the dejected borderlands of consumer capitalism has culminated in the everyday practices of physical fitness and weight loss becoming implicit within technologies of self-governance and the personalization of health. Within this chapter we explicate the powerful role played by the self-help genre of reality television in the making and remaking of citizens (Ouellette and Hay 2008a, 2008b). We interrogate *The Biggest Loser* (*TBL*) as a highly politicized and contested space that educates subjects, disciplines the noncompliant, and becomes part of a moral economy that differentiates between "good" and "bad" citizens.

Real Governmentality: Reality TV as a Cultural Technology

We are not alone in theoretically grounding the genre of reality television within this neoliberal conjunctural moment; finding solace and instruction, we owe a debt in particular to the work of Laurie Ouellette and James Hay (2008a, 2008b), Toby Miller (2008) and Gareth Palmer (2003). Drawing inspiration from Foucault's conception of governmentality—the processes through which individuals shape and guide their own conduct (and that of others) and are instilled with a willing acquiescence to surveillance and self-monitoring, and in which capillary-like institutions (such as the media) do the work of government

A version of this chapter was previously published as M. Silk, J. Francombe, and F. Bachelor, "The Biggest Loser: The Discursive Constitution of Fatness," *Interactions: Studies in Communications and Culture* 1, no. 3 (2009): 369–390.

agencies in encouraging a focus on issues of responsibilization and self-discipline (Andrejevic 2004; Foucault 1991; Palmer 2003)—our theoretical grounding involves looking beyond the formal institutions of official government. In essence, we are emphasizing the proliferation and diffusion of the everyday techniques through which individuals and populations are expected to reflect on, work on, and organize their lives and themselves as an implicit condition of their citizenship (Ouellette and Hay 2008b).

Techniques of governmentality circulate in a highly dispersed fashion by social and cultural intermediaries and the institutions (schools, social work, and the medical establishment) that authorize their expertise. This involves techniques, technologies, and discourses that are constructed to render problems thinkable and hence governable—that conceptualize various populations to be subject to governance and that characterize the different spaces and technologies of government in, through, and around which political agendas are operationalized and institutionalized (MacLeod, Raco, and Ward 2003; Rose 1999). These initiatives stress the problems deemed appropriate to be governed, the sites within which these problems come to be defined, the diversity of authorities that have been involved in the attempts to address them, and aspirational (technical) devices that aim to produce certain outcomes. These are practices and processes of governance that are, in many respects, far removed from the political apparatus as was traditionally conceived (Rose 2000). As Peck and Tickell (2002) eloquently surmise, these are *new* technologies of government that fashion *new* institutions and modes of delivery within which *new* social subjectivities are being fostered. They are extensions of the logic of the marketplace that socialize individualized subjects and discipline the noncompliant. Following Rose (1999), we are talking here about an array of other practices for shaping identities and forms of life: advertising, marketing, the proliferation of goods, the multiple stylizations of acts of purchasing, cinemas, videos, pop music, lifestyle magazines, television soap operas, advice programs, talk shows, and reality television.

Television and other popular media are an important—if much less examined—part of this mix in that they too have operated as technologies called on to assist and shape citizens (Ouellette and Hay 2008a, 2008b). For instance, Ouellette and Hay observe that in a given week of television programming, the viewer engages with numerous examples of

> how to succeed at work (*The Apprentice, America's Next Top Model, Project Runway*), how to win a desirable mate (*The Bachelor/Bachelorette, Joe Millionaire*), how to be stylish (*What Not to Wear*), sophisticated (*Queer Eye for the Straight Guy*) and personable (*Beauty and the Geek*), how to survive natural and manmade challenges (*Survivor, Big Brother*), how to nourish our health and psyche (*The Biggest Loser, Starting Over*), how to put our personal finances in order (*Suze Orman, Mad Money with Jim Cramer*), how to enhance an ordinary house or car (*Trading Spaces, Pimp My Ride*), how to transform our bodies (*Extreme Makeover, The Swan,* the Fitness

Channel), how to maximise sexual performance and intimacy (*Sex Inspectors, Berman and Berman*), how to manage our families and domestic lives (*Supernanny, Wife Swap*, the Food Network), how to prepare for emergencies (*Storm Stories, What Should You Do?*), and even how to restore blighted cityscapes (*Town Haul*). (2008a, 3)

In this sense, and as part of an array of private-sector interests capable of socializing subjects, television operates as a "powerful public pedagogy" (see H. Giroux 2003), an educator of sorts, or what Ouellette and Hay (2008a) term a "cultural technology," in the production of good citizens. As Rose (1996, 58) put it, television is able to translate the "goals of authorities" into guidelines for enterprising living.

Significantly, Toby Miller (2008) highlights that the genre of reality TV is suffused with the deregulatory nostra of individual responsibility, avarice, possessive individualism, hypercompetitiveness, and commodification, which are all played out in the domestic sphere rather than the public world. Embroiled as a component of the "outsourcing" and outreach through which the current stage of liberal government rationalizes public welfare and security, reality television offers a cultivation of sorts, a space for putting things in order to ensure maximum productivity and the achievement of goals (Ouellette and Hay 2008a)—that is, instruction on how the little, banal tasks of daily life link knowledge and skill to the administration of one's household, family, and self. Reality entertainment facilitates the articulation of lifestyle governance and everyday regimes of self-care. Acting as a kind of "meme" (Redden 2008), the proliferation of the genre points to the changing relationship between television and social welfare, in which television viewers are molded into active and healthy citizens—part of the "'reinvention' of government in neoliberalist capitalist democracies" (Ouellette and Hay 2008b, 471). Indeed, Nick Couldry (2008) suggests that reality television is the secret theater of neoliberalism, given that it obscures the links to "labor" conditions—"self-work"—normalized under neoliberalism.

Providing *education* in the better use of symbolic resources, citizens are *given the chance* to achieve social recognition—whether that is in showing off a beach body, a home, or an obedient toddler or pet or learning how to become a (moral) entrepreneur (Hollows and Jones 2010; Redden 2008; Stevenson 2010). Thus, and in a neoliberal conjuncture where civic well-being is commodified and tied to market imperatives, reality television aids in the production of a privatized system of welfare, one that is significantly more aligned with a market logic than was the case in the previous states of welfare (Ouellette and Hay 2008b).[1] The political rationality of contemporary reality programming, then, acts as a resource for achieving the changing demands of citizenship in our national ordinary (Bonner 2005, cited in Lewis 2008). In our present moment, "the impetus to facilitate, improve and makeover people's health, happiness and success through television programming is tied to distinctly neoliberal reasoning about governance and social welfare" (Ouellette and Hay 2008b, 471).

As the proliferation of the genre itself may suggest, responsibility for self and family development and control on television is separated into its constituent parts (cleaning, caring, education, eating, exercising, manners) and subjected to surveillance and judged accordingly (Skeggs and Wood 2008). By repeatedly distinguishing, defining, and attributing moral values—middle-class values at that (see Palmer 2003)—to specific practices, the schema of this moral value becomes apparent as it identifies people in need of transformation: predominantly working-class populations (Skeggs and Wood 2008). Within this context, cultural technologies such as television, which have always played an important role in the formation of idealized citizen-subjects, become instrumental as resources of self-achievement in different and politically significant ways (Ouellette and Hay 2008a). In sum, then, reality television has emerged in a context of deregulation, welfare reform, and other attempts to reinvent government as the quintessential technology of citizenship of our age.

The Biggest Loser: The Social Currency of Slenderness

Know that by deciding to take charge of your health and lose weight, you're doing the right thing. Try and focus on what you're gaining—years of your life, more energy, and a sleeker look—instead of what you're missing out on. Losing is not about beating yourself down, but lifting yourself up. (NBC 2008)

Reality television does not often venture into the territory of serious illness, yet it isolates the travails of drinkers, smokers, junk food addicts, the overweight, the sedentary: those who can be seen as victims of their own lifestyle choices (Redden 2008).[2] Following those in disciplines such as medical geography and public health, it is important to take a critical and interdisciplinary approach to thinking about obesity lest we reify and legitimize the stigmatization, medicalization, and labeling as deviant of some bodies, spaces, and places (Evans 2006; Jutel 2005). With Evans (2006), this does not mean a questioning of medical knowledge per se, but thinking through how the ideas about "right" and "wrong" and the association of guilt with some practices, are formed through and rooted in the discourse surrounding medical interpretations of obesity. In the next section of this chapter, then, as we address the mediated discursive constitution of corpulence, we are referring to specific (re)presentations of fat bodies that (re)produce ideas about (im)morality (Evans 2006; Longhurst 2005).

Previously, scholars such as Mosher (2001) and Sender and Sullivan (2008) have suggested that when larger people are portrayed on television, fat women are frequently figures of fun, occasionally villainesses, often "bad" examples of people with no self-control or low self-esteem (take, for example, Maggie's mother in the film *Million Dollar Baby*). Conversely, fat men tend to appear in situation comedies (*Drew Carey, The King of Queens*) in which the impotence of patriarchal power invests male fat with an effeminacy or sensitivity against the dominant heterosexual masculine ideal (see also Greenberg et al. 2003; Himes and Thompson 2007).

Despite the perversity of focusing on television—so castigated for both its fatty commercial content and its role as a sedentary social technology (see, e.g., Jenvey 2007)—in this chapter our interests lie with addressing how a program that lauds physical activity discursively constitutes (ill) health. Somewhat rearticulating Palmer (2003), we interrogate the way in which reality television, centered on weight loss, organizes discourse that forms the citizen-subject.

NBC's *The Biggest Loser* allows its contestants, as well as the viewing public, to take charge of their health and lose weight. Via an established reality television series, a comprehensive website, and a cornucopia of new social media interfaces, individuals can attend boot camps; post diet blogs; attach pictures to the *Biggest Loser* gallery; learn recipes from the new *Biggest Loser* cookbook; listen to the *Biggest Loser* workout mixes; join the *Biggest Loser* club; access the *Biggest Loser* meal plan; purchase from the *Biggest Loser* store; sign up for the *Biggest Loser* weight-loss League; "like" *The Biggest Loser* on Facebook; "follow" *The Biggest Loser* on Twitter; stay at the *Biggest Loser* ranch and resort spa at Fitness Ridge, Utah; play *The Biggest Loser* on Wii or Nintendo DS consoles; download the *Biggest Loser* "app," featuring a fitness tracker and healthy recipes; and subscribe to receive weight-loss text alerts direct to a mobile phone. The show debuted on NBC in the United States and at the time of writing is entering its twelfth season. With subtle local adaptations pointing to glocal resonances (see Ritzer 2004), the format can be viewed in twenty-two media territories,[3] including in fourteen countries in the "Arab World" version (*Ar Rabeh ElAkabar*), India (*Biggest Loser Jeetega*), the Philippines (*The Biggest Loser: Pinoy Edition*), Brazil (*Quem Perde Ganha*), the Netherlands (*De Afvallers*), Australia, the United Kingdom, and Asia. Recruiting male and female applicants—often from the lower middle classes (Sender and Sullivan 2008)—who "desire" to lose weight, personal trainers (Jillian Michaels, Bob Harper, and Kim Lyons) provide "expertise" to resculpt and reshape the bodies of participants. In terms of viewing figures, the show regularly attracts more than ten million viewers in the United States (although there does appear to be a slight decline in numbers in 2011), boosts ratings of follow-on shows, and has consistently delivered the desired eighteen-to-forty-nine age group to NBC (see, e.g., Gorman 2010). In the U.S. version of the show, which forms the essence of our commentary,[4] the contestants spend up to three months at a Southern California ranch where they eat, live, and work out before returning home to finish losing weight (Sender and Sullivan 2008).

The program is highly structured, offering a narrative flow that fragments each episode into a series of distinct scenes. The first scene of each episode starts by introducing the viewers to the contestants and giving a heartfelt, emotive recap on their background. The second segment centers on exercise sessions, meal times, weekly weight loss, and physical challenges. The climactic conclusion—the money shot (Grindstaff 2002)—is the dramatic "weigh-in" where the weight loss of each contestant is revealed and the problems of the self are solved through a quick and simplistic solution (Sender and Sullivan 2008). Of course, all these narratives are left "hanging" through the insertion of commercial breaks, another element that enhances the drama (and indeed marketization) of each broadcast. This climax provides the conclusion to each week, offering a storytelling element designed to engage the audience to feel a part of the experience (Gruneau, Cantelon, and Whitson 1988). The "internal composition" of the show offers a definitive rhythm and facilitates the governance of "underlying messages" (Gruneau, Cantelon, and Whitson 1988). *TBL* then presents individuals' experiences and understandings of their embodied selves as fat, thin, underweight, overweight, obese, or normal. It centers on "correcting" the obesity "disease" through structured, competitive weight loss achieved through diet and exercise. From this juncture, we mobilize *TBL* as emblematic of reality media products that conduct the corpus toward particular ends. Our discussion is concerned with the mediated discursive constitution of fatness—the biopedagogies of obesity that do little but pathologize anything other than the white, heterosexual, militarized, gendered, and slender normalized consumer-citizen.

Biopedagogies of Fatness: "What Have You Done Today to Make Yourself Feel Proud?"

Obesity is a complex potpourri of science, morality, and ideological assumptions—an embodied and situated experience as much as it is a biomedical condition (Herrick 2007). It is writ large on our bodies, a part of the intimate private sphere that has now been marshaled into public spaces "for the operation of power, using it to reinforce arguments of normalcy against the ruptures of social and cultural tensions" (Skeggs and Wood 2008, 559). *TBL* is emblematic of the individualization of obesity discourse; it suggests that individual choices—or, more accurately, wrong choices—must be solved through an ethic of responsibilization and subject self-sufficiency. Emphasis is placed on the contestants' careers, lifestyles, targets, and previous experiences. Framed within a soundtrack announcing, "What have you done today to make yourself feel proud," the focal point of the narrative is based on how the individuals will "get with the program" and lose the weight they have gained. Eschewing any mention of support (or indeed lack thereof) from health care services, or indeed any views the contestants may have on the obesity epidemic, *TBL* individualizes fatness. This approach is most visibly evident in the workouts that the contestants attend daily. The personal trainers situate all the blame on the individuals for being obese; the way out, the escape from this condition, is a renewed focus on the self and the need to take "100 percent responsibility." Insults, if not outright victimization and humiliation (McRobbie 2004; see also Bonner 2008), revolve around exercise, presumably to motivate the contestant: "Being fat is your fault"; "You are letting down your family." These lipoliteracies—the dominant cultural meanings attached to "fat" bodies in Western societies (Graham 2005)—circulate within *TBL* around themes of inactivity, laziness, defiance, lack of control, moral failings, ill health, unhappiness, food addiction, lack of willpower, inability to manage desire, and lower than normal levels of intelligence (Crandall 1994; McMurria 2008; Murray 2008).

TBL conceives the fat body as a site of numerous discursive intersections, the effect of normative beauty standards, health, gendered (hetero)sexual appeal, self-authorship, moral fortitude, fear of excess, and addiction—roughly translated as white, male, heterosexual, and able-bodied. A cared-for, thin body is recognized as reflecting control, virtue, and goodness (Bordo 1993; Evans 2006; Evans, Davis, and Rich 2008; Rich and Evans 2005). To be fat in *TBL* is to conceive the individual as unfit and unhealthy, a moral failure (Hearn 2008). In *TBL*, unquestioned medical narratives bring these normative discourses and assumptions together under the ontological umbrella of the obesity epidemic (see Gard and Wright 2005). That is, anxieties about body difference constitute both medical narratives of endangering health and narratives concerned with the fraying of the (moral) fabric of society (Murray 2008), amounting to a moral panic.

In essence, and drawing on the Cartesian separation of mind and body, fat and obese bodies are conceptualized as unruly, uncivilized, dangerous, and in need of control, the result of inaction or complacency. *TBL*, of course, provides the fictive solution; abject bodies are, quite literally, put on trial to ascertain if they can be induced to become fully participating consuming, proper subjects in the neoliberal economy (see, e.g., McMurria 2008). In this sense, *TBL* operates as part of what Rail (2009) terms the biopedagogies of obesity discourse that act to regulate life and bodily practices, focus on controlling bodies to reduce obesity, and work to protect everyone from the risks of obesity—a discourse that places individuals under constant surveillance and presses them toward monitoring themselves. In this regard, as a discursive biopedagogy, *TBL* does little but pathologize and ascribe obesity as deviant (Rail 2009) yet perversely offers the lucky contestant the way out.

Public Pedagogies of Normalcy: "Do You Have the Willpower?"

TBL provides a life intervention that circulates the techniques for a government of the obese self; it is a technology operating as part of the ethics of neoliberal citizenship. As the insecure "other" is massaged into the narrative, viewers get helpful hints about how to become productive, stable, culturally legible individuals (Hearn 2008; Sender and Sullivan 2008). *TBL*, then, is part of an overtly pedagogical process that positions some bodies as more equal than others (Evans 2006; Hearn 2008; Jutel 2005); it "diffuse[s] and amplif[ies] the government of everyday life, utilising the power of television (and its convergence with new media) to evaluate and guide the behaviours of ordinary people, and, more importantly, to teach us how to perform these techniques on ourselves" (Ouellette and Hay 2008b, 472). In saying *something* about the reshaping of citizens' bodies—a *something* concerned with the transformation of faltering, uneasy, anti-neoliberal citizens—there is, as Jameson (1981) reminds us, something left out. This is the unconscious of the text, the silences, that which is not said (Johnson et al. 2004). *TBL* neglects to offer any narrative on the health implications relating to intense workouts, extreme dieting, mental or physical challenges. *TBL* does not deem itself responsible or accountable for informing the public on healthy living or how to reduce the occurrence of obesity; there is no narrative concerned with any of the classed and social dimensions associated with the epidemic. This latter point is epitomized by the lack of information on the right foods to consume and the explicit verbal and visual demonization of the wrong foods, those that are most readily available in poorer neighborhoods. As Sender and Sullivan's (2008) audience research on *TBL* has suggested, it is far more gratifying to see contestants' sweat and tears than it is to see a lesson in how to gauge the calorie content of various foods. In this sense, *TBL* enacts the reasoning that people who are floundering can and must be "taught" to develop an ethic of self-sufficient citizenry (Ouellette and Hay 2008b), maximizing their capacities for normalcy, happiness, and mental stability, and refuting reliance on a public safety net. As inferred through the work of Jones (2008), *TBL* is a panoptic—self-regulating, disciplining, normalizing—part of the new formations of welfare that mask the social forces that position citizen-subjects (Ouellette and Hay 2008a, 2008b).

Accordingly, responsibility for obesity is firmly placed at the level of the individual; contestants are held accountable for being obese and constantly reminded of this throughout the program. Herein lies the winning neoliberal formula for the biggest losers. Obese bodies represent the failure of will in a culture in which self-direction and choice are paramount; fatness is proof of and produces laziness, a lack of willpower, and a failure of self-esteem (Sender and Sullivan 2008). The opening montage's text challenges, "Do you have the willpower?" and each episode tests contestants' will through the show's challenges (competitions of physical endurance) and its temptations (trials of psychological commitment). *TBL* provides a discursive space for learning balanced and "disciplined" eating habits and for carrying out intense physical exercise regimes; at the same time, it tempts contestants with vast displays of decadent food to test determination and willpower (Ouellette and Hay 2008a, 2008b). Notably, *TBL* format allows contestants back into their domestic sphere where their choices and will are tested by the temptations of their own larders and lifestyles. Further, and as with other reality shows whose narratives are predicated on the pathologization of the inadequate ability to make choices (Redden 2008), *TBL* offers a seductive, if not peccable, repast in the form of a vacation.

In the season that formed the focal point for this analysis, the contestants are taken to Jamaica for a week, the narrative centering on their will to avoid the tempting food and drink on offer. Following Sender and Sullivan (2008, 580), this narrative strategy positions the ideal neoliberal citizen, governed by free will and consumer choice, in relation to the figure of the contestant/addict (as long as we are able to put aside the contradictions and problems with exercise addiction), unable to cope with the endless freedom on offer: "The neoliberal moment that demands self-disciplined, self-directed, willing citizens both produces and requires their nemesis: the undisciplined, food-addicted, lazy fatty." In this sense, the discursive constitution of the healthy body politic and those who do not properly belong (Butler 1993; Zylinska 2004) operates as a form of ocular authoritarianism that renders even more visible—and thus subject to control and regulation—those bodies that are deemed or perceived to threaten normalized, consumerized, healthy bodies and social practices (see Silk and Andrews 2006, 2008).

The idealized, normalized citizen-subject in *TBL* is an entrepreneur of the self given the exaggerated capacity afforded to the correct use of commodities in the improvement of individuals lives (Bonner 2008; Redden 2008). In the process of making one's body anew, *TBL* offers a whole array of consumables and autocritique in place of adequate social security (Miller 2008). Consumption is transformed into a form of citizenship, options for living become bound with regimes of status values, and the codes of propriety that are depicted as leading to personal betterment are largely reflective of consumption practices (Miller 2008; Ouellette and Hay 2008a, 2008b; Redden 2008). In such a formulation, any notion of self-expertise is obscured; productive citizenship is instead formed through a belief in the norm (Palmer 2003). This norm—the ways in which people come to think of themselves—is of course nourished by the desire for self-development and private self-empowerment, a desire that can be ensured through a combination of the market, a regulated autonomy, and expertise (Bonner 2008; Ouellette and Hay 2008a, 2008b; Redden 2008; Rose 1996, 1999). A certain amount of pseudo-expertise can be gathered from the *Biggest Loser* club, through which members can gain diets and exercise routines. The Will Power Bash on the official NBC *Biggest Loser* website also provides the opportunity to smash hamburgers, pies, and broccoli. A bad score in this online game is rewarded with a message telling the surfer to keep dieting and try again when in better shape. As Palmer (2003, 2004) proposed, this form of technological governmentality is dependent on experts (see also Rich 2011) in exercise, diet, and nutrition. These are the new authorities that preach from the same neoliberal text about the keys to happiness and self-fulfillment. As Miller and Rose implied, programs such as *TBL* rely "in crucial respects upon the intellectual technologies, practical activities and social authority associated with expertise . . . the self-regulating capacities of subjects, shaped and normalised through expertise, are key resources for governing in a liberal democratic way" (1993, 75). *TBL*'s experts (Jillian Michaels, Bob Harper, and Kim Lyons) not only provide onscreen training in everyday life; they constitute winners as "beneficiaries of consumer advice about 'improving practices'" (Bonner 2003, 106). Of course, as both Rose (1999) and Redden (2008) have suggested, such expert advice is exploited and enhanced in the new markets of health and welfare. Professional lifestyle coaches germane to the task of resculpting bodies have an array of services for sale. Kim Lyons, for example, offers a twelve-week exercise program for enhancing your life in her book, *Your Body, Your Life*.

You could, if desired, also purchase her upcoming DVD exercise series or the all-natural line of health supplements and sweeteners. With a more nutritional focus, Jillian Michaels offers a thirty-day shred instead of the twelve-week approach. Furthermore, you could take the "Jillian Michaels Fitness Ultimatum 2009" test, available on the Nintendo Wii console. There is also an array of "official" pedagogical devices, such as *TBL*'s *Cardio Max* DVD or the *Power Sculpt* DVD, as well as the range of *Biggest Winner* DVDs. As a telling exemplar in the new formations of welfare, these *TBL* products, fronted by "heroic" professionals who deliver ignorant and ugly people from the dross of everyday life, provide technologies of the self that can transcend what offscreen primary care professionals have been able to do for them (Miller 2008).

Living Properly: Breaking Bodies

On *TBL*, depictions of the normalized (read consumerized) citizen are bound with the power relations inherent in the constitution of body size—particularly with regard to the assumptions about the relationship between class, race, gender, and obesity (Evans 2006; Jutel 2005). Through the processes of normalizing the body, *TBL* offers the pathway toward "living properly" (Bonner 2008, 549) in a neoliberal world. However, living properly involves consumption (of personal trainers, exercise regimes, correct foods), and the positioning of middle-class tastes (literally), lifestyles, and values as normative. In this regard *TBL* acts to police and regulate the working classes, modifying class tastes through the humiliation of those evincing working or lower-middle-class preferences by those possessing middle or even upper-middle-class social capital (Bonner 2008; Lewis 2008; McRobbie 2004: Ouellette and Hay 2008a, 2008b; Palmer 2003, 2004). Indeed, the tips provided by experts and their range of commercial accoutrements offer strongly class-inflected modes of guidance around questions of style, taste, and social distinction (Palmer 2003). That such tastes, values, and preferences may not be available—given the long-established disparities in health and wellness of populations disadvantaged by class, race, and social location—is, of course, conveniently ignored.

Living properly on *TBL* also means living like a man. The cast is equally split between men and women, yet masculine values of hard work prevail; trainers emphasize the need for contestants to push beyond their perceived limits and to work out like a man (Sender and Sullivan 2008). Working out like a man, however, is depicted, somewhat ironically, as "required" to achieve what we could term a feminized corporoeconomicus—the *correct* or *proper* female body, invested from head to toe, from the surface of its skin to the gastrointestinal tract, with a middle-class consumption ethic. In this sense, *TBL* further reconstitutes the ways in which women's bodies are presented as being in constant need of monitoring, surveillance, disciplining, and remodeling (and consumer spending) in order to conform to ever narrower judgments of female attractiveness (Gill 2007; Jones 2008). Yet while we agree with Jones (2008) and McRobbie (2004) that gender binaries on reality television appear stricter and more regressive than other television genres, *TBL* offers a further dimension. Men are told to work out like a man, however, and, often through humiliation of their obese bodies (especially with regard to heterosexual carnal performance), are broken through recourse to the affective/feminine. Within the episodes, "read" men were often seen crying, offering emotive responses to trainers' judgments and feminized and domesticated in certain respects (such as through cooking correct foods or completing feminine forms of physical activity) to solve their aberrant body. While these men were being inducted into middle-class, feminized dispositions (Redden 2008), these passages were often framed in terms of the male being able to return to the domestic order, taking up responsibility as head of the traditional nuclear family through reaffirmation of heterosexual sexual activity—a counter to the impotence and lack of sexual desire assigned to the obese body.

Normalcy in *TBL* also affirms an ugly and repressive racial politics—part of what Goldberg (2008) termed the architecture of neoliberal racism that separates and partitions based on notional distinction and predetermined difference (S. Giroux 2010; Goldberg 2008, 2010). Extending Sender and Sullivan's (2008) account of audience reaction to *TBL*, our observations suggest that although *TBL* is somewhat more racially diverse than much network television, the link between obesity and social, racial, and geographical patterns of polarization and neglect are "whitewashed." In this regard, and contributing to the privatization and individualization of racial politics, power is further disconnected from social obligation, making it progressively more difficult for disadvantaged groups to gain equality and justice (H. Giroux 2004a). In accordance with McMurria (2008), *TBL* never identifies race as a factor for why families are struggling, obfuscating the structures of racial discrimination that position them there in the first place and offering neoliberal solutions as being equally beneficial to all. Indeed, the show cites tolerance of obesity in black communities, suggesting that such a cultural heritage must be overcome in order to save oneself—a reinstatement of implicitly white norms of size and appearance (Sender and Sullivan 2008). Somewhat reworking H. Giroux (2004b), then, we find that *TBL*'s discursive power serves to reconstitute whiteness, blames those abject "others" deemed less responsible for their bodies, offers a corporatized solution to their condition, and eludes any form of social responsibility for improving their lifestyles. "Otherness," in this sense racial and ethnic difference, is treated as an unremarkable contingency of social life, an incidental occurrence in a televisual reality culture that has seemingly moved beyond race (Gilroy 2005; Sender and Sullivan 2008).

TBL Boot Camp: The Biopolitics of Militarization

H. Giroux (2008) suggests that while both militarism and neoliberalism have a long history in the United States, the symbiotic relationship into which they have entered and the way in which this authoritarian ideology has become normalized constitute a distinct historical moment. The ever-expanding militarized neoliberal state is a vast war machine that stresses military-oriented measures over social programs such as health care and, as a culture of force, serves as a powerful pedagogical thrust that shapes our everyday lives and memories (H. Giroux 2004b, 2008; Newfield 2006). The synergies between neoliberalism and militarization are evident in a range of diverse institutions and organizations—for example, schools with "zero-tolerance policies," media broadcasts (*Jag, Army Wives*), and our leisure activities: paintballing, computer games, or attendance at a NASCAR event (Silk 2011). Moreover, and importantly for this chapter, the neoliberal militarization of everyday life is enmeshed within the genre of reality television: *American Fighter Pilot* on CBS; *Boot Camp* and *Celebrity Boot Camp* on Fox; *The Last 10 Pounds Boot Camp* on the Slice Network; the BBC's *Bad Lads Army*; DVDs such as *Special Ops Fitness, Semper Fit: The Marine Corps Workout, NikkiFitness: Military Life Workout*, and Sergeant Ken Weichert's *Boot Camp Fitness Trilogy*; the various boot camp weeks on various versions of *The X Factor* or *American Idol* competitions; and, indeed, the boot camps for troubled or overweight teens on "advice" programs such as *The Jeremy Kyle Show* and *The Jerry Springer Show*.

Unsurprisingly, *TBL* deploys the same narrative structure, even naming one of its patented workouts *The Biggest Loser Boot Camp*. Subsequently, in doing little to dispel the gendered nature of neoliberal militarized citizenship, a special edition of the show was centered on the battle between military wives. The narrative is dispersed throughout episodes; contestants' behavior is governed by what the trainers dictate, fostering a sense of fear. They are marched in formation across the desert toward the waiting officers (trainers) and instructed not to speak out of turn or question anything the trainers commanded them to do, as in real boot camp. The contestants are led through physical torture by the experts, subject to stress and emotional bullying, which often induces emotive reactions. Broadcasts were structured around the battle between teams, trainers emphasized the notions of sacrifice and team "spirit," discussion focused on gaining "territory" and being "warriors" during challenges, and trainers often used phrases such as "Who wants a beating?" to scare contestants during workouts. Moreover, building on discussions of the place of mediated sport within the war on terror (see, e.g., Falcous and Silk 2005; Hogan 2003), we see that *TBL* uses the "evocative iconography" (Biltekoff 2007, forthcoming) of patriotism—the theme song by Heather Small, "Proud," provides the perfect slippage between individual self-responsibility and freedom. In this sense, *TBL* can be read as a powerful, militarized, and neoliberal form of public biopedagogy, a normalizing cultural technology in the formation, shaping, and production of good consumer-citizens.

Conclusion: The Neoliberal Menu, or "I'm Sorry; We're Out of Welfare"

Critical engagement with contested media spaces, such as the self-help genre of reality television, bestows rich theoretical insight into modes of neoliberal governance. *The Biggest Loser*—a site that provides us with a nexus of transformed bodies that are at once fleshy and digital, hybrid-mediated bodies that exist on the screen and in the living world (Jones 2008)—provides a site for the excavation of the neoliberal ethic and its implications for and explanations of both poverty and health. Informed by H. Giroux (2001, 2003, 2004b, 2008), *TBL* is emblematic of what he terms the death of the social—the war waged on the domestic front that feeds off the general decay of politics; a virulent contempt of social needs; the destruction of a liberal political order; a growing culture of surveillance, inequality and cynicism; and a growing dislike for all things public, social, and collective under the power, influence, and spread of neoliberalism. Reality television programs like *TBL* act as a form of governance, a key pedagogical site in our neoliberal conjunctural moment framed by the massive retrenchment of social welfare sensibilities and programs (H. Giroux 2005; McMurria 2008). While the doses vary, the basic menu for this new neoliberal governance is the same: purge the system of obstacles to the functioning of free markets; celebrate the virtues of individualism; recast social problems such as drug use, obesity, and inadequate health insurance as individual problems; foster economic self-sufficiency; abolish or weaken social programs; include those marginalized (often by this shift in the role of government) or the poor in the labor market; and criminalize the homeless and the urban poor (subject this population to curfew orders, increased surveillance, or "zero-tolerance" policing) (H. Giroux 2005; Peck 2003; Rose 2000). This then entails a greater reliance on the privatization and personalization of welfare (through, for example, reality television) as the state entrusts pastoralism to private entities (including media) and emphasizes that citizens are not only active but also enterprising in the pursuit of their own empowerment and well-being (Ouellette and Hay 2008a).

Of most concern, perhaps, is the transference of health provision to private individuals. It is well documented that poverty can cause poor health through connection with inadequate nutrition, substandard housing, exposure to environmental hazards, unhealthy lifestyles, and decreased access to and use of health care services (e.g., access to clean air and water, exposure to lead paint, stress, obesity, smoking habits, diet, social isolation, availability of public spaces [such as parks and recreation facilities], proximity to hospitals and other medical treatment facilities, and availability of health insurance). In this regard, health disparities may well constitute one of the most concrete disadvantages associated with the social and racial patterns of polarization and postwar neglect (Squires and Kubrin 2005). That is, the privatization and individualization of health care as part of the neoliberal menu leaves a bitter taste that produces, legitimates, and exacerbates the existence of persistent poverty and inadequate care, leading to growing inequalities between the rich and the poor (II. Giroux 2005). Furthermore, a diversity of traditionally public health issues and concerns have become incorporated into the reach of the private sector, such as disease prevention, health promotion, personal and public health, juvenile curfews, medical services, day care, nutrition, substance abuse prevention, mental health and family counseling, teen pregnancy, services for the homeless, family abuse, improvement of infrastructures, and economic revitalization (Andrews, Silk, and Pitter 2008). For us, our concern is the ways in which alternative technologies of governance, such as the genre of reality television, seem to be a conduit for this transfer of health patterns from public to private priorities.

TBL individualizes, blames, and privatizes contestants for being obese, a central part of a neoliberal menu that acts to sustain the boundaries between the *bodies proper* that fulfill the obligations of participatory democratic citizenship (in this sense through the appropriate rates and acts of fitness consumption and the health and wealth connotations these infer) and those constitutive socially, morally, and economically pathologized *outsiders*: the public pollutants (Zylinska 2004). Acting as a justification for the systematic evisceration of welfare, and indeed, those bodies that do not count, *TBL* provides the obese, quite literally, with the digital currency with which they should conduct their everyday lives. Failure to conform, to conduct oneself in line with this menu, positions one as abject, personally responsible for a body that does not *belong* to a consumerized neoliberal and militarized society.

NOTES

1. See Corner 2004 for complementary reasons for television's turn toward the "everyday terms of living" (a deregulated market and fragmented audience, the relatively inexpensive production of the genre, and "free" nonunionized labor [in the form of contestants]).

2. Of course, obesity is a serious and increasingly prevalent condition, a costly and deadly "epidemic," and regarded as one of the major public health problems in the world (e.g., Gard and Wright 2005).

3. There are differences in the discursive meanings within the localized formatting of *TBL*. Lewis (2008), for example, points to the Australian contexts where the hosts are "resolutely average" and the focus is on losing weight for family and community. While we contend that there is a global currency of certain types of consumerist and neoliberal models of selfhood and citizenship (Lewis 2008), our comments in this chapter extend only to the U.S. version. A comparison between localized inflections of *TBL* is a project that we are seeking to develop.

4. Our method in this chapter is based on the approach of Johnson et al. (2004) to reading texts for dominance.

REFERENCES

Andrejevic, M. 2004. *Reality TV: The Work of Being Watched.* New York: Rowman and Littlefield.

Andrews, D. L., M. Silk, and R. Pitter. 2008. "Physical Culture and the Polarized American Metropolis." In *Sport in Society*, ed. B. Houlihan, 284–304. London: Sage.

Biltekoff, C. 2007. "The Terror Within: Obesity in Post 9/11 U.S. Life." *American Studies* 48 (3): 29–48.

Biltekoff, C. Forthcoming. "The Terror Within." In *Physical Cultural Studies: A Constitutive Anthology*, ed. M. Silk and D. Andrews. Philadelphia: Temple University Press.

Bonner, F. 2003. *Ordinary Television: Analyzing Popular TV.* London: Sage.

———. 2008. "Fixing Relationships in 2-4-1 Transformations." *Continuum: Journal of Media and Cultural Studies* 22 (4): 547–557.

Bordo, S. 1993. *Unbearable Weight: Feminism, Western Culture, and the Body.* Berkeley: University of California Press.

Butler, J. 1993. *Bodies That Matter: On the Discursive Limits of "Sex."* London: Routledge.

Corner, J. 2004. "Afterword: Framing the New." In *Understanding Reality Television*, ed. S. Holmes and D. Jermyn, 57–74. New York: New York University Press.

Couldry, N. 2008. "Reality TV or the Secret Theatre of Neoliberalism." *Review of Education, Pedagogy, and Cultural Studies* 30 (1): 3–13.

Crandall, C. 1994. "Prejudice against Fat People: Ideology and Self-Interest." *Journal of Personality and Social Psychology* 66 (5): 882–894.

Evans, B. 2006. "'Gluttony or Sloth': Critical Geographies of Bodies and Morality in (Anti)obesity Policy." *Area* 38 (3): 259–267.

Evans, J., B. Davis, and E. Rich. 2008. "The Class and Cultural Functions of Obesity Discourse: Our Latter-Day Child Saving Moment." *International Studies in Sociology of Education* 18 (2): 117–132.

Falcous, M., and M. Silk. 2005. "Manufacturing Consent: Mediated Sporting Spectacle and the Cultural Politics of the 'War on Terror.'" *International Journal of Media and Cultural Politics* 1 (1): 59–65.

Foucault, M. 1991. "Governmentality." In *The Foucault Effect: Studies in Governmentality*, ed. G. Burchell, C. Gordon, and P. Miller, 87–104. London: Harvester Wheatsheaf.

Gard, M., and J. Wright. 2005. *The Obesity Epidemic: Science, Morality and Ideology.* New York: Routledge.

Gill, R. 2007. *Gender and the Media.* Cambridge, UK: Polity Press.

Gilroy, P. 2005. "Multiculture, Double Consciousness and the 'War on Terror.'" *Patterns of Prejudice* 39 (4): 431–443.

Giroux, H. 2001. "Cultural Studies as Performative Politics." *Cultural Studies ↔ Critical Methodologies* 1 (1): 5–23.

———. 2003. *Public Spaces, Private Lives: Democracy beyond 9/11.* Lanham, MD: Rowman and Littlefield.

———. 2004a. *The Terror of Neoliberalism: Authoritarianism and the Eclipse of Democracy.* Boulder, CO: Paradigm.

———. 2004b. "War on Terror: The Militarising of Public Space and Culture in the United States." *Third Text* 18:211–221.

———. 2005. "The Terror of Neoliberalism." *College Literature* 32 (1): 1–19. Available at http://muse.jhu.edu/journals/college_literature/v032/32.1giroux.html.

———. 2008. "The Militarization of US Higher Education after 9/11." *Theory, Culture and Society* 25 (5): 56–82.

Giroux, S. 2010. "Sade's Revenge: Racial Neoliberalism and the Sovereignty of Negation." *Patterns of Prejudice* 44 (1): 1–26.

Goldberg, D. 2008. *The Threat of Race: Reflections on Racial Neoliberalism.* Oxford: Wiley-Blackwell.

———. 2010. "Call and Response." *Patterns of Prejudice* 44 (1): 89–106.

Gorman, B. 2010. "TV Ratings: Biggest Loser Weighs In Huge." Zap2It, January 6. Available at http://tvbythenumbers.zap2it.com/2010/01/06/tv-ratings-biggest-loser-weighs-in-big-nbc-tops-ncis-lead-cbs/37780/.

Graham, M. 2005. "Chaos." In *Fat: The Anthropology of an Obsession*, ed. D. Kulick and A. Meneley, 169–184. New York: Tarcher/Penguin.

Greenberg, B. S., M. Eastin, L. Hofschire, K. Lachlan, and K. D. Brownell. 2003. "Portrayals of Overweight and Obese Individuals on Commercial Television." *American Journal of Public Health* 93:1342–1348.

Grindstaff, L. 2002. *The Money Shot: Trash, Class, and the Making of TV Talk Shows.* Chicago: University of Chicago Press.

Gruneau, R., H. Cantelon, and D. Whitson. 1988. "Methods and Media: Studying the Sport/Television Discourse." *Leisure and Society* 11:265–281.

Hearn, A. 2008. "Insecure: Narratives and Economies of the Branded Self in Transformation Television." *Continuum: Journal of Media and Cultural Studies* 22 (4): 495–504.

Herrick, C. 2007. "Risky Bodies: Public Health, Social Marketing and the Governance of Obesity." *Geoforum* 38:90–102.

Himes, S. M., and J. K. Thompson. 2007. "Fat Stigmatization in Television Shows and Movies: A Content Analysis." *Obesity* 15 (3): 712–718.

Hogan, J. 2003. "Staging the Nation: Gendered and Ethnicized Discourses of National Identity in Olympic Opening Ceremonies." *Journal of Sport and Social Issues* 27 (2): 100–123.

Hollows, J., and S. Jones. 2010. "'At Least He's Doing Something:' Moral Entrepreneurship and Individual Responsibility in *Jamie's Ministry of Food.*" *European Journal of Cultural Studies* 13 (3): 307–322.

Jameson, F. 1981. *The Political Unconscious: Narrative as a Socially Symbolic Act.* London: Methuen.

Jenvey, V. B. 2007. "The Relationship between Television Viewing and Obesity in Young Children: A Review of Existing Explanations." *Early Child Development and Care* 177 (8): 809–820.

Johnson, R., D. Chambers, P. Raghuram, and E. Tincknell. 2004. *The Practice of Cultural Studies.* London: Sage.

Jones, M. 2008. "Media-Bodies and Screen-Births: Cosmetic Surgery Reality Television." *Continuum: Journal of Media and Cultural Studies* 22 (4): 515–524.

Jutel, A. 2005. "Weighing Health: The Moral Burden of Obesity." *Social Semiotics* 15 (2): 113–125.

Lewis, T. 2008. "Changing Rooms, Biggest Losers and Backyard Blitzes: A History of Makeover Television in the United Kingdom, United States and Australia." *Continuum: Journal of Media and Cultural Studies* 22 (4): 447–458.

Longhurst, R. 2005. "Fat Bodies: Developing Geographical Research Agendas." *Progress in Human Geography* 29 (3): 247–259.

MacLeod, G., M. Raco, and K. Ward. 2003. "Negotiating the Contemporary City: Introduction." *Urban Studies* 40 (9): 1655–1671.

McMurria, J. 2008. "Desperate Citizens and Good Samaritans: Neoliberalism and Makeover Reality TV." *Television and New Media* 9 (4): 305–332.

McRobbie, A. 2004. "Notes on 'What Not to Wear' and Post-Feminist Symbolic Violence." In *Feminism after Bourdieu*, ed. L. Adkins, and B. Skeggs, 99–109. Malden, MA: Blackwell.

Miller, P., and N. Rose. 1993. "Governing Economic Life." In *Foucault's New Domains*, ed. M. Gane and T. Johnson, 75–105. London: Routledge.

Miller, T. 2008. "Afterword: The New World Makeover." *Continuum: Journal of Media and Cultural Studies* 22 (4): 585–590.

Mosher, J. 2001. "Setting Free the Bears: Refiguring Fat Men in Television." In *Bodies Out of Bounds: Fatness and Transgression*, ed. J. E. Braziel and K. LeBasco, 166–194. Berkley: University of California Press.

Murray, S. 2008. "Pathologizing 'Fatness': Medical Authority and Popular Culture." *Sociology of Sport Journal* 25:7–21.

NBC. 2008. *The Biggest Loser* home page. Available at http://www.nbc.com/The_Biggest_Loser/.

Newfield, C. 2006. "Culture of force." *South Atlantic Quarterly* 105 (1): 241–263.

Ouellette, L., and J. Hay. 2008a. *Better Living through Reality TV.* Oxford: Blackwell.

———. 2008b. "Makeover Television, Governmentality and the Good Citizen." *Continuum: Journal of Media and Cultural Studies* 22 (4): 471–484.

Palmer, G. 2003. *Discipline and Liberty Television and Governance.* Manchester, UK: Manchester University Press.

———. 2004. "The New You: Class and Transformation in Lifestyle Television." In *Understanding Reality Television*, ed. S. Holmes and D. Jermyn, 173–190. London: Routledge.

Peck, J. 2003. "Geography and Public Policy: Mapping the Penal State." *Progress in Human Geography* 27 (2): 222–232.

Peck, J., and A. Tickell. 2002. "Neoliberalizing Space." *Antipode* 34 (3): 380–404.

Rail, G. 2009. "Canadian Youth's Discursive Constructions of the Body and Health." In *Biopolitics and the "Obesity Epidemic": Governing Bodies*, ed. J. Wright and V. Harwood, 141–156. London: Routledge.

Redden, G. 2008. "Economy and Reflexivity in Makeover Television." *Continuum: Journal of Media and Cultural Studies* 22 (4): 485–494.

Rich, E. 2011. "I See Her Being Obesed! Public Pedagogy, Reality Media and the Obesity Crisis." *Health* 15 (1): 3–23.

Rich, E., and J. Evans. 2005. "'Fat Ethics'—The Obesity Discourse and Body Politics." *Social Theory and Health* 3:341–358.

Ritzer, G. 2004. *The Globalisation of Nothing.* Thousand Oaks, CA: Sage.

Rose, N. 1996. *Inventing Our Selves.* Cambridge: Cambridge University Press.

———. 1999. *Governing the Soul: The Shaping of the Private Self.* London: Free Associations Books.

———. 2000. "Community, Citizenship, and the Third Way." *American Behavioral Scientist* 43 (9): 1395–1411.

Sender, K., and M. Sullivan. 2008. "Epidemics of Will, Failures of Self-Esteem: Responding to Fat Bodies in *The Biggest Loser* and *What Not to Wear.*" *Continuum: Journal of Media and Cultural Studies* 22 (4): 573–584.

Silk, M. 2011. *Television, Sport and the Cultural Politics of Post-9/11 America: Power, Pedagogy and the Popular.* New York: Routledge.

Silk, M., and D. Andrews. 2006. "The Fittest City in America." *Journal of Sport and Social Issues* 30 (3): 315–327.

———. 2008. "Managing Memphis: Governance and Regulation in Sterile Spaces of Play." *Social Identities* 14 (3): 395–414.

Skeggs, B., and H. Wood. 2008. "The Labour of Transformation and Circuits of Value "around" Reality Television." *Continuum: Journal of Media and Cultural Studies* 22 (4): 559–572.

Squires, G. D., and C. E. Kubrin. 2005. "Privileged Places: Race, Uneven Development and the Geography of Opportunity in Urban America." *Urban Studies* 42 (1): 47–68.

Stevenson, N. 2010. "Education, Neoliberalism and Cultural Citizenship: Living in X-Factor Britain." *European Journal of Cultural Studies* 13 (3): 341–358.

Zylinska, J. 2004. "The Universal Acts: Judith Butler and the Biopolitics of Immigration." *Cultural Studies* 18 (4): 523–537.

15

Technologies of the South

Sport, Subjectivity, and "Swinging" Capital

JOSHUA I. NEWMAN

> Neoliberal globalization will be written about ten
> years from now as a cyclical swing in the history of the
> capitalist world-economy. The real question is not whether
> this phase is over but whether the swing back will be able,
> as in the past, to restore a state of relative equilibrium in
> the world-system. Or has too much damage been done?
> —IMMANUEL WALLERSTEIN, "2008: The Demise
>   of Neoliberal Globalization"

For all intents and purposes, Immanuel Wallerstein's 2008 declaration of an impending turn away from the free market echoes an accord shared by many globalization theorists and political economists (see Geier 2008; Li 2008)—one that suggests that the developed national nodes of the global capitalist "world economy" are on the verge of, or are already in the process of, retracting to what David Harvey (2005a, 2007) refers to as an "embedded" state (e.g., new formations of the Keynesian welfare state) and thereby away from the recent mutations of laissez-faire globalization. Indeed, the recent election of Democrat Barack Obama in the United States—as well as the resounding 2010 election day triumphs of the French Socialist Party and the overwhelming majority of votes shared by the Labour and Liberal Democrat Parties in the U.K. elections that same year—may be suggestive of such a leftward turn in the political economies of many developed nation-states.

My interest in this chapter is on the cultural logics of that turn. I make the case that as we "swing" away from neoliberalism, we find a contextually residual assemblage of spectacles (e.g., those of the military-industrial-complex, spectacles of the biopoliticized body, spectacles of the global popular, the spectacles of terror and terrorism, and the spectacularized sporting events that draw the focus of this edited collection), which have incubated and continue to incubate pedagogies attendant to the neoliberal imperative. More specifically, this chapter focuses on sport spectacles distinctive to the U.S. South and the role they play in reproducing power and manufacturing consent before (and during) this macroeconomic *swing*. As will become more apparent through what follows, my focus on this imaginary "South"—at once a media formation dominated by images such as George W. Bush as sportsman and narratives of Bible Belt–infused "family values"—is not necessarily a means of delimiting for a more manageable scope of analysis. Rather, the South has been an important feature in the social production of free-market conjuncturalism: conjoining the logics of individualization, American exceptionalism, and market freedom.

Cursorily, we need look no further than the pastoral machinations of footballing brothers Peyton and Eli Manning, the bucolic stylings of "new New South" cinema (e.g., *Dukes of Hazzard* or *Talladega Nights*), or the valorization of country western singers such as Tim McGraw and Gretchen Wilson to realize that in the contemporary U.S. popular, the South matters. This southerly shift is also bolstered by the increased relevance of southern politicians such as Texan Rick Perry, Rand Paul, or Haley Barbour—each advocating in Fox News vernacular a need to return to "core American values" of faith, family, and free enterprise. Looking back over the past decade, it would be hard to argue against the notion that this aestheticized, mythologized South emerged an important (mediated) cultural space for articulating identities, ideologies, and discourses of neoliberal political and cultural economies (see Phillips 2006). If the national narratives dominating the U.S. mediascape tell us anything in recent years, it is that through Tea Party rallies, political conventions, rock concerts, sporting fetes, megachurch revivals, Senate hearings, and board of education meetings, the new lexicon of U.S. free-market conservatism has taken on a southern drawl.

The intersection of free-market hegemony and southern culture, however, is not a matter of happenstance. Rather, it was the southern-inflected political right's fetish with the free market, coupled with a fascination for Antonio Gramsci's notion of hegemony, that many scholars argue successfully forged this systematic "southerly" shift within U.S. cultural and political discourse (Denzin and Giardina 2007a; Giroux 2004; Harvey 2005b, 2006; Kincheloe and Steinberg 2006; McLaren 2005)—those of the "Moral Majority," "Republican Revolution," the "Bible Belt," the "electorate mandates" of "Red State America," and most recently the "Tea Party movement." Indeed, the connections between economic polity and cultural hegemony are not loose ones. Right-wing politico-intermediaries such as Pat Buchanan (see Buchanan 2002) and Rush Limbaugh have strategically reorganized a number of cultural institutions within the American popular over recent decades, with the latter outright declaring in his 1993 memoir, *See, I Told You So*:

> In the early 1900s, an obscure Italian communist by the name of Antonio Gramsci theorized that it would take a "long march through the institutions" before socialism and relativism would be victorious. . . . Gramsci theorized that by capturing these key institutions and using their power, cultural values would be changed, traditional morals would be broken down, and the stage would be set for the political and economic power of the West to fall. . . . Gramsci succeeded in defining a strategy for waging cultural warfare. . . . [W]hy don't we simply get in the game and start

competing for control of these key institutions? In other words, why not fight back? (Limbaugh 1993, 87)

If Wallerstein is correct, and the cycle of liberal capitalism is nearing an end, then now is an opportune time to reflect on the role of those "key institutions" mobilized by the hegemons of neoliberalism to sustain their macroeconomic order of things. Time to ask: What role do such institutions play in shaping identity and ideology in contemporary America? I make the case that at the twilight of neoliberal prosperity, it has become increasingly evident that the southern sport spectacle (and its effusive identity politics) has been one such key institution. Leaving discussions of the fragile state of neoliberalism to other contributors in this volume, I turn my attention to two important features of the contemporary U.S. South sportscape. First, I turn the klieg light on the sporting spectacles of the University of Mississippi's intercollegiate football team and the social conditions for reproducing the ideologies and identities of the Dixie South's elite class. I then offer partial answers to two central interrogatives postulated by David Harvey (2005a) in *A Brief History of Neoliberalism*: "How was sufficient popular consent generated to legitimize the neoliberal turn?" (40) and how do the market's "captains of industry and finance" continue to sustain ideological sway over the disenfranchised laboring masses in spite of the failures of such a free-market system (60)? Again, I turn to the South as I review the ascent of stock car racing (most often referred to by its overarching governing and corporate body, NASCAR)—site of preeminent sporting nomenclature within the contemporary U.S. South—during the George W. Bush presidency.

In and between the two, I contemplate the ways in which myths of the neoliberal nation have been dialectically articulated through the identity politics and bodily practices of a normalized (conservative, white, masculine, Christian, working-class, heteronormative) "southern" subject position. Following Foucault (1977), I then explore how the subject of the sporting spectacle is *subjected to* broader formations of neoliberalism but also how out of that subjectivity the spectator constitutes the *self* and *self-understanding*. I argue that in both cases the local sporting spectacle, saturated with paradoxes of inclusivity and exclusivity, is not simply projected onto the sporting masses but *consumed* as a technology of individualization, exceptionalism, and ultimately *empowerment* at the neoliberal turn.

The Grove Society: The Spectacle of Post-plantation "Good Ol' Boy" Exceptionalism

To better understand the contemporaneous fulcrum of neoliberalism's cultural and "political politics" (Morris 1989), one need look no further than a "key institution" of the educative South—a place that has been referred to as the "training ground" for America's most strident free-market politicos (e.g., former Republican National Committee chairperson Haley Barbour; prominent

U.S. senators Trent Lott and Thad Cochrane; and Admiral John S. McCain, Sr., patriarch of the family of 2008 Republican presidential nominee John Mc-Cain). Affectionately referred to by university constituents as "Ole Miss," the University of Mississippi has been described as everything from an institution of higher education, to a "longstanding pillar of the Old South" (Sansing 1990, 1999), to the "Country Club of the South" (Read and Freeland 1983). It is at once a university, an intercollegiate athletic brand, and a mythologized institution of the Old South. As one famous alumnus put it, Ole Miss is "an intangible experience rather than just a place. It is the beauty of the Grove, the sound of 'Dixie,' and the charm of Oxford itself" (Evans 2004, 2). As I and others have argued elsewhere, the institution is a physical and cultural space where histories of racial exclusivity, Old South patriarchy, and a formalized "good ol' boy" network incessantly converge on the everyday experiences of the present, constituting *a dreamworld of the "new Old South"* (King and Springwood 2001; Newman 2007a, 2007c; Weeks 1999). As I have also suggested, perhaps no other spectacle of the "new sporting South" during the George W. Bush presidency brought those politics to life quite like that of the intercollegiate football matches hosted on the Ole Miss campus (Newman 2007a).

Here I want to focus on the spectator practices of "tailgating" that materialize in the hours leading up to each home football game on the Ole Miss campus. As a *Sports Illustrated on Campus* writer in a 2003 article titled "The 100 Things You Gotta Do before You Graduate (Whatever the Cost)" made clear, there is no greater pregame carnival offered anywhere in college sport that trumps the experience of "tailgating in the Grove" of the University of Mississippi (4). The Grove, a "10-acre, debutante-stacked meadow" ("The 100 Things You Gotta Do" 2003, 4) situated in the middle of the University of Mississippi campus, is dominated by the ingestion of pregame mixtures of whiskey and the racial and habitus homogeneity. In what can perhaps best be described as a "cathedral of pleasure" (Foucault 1984, 251), the Grove constitutes a highly regulated social space in which its constituents imbibe in sport, carnival, and the sociospatial power dynamics borne thereof. It is a place where the myths of sporting egalitarianism and collegial meritocracy collide in the performance of the South's "simplified," "traditional" identity politics.

As a touring journalist from *Sports Illustrated* deduced, "There are rules here in the Grove. And ways of communicating that I couldn't comprehend" (Duerson 2004, 10). The code of a unifying (divisive) "southern ethic" is both encoded and decoded in an inimitable play of signifiers unique to the Grove: embodied signifiers, Confederate symbols, patriarchal parlance, and genteel bodily praxis. In sum, the Grove is the spectacularized space through which the localized politics of race and social class (as well as gender) are filtered into the spectating practice:

> They drink bourbon and eat boiled peanuts and finger sandwiches from sterling-silver platters and serving dishes arranged by caterers and frantic moms on elaborate tabletops. They partake in front of flat-screen TVs with

DirecTV, underneath chandeliers and amongst intricate candelabras and ornate flower arrangements. And when football calls, they pay people like Andre, at the Rebel Rousers tent, to stand guard. (Duerson 2004, 11)

In this way, the distinctive cultural practices within the Grove are more than a metaphor of the centrality of whiteness or class privilege in the spectrum of representative power at Ole Miss. Foucault (1984), theorizing the governance space and the spatialized body, emphasizes that no one can enter or leave such a spectacularized geometric configuration "without being seen by everyone—an aspect of the architecture that could be totally oppressive. But it could be oppressive only if people were prepared to use their own presence in order to watch over others" (246). The architecture of these spectacular practices and signifying acts marks territory, allows or denies access, and delineates its exclusively white—and white-collar—membership around what the university's sport marketing department proudly refers to as "the Grove Society."

For the spectator of the Grove Society, the symbolic unification of the racialized body creates a spectacular panoptic space, whereby the fetishization of white exclusivity is materialized through the possibilities of an atomized corporeal collective. In other words, the reign of an uncontested white space (the Grove) creates a codified solidarity, as the embodied signification of localized whiteness permeates throughout (Frederick 1999). A writer for the *Chronicle of Higher Education* observes, "Just as at the game, blacks are virtually invisible in the Grove—except when the football squad . . . parades through the crowd en route to the stadium" (Lederman 1993, A52). It is the spatial and spectacular aggregate of otherwise disconnected embodied subjects linked together by their nonneutral common (imaginary) whiteness. Albeit more imagined than real, that collective sense of identity is made all the more powerful by the institutional and lived histories of slavery, segregation, and lynch-mob terrorism that has shaped race relations in the region for centuries (and has constituted a source of white supremacy).

Further, for spectator-members of the Grove Society, the "burden of whiteness" (Giroux 1997; Kincheloe et al. 1998) becomes a form of governance, as the prescriptions of expressive whiteness and the politics of "enfleshment" (McLaren 1988) shape social action. In this way, subjectivities within the Grove spectacle are grafted out of the discourse of sameness and difference. One might argue that, surrounded by embodied and signified forms of southern whiteness, "social life is so colonized by . . . administrative techniques, so saturated in an accumulation of spectacles, that people are more like spectators than active agents, occupying roles assigned to them in a state of passive contemplation" (Pinder 2000, 361–362).

That exclusive, mass inhabitation of white bodies within the Grove resuscitates the histories of an antebellum, plantation-based market economy while simultaneously resurrecting the racial politics that afforded Grove Society members the genealogical advantage over nonwhite subjects excluded from, and subjected to, the reign of the spectacle. Thus the lived experiences of the postplantation Grove spectacle constitute a perfect mélange of power. It is at once a distinctive "rhythm of time and space" (Lefebvre 2004), class, and race—as twill and plaid trousers, penny loafers, and red Ole Miss–themed polo shirts dominate a monomorphic, hyperwhite geometric topography.

Written into the text of this multifarious tentscape and bodyscape, the politics of race invoke performances of memorialized politics (and the politics of memory) of "Dixie South whiteness" (Newman 2007c) through the symbolic (i.e., a space cloaked with Confederate flags), the conversant (the soft murmur of the white masculine communal), and the embodied (phenotypical homogeneity). As Debord suggests—following Marx—history comes to life through such spectacles:

> It is because human beings have thus been thrust into history, and into participation in the labor and the struggles which constitute history, that they find themselves obliged to view their relationships in a clear-eyed manner. . . . As for the subject of history, it can only be the self production of the living: the living becoming master and possessor of its world—that is, of history—and coming to exist as consciousness of its own activity. (1994, thesis 74)

While the collective conscious of Ole Miss spectators (and the identification of the agent to that collectivity) is a product of imagined historical activity, the racialized power/knowledge complex exists and is preponderated through the active subjectification of humans in the language of history, hierarchy, and privilege (see Best and Kellner 1999). In Debord's words, such a cultural formation is "the reflection and prefiguration of the possibilities of organization of everyday life in a given historical moment; a complex of aesthetics, feelings and mores through which a collectivity reacts on the life that is objectively determined by its economy" (1981, 45).

Thus, the locus of race- and class-based privilege at the neoliberal turn comes to life in the Grove Society: a contextually unique mythscape which weaves together spectacularized white bodies, revisionist/absolutionist histories, and (ahistorical) false idioms of neoliberal meritocracy. Ole Miss is known throughout the state and region as a producer of state and federal politicians, high-ranking lawyers and judges, and powerful businessmen. At Ole Miss, affiliation leads to access of the "Good Ole Boy" network (Weeks 1999, C1). This network is the conduit to political and economic power in the state of Mississippi and has long used the campus Greek system as a means of cordoning off access from racialized, gendered, and social-classed "undesirables." In the closed halls of their fraternity houses, these men of campus power shape the social livelihood on campus (almost all campus leaders annually are elected by the will of the Greek system) and the cultural import flowing through the campus space (Cohodas 1997; Dodson 1997). The discursive terrain constructed by the uninterrupted fluidity with which these bodies flow through the Grove space reiterates the territoriality of white hegemons within the context. Through the spectacle, "identity is . . . a property. It is something you can purchase, or purchase a relation to" (Berlant 1997, 17). And yet, by way of its very existence and frames thereof, the Grove spectacle denies the histories and the legacies of accumulation on which these identities rest.

From this "brotherhood" on purchase—which has been referred to as a "statewide network of money and influence that began at the University of Mississippi in the late 1950s and early 1960s" (Weeks 1999, C1)—aspirant political leaders, sporting icons (e.g. Archie and Eli Manning), and postplantation aristocrats accumulate and engage racially exclusive, patriarchal pedagogies and subjectivities of genteel performance within this southern local. In the halls of Fraternity Row, the grandstands of Vaught-Hemingway Stadium, and the green space ballroom of the Grove, the region's patriarchs in training learn how to mobilize the social and cultural capital developed in the linguistic and deportmental codes of Ole Miss. By way of this "network," one that both is exclusive to white men and fostered the antiquated hegemonic masculinities of the Old South, Ole Miss student subjects have grafted a system of embodied knowledge by which this patriarchal, race-based capital could be encoded, decoded, and made powerful (Meredith, Marshall, and Doar 2002). In other words, for many within the spectacle of Ole Miss, the Grove spectacle is both an exercise in postplantation power and a rite of inheritance to the privilege embedded in their racialized and class-based subject position. In short, it is the canvas on which a posthistoric future with modern racist resonance can be written.

In the first instance, that posthistoric future and its antecedent power/knowledge relationships forged through the Grove spectacular give local credence to the central premise of Milton Friedman's ([1962] 2002) neoliberal theory: that of *protecting private property*. It projects a modern-day mytharc that has disconnected the wealth and "private property" inherited by the Grove's "good ol' boy" class from the historical processes by which that property was seized (mass genocide of the native peoples of the region) and made valuable (plantation-based slavery). In turn, it extends the basic "crony capitalist" (Hedges 2007) false consciousness within neoliberalism's personal histories: that of the false idiom of meritocracy. Filtering from its forerunning pedagogues at the University of Chicago down through the "grassroots" rhetoric of Ron Paul, the baseline assumption among neoliberalism's strident power elites is that wealth, power, and privilege are solely determined by endeavor, ingenuity, and value to the market. More importantly, it naturalizes the dialectics of identity and power such that the spectacular and pedagogical discourses that blanket the Grove spectacle seemingly revise the material histories of oppression whilst simultaneously rationalizing, if not glorifying, the uneven access to education, to power, and to the spectacle afforded those spectators who have put their postplantation capital to use in the neoliberal market. Like the broader panoply of power relations floating about the nation at the neoliberal turn, the subjectivities of the Grove Society consecrate the pseudo-pragmatic "southernized" neoliberal discourses of "individual freedom," American exceptionalism, and the meritocracies of the free market and at the same time reject the regimes of subjectivity (both empowering and oppressive) and subordination acting within that historical moment.

Second, and more important, the individualization of the atomized Grove spectacle disarticulates the spectator from the social formations that his or her relative autonomy has seemingly created. As such, the men of the "good ol' boy" network and icons of Dixie South whiteness emerge out of various historical moments always already bound to economic, sociopolitical, and institutional chains of interdependency, chains that link each—whether through a shared physicality, cerebralism, or genealogy—to the knowledge-power formations of Dixie South whiteness. And yet in recent years, and particularly in the context of a neoliberal individualist hegemony (see Beck and Beck-Gernsheim 2002), men of the South have not come to reemphasize those structures from which their intertextual positionality is made relevant, but rather their individuality and individual accomplishment. These are the subjects of structural absolution, icons of a "new New South" whiteness somehow detached from histories and systems of plantation-accumulation and segregation-privilege.

Inventing NASCAR Nation: Consuming the Cultural Politics of Neoconfederate Individualism

Much like the spectacles of the "Grove Society," the weekly conglomeration of mass-media intermediaries, iconized southern sporting bodies (and their industrialist vassal-machines), nearly two hundred thousand "southern" sport spectators, omnipresent "corporate sponsors," and right-wing politico-sportsmen of NASCAR has played an equally important role in defining the boundaries of sport subjectivity in the lead-up to the neoliberal turn. A sport that has historically been marginalized by the "big four" U.S. sporting oligarchy as a local, southern, "small-time," "redneck," southern pastime, NASCAR and its parent corporate umbrella, International Speedway Corporation (ISC), emerged as a significant force in the highly competitive North American sport marketplace over the past decade. Under the centralized stewardship of the sporting-entrepreneurial France family, stock car racing's authoritative organizing body has guided the sport into the heights of corporate wealth and cultural import. In perfecting the "NASCAR Way," as author Robert Hagstrom (1998) observed more than a decade ago, NASCAR officials have been more successful than those of any other professional North American sport in transforming spectator allegiance into active forms of consumption.[1]

Indeed, NASCAR has moved from the periphery of sport and cultural relations in the United States to the center of "SportsNation"—much like the broader spectacle of neoliberalism—and has done so by extending its import through an assemblage of media discourses, celebrity intonations, and a harnessed, commercialized sense of collectivity among its spectatorship. However, the NASCAR empire is more than an emerging cultural destination in the now-crowded sport marketplace. The sport most entangled in free-market enterprise has prospered under the neoliberal condition because it is directly constituent to, and constitutive of, this dominant economic order. This dialectic relationship between stock car racing and the market forces that have ushered in a new era of profitability is a consequence of a brazenly triangulated conglomeration of sport spectatorship, southern identity, and political economy grafted under the journalistic aegis "NASCAR Nation."

In other forums, my colleagues and I have argued that "NASCAR Nation" has become a collective configuration defined by its southern aesthetic, exclusive white racial identities, and auto-culture hypermasculinity (Denzin and Giardina 2007b; Kusz 2007; Newman 2007b; Newman and Giardina 2008, 2011). "NASCAR Nation" is a double entendre that refers to both an imagined spectator community dominated by "rural, small-town, mostly white, southern fans of America's fastest growing spectator sport" (Derbyshire 2003, 29) and to the broader idioms of American nationalism, which are concurrently and dialectically bound to the same precepts of neoliberalism and paleoconservatism/ neoconservatism. It is quite common within the sport and beyond to refer to stock car racing fans as members of NASCAR Nation, and also to evoke the term in describing the political and cultural trajectory of a national imaginary mesmerized by a strategically controlled, theocratized cultural technology that normalizes the moral, political, economic, and ideological dimensions of George W. Bush's post-9/11 brand of market-doctrined, security state polity. In what follows, I locate how these subjectivities come to life within stock car spectacles and how race- and social class–based signifying acts and signified praxis intersect within the spectacle to enhance twinned neoliberal/conservative hegemony.

First, and particularly at races held in the U.S. South (Talladega, Alabama; Bristol, Tennessee; Daytona, Florida; Darlington, South Carolina; and Richmond, Virginia), the spaces and spectacles of "NASCAR Nation" are blanketed by signifiers of neo-Confederate citizenship. As most NASCAR fans would attest, if the number of Confederate symbols at each race is any indicator, NASCAR Nation is very much an exclusively white, if not "neo-Confederate," collective. Such a neo-Confederacy, writes Tony Horwitz (1999), is a recalcitrant identity politics resurrected in two parts: (1) as a reclamation of masculine, white privilege resuscitated in imaginaries of a modern-day supremacist southern faction and (2) as a much softer romanticization of southern "tradition," the gentility of plantation life, and—to quote from the slave song "Dixie"—"old times there are not forgotten." Sports journalist Dan Wetzel recently noted the symbolic homogeneity of this neo-Confederacy after attending a NASCAR race in Talladega, Alabama: "In America . . . a NASCAR race is the last major sporting event where the Stars and Bars is still so prevalent, still so prominent" (2006, 1). In the best reading, this signifying system thus transforms the praxis and symbols of NASCAR Nation into what Umberto Eco (1976) refers to as "a lie," or "something that stands for something else" (Gottdiener 1994, 156). Problematically, the neo-Confederate symbolic "liquidates the real" (Bishop 2001)—becoming a simulacrum of the racist impetuses it has come to represent whilst simultaneously reinforcing the hierarchical desires of this form of ethnic nationalism or "neotribalism" (Cova 1997; Maffesoli 1995).

Much like the Grove, this selective encoding and decoding (Hall 2001) of NASCAR signifiers is thus two degrees separated from the Confederacy, slavery, segregation, and so on. Consumer subjects are confronted by intermediaries' attempts to erase the realities of a sport that to this day has no regular women drivers and only one driver of color—the accomplished Formula One racer Juan Pablo Montoya (or, as NASCAR commentators have recently nicknamed him in the linguistic "whiting out" of his ethnic difference, JPM or Jonnie Montoya). To wit, the sport maintains an almost exclusively white fan base at most races and is dominated by the same symbols that signified the cause of slavery in the antebellum, Jim Crow, and Civil Rights–era South. NASCAR Nation's "diversity dearth," wrote one *Washington Post* journalist, is a product of the sport's "exclusionary athletic enterprise in terms of race and sex" (W. Brown 2004, G02).

This leads me to the point I have made elsewhere (Newman 2007b, 2010): despite its blatant practices of symbolic violence and exclusivity, the sport thrived during the George W. Bush presidency. As numerous observers have suggested (E. Brown 2000; Hale 1998, 1999; hooks 1992; Reed 1986; Rubin 2002; Winders 2003), this and other spectacles of the neo-Confederacy are perhaps more than simply a symbolic and embodied proclamation of the "southern," sporting, or "white identities." In banal terms, we might surmise that these southern sporting spectators mobilize the Confederate symbolic as a symbol of white identities in an age when whiteness is marked as an identity, inasmuch as these individuals "sense that they now have *identities*, when it used to be just other people who had them" (Berlant 1997, 2). But more importantly, the racially divisive overtones layered onto these signified spaces create power, and particularly at a time when the everyday lives of the South's white working class (and NASCAR's "target market") have deteriorated amid the thrusts of the global neoliberal imperative. Under such a condition, NASCAR fans laud the same Exxon-dominated, Walmart-ized neoliberal market that both mesmerizes their consumer sensibilities while simultaneously decimating their own postindustrial labor conditions (see Giroux 2004; Harvey 2005a; Kincheloe 2004).

For example, recent NASCAR marketing research suggests that most stock car racing fans live in households with less than $40,000 annual income, with the most overrepresented "household earning" category being that of the $20,000–$39,000 range ("Loyal and Ready to Buy" 2000). While most NASCAR fans draw employment from the expanding universe of low-paying, unskilled, no-benefit service jobs—or what George Ritzer (1998) refers to as "McJobs"—and increase their credit card debt on holidays spent in NASCAR Nation, they produce the conditions of neoliberal capitalism through (1) accelerated forms of sport-themed consumerism and (2) the collective identity of NASCAR Nation. And while neoliberal corporate goliaths—which many commentators have argued are the most "anti-humane" social technologies of our time (Bakan 2004; Klein 2007)—alienate and oppress most of these contemporary wage laborers by way of uneven distribution of capital, discontinued access to health care, "fat-trimming" layoffs, fraudulent accounting practices, deskilling/dehumanizing labor conditions, and unsafe and unhealthy working environments, the further compromising of the planet's environmental stability, and the proliferation of antidemocratic political lobbying in favor of greater surplus value (Albert 2003; Giroux 2004; Hardt and Negri 2000; Negri 2003). And yet among the massive horde of NASCAR faithful, the consensus seems to lie on the side of pro-corporate neoliberalism.

Warren Brown (2004) posits that the commercial pursuits of NASCAR have led to an exclusionary condition whereby the equilibrium among drivers, sponsors, and spectators has necessitated an overreliance on a "traditionalist" view of NASCAR subjectivity. He writes, "NASCAR fans see their drivers as 'people like me.' . . . They see them as having 'regular physiques,' and being 'regular guys' and 'role models'" (W. Brown 2004, G02). He concludes that NASCAR has failed to put minority drivers behind the wheel as a result of sponsors' "fear of alienating" their predominately white market segment. This commodified (southern) whiteness, the author would argue, is the signature identity of NASCAR Nation—the preferred order of a subjectivity that still alienates and oppresses individuals based on race and gender and gains strength and value from the allegiances of a hyperwhite, hypermasculine "target market."

The subject as spectator is thus transformed into both an embodiment of the hierarchical body politic and the governmentalities of corporeality that reaffirm the impulses of such a hierarchy. Much as in the Grove Society, the unity of practice overdetermines spatial autonomy, and thus the geometric space creates an enclosure in which the body becomes a site for governance through normalizing judgments and surveillance. And out of such praxis, the defining feature of the Debordian spectacle comes to the surface: through the practices of consumption and submitting to the discourses of "belonging," the individual spectator in NASCAR Nation is seduced by the collective spectacles of southern whiteness and sporting solidarity (as materialized through the sporting spectacle), and at the same time subjected to, and reminded of, the laws of alienation inherent in the pillars of neoliberalism. Individuals are brought together through consumption, through engagement with the spectacular commodity, and yet are made to realize that their access to the spectacle is a necessary product of their ability to reproduce (reproduce free-market capital, reproduce the conditions of their existence in such an order, and reproduce the iniquitous social history from which these conditions were "made").

In this way, following Deleuze and Guattari (1987), the rhizomatic pluralities of consumer-based identities with NASCAR Nation collapse under the auspices of a unified subjectivity—that of patriarchal, conservative southern whiteness. That adhesive quality, or the defining unifying feature (what Deleuze and Guattari refer to as *unité*) of NASCAR fandom, is performed in and through the spectacularized spaces of NASCAR Nation and molded out of a hyperwhite southern discursive locale. When assembled at these races, NASCAR fans act as semiotic organisms of spatialized norms/normalizing space, subjected to the laws of what Michel de Certeau (1984) refers to as a cultural "strategy" and thus subjects that facilitate the "imposition of power through the disciplining and organizing of space" (Crang 2000, 137). As "space is fundamental in any exercise of power" (Foucault 1984, 252), the proliferation of southern identities and southern aesthetics within NASCAR spaces has been used to authorize neoliberal economics and paleoconservative/neoconservative polity. Most significantly, this *unité* denies the alienating processes at work within the spectacle—those that operate on behalf of neoliberal accumulation.

In the most basic sense of subjectivity, then, members of NASCAR Nation are being subjected to what Jacques Derrida (1987) refers to as "the logics of parergonality," whereby knowledges of citizenship are produced, shared, contested, and made meaningful within a contextually specific plasticity of conservative/neoliberal conjuncture. The NASCAR spectacle thus offers parergonal legitimacy: legitimacy to be white (and guilt free) at the turn toward "Obama's America"; legitimacy to stand against equal marital rights for all U.S. citizens; legitimacy for "white man falling" paranoia; legitimacy to clog the roadways and airways with planet-destroying sport-utility vehicles (God's gift of safety and conspicuous consumption); legitimacy to believe in a market structure that, while bursting at the seams, is too natural, and indeed "too big," to fail.

Southern (Neo)Liberations

In oversimplified terms, what I have argued thus far is that the much like Michel Foucault's notion of "technologies of the self," *technologies of the (sporting) South* produce subjects. Those subjects, in turn, produce the discursive formations of which the subject is only one part. Foucault's definition of subject position highlights the productive nature of disciplinary power—how it names and categorizes people into hierarchies (of normalcy, health, morality, etc.). Similarly, I have argued that through the "southern" sport spectacles of the Grove Society and NASCAR Nation, racial, national, and class-based norms are shaped around the imperatives of the (failing) free market (by at once celebrating and denying its existence). This chapter has dealt with the *subject* of whiteness and the productive qualities of the sporting spectacle within the contemporary market-based U.S. South. Following Michel Foucault (1988, 1994), I have endeavored to illustrate how the southern sporting subjectivities within these contexts are made polyvalent: First, the subject cannot create his or her identity outside discourse meaningfully, and therefore each spectator is the subject of discourse. Second, the spectator becomes subjected to the discourses of neoliberalism if he or she puts himself or herself at the position from which discourse makes most "sense" (as postplantation elite sans the burden of history, as a member of the atomized masses of the working-class "Nation").[2] In short, the southern sporting spectacle brings people together to remind them that they are individuals, mythologically reprieved from the social and economic histories in which they make their own lives.

What I perhaps have not made clear up to now is that these technologies are not unique to the Grove at Ole Miss or the super speedways of NASCAR. In the context of neoliberal market hegemony, each form of subjectivity penetrates many aspects of everyday life in America. Written in political shorthand, one might suggest that these subjectivities lie in the (albeit fluctuating) chasm between Texan Ron Paul (neoliberalism as myth and posthistoric absolution) and Texan George W. Bush (neoliberalism as flawed policy and performative southern identity). In other words, neoliberal economic polity has necessarily spilled over into, and made use of, the "American" superstructure as a way of producing the conditions of its existence. It has manufactured, within both those who profit from its uneven distribution schemes and those who do not, the *privatization of citizenship*: the ultimate free-market ethos of "conservative Republicanism" that creates the myth of identity as private property. This "southern" sporting identity exists in the age of privatization as a reified, abstract technology that can be marketed, mediated, and sold to buyers of the free-market spectacle. But the sport and southern foci discussed here give these technologies traction within the popular sphere. Consumers are purchasing ownership of a vast network of neoliberalized identity politics within postmodern America and beyond.

These technologies of the South are significant for this and other reasons. They have been normalized, contested, and spectacularized to create a singular identity politic of the contemporary national imaginary. They are made powerful by both the spectacle and the processes of spectacularization that make them "normal." These technologies privilege whiteness, masculinity, and market hegemony, defining whose identities matter within the neoliberal market: "Condensed into the image/hieroglyph of the innocent or incipient American, these anxieties and desires are about whose citizenship—whose subjectivity, whose forms of intimacy and interest, whose bodies and identifications, whose heroic narratives—will direct America's future" (Berlant 1997, 6). And so it might be argued that members of the "Grove Society" and "NASCAR Nation" are not the dupes or victims they have been made out to be in the scholarly discourse, but rather are acutely aware of the benefits or detriments of neoliberalism and the effects its policies have had on their everyday lives. This hypothesis is given partial credence in the cultural political tensions that have come to define Barack Obama's presidency, whereby political transformation (and the cyclical turn) has been met, and prolifically opposed, by an entrenched (if residual) cultural logic rooted to the reimagined local, to tradition (without history), to "values" and "faith" (in both God and market), to patriarchy and whiteness—in short, to the *technologies of the South*. Here, at the "cyclical swing," these technologies of the South offer but a lie, yet it is a powerful, spectacular lie that brings about the truths of privilege for those who have invested most significantly in their own free-market identity politics. In cultural terms, then, to answer Wallerstein's (2008) epigraph, one might surmise that amid these fractures of spectacle and capital, perhaps too much damage has been done.

NOTES

1. Such an intensive hypercommercialization led one *Sports Illustrated* writer to declare NASCAR "the most commercially saturated sport in the U.S." (Hinton 1999, 66): Membership in "NASCAR Nation" is signified by spectators' adornment with the corporate logos of their favorite driver-celebrity; tracks, events, and televisual texts bear the imprint of corporate "facilitators" through an omnipresent universe of symbolic, narrative, and imaged promotional technologies; and on any given race weekend, spectators at NASCAR racetracks will be exposed to more than forty thousand corporate logos and intellectual properties (not including those existing in hypermediated spaces such as telecasts).

2. As such, these new technologies of the self—constructed in and through the southern sporting spectacle—perhaps do hold some of the emancipatory promise theorized by Michel Foucault. By changing or rejecting the spectacle, the overrepresented faction of southern working-class spectators at NASCAR races can create alternatives to their normalizing systems of representation and subjectification; rejection through nonconsumption, if you will. In much the same way, by clinging to the vestiges of Old South gentility and the rituals of white privilege interwoven into the cultural fabric of the Grove Society, spectators at Ole Miss share some degree of agency in molding their existence in this recapitulated Old South spectacle.

REFERENCES

Albert, M. 2003. *Parecon: Life after Capitalism*. London: Verso.

Bakan, J. 2004. *The Corporation: The Pathological Pursuit of Profit and Power*. New York: Free Press.

Beck, U., and E. Beck-Gernsheim. 2002. *Individualization: Institutionalized Individualism and Its Social and Political Consequences*. London: Sage.

Berlant, L. 1997. *The Queen of America Goes to Washington City: Essays on Sex and Citizenship*. Raleigh, NC: Duke University Press.

Best, S., and D. Kellner. 1999. "Debord, Cybersituations, and the Interactive Spectacle." *Substance* 90:129–154.

Bishop, R. 2001. "Stealing the Signs: A Semiotic Analysis of the Changing Nature of Professional Sports Logos." *Social Semiotics* 11 (1): 23–41.

Brown, E. B. 2000. "Negotiating and Transforming the Public Sphere: African American Political Life in the Transition from Slavery to Freedom." In *Jumpin' Jim Crow: Southern Politics from Civil War to Civil Rights*, ed. J. Dailey, G. E. Gilmore, and B. Simon, 28–66. Princeton, NJ: Princeton University Press.

Brown, W. 2004. "NASCAR's Diversity Dearth May Be Sponsor-Driven." *Washington Post*, July 25, G02.

Buchanan, P. 2002. *The Death of the West*. New York: St. Martin's Press.

Certeau, M. de. 1984. *The Practice of Everyday Life*, trans. S. F. Rendall. Berkeley: University of California Press.

Cohodas, N. 1997. *The Band Played Dixie: Race and the Liberal Conscience at Ole Miss*. New York: Free Press.

Cova, B. 1997. "Community and Consumption: Towards a Definition of the "Linking Value" of Product or Services." *European Journal of Marketing* 31 (3/4): 297–316.

Crang, M. 2000. "Relics, Places and Unwritten Geographies in the Work of Michel de Certeau." In *Thinking Space*, ed. M. Crang and N. Thrift, 136–153. London: Routledge.

Debord, G. 1981. "Definitions," trans. K. Knabb. In *Situationist International Anthology*, ed. K. Knabb, 45. Berkeley, CA: Bureau of Public Secrets.

———. 1994. *The Society of the Spectacle*, trans. D. Nicholson-Smith. New York: Zone.

Deleuze, G., and F. Guattari. 1987. *A Thousand Plateaus: Capitalism and Schizophrenia*. Minneapolis: University of Minnesota Press.

Denzin, N. K., and M. D. Giardina, eds. 2007a. *Contesting Empire, Globalizing Dissent: Cultural Studies after 9/11*. Boulder, CO: Paradigm.

———. 2007b. "Introduction: Cultural Studies after 9/11." In *Contesting Empire, Globalizing Dissent: Cultural Studies after 9/11*, ed. N. K. Denzin and M. D. Giardina, 1–19. Boulder, CO: Paradigm.

Derbyshire, J. 2003. "NASCAR Nation." *National Review*, November 10, 29–32.

Derrida, J. 1987. *The Truth of Painting*, trans. G. Bennington and I. McLeod. Chicago: University of Chicago Press.

Dodson, J. 1997. "Ole Miss Continues Struggle with History." *Daily Mississippian*, March 21, 1, 8.

Duerson, A. 2004. "Roadtrip: University of Mississippi." *Sports Illustrated on Campus*, September 23, 10–11.

Eco, U. 1976. *A Theory of Semiotics*. Bloomington: Indiana University Press.

Evans, E. 2004. "What's Your Ole Miss?" *Daily Mississippian*, August 23, 2.

Foucault, M. 1977. *Discipline and Punish: The Birth of the Prison*, trans. A. Sheridan. New York: Vintage Books.

———. 1984. "Space, Knowledge, and Power." In *The Foucault Reader*, ed. P. Rabinow, 239–256. New York: Pantheon Books.

———. 1988. "Technologies of the Self." In *Technologies of the Self: A Seminar with Michel Foucault*, ed. L. H. Martin, H. Gutman, and P. H. Hutton, 16–49. Amherst: University of Massachusetts Press.

———. 1994. *The Order of Things: An Archaeology of the Human Sciences*. New York: Vintage Books.

Frederick, C. R. 1999. *A Good Day to Be Here: Tailgating at the Grove at Ole Miss*. Doctoral dissertation, Indiana University.

Friedman, M. (1962) 2002. *Capitalism and Freedom*. Chicago: University of Chicago Press.

———. 1993. *Why Government Is the Problem*. Palo Alto, CA: Stanford University/Hoover Institution.

Geier, J. 2008. "The Coming Economic Meltdown." *International Socialist Review*, no. 57. Available at http://www.isreview.org/issues/57/feat-economy.shtml.

Giroux, H. A. 1997. "Rewriting the Discourse of Racial Identity: Towards a Pedagogy and Politics of Whiteness." *Harvard Educational Review* 67 (2): 285–320.

———. 2004. *The Terror of Neoliberalism: Authoritarianism and the Eclipse of Democracy*. Aurrora, Canada: Garamond Press.

Gottdiener, M. 1994. "Semiotics and Postmodernism." In *Postmodernism and Social Inquiry*, ed. D. R. Dickens and A. Fontana, 155–181. New York: Guilford Press.

Hagstrom, R. 1998. *The NASCAR Way: The Business That Drives the Sport*. New York: Wiley.

Hale, G. E. 1998. *Making Whiteness: The Culture of Segregation in the South, 1890–1940*. New York: Vintage Books.

———. 1999. "We've Got to Get Out of This Place." *Southern Cultures* 5 (1): 54–66.

Hall, S. 2001. "Encoding/Decoding." In *Popular Culture: Production and Consumption*, ed. C. L. Harrington and D. D. Bielby, 123–132. Malden, MA: Blackwell.

Hardt, M., and A. Negri. 2000. *Empire*. Cambridge, MA: Harvard University Press.

Harvey, D. 2005a. *A Brief History of Neoliberalism*. Oxford: Oxford University Press.

———. 2005b. *The New Imperialism*. New York: Oxford University Press.

———. 2006. *Spaces of Global Capitalism: A Theory of Uneven Geographic Development.* London: Verso.

———. 2007. *The Limits to Capital,* new ed. London: Verso.

Hedges, C. 2007. *American Fascists: The Christian Right and the War on America.* New York: Free Press.

Hinton, E. 1999. "Goodbye Sweet Charlotte." *Sports Illustrated,* February 22, 66.

hooks, b. 1992. *Black Looks: Race and Representation.* Boston: South End Press.

Horwitz, T. 1999. *Confederates in the Attic: Dispatches from the Unfinished Civil War.* New York: Vintage Books.

Kincheloe, J. 2004. *Critical Pedagogy.* New York: Peter Lang.

Kincheloe, J. L., and S. R. Steinberg. 2006. "An Ideology of Miseducation: Countering the Pedagogy of Empire." *Cultural Studies ↔ Critical Methodologies* 6 (1): 33–51.

Kincheloe, J. L., S. R. Steinberg, N. M. Rodriguez, and R. E. Chennault, eds. 1998. *White Reign: Deploying Whiteness in America.* New York: St. Martin's Griffin.

King, C. R., and C. F. Springwood. 2001. *Beyond the Cheers: Race as Spectacle in College Sport.* Albany: State University of New York Press.

Klein, N. 2007. *The Shock Doctrine: The Rise of the Disaster Economy.* New York: Metropolitan Books.

Kusz, K. 2007. "From NASCAR to Pat Tillman: Notes on Sport and the Politics of White Cultural Nationalism in Post-9/11 America." *Journal of Sport and Social Issues* 31 (1): 77–88.

Lederman, D. 1993. "Old Times Not Forgotten." *Chronicle of Higher Education* 15 (October 20): A51–A52.

Lefebvre, H. 2004. *Rhythmanalysis: Space, Time and Everyday Life.* London: Continuum.

Li, M. 2008. "An Age of Transition: The United States, China, Peak Oil, and the Demise of Neoliberalism." *Monthly Review* 59 (11): 20–34.

Limbaugh, R. 1993. *See, I Told You So.* New York: Simon and Schuster.

"Loyal and Ready to Buy: Las Vegas Motor Speedway 2000." Report prepared by NASCAR, Las Vegas, NV.

Maffesoli, M. 1995. *The Time of Tribes.* London: Sage.

McLaren, P. 1988. "Schooling the Postmodern Body: Critical Pedagogy and the Politics of Enfleshment." *Journal of Education* 170 (3): 53–83.

———. 2005. *Capitalists and Conquerors: A Critical Pedagogy against Empire.* New York: Rowman and Littlefield.

Meredith, J., B. Marshall, and J. Doar. 2002. *James Meredith and the Integration of Ole Miss.* Boston: John F. Kennedy Library and Foundation.

Morris, M. 1989. "Tooth and Claw: Tales of Survival and 'Crocodile Dundee.'" *Social Text* 21:105–127.

Negri, A. 2003. *Time for Revolution,* trans. M. Mandarini. New York: Continuum.

Newman, J. I. 2007a. "Army of Whiteness? Colonel Reb and the Sporting South's Cultural and Corporate Symbolic." *Journal of Sport and Social Issues* 31 (4): 315–339.

———. 2007b. "A Detour through 'NASCAR Nation': Ethnographic Articulations of a Neoliberal Sporting Spectacle." *International Review for the Sociology of Sport* 42 (3): 289–308.

———. 2007c. "Old Times There Are Not Forgotten: Sport, Identity, and the Confederate Flag in the Dixie South." *Sociology of Sport Journal* 24 (3): 261–282.

———. 2010. "Full-Throttle Jesus: Toward a Critical Pedagogy of Stockcar Racing in Theocratic America." *Review of Education, Pedagogy, and Cultural Studies* 32 (3): 263–285.

Newman, J. I., and M. D. Giardina. 2008. "NASCAR and the 'Southernization' of America: Spectatorship, Subjectivity, and the Confederation of Identity." *Cultural Studies ↔ Critical Methodologies* 8 (4): 479–506.

———. 2011. *Sport, Spectacle, and NASCAR Nation: Consumption and the Cultural Politics of Neoliberalism.* New York: Palgrave Macmillan.

"The 100 Things You Gotta Do before You Graduate (Whatever the Cost)." 2003. *Sports Illustrated on Campus*, September 30, 4.

Phillips, K. 2006. *American Theocracy: The Peril and Politics of Radical Religion, Oil, and Borrowed Money in the 21st Century.* New York: Viking.

Pinder, D. 2000. "'Old Paris Is No More': Geographies of Spectacle and Anti-Spectacle." *Antipode* 32 (4): 357–386.

Read, S., and L. Freeland. 1983. "The Needed Symbol?" *Daily Mississippian*, April 12, 2.

Reed, J. S. 1986. *The Enduring South: Subcultural Persistence in Mass Society.* Chapel Hill: University of North Carolina Press.

Ritzer, G. 1998. *The McDonaldization Thesis: Explorations and Extensions.* London: Sage.

Rubin, R. 2002. *Confederacy of Silence: A True Tale of the New Old South.* New York: Atria Books.

Sansing, D. G. 1990. *Making Haste Slowly: The Troubled History of Higher Education in Mississippi.* Jackson: University of Mississippi Press.

———. 1999. *The University of Mississippi: A Sesquicentennial History.* Jackson: University of Mississippi Press.

Wallerstein, I. 2008. "2008: The Demise of Neoliberal Globalization." *MR Zine*, February 1. Available at http://mrzine.monthlyreview.org/2008/wallerstein010208.html.

Weeks, L. 1999. "Two from Ole Miss, Hitting It Big." *Washington Post*, January 7, C1.

Wetzel, D. 2006. "Red Flag." Yahoo! Sports, October 9. Available at http://sports.yahoo.com/nascar/news?slug=dw-confederateflag100906&prov=yhoo&type=lgns.

Winders, J. 2003. "White in All the Wrong Places: White Rural Poverty in the Postbellum US South." *Cultural Geographies* 10 (1): 45–63.

16

Hijacking Canadian Identity

*Stephen Harper, Hockey, and
the Terror of Neoliberalism*

JAY SCHERER
LISA McDERMOTT

The CBC [Canadian Broadcasting Corporation] usually has a half-hour with the Prime Minister [PM] for his year-end interview. This year, however, the Corp. was offered 15 minutes . . . with Stephen Harper. Now this is revealing as the Harper government is no fan of the media and many Conservatives especially don't like the CBC, believing it is left-of-centre and does not treat the Harper government fairly. Compare this with CTV. The [private] network got its usual hour-long interview. . . . [Its] journalists asked the Prime Minister about his love/hate affair with the national media. Mr. Harper said he likes to do interviews "when I have something to say. Otherwise, I don't . . . I think that's what Canadians expect. . . . They don't expect the prime minister to aspire to be a media star as an end in itself." Meanwhile, the reluctant media star is appearing in two 15-second spots on TSN [The Sports Network] to promote the IIHF World Junior Championship, which is taking place over the holidays in the Czech Republic. The hockey-fan PM asks Canadians to watch the series. (Taber 2007, A6)

Political pundit Jane Taber's year-end column in 2007 revealed a host of fascinating tensions within the Canadian political landscape. Beyond highlighting the PM's well-documented antagonistic relationship with the Canadian media (e.g., Delacourt 2007; L. Martin 2010),[1] Taber identifies Harper's less-than-subtle rebuke of the public broadcaster, the CBC, in favor of the privately owned CTV network (owned by telecommunications giant Bell Canada Enterprises [BCE]). For many conservatives, including Harper, the CBC is a leftist monolith of the welfare state that holds little relevance in an age of globalization and media deregulation. Ironically, though, Harper's affection for the national game of hockey, like that of many other middle-aged Canadian men, was cultivated every Saturday night when he watched the CBC's legendary program *Hockey Night in Canada* (Johnson 2005). Germane to this chapter, Taber also adroitly illuminates a consistent media tactic in the political arsenal of both Harper and his Conservative strategists: the ongoing representation of Harper as a hockey fan and scholar of the game, and the (re)production of an imagined national culture as common sense in an effort to target various Canadian electoral constituencies.

Throughout this chapter, we argue that these representational strategies are an extension of what Andrew Wernick (1991) has described as "promotional politics"—a new stage of promotion within the mainstream politics of advanced capitalist democracies through which political dialogue has been subsumed by the language and practices of contemporary marketing and image-making spectacles. Of course, the personalization of political figures from across the political spectrum via well-rehearsed and enduring links between nationalism and the mythology (to use Roland Barthes's [(1957) 2000] terms) of hockey is certainly not unprecedented in Canadian history (Macintosh and Hawes 1994; "Golden Nation" 2002). However, in the context of the current Conservative government's unabashed commitment to an increasingly divisive neoliberal and socially conservative agenda, it is vital to hold up Harper's hegemonic hijacking of Canadian identity and its articulation to hockey for critical reflection. Indeed, as Canadians increasingly confront the "terror of neoliberalism" (Giroux 2004) under the Harper government, there is an unprecedented urgency to examine when the cultural/sporting nation is conjured up by various politicos so that "an affective unity can be posited against the grain of structural divisions and bureaucratic taxonomies" (Rowe, McKay, and Miller 1998, 120).

To begin this chapter, then, we provide background to Canada's right-wing political resurgence and the emergence of Stephen Harper as this country's political leader. In what follows, we discuss the public relations strategy of the Conservative Party (CP), which, since 2004, has been carefully crafted by political strategists to soften Harper's image as an uncharismatic, right-wing ideologue, making the PM and the CP more palatable to middle- and working-class Canadian voters. We suggest that these promotional tactics have focused specifically on articulating Harper's mediated identity with the national sport of hockey and constructing the PM as a passionate hockey fan, an avid hockey historian, and an "ordinary" Canadian hockey dad. All of these developments, moreover, work to obscure Harper's ideological leanings and the profound effects of the CP's neoliberal and socially conservative agenda on Canadians.

The Rise of Stephen Harper: The Right Strikes Back

The emergence and rebranding of Stephen Harper as a federal political leader is a direct result of the reunification of the Canadian right, in the form of the CP of Canada,[2] and the Liberal Party's downfall under the weight of a devastating sponsorship scandal. Regarding the former, since the late 1980s, the right-wing vote has been divided between the Reform Party/Canadian Alliance Party and the PC Party which, under PM Brian Mulroney, governed Canada from 1984 to 1993. Led by Albertan Preston Manning, the Reform Party was formed in 1987 by a range of western Canadian interest groups that were disillusioned with what they argued was the PC's favoritism toward the province of Quebec, a lack of federal fiscal responsibility, and the PC's failure to meet western Canadians' needs. For example, at a 1989 Reform convention, Manning delivered his (in)famous "House Divided" speech that disparaged the PC government's 1986 decision to award a billion-dollar maintenance contract for CF-18 fighter planes to Montreal's Canadair, even though a Winnipeg consortium's bid was cheaper and judged by the federal government's own experts to be technically superior. Manning opened his speech with a joke that played on the Calgary Flames' Stanley Cup championship that temporarily disrupted the Edmonton Oilers' legacy in the late 1980s:

> Last year, in a magnanimous effort to redress regional disparities, Edmonton allowed Calgary to win the Stanley Cup. While it is Edmonton's nightmare that this might be repeated this season, Les MacPherson of the Saskatoon *Star Phoenix* had an even worse nightmare. He dreamt that Mulroney and the federal government intervened after last year's Stanley Cup final to give the cup to Montreal even after Calgary had won the series. (Quoted in Johnson 2005, 149)

Although initially a PC supporter, Harper[3] became disenchanted with Brian Mulroney's brand of conservatism and, thus, found a welcome home in the Reform Party, where, in 1987, he became the party's Chief Policy Officer.[4] In a 1997 speech to the right-wing U.S. Council for National Policy, Harper described Canada as a "welfare state in the worst sense of the word" ("Canada through Stephen Harper's Eyes" 2011) and likened Mulroney's conservatism to that of a liberal Republican version. In Harper's own words:

> The [Progressive] Conservative party was running the largest deficits in Canadian history. They were in favour of gay rights officially, officially for abortion on demand. . . . Officially for the entrenchment of our universal, collectivized health-care system and multicultural policies in the constitution of the country. . . . This explains one of the reasons why the Reform Party has become such a power. ("Canada through Stephen Harper's Eyes" 2011)

Elected as a Calgary MP in 1993, Harper had a strained relationship with the Reform Party and Preston Manning over the next four years. While Manning embraced a populist approach and represented the rural resource-producing regions, Harper believed that the Reform Party needed to target a broader constituency of Canadians by emphasizing conservative social values consistent with the traditional family, the market economy, and patriotism to appeal to those parts of the urban middle and working classes and rural constituents who agreed with those values (Wells 2006). After concluding that he was unlikely to defeat the populist Manning, Harper quit the Reform caucus in 1997 and became president of the National Citizens Coalition (NCC).

Despite Harper's departure from federal political circles, he maintained close ties with other western-based conservatives and carefully followed the Reform Party's trials and tribulations. During this time, Harper was a frequent commentator in the media; unsurprisingly, his columns found a home in the conservative-leaning national newspaper the *National Post*. In one column, Harper praised Alberta's[5] conservative culture and openly critiqued Canada: "Alberta has opted for the best of Canada's heritage—a combination of American enterprise and individualism with the British traditions of order and cooperation. We have created an open, dynamic, and prosperous society in spite of a continuously hostile federal government. Canada appears to be content to become a second-tier socialistic country" (quoted in Johnson 2005, 282). However, his most infamous column, titled "The Alberta Agenda," appeared in 2001 as an "open letter" to then Alberta premier Ralph Klein. Harper and other prominent conservatives, including University of Calgary[6] political scientists Tom Flanagan and Ted Morton, argued that Alberta should withdraw from the Canada Pension Plan and the Canada Health Act, collect revenue from personal income (a federal responsibility), and create an Albertan provincial police force to replace the Royal Canadian Mounted Police (RCMP). Or, as the authors argued, "It is imperative to take the initiative, to build firewalls around Alberta, to limit the extent to which an aggressive and hostile federal government can encroach upon legitimate provincial jurisdiction" (quoted in Flanagan 2007, 23). While the "Alberta Agenda" was widely lambasted and discredited in the media as little more than a separatist platform, Harper and his coauthors continued to promote a far-right perspective and argued that Canadian provinces needed "to block further expansion of the welfare state" (quoted in Flanagan 2007, 23). All of these manifestos, though, did little more than tarnish Harper's political reputation as an angry, uncharismatic, right-wing zealot, a persona that continues to haunt him to this day.

By the end of the last millennium, the Reform Party had been officially disbanded and replaced by the Canadian Alliance Party, led by Albertan Stockwell Day. However, the right-wing vote continued to be divided, and conservative politics reached its nadir in November 2000 when Canadians awarded Jean Chrétien his third consecutive majority government, although the Alliance remained the official opposition party. The Alliance's failure to make inroads in Ontario, Canada's most populous region, along with concerns about Day's leadership, opened the door for Harper's return to federal politics. After receiving encouragement from a range of conservative supporters, Harper resigned his NCC position; formally declared his leadership candidacy on December 2, 2001; and was elected leader of the Canadian Alliance in March 2002. Harper's ideological leanings in his post as opposition leader were clear for most Canadians to see. When Jean Chrétien announced in 2003, to widespread public support, that Canada had declined to join the "Coalition of the Willing" and the U.S.-led invasion of Iraq, Harper responded in a House of Commons speech by castigating the Liberals' position:

> "We will not be neutral. We will be with our allies and our friends, not militarily but in spirit we will be with them in America and in Britain for a *short and successful conflict* and for the liberation of the people of Iraq. We will not be with our government, for this government, in taking the position it has taken, had betrayed Canada's history and its values . . . and for the first time in our history, left us outside our British and American allies in their time of need." (Quoted in Flanagan 2007, 88; emphasis added)

There were, of course, individuals in the Canadian public who supported Harper's stance, most notably hockey and media personality Don Cherry, who devoted an entire episode of his popular weekly show *Coach's Corner* to promote his position that Canada should have supported the United States. Wearing a star-spangled tie, Cherry, who also scolded Montreal hockey fans for booing the U.S. anthem, extolled, "I hate to see them [the United States] go it alone. We have a country that comes to our rescue, and we're just riding their coattails" (quoted in Matte 2003).[7]

As opposition leader, Harper was well aware that he could not defeat the Liberals without giving "unity a try" (Wells 2006, 49), which meant reaching out to the PC Party to coalesce the Canadian right. After protracted negotiations with PC leader Peter MacKay in October 2003, the two parties announced a merger to form the rebranded CP of Canada. Equally significant, on March 20, 2004, Stephen Harper was elected as leader of the new party, completing a remarkable rise through the federal political ranks.

Selling Harper to "Ordinary" Canadians

In June 2004, after an exhausting leadership campaign, Harper lost a hastily called federal election to the Liberals and former finance minister Paul Martin, who had succeeded Jean Chrétien as PM. While the Conservatives remained the official opposition party, having made some inroads in Ontario, they were completely shut out in Quebec. This was the first time a center-right party had failed to win a seat in Quebec. Nevertheless, the Liberals were reelected with only a minority government thanks to revelations that between 1997 and 2002, up to $100 million of a $250 million sponsorship program was awarded to Liberal-friendly advertising firms and Crown corporations for little or no work. Despite this disturbing publicity, the Liberals inflicted considerable damage to the CP's credibility in a number of attack ads that played on Harper's image as a right-wing ideologue and accused the Conservatives of a "hidden agenda" (notably regarding public health care) that was in line with U.S. interests. While Harper was despondent over the loss, he responded to it by shifting his CP party closer to the political center and attempted to "rectify" his image to make him more palatable to non-western Canadians, especially those in Ontario and Quebec. As one of the "Calgary School" players, David Bercuson, explained: "I think there was a sharp epiphany after the last election. The people around Stephen Harper realized the only way to win power was to transform themselves and their message" (quoted in Walkom 2006, F1). A key element in this political "makeover" was the Conservative Convention in March 2005. As one Conservative adviser recalled, "It was a giant PR exercise. The goal was to go into the convention, come out of the convention, not fuck up, and come up with moderate centre-right policies and show the public that we were not a scary prospect" (Wells 2006, 140). That summer, Harper also took his PR exercise on the road and traveled across Canada in a promotional mission nicknamed the "Glad as Hell Tour." As the CBC reported, Harper's reimaging strategy was clear: "'Conservative Stephen Harper will hit the festival and barbeque circuit across Canada this summer to persuade voters he's a nice, warm guy with a good sense of humour'" (Johnson 2005, 426).

Beyond these efforts, in 2005, the Conservatives began to rethink their advertising strategies to woo "ordinary" (a staple of Harper's rhetorical devices) lower-middle-class and working-class Canadians. Taking their cue from Australian PM John Howard's successful 1996 campaign manual,[8] the Conservative's focus on these demographics signaled Harper's recognition that, just as center-left parties had made inroads into wealthier and more urban sections of the electorate, Conservative success hinged on their ability to disconnect lower-middle and working-class voters from their traditional center-left positions (Montgomerie 2007; Barns 2006). The Conservatives were particularly impressed with Howard's appeals to the Australian constituency nicknamed "the battlers": middle-class families struggling to raise their children on a modest income. The Conservatives subsequently rearticulated their platform to Canadians through an advertising strategy that revolved around groups of fictional people who reflected *core voters*, *non-Conservative voters*, and potential *swing voters*. Identified as *core voters*, "Steve and Heather" were a married couple in their forties with three children who owned their own business. "Zoey," cast as the *non-Conservative voter*, was a single, twenty-five-year-old urban resident who ate organic food and practiced yoga. *Swing voters*, however, represented an interesting snapshot of the CP's interpretation of middle- and working-class Canadians, a constituency to which the Conservative policy book made a number of appeals (Flanagan 2007). "Mike and Theresa," cast as having "a mortgage and two kids . . . moved out of Toronto to suburban Oakville because they hated the bustle of downtown" (Wells 2006, 214). "Dougie," however, represented the "Conservatives' fondest hope" (214): a single, male tradesperson in his late twenties, "Dougie" agreed with Conservative policies on crime and welfare abuse but was "more interested in hunting and fishing than politics and often didn't bother to vote" (Flanagan 2007, 224). The Conservatives concluded that targeting the likes of "Dougie" through a new round of brand advertising and enticements (e.g., a tax credit for his imagined tools and an environmental tax exemption on the invented truck that he drove to his fictional job) would provide electoral dividends. The CP's strategy of attempting to understand its "market" by pinning down the predilection of Canadian voters is, of course, emblematic of Wernick's (1991) observation of the increasing incorporation of sophisticated advertising practices (e.g., voter analyses and predictions) from the field of market research into the political realm.

On November 1, 2005, Justice John Gomery's report on the Liberal sponsorship scandal greeted Canadians. While the Gomery Report exonerated PM Paul Martin, it concluded that a culture of entitlement existed within the federal government and described an elaborate kickback scheme designed to benefit the Liberals' Quebec wing. These revelations prompted Harper to initiate a motion of nonconfidence that was seconded by the left-of-center New Democratic Party's then leader, Jack Layton, forcing Martin to call an election for Monday, January 23. The Conservatives were well prepared and had gained valuable electioneering experience from the 2004 federal election. Promoting their neoliberal policy platform under the rubric "Stand Up for Families" (quoted in Porter 2006), they proposed cutting the federal Goods and Services Tax and replacing the Liberal's embryonic "Universal Childcare Program" with a "Choice[9] in Child Care Plan," while simultaneously rebranding Harper's identity to appeal to various swing voters. Building on their earlier strategic reformulations, the Conservatives released an advertising strategy that targeted "ordinary" Canadians. Titled "Stand Up for Canada," the ads featured a woman posing a series of scripted questions and receiving equally scripted answers from Harper about pensions, taxes, and government ethics as the sponsorship scandal continued to engulf the Liberals. Despite their simple, direct, and hokey nature (Wells 2006), the ads represented an important discursive shift in Conservative strategy that now explicitly targeted core and potential swing voters; in Flanagan's terms, they were looking to capture voters who "get their coffee at Tim Hortons"[10] (2007, 225) rather than Starbucks. Conservative pundit Tim Powers likewise used a hockey analogy to explain the new ad strategy: "There's a school of thought that we're more Don Cherry than Giorgio Armani. And the ads reflect that. Look at the success that Don Cherry has had with Rock'em Sock'em Hockey [videos]. A low-tech production, but a messenger with a product people wanted" (Wells 2006, 182). Such comments provide a window to the CP's framing and reimagining of Harper through symbols of Canadian identity to capture swing wing voters like "Dougie" with his "workaday concerns" (Wells 2006, 221). Significantly, "Dougie" was (and remains) likely white, presumably heterosexual, and from a working-class background: arguably the precise constituency of Canadians for whom the deeply conservative and hypermasculine Don Cherry still holds considerable appeal. Importantly, "Dougie" was also cast by the Conservatives as a neoliberal citizen—an economic actor and consumer who seeks neither special status nor special treatment from the state and has the ability to provide for his own needs and to service his own ambitions (Brown 2006).

Harper's tactics are noteworthy on three additional fronts. First, they point to the ascendency of marketing discourse in contemporary promotional

Jay Scherer and Lisa McDermott

politics, which has been transformed into a continual advertising campaign that is commonly fought via the terrain of popular culture. Second, Harper's relatively recent embrace of popular symbols of Canadian identity (e.g., hockey and Tim Hortons) is ironic. Before this shift, Harper was, in fact, loath to admit that such things as Canadian identity and culture[11] even existed ("Federal Leaders" 2005). Third is the profoundly penetrating, essentializing, and divisive "us versus them" binary logic used by Harper and his Conservative colleagues to represent not only various target demographics but also rival political parties: the Tim Hortons (versus the Starbucks) electorate, the "Dougies" (versus the "Zoeys") demographic, or more recently, supporters of popular cultural practices (e.g., hockey versus the "highbrow" performing arts community).[12] As with all binaries, though, the Conservative "Other" is framed through mutually exclusive oppositional terms that work to devalue and denigrate critical perspectives and rival images. All of these issues are glaringly apparent in Harper's approach to non–Tim Hortons, pro-CBC, anti–Don Cherry, non-hockey-loving Canadians who, for the Conservatives, are represented as unsympathetic to a neoliberal vision.[13] Central to the workings of the CP's very public discursive "us versus them" strategy, then, is a "cultural war" (Chase and Vu 2010) that continues to foment in an effort not only to attract particular swing voters but also to pin down what it means to be a "real" Canadian in terms of the terrain of values, ideology, and convictions, areas in which, as Caplan (2010) argues, "Canadians have [historically] disagreed."

On January 23, 2006, the Conservatives were elected with a minority government, thirty-one ridings short of a majority.[14] While the Conservatives made substantial progress in Ontario and Quebec, they captured only a handful of seats in Atlantic Canada and were shut out in Canada's three largest cities (Toronto, Montreal, and Vancouver), revealing an enduring urban-rural divide. Despite the use of attack ads that "revealed" Harper's ties to right-wing groups in the United States and Canada, the Liberals were unable to recover from the Gomery Report's damning revelations. However, Harper's victory cannot be solely attributed to public anger over the sponsorship scandal; rather, over the last two decades a salient shift has occurred in Canadian political ideology, public policy, and attitude (Cameron 2001). Since the 1990s, parties on the political right have been steadily climbing in popularity and influence, and the Canadian Alliance-PC Parties' merger ultimately solidified this trend in "which conservative parties slowly displaced the Liberals as the party of the average working Canadian" (Wells 2006, 264).

Massaging the Voter: Manufacturing Harper's Hockey Identity

MP's Christmas cards have been arriving in mailboxes during the past couple of weeks. . . . Stephen Harper's card shows him gazing at a collage of photos of himself from the past year—the Prime Minister with his family, hoisting the Stanley Cup, holding up a hockey jersey, posing with the Queen and various foreign leaders. (Smyth 2007, A3)

Building on his successful electioneering strategy, less than a month after being sworn in as PM, Harper's promotional identity was reinforced in an article that discussed how the RCMP now drove Harper to hockey rinks to watch his son, Ben, play hockey. This questionably newsworthy story was accompanied by photos of Harper walking with his son to his hockey practice and sitting in the stands with the other, "ordinary" hockey parents. In the article Harper was quoted as saying, "No matter how tired I am, no matter how many things I have on my agenda, if I can find time, I can always get up and always make it to the hockey rink" ("Stephen Harper" 2006).[15] Also referenced were comments from other parents, including one father who remarked that Harper was simply "a regular guy like all the rest of us, he still walks, talks and chews gum the same way as we do" (quoted in "Stephen Harper" 2006). Central to these media narratives is the Conservative frame of not only "ordinary Canadians" juxtaposed to the "elite" supposedly favored by the Liberal Party, but also the "ordinariness" of Harper and his family (Taylor 2007; Hunt 2007): "Ben and Rachel are the ordinary kids in hockey and gymnastics, Stephen and Laureen are such an ordinary couple that one or the other may forget an anniversary, similar to . . . any other ordinary Canadian couple" (Taylor 2007).[16] Discursive promotional strategies such as these, however, function to obscure the glaring class differences and the growing socioeconomic divide between "ordinary" Canadians and their counterparts in Canada's business establishment and political circles who, in the sociologist Zygmunt Bauman's (2001) terms, have effectively seceded from the Canadian commons and openly advocate for the welfare state's dismantlement.

Harper's routine embracement of national symbols such as hockey has been further emphasized through his promotion of his identity as a hockey "historian." For example, in 2006, while attending hockey games in Toronto and Calgary, Harper was referred to as a "hard-core hockey fan" and a "member of the *Society for International Hockey Research*" who is currently "penning a book about the pre-NHL history of the game" ("PM's Hockey Book" 2006). Harper did, however, readily admit to the challenge of being PM and completing this scholarly endeavor: "My original plan was to have that published by the end of this year, but I have to admit, that since Jan. 23, I've been spending a little less time on it than before so we'll have to see" ("PM's Hockey Book" 2006).[17] Similarly, in an exclusive one-on-one interview for TSN, Harper reiterated his identity as a proud hockey dad and creatively extolled, "I love my job as Prime Minister, but if you could be a hockey player, I mean, what could be better than that" ("PM's Hockey Book" 2006).

Harper's fondness for representing himself via an affective national symbol is, of course, far from unintentional and little more than an adaptation of the discursive strategies of the George W. Bush administration. Indeed, in May 2006, Harper met with Frank Luntz, a U.S. Republican pollster, communications adviser, and adjunct fellow at the Hudson Institute.[18] Credited with having a momentous impact on contemporary U.S. political and public discourses and being the mastermind behind the Republican rise in fortunes dating back to its 1994 sweep of Congress (Berkowitz 2006a; Moxley 2007), Luntz was also the wordsmith who underpinned Bush's carefully crafted successive wins and policies (Berkowitz 2006a, 2006b; Mason 2006). For his part, Luntz promotes his services as "language guidance": "'my job is to look for the words that trigger the emotion. Words alone can be found in a dictionary or telephone book, but words with emotion can change destiny, can change life as we know it'" (Mason 2006, A5). Accordingly, Luntz's central promotional strategy is to use carefully tested and often repeated simple messages, along with deploying key words, images, pictures, and national symbols "to deflect suspicions of unpopular policies" (Moxley 2007; "Tories Influenced" 2006). In 1997, Luntz fashioned a communications how-to guide, *Language of the 21st Century*, which became the Republican Party's "language bible" (Mason 2006) from which the Harper government now "worships" (Berkowitz 2006a, 2006b; "Tories Influenced" 2006; Dobbin 2006; Mason 2006). Luntz's interest in Canadian politics and his relationship to western Canadian economic and social conservatives, in fact, dates back to Reform Party days when he was hired by Preston Manning's political advisers as an official election pollster and strategic adviser. Indeed, Luntz's primary task was "to coach" Manning on the art of negative political campaigning (Walker 1992).

Harper's 2006 meeting with Luntz occurred the day before the Republican pollster (Doskoch 2006) gave the keynote address at the tenth-anniversary conference of the Civitas Society (Gairdner 2006), lauded as "the premier venue in Canada where people interested in conservative, classical liberal and libertarian ideas can not only exchange ideas, but meet others who share an interest in these rich intellectual traditions" (Civitas Society, n.d.). Its founder, William Gairdner, described the conference as such: "there were about 250 members of Civitas there from all across Canada drawn from a membership that constitutes a kind of lonely platoon of conservative/libertarian thinkers, journalists, professors and policy wonks who are pretty excited to find one of their own as Prime Minister of Canada [Stephen Harper]" (Gairdner 2006). As Gairdner alluded to, the Civitas Society has particularly close ties to the PM; Harper's former chief of staff (2006–2008), Ian Brodie, is a Civitas director, and Harper's mentor and former campaign manager, Tom Flanagan, was a founding director and past president.

Luntz's speech, "Massaging the Conservative Message for Voters,"[19] was a communications blueprint that outlined a range of public relations strategies for "tailoring a conservative message and selling it to moderate voters" (Moxley 2007). Its objective was nothing less than to solidify the conservative minority government with a view to expanding it to a majority in the next election. The pillars of Luntz's "message" to Civitas members were accountability,[20] opportunity (read: the neoliberal favorite of "choice"), security, and families. "Massaging," meanwhile, encompassed language, images, and national symbols. Or, as Luntz explained, "language is your base. Symbols knock it out of the park" (quoted in Mason 2006). To this end, Luntz simply encouraged Harper to link his identity and right-wing agenda to national symbols such as hockey: "If there is some way to link hockey to what you all do, I would try to do it" (quoted in Thompson 2006, A6). According to Luntz, these types of personal appeals to national popular culture play a critical role in appealing to "average voters," the "Mikes and Theresas" and "Dougies" of the Conservative playbook, who may not traditionally vote Conservative: "You have a gentleman who may well be the smartest leader intellectually. Now, that is half the battle. The other half of the battle is to link that intelligence to the day-to-day lives of the average individual" (quoted in Thompson 2006, A6). The American linguist George Lakoff's work on framing within political and public discourses is constructive in making sense of Luntz's counsel to Civitas, and the CP of Canada. For Lakoff (2006), what is central to deconstructing contemporary political discourse is an understanding of how issues are framed through particular commonsense values that resonate within a political context. As Lakoff elucidates, "Politics is about values; it is about communication. . . . And it is about symbolism" (8); the positioning of an issue follows "from one's values, and the choice of issues and policies should symbolize those values" (8).[21]

Building on these ideas, Luntz also encouraged the Conservatives to promote neoliberal policy initiatives through carefully manipulating discourse by deploying less threatening terms like "tax relief" rather than "tax cuts," "personalization" instead of "privatization." Such discursive tactics represent an Orwellian version of Newspeak designed to massage Canadian voters, particularly as those terms are embraced and uncritically transmitted by right-leaning corporate media conglomerates or through alternative (i.e., "unfiltered") media sources. Neoliberalism is, in this instance, clearly so much more than an economic theory; it "constitutes the conditions for a radically refigured cultural politics" (Giroux 2004, 107) that reinforces dominant values, social relations, and understandings of citizenship.

Given Luntz's longstanding relationship with the CP and its political forerunners, it is likely that Harper was well aware of the strategy of making potentially divisive conservative policies palatable through their articulation to popular national symbols like hockey. However, since 2006, those strategies have been driving Harper's media activity. For example, two days after Luntz's presentation, Harper appeared during the Game 2 second intermission of the Ottawa Senators–Buffalo Sabres NHL playoff series, where he posed for photos with other hockey fans and signed autographs (St. Martin 2006). Such practices, of course, juxtapose with Harper's assertion, noted previously, that Canadians do not expect their PM "to aspire to be a media star as an end in itself" (quoted in Taber 2007, A6), not least of which would contradict Harper's "ordinary" rebranding process and the strategy of appealing to "ordinary" Canadians through national symbols.

Returning to our initial remarks about Luntz's discursive philosophy, such articulations are readily apparent in the ongoing attempts by Conservative strategists to "massage" and market various right-wing policies to moderate voters who are now continually encouraged to embrace new identities as neoliberal citizens. In a move to address the childhood "inactivity" and "obesity" "epidemics," for example, federal finance minister Jim Flaherty, clad in skates and a hockey jersey after playing hockey with a group of peewees in his home riding of Whitby, Ontario (Department of Finance 2007), announced a Children's Fitness Tax Credit in 2006 to provide families with up to $500 per child for registration fees. At a tax rate of 15.5 percent, the savings amount to $77.50. Yet, as McDermott (2008) points out, like other policies emphasizing tax cuts rather than investment in public infrastructure and social services, such initiatives further entrench class differences by predominantly supporting families whose children are already registered in sports programs. Indeed, a tax credit is simply a moot point for less affluent families that cannot afford registration fees in the first place.

Luntz's strategy of massaging unpopular (neoliberal) policies with national symbols were routinely on display in Flaherty's initial federal budgets. On the one hand, these budgets were peppered with popular hockey metaphors. On the other hand, though, they contained the hallmarks of neoliberal social engineering: expanded military and law and order funding, substantial corporate subsidies and tax breaks, and a combination of debt reduction and personal tax "relief." In Flaherty's words, "We believe in reducing taxes. We've reduced taxes of every kind—consumption taxes, income taxes, corporate taxes dramatically, excise taxes, the GST by two full percentage points. . . . We believe in controlling the size of government and controlling the growth of government" (quoted in Whittington 2008). Such an agenda represents an ongoing erosion of the tax base to finance public services, developments that effectively preclude future governments from implementing social service programs without increasing taxes (Evans 2008). Similarly, Flaherty's 2007 budget speech announced a Working Families Tax Plan to "support hard-working families." Personalizing "tax relief" measures with a familial example, Flaherty simply noted that tax cuts provide "money families can use to buy new shoes or clothes for their children . . . [o]r even . . . a new pair of hockey skates—just like I did yesterday for my son John" (Flaherty 2007).

Characteristic of a neoliberal agenda is an anathema for governmental regulations, viewed as roadblocks to economic growth. Nowhere is this ideology so conspicuous for Harper than in the case of global warming and Canada's commitment to the Kyoto Accord. In a 2002 fund-raising letter to Canadian Alliance members, Harper decried the Kyoto Accord as an "economy destroying . . . socialist scheme to suck money out of wealth-producing nations" ("Harper Letter" 2007). Harper's perspective is arguably unsurprising given his longstanding connections to the Alberta oil industry and his resolute commitment to aggressive oil sands development (McQuaig 2007). Harper's opposition to the Kyoto Accord followed him into office, where he demonstrated his environmental disdain through frequent denials of global warming and his appointment of Rona Ambrose[22] as Canada's environment minister. In 2006, Ambrose announced that Canada would not meet its Kyoto commitments and, instead, would implement a "Made in Canada" solution to "climate change."[23] Opposition Liberals, who had originally committed Canada to the Kyoto Accord, responded by introducing a private members' bill to force Canada to maintain its Kyoto commitment. Significantly, Harper skipped this bill's parliamentary vote to fly to Toronto on the Department of National Defence's executive jet with his son to watch the Maple Leafs' season opener against the Ottawa Senators (McGregor 2006).[24]

On January 5, 2007, TSN interviewed the PM during the first intermission of the gold medal game of the World Junior Hockey Championships between Canada and Russia. Referenced, yet again, as a hockey historian, he offered his analysis of both the opening period and various rules and regulations. Following a 4–2 Canadian victory, TSN covered a congratulatory phone call from Harper to Canadian head coach Craig Hartsburg, while the next day various newspapers carried a photo of Harper calling from his office with the Canadian flag behind him. These particular stories and images, arguably, served to draw attention away from Harper's recent removal of the much maligned Ambrose from her environment portfolio to neutralize national and international criticism against his government's abandonment of the Kyoto Accord and the subsequent introduction of the Luntz-inspired "Made in Canada" solution: the Clean Air Act. Lamenting Canada's rapidly declining environmental reputation, opposition parties and environmentalists resoundingly attacked the new act (Simpson 2008). Harper's approach to pressing environmental concerns, however, has not deterred the PM from various promotional efforts designed to massage his party's environmental policies and depoliticize the issue of global warming. When former California governor Arnold Schwarzenegger, widely lauded for implementing stringent greenhouse gas emissions caps, traveled to Ontario in 2007 to sign an agreement coordinating fuel efficiency standards to reduce greenhouse gases, Harper also took the opportunity to meet with the governor. While a similar agreement was not forthcoming at the federal level, Harper and Schwarzenegger managed to discuss the Ottawa Senators–Anaheim Ducks Stanley Cup finals and exchanged hockey jerseys in a photo op ("Arnie to Automakers" 2007).

Conclusion

Prime Minister Stephen Harper's reticence toward the media apparently doesn't apply to sportscasters. Harper invited TSN's Gord Miller to 24 Sussex Drive [PM's residence] on Wednesday night so he could be filmed watching Game 2 of the Stanley Cup final. The Prime Minister hasn't held a news conference in Ottawa this year, and only rarely stops on the staircase outside the House of Commons to deliver a message to the news media. His relationship with the parliamentary press is charitably described as frosty. . . . But when it comes to hockey, Harper is expansive and accommodating. ("Harper Makes Time for TSN's Miller" 2006, A13)

We draw this chapter to a close by revisiting our main observation: Stephen Harper's symbolic hijacking and mobilization of hockey as a preeminent signifier of "Canadian-ness" in the pursuit of political fortunes and the remaking of the Canadian social fabric as common sense. Of course, Harper is far from the only political figure to have deployed the iconic status that hockey holds within the Canadian imaginary for political gain. However, in the new millennium, there has been a notable expansion of these carefully crafted promotional practices that Harper and the CP have deployed for personal image-making and relentless partisan advertising, with the ultimate goal of ideologically shifting the Canadian political center to the far right. In so doing, Harper and the CP have masterfully executed Luntz's promotional blueprint of often-repeated messages invoking national symbols to reimagine the PM's political persona as an "ordinary" Canadian hockey fan and scholar of the game, and to articulate the CP as the political choice of middle- and working-class Canadians. Here we suggest that Harper is keenly perceptive to Nagata's (2011) observation that "hockey does two things very well. It serves as a symbolic stand-in for political struggles, and it also distracts from them.... Hockey doesn't matter, and yet it does—to politicians dependent on a discourse of 'us' versus 'them.' What goes on at ice level is insignificant. The real work is happening in the stands."

In the spring of 2011, the CP realized its political objective of forming a majority government, and Stephen Harper's remaking of the Canadian social fabric has continued in full force. With minority status, the Harper government closed more than half of the Status of Women's regional offices, changed the government criteria for funding women's groups, removed the word *equality* from its objectives, refused to adopt pay equity legislation, withdrew funding for a national child-care program ("1,000 Protesters" 2006), and canceled the Liberal Kelowna Accord. The Kelowna Accord sought to improve the education, employment, and living conditions of Canadian Aboriginal peoples through government funding. Within a year of being elected with a majority government, Harper deregulated the Canadian Wheat Board and dismantled the long-gun registry despite opposition from police and medical organizations as well as victims' groups. Finally, during a time of fiscal austerity in which sixty thousand public-sector jobs will be eliminated because of the impact of the 2010 and 2011 federal budgets (Macdonald 2012), the Harper government has indicated its intention to continue to expand military spending (e.g., $16 billion on new F-35 fighter jets—a highly underestimated cost estimate) and, following the widely discredited U.S. crime prevention model, has committed to dedicating $2 billion over the next five years for the construction of new prisons across the country.

The political commentator Lawrence Martin has pointed to the radical transformation of the Canadian political landscape that has occurred under the Harper government in just over six years:

> Under the Conservatives, Canada is a country that venerates the military, boasts a hardened law-and-order and penal system, is anti-union and less green. It's a government that extols, without qualms of colonial linkage,

the monarchy, that has a more restrictive entry policy, that takes a narrower view of multiculturalism, that pursues an adversarial approach to
the United Nations. In a historical first, Canada's foreign policy . . . can be
said to be to the right of the United States. In a nutshell, the cliché about
Canada's being a kinder, gentler nation is being turned on its head. In
hockey parlance . . . we're shifting, with [seemingly] voter approval, from
a country of Ken Dryden[25] values to one closer to those of Don Cherry. . . .
The Cherry brand sells. The Dryden spirit—the tolerance, inclusiveness,
modesty, quiet striving for excellence—are values less heard. (2011)

Most Canadians, however, do not support these developments: Harper and the
CP captured under 40 percent of the popular vote in the 2011 federal election.
Still, the sheer speed at which the Harper government continues to realign the
Canadian political landscape points to the urgent need for progressives to put
forward and promote alternative and more enduring kinds of common interests to challenge the neoliberal and social conservative agenda that is now
ascendant. Undoubtedly, the terrain of popular culture will continue to be a
critical battleground—as it has always been—in the ongoing struggle over national common sense.

NOTES

1. Symptomatic of a neoliberal policy agenda is the decline in democracy, notably in
terms of access to information about government activities. Since becoming PM, Harper
has actively limited the flow of information to the public, particularly through mainstream
media (see, e.g., the Access to Information Commissioner's 2008–2009 report assessing
the responses of twenty-four federal departments to public information request, largely
by the media: thirteen of the departments were rated below average or worse [Office of
the Information Commissioner Canada 2010]). Harper's government-media relations approach enacts what Rosen (2005) calls a "decertification of the press," which he suggests
has two faces. The first involves putting journalists in a diminished position (i.e., "Don't
answer their questions; it only encourages the askers to think they're legitimate interlocu-
tors and proxies for the public"). The second involves describing government efforts to
inform the public as purely factual while dismissing mainstream media as inherently
biased and unable to serve the general interests of Canadians. Decertification, as a Harper
government strategy, encompasses "getting its message" to the public unencumbered by
"negative" media filters and often involves tapping into alternative media venues (e.g.,
blogs, YouTube).

2. The federal Canadian Conservative Party has existed since 1867, although it has
undergone several name changes between then and 1942, when it adopted the name
the *Progressive* Conservative (PC) Party of Canada ("The PC Party" 2005), a term that
Harper has referred to as "an oxymoron" ("Canada through Stephen Harper's Eyes" 2011).
Historically, the PC Party of Canada has adopted a center-right position on economic issues
and a centrist stance on social ones. One of the first tasks of the unified right was to drop
Progressive from the party's name, evidence to "Red" Tory supporters of a political shift to
the right (Plamondon 2006), particularly regarding social issues. As Harper prophetically
argued earlier, "The real challenge is therefore not economic, but the social agenda of the
modern Left. Its system of moral relativism, moral neutrality and moral equivalency is
beginning to dominate its intellectual debate and public-policy objectives. . . . The truth of

the matter is that the real agenda and the defining issues have shifted from economic issues to social values, so conservatives must do the same" (2003, 6). Indeed, Porter (2006) suggests that central to Harper's agenda is the intertwined focus of neoliberalism and social conservatism, a focus that is intent on reformulating how the "social" historically has been understood within Canada. Principal to this "double tendency" is "a continued shift both from the state to the market and from the state to the family; a reconfiguration of what are public goods and what are private goods and responsibilities" (1).

3. Harper completed graduate studies in economics at the University of Calgary, where he became highly enamored with neoliberal guru, Austrian economist, and political philosopher Friedrich Hayek (Rose 1999). Harper is also a noted Thatcher and Reagan admirer.

4. In a 1997 interview, Harper noted, "The agenda of NCC [National Citizens' Coalition] was a guide to me as the founding policy director of Reform" (quoted in Dobbin 2006). Harper would later (1998–2001) become the president of the NCC, which "stands for the defence and promotion of free enterprise, free speech and government that is accountable to its taxpayers" (National Citizens Coalition 2006). Central to its agenda is eliminating "the government's monopoly on healthcare," tax cuts, an economically sound climate change policy, and privatizing the CBC (National Citizens Coalition, n.d.).

5. In Canada, Alberta is frequently referred to as the "Texas of the North."

6. Flanagan and Morton, along with others (Barry Cooper, Roger Gibbins, and Rainer Knopff), are a group of political science professors from the University of Calgary known as the "Calgary School" who are attributed with Harper's swift rise to lead the CP of Canada and ultimately become PM. Marci McDonald (2004) describes the "Calgary School" as being bound by a "neo-conservative agenda [that] read as if it has been lifted straight from the dusty desk drawers of Ronald Reagan: lower taxes, less federal government, and free markets unfettered by social programs such as Medicare that keep citizens from being forced to pull up their own socks."

7. In a CTV interview, hockey icon Wayne Gretzky also openly supported the U.S. invasion: "I live in the United States right now. I elected the president. I happen to think he's a great leader and a wonderful president. And if he believes that we need to be where we are right now, for the freedom of the world, I back him 100%" ("Gretzky Says He Backs Bush" 2003).

8. A key CP adviser in its 2006 election was Brian Loughnane, Howard's national campaign director.

9. Nikolas Rose's (1999) discussion of freedom is relevant here. Central to the workings of a neoliberal rationality is an understanding of freedom whereby the individual is represented as an autonomous, entrepreneurial self who has "the capacity to realize one's desires . . . to fulfill one's potential through . . . acts of choice" (84). Thus, the neoliberal subject is conceived in terms of self-responsibility (rather than social responsibility) and self-actualization through choice. "Choice," within conservative discourse is, therefore, far from an innocent word.

10. Tim Hortons is a coffee and doughnut fast-food restaurant chain that is represented as symbolic of Canadian identity.

11. Harper rarely uses the term "culture," which was noticeably absent in the CP's 2006 election campaign policy document (Dobbin 2006). A 1997 CBC interview provides insight into Harper's views on the notion of Canadian culture. When asked, "Is there a Canadian culture?" Harper responded, "Yes in a very loose sense. It consists of regional cultures within Canada, regional cultures that cross borders with the US. We're part of a worldwide Anglo-American culture. And there is a continental culture" (quoted in Dobbin

2006). Such an understanding of culture aligns well with the interests of global corporations, furthering the entrenchment of globalized economic relations.

12. In explaining why no members of Harper's Conservative cabinet attended the 2008 Governor-General's Performing Arts Award Gala, a Conservative MP noted that "he and many of his fellow Tories don't get 'jacked up' by meeting arts and cultural celebrities, but would if they were honouring 'hockey players'" (Taber 2008, R7).

13. According to a *Vancouver Sun* poll, Harper's political fortunes are grounded in male Tim Hortons–supporting voters who view Don Cherry as a "national icon," watch more sports, and are most likely to fear a terrorist attack (O'Neil 2007).

14. Since 2006, when the CP formed a minority government in Canada, two subsequent federal elections have been called: one in 2008, which resulted in the CP being re-elected as minority government; and a second that occurred in the spring of 2011 and saw the CP reach its objective of forming a majority government.

15. Despite Harper's regularly stated noninterest in being a celebrity, it is ironic that he willingly incorporates his private family life into CP promotional efforts. On the other hand, such measures shore up his representation as a "family" man.

16. Stephen Taylor is an example of the CP's attempt to "decertify" mainstream media as a source for political information and analysis. Taylor, the founder of the blog the *Blogging Torries*, provides a platform for Conservative messages "to get out" "unfiltered" (Delacourt 2007).

17. Azpiri (2007) astutely notes that Harper regularly self-promotes his hockey book in interviews. Azpiri goes on to disclose, however, that when pressed on the book's details, Harper explains that he "only spends about 15 minutes a day working on it," to which Azpiri observes, "It sound[s] more like a hobby than a serious work of historical research."

18. The Hudson Institute is a Washington-based free-market conservative think tank whose financial support comes largely from the corporate sector. According to its 2002 annual report, funders included Cargill, DuPont, ExxonMobil, GE, Merck, and Monsanto (SourceWatch 2008).

19. Gairdner (2006) describes Luntz's speech as follows: "A fascinating political spin-doctor showed us ample polling evidence that what voters want more than even a politician who supports their policies, is someone who is genuine and walks his own talk. Insofar as he is permitted, our PM is doing just that."

20. Luntz urged conservatives to take every opportunity to remind Canadians, "Your Liberal government was corrupt. . . . The way they wasted your hard-earned tax dollars was a disgrace. I want you to leave here committed to insisting that the Conservative government hold that previous Liberal government accountable . . . that you continue doing it for the next year so that every Canadian knows and will never forget and will never allow another government to steal more from them" (quoted in Doskoch 2006).

21. While appearing on a *Global National* newscast, Harper illustrated his understanding of the centrality of values to politics when he described his reticence to interact with the media: "I have no desire to be a celebrity or media star. I'm not in *People* magazine, talking about my hopes and fears as an individual. . . . While I don't go on interviews and unburden my inner soul, at the same time I think Canadians know about me what most people know about me. I think they know that I'm a family man, they know that I'm a hockey fan. They know the kind of values I have, whether they agree with them or disagree with them" (quoted in Mayeda and Martin 2007, A1).

22. Before running as a federal Conservative, Ambrose, whose father was an oil industry executive (Thomson, n.d.), was Alberta's (Canada's most vocal Kyoto critic) Conservative government's senior intergovernmental officer. Her responsibilities

encompassed fiscal, social, and constitutional policy issues, including Alberta's position on the Kyoto Protocol ("Ministers in the Harper Cabinet" 2007).

23. "Climate change" is but another example of Luntz's wordsmithing for Bush's Republicans in an effort to avoid "'frightening'" phrases like *global warming* (Burkeman 2003), which has made its way north of the border. Similarly, the "Made in Canada" climate change solution reproduces Luntz's "made in America" one.

24. The CP repetitively conveyed to the public that it paid for the jet expense to Toronto and Harper's two platinum-level ($182 per seat [Kernaghan 2008]) seats next to Leafs owner Larry Tanenbaum (McGregor 2006). The flight, ticket cost, and company shared at the game arguably debunk Harper's appeal to being an "ordinary" Canadian. His appearance at the game, however, did provide another Harper-hockey photo op.

25. Dryden is the venerated former goalie for the Montreal Canadiens who won six Stanley Cups. Outside of professional hockey, though, he is well known as a federal Liberal politician, lawyer, and celebrated author.

REFERENCES

"Arnie to Automakers: 'Get Off Your Butts.'" 2007. CBC News, May 30. Available at http://www.cbc.ca/canada/story/2007/05/30/schwarzenegger-green.html.

Azpiri, J. 2007. "Harper Taps into Hockey to Aid Political Game." Straight.com, May 10. Available at http://www.straight.com/article-90247/harper-taps-into-hockey-to-aid-political-game.

Barns, G. 2006. "Stephen Harper's Canada?" *Globe and Mail Update*, January 17. Available at http://www.theglobeandmail.com/servlet/story/RTGAM.20060117.wcomment0117/BNStory/National/.

Barthes, R. (1957) 2000. *Mythologies*. London: Vintage.

Bauman, Z. 2001. *Community: Seeking Safety in an Insecure World*. Cambridge, UK: Polity Press.

Berkowitz, B. 2006a. "Politics: Republican Über-Strategist Takes Canada for a Spin." Inter Press Service News Agency. Available at http://ipsnews.net/news.asp?idnews=33457.

———. 2006b. "Spurned by Washington's Republicans, Frank Luntz Turns to Canada." Media Transparency, May 27. Available at http://old.mediatransparency.org/story.php?storyID=129.

Brown, W. 2006. "American Nightmare: Neoliberalism, Neoconservatism, and De-Democratization." *Political Theory* 34 (6): 690–714.

Burkeman, O. 2003. "Memo Exposes Bush's New Green Strategy." *The Guardian*, March 4. Available at http://www.guardian.co.uk/environment/2003/mar/04/usnews.climate change.

Cameron, D. 2001. "Putting the 'Public' Back in Government and the Economy Back in Its Place." Paper presented at Beyond the Washington Consensus: Governance and the Public Domain in Contrasting Economies: The Cases of India and Canada, York University, Toronto, February 3. Available at http://www.yorku.ca/robarts/archives/chandigarth/pdf/cameron_delhi.pdf.

"Canada through Stephen Harper's Eyes." 2011. *The Tyee*, March 23. Available at http://thetyee.ca/News/2011/03/23/StephenHarpersEyes/.

Caplan, G. 2010. "Deciphering Sides in Canada's 'Culture Wars.'" *Globe and Mail*, May 28. Available at http://www.theglobeandmail.com/news/politics/deciphering-sides-in-canadas-culture-wars/article1584647/.

Chase, S., and L. Vu. 2010. "Ignatieff Accuses Tories of Division." *Globe and Mail*, May 18, A4.

Civitas Society. n.d. "Welcome to the Home Page of Civitas." Available at http://www.civi
    tascanada.ca/public/ (accessed March 30, 2012).
Delacourt, S. 2007. "PM Can't Hide His Media Obsession." TheStar.com, April 14.
    Available at http://www.thestar.com/article/202992.
Department of Finance. 2007. "Canada's New Government Encourages Parent to Take
    Advantage of the Children's Fitness Tax Credit." January 5. Available at http://www
    .fin.gc.ca/n07/07-002-eng.asp.
Dobbin, M. 2006. "Will the Real Stephen Harper Please Stand Up?" *Murray Dobbin's Word
    Warriors*, January 10. Available at http://www.canadians.org/wordwarriors/2006/
    jan-10.html.
Doskoch, B. 2006. "Tories Influenced on Climate Change by U.S. Pollster: Environ-
    mentalists." *Bill Doskoch: Media, BPS*, Film, Minutiae*, May 15. Available at http://
    www.billdoskoch.ca/2006/05/15/tories-influenced-on-climate-change-by-u-s-poll
    ster-environmentalists/.
Evans, B. 2008. "Canada's Budget 2008: Taxes and the Forward March of Neoliberalism."
    Centre for Research on Globalization, March 1. Available at http://www.globalre
    search.ca/index.php?context=va&aid=8235.
"Federal Leaders Come Out Swinging as Jan. 23 Election Set." 2005. CBC, November
    29. Available at http://www.cbc.ca/story/canadavotes2006/national/2005/11/29/
    elxn-called.html.
Flaherty, J. 2007. "The Budget Speech 2007: Aspire to a Stronger, Safer, Better Canada."
    Department of Finance Canada, March 19. Available at http://publications.gc.ca/
    collections/Collection/F1-23-2007-1E.pdf.
Flanagan, T. 2007. *Harper's Team: Behind the Scenes in the Conservative Rise to Power.*
    Montreal: McGill-Queen's University Press.
Gairdner, W. 2006. "Civitas, Harper and Free Speech." Available at http://www.william
    gairdner.com/journal/2006/5/8/civitas-harper-and-free-speech.html.
Giroux, H. 2004. *The Terror of Neoliberalism: Authoritarianism and the Eclipse of
    Democracy.* Boulder, CO: Paradigm.
"Golden Nation: Canada Takes to the Streets to Celebrate Hockey Gold." 2002. Sports
    Illustrated/CNN.com, February 24. Available at http://sportsillustrated.cnn.com/
    olympics/2002/ice_hockey/news/2002/02/24/canada_celebration_ap/.
"Gretzky Says He Backs Bush on U.S.-Iraq War." 2003. CTV News, March 25. Available
    at http://www.ctv.ca/servlet/ArticleNews/story/CTVNews/1048585693197_256/?hub
    =TopStories.
Harper, S. 2003. "Rediscovering the Right Agenda." *Report Magazine*, June. Available at
    http://archive.rabble.ca/babble/ultimatebb.cgi?ubb=get_topic&f=1&t=001910.
"Harper Letter Called Kyoto 'Socialist Scheme.'" 2007. TheStar.com, January 30. Available
    at http://www.thestar.com/article/176382
"Harper Makes Time for TSN's Miller." 2007. *Kamloops Daily News*, May 31, A13.
Hunt, B. 2007. "Fitzsimmons, PM Share Passion for Hockey History." *Daily Gleaner*
    (Fredericton, NB), May 31, B3.
Johnson, W. 2005. *Stephen Harper and the Future of Canada.* Toronto: McClelland and
    Stewart.
Kernaghan, J. 2008. "Leaf Ticket Price Cuts Just a Token Gesture." Slam! Sports. Available
    at http://slam.canoe.ca/Slam/Columnists/Kernaghan/2005/07/30/1153755-sun.html.
Lakoff, G. 2006. *Thinking Points: Communicating Our American Values and Vision.* New
    York: Farrar, Straus and Giroux.
Macdonald, D. 2012. *The Cuts behind the Curtain: How Federal Cutbacks Will Slash Services
    and Increase Unemployment.* Ottawa, ON: Canadian Centre for Policy Alternatives.

Macintosh, D., and M. Hawes. 1994. *Sport and Canadian Diplomacy.* Montreal: McGill-Queen's University Press.

Martin, L. 2010. *Harperland: The Politics of Control.* Toronto: Penguin Canada.

——. 2011. "A Country of Dryden's Values Shifts to Cherry's." *Globe and Mail*, October 18. Available at http://www.theglobeandmail.com/news/politics/lawrence-martin/a-country-of-drydens-values-shifts-to-cherrys/article2204000/.

Mason, J. 2006. "Lord of the Lingo: How to Pick Your Words Carefully and Influence Everyone." The Council of Canadians, November 4. Available at http://www.canadians.org/publications/CP/2006/summer/lingo.html.

Matte, A. 2003. "War a Necessary Evil, Some Canadians Argue." *My Town Crier*, May 1. Available at http://www.mytowncrier.ca/war-a-necessary-evil-some-canadians-argue.html.

Mayeda, A., and D. Martin. 2007. "Harper Predicts Economic Hangover: Green Laws Could 'Bite' into Growth." *Calgary Herald*, December 21, A1.

McDermott, L. 2008. "A Critical Interrogation of Contemporary Discourses of Physical (In)activity amongst Canadian Children: Back to the Future." *Journal of Canadian Studies* 42:5–42.

McDonald, M. 2004. "The Man behind Stephen Harper." *Walrus Magazine*, October. Available at http://www.walrusmagazine.com/articles/the-man-behind-stephen-harper-tom-flanagan/.

McGregor, G. 2006. "Hockey Trumps Kyoto for Harper: Skips Climate Vote in Order to Take Son to Maple Leafs Game." *The Gazette* (Montreal), October 6, A4.

McQuaig, L. 2007. *Holding the Bully's Coat: Canada and the U.S. Empire.* Toronto: Doubleday Canada.

"Ministers in the Harper Cabinet." 2007. *Globe and Mail*, August 13. Available at http://www.theglobeandmail.com/servlet/story/RTGAM.20060121.wxtorycabinet/BNStory/specialNewTory2006/national.

Montgomerie, T. 2007. "Canada Provides All Conservatives with Hope." ConservativeHome Tory Diary. August 3. Available at http://conservativehome.blogs.com/torydiary/2007/08/a-special-profi.html.

Moxley, M. 2007. "Minority Report." *This Magazine: Because Everything Is Political*, January–February. Available at http://www.thismagazine.ca/issues/2007/01/minorityreport.php.

Nagata, K. 2011. "Why Harper Wants You to Know He Loves Hockey." *The Tyee*, October 6. Available at http://thetyee.ca/Opinion/2011/10/06/Harper-Loves-Hockey/.

National Citizens Coalition. 2006. Home page. Available at http://nationalcitizens.ca/index.html.

——. n.d. "Agenda for Canada: The Power of Free Enterprise and Common Sense." Available at http://nationalcitizens.ca/doc_bin/agenda_canada.pdf (accessed April 22, 2008).

Office of the Information Commissioner Canada. 2010. "Interim Information Commissioner Renews Call for Action to Stem Delays in Federal Access to Information System." Available at http://www.infocom.gc.ca/eng/med-roo-sal-med_nr-cp_2010_5.aspx.

O'Neil, P. 2007. "'Harper's Canadians' Prefer Double-Double, Cherry on Top: Poll." *Edmonton Journal*, February 3, A8.

"1,000 Protesters Attack Tory Policies on Women's Rights." 2006. *Edmonton Journal*, December 11, A7.

"The PC Party." 2005. CBC News, May 3. Available at http://www.cbc.ca/news/background/conservativeparty/pcparty.html.

Plamondon, B. 2006. *Full Circle: Death and Resurrection in Canadian Conservative Politics.* Toronto: Key Porter Books.

"PM's Hockey Book Shut Out by Job Duties." 2006. CBC News, April 14. Available at http://www.cbc.ca/canada/story/2006/04/14/harper-hockey060414.html.

Porter, A. 2006. "The Harper Government: Towards a New Social Order?" Centre for Research on Globalization, May 22. Available at http://www.globalresearch.ca/index.php?context=va&aid=2494.

Rose, N. 1999. *Powers of Freedom. Reframing Political Thought.* Cambridge: Cambridge University Press.

Rosen, J. 2005. "From Meet the Press to *Be* the Press." PRESSthink, March 21. Available at http://journalism.nyu.edu/pubzone/weblogs/pressthink/2005/03/21/be_press.html.

Rowe, D., J. McKay, and T. Miller. 1998. "Come Together: Sport, Nationalism, and the Media Image." In *MediaSport*, ed. L. Wenner, 119–133. London: Routledge.

Simpson, J. 2008. "Turning Our Back on the UN." *Globe and Mail*, May 21, A13.

Smyth, J. 2007. "No Offence Sent; Garth Turner's Troll the Most Animated of Political Greeting Cards." *National Post*, December 20, A3.

SourceWatch. 2008. "Hudson Institute." May 1. Available at http://www.sourcewatch.org/index.php?title=Hudson_Institute.

"Stephen Harper Balances Job, Hockey Dad Duties." 2006. CTV News, March 1. Available at http://www.ctv.ca/servlet/ArticleNews/story/CTVNews/20060228/harper_hky_dad_060228/20060228?hub=TopStories.

St. Martin, R. 2006. "Harper Night in Canada." PoliticsWatch, May 9. Available at http://www.politicswatch.com/harper-may9-2006.htm.

Taber, J. 2007. "Stephane Dion Gives Us Something to Chew On." *Globe and Mail*, December 22, A6.

———. 2008. "Why Tories Are Blowing Off G-G's Arts Party." *Globe and Mail*, May 3, R7.

Taylor, S. 2007. "Harpers and Dions Contrasted." Stephen Taylor—Conservative Party of Canada Pundit. June 12. Available at http://www.stephentaylor.ca/2007/06/harpers-and-dions-contrasted/.

Thompson, E. 2006. "U.S. Guru Tells Tories to Talk Hockey." *Edmonton Journal*, May 7, A6.

Thomson, T. n.d. "A Threat to Our Environment." *The Peak: Student Newspaper of Simon Fraser University.* Available at http://www.the-peak.ca/2006/05/a-threat-to-our-environment/ (accessed March 30, 2012).

"Tories Influenced by U.S. Pollster: Activists." 2006. CTV News, May 14. Available at http://www.ctv.ca/servlet/ArticleNews/story/CTVNews/20060514/tories_luntz_060514/20060514?hub=Qperiod.

Walker, W. 1992. "First of Four Parts." *Toronto Star*, April 13, A15.

Walkom, T. 2006. "Is He a Changed Man?" *Toronto Star*, January 7, F1.

Wells, P. 2006. *Right Side Up: The Fall of Paul Martin and the Rise of Stephen Harper's New Conservatism.* Toronto: McClelland and Stewart.

Wernick, A. 1991. *Promotional Culture: Advertising, Ideology and Symbolic Expression.* London: Sage

Whittington, L. 2008. "It's Politics as Usual for Flaherty." TheStar.com, March 10. Available at http://www.thestar.com/News/Canada/article/326788.

17

Global Smackdown

Vince McMahon, World Wrestling
Entertainment, and Neoliberalism

TED BUTRYN

Vince McMahon's World Wrestling Entertainment (WWE) is the most lucrative professional wrestling organization in North America. Its flagship show, *Raw*, which airs on Monday nights on the USA network, regularly ranks among the better-rated cable television programs weekly, with men making up more than 70 percent of viewers. Additionally, around half a million children ages two to fourteen watch WWE programming each week (Tamborini et al. 2005). The WWE also airs two other moderately successful programs nationally on cable television: *Smackdown!* on Friday nights on MyNetworkTV and *NXT* on Tuesday nights on the SyFy Channel. The company itself, which until the late 1980s was a mainly regional enterprise, is now a favorably rated, publicly traded multimedia platform company with an increasingly global business plan (Show 2006). According to information provided to its shareholders, almost a quarter of the company's profits are derived from markets outside the United States. Over the past several years, the company has run successful tours, often to sell-out audiences, around the world, including South Africa, Australia, New Zealand, England, Ireland, Italy, the Philippines, Belgium, Japan, Germany, Canada, Brazil, Peru, Chile, El Salvador, and Mexico. Most recently, in February 2012, the WWE performed for record-setting crowds in Abu Dhabi ("WWE Breaks Records" 2012). In fact, when the massive earthquake struck mainland China in 2008, WWE capitalized, seizing the marketing opportunity by sending one of its biggest stars, Rey Mysterio, who was doing promotional work in the country, to the quake zone.

Despite WWE's ongoing popularity, lucrative profit margins, and international expansion, however, little research has been conducted on the cultural meaning of WWE until relatively recently (Atkinson 2002; DeGaris 1999; H. Jenkins 1997; Maguire 2005; Sammond 2005; Spark 1996). In addition, the business of the WWE has received little attention from academics, and in fact, most of the information to be garnered on the business of professional wrestling must be gathered from trade publications and "insider" newsletters that report on the finances of wrestling organizations, and more recently, data presented to WWE shareholders. Further, the politics of the WWE, both in terms of storylines and considering their right-leaning political stance as typified by the explicit support of U.S. troops, has yet to be addressed in any depth by scholars in sport, communication, or cultural studies.

Drawing from Giroux (2004, 2008) and other cultural studies and critical sport studies scholars, I situate the WWE squarely within the framework of neoliberalism. More specifically, I examine how the business practices of the WWE, as well as the use of particular gimmicks, characters, and storylines, work to align this corporate wrestling juggernaut with the principles of neoliberalism. In addition, I explore how the company's global expansion can be viewed as part and parcel of the larger U.S. entertainment and sport hegemony. As McLaren and Martin note, the mass media's role in the Iraq war was, in part, to get people "to subjectively identify with ideas that were not objectively in their interests, for example nationalism, racism, and war" (2004, 286). It is clear that when one examines the scripted representations of racial and ethnic minorities in WWE broadcasts with participatory citizenship programs like the WWE's ongoing "Smackdown Your Vote" campaign that has registered thousands of young voters, one prominent function of WWE programming relates to neoliberal agendas. From the decimation of the wrestling territories in the 1980s to current images of WWE personnel performing for troops overseas during their "Christmas in Baghdad" special, the emergence, albeit a chaotic and at times uncertain one, of an increasingly globalized, politicized, and monopolistic WWE is not all that far removed from what some on the left have termed the "Bush Gang." I also briefly discuss the issue of steroids in wrestling and the discourses that emerged following the controversial deaths of two of the company's top stars. I argue that McMahon's stance toward steroid use and abuse over the years is characteristic of the ways that issues such as public health and personal choice are framed within the rationale of neoliberalism. Before moving to a brief, but necessary, overview of how McMahon's company became what it is today, it is first worth noting that at first glance, a chapter on neoliberalism and pro wrestling, often referred to by my own colleagues as "fake" or "pseudo" sport, may seem absurd for several reasons. Indeed, in their documentary "Wrestling with Manhood: Boys, Bullying, and Battering," Jhally and Katz (2002) begin with an admission that their own colleagues wonder about their interest in wrestling. While significant attention has been given to the global politics of, for instance, baseball, basketball, and soccer, pro wrestling, and the WWE specifically, has had few academic points of insertion into discourses on globalization, postcolonialism, cultural imperialism, and the like. In fact, as DeGaris (2005) notes, much of the work on wrestling has been textual analysis, with mixed results and application. In addition, the WWE has been picked apart by both media critics and academics for its relationship to, and perpetuation of, violent content, as well as racist, sexist, and homophobic representations (Jhally and Katz 2002). Thus, some may question whether this seemingly profane and, within sport studies and cultural studies at least, peripheral topic warrants serious treatment in a text on sport and neoliberalism.

When examined more closely, however, with an eye toward the carnivalesque aspects of the actions and commentary of the "Bush Gang" following the events of September 11, 2001, I argue that the success of Bush, Cheney, and Rumsfeld in "working" (i.e., "fooling" in pro wrestling parlance) the collective audience of the United States was, taken together, a performance right out of a WWE script. The administration's story of uranium in mysterious tubes, which floated to media to the *New York Times* and then was used as part of the basis for invading Iraq, is in one sense similar to the well-worn wrestling storyline involving the heel (i.e., "bad guy") wrestlers incapacitating the babyface (i.e., "good guy") with brass knuckles. Both are comical in that they employ deceit that, when watched closely enough, eventually becomes an obvious ruse.

As many performers and wrestling writers have noted of Vince McMahon's "performance" as his onscreen alter ego, the generally despicable "Mr. McMahon," it is difficult to tell where one leaves off and the other begins. It is interesting to consider some of the leading figures in the Bush administration in the same light. What, for instance, of Dick Cheney unceremoniously telling Democratic senator Patrick Leahy to "fuck yourself"? Indeed, I argue that the Bush Gang oddly resembles a pro wrestling stable of "heel" characters, a group of performers held together by their desire for power, their arrogance and systematic abuse of the rules, a willingness to do anything to get the championship belts. At the same time, using wrestling lingo, George W. Bush plays the populist good ol' boy character for all it is worth, selling himself to the "marks" as the "morally guided" good guy you'd like to have a beer with.

Enter Sports Entertainment, Exit Employment

The rise of Vince McMahon and World Wrestling Entertainment began when McMahon bought the company, then named the World Wrestling Federation (WWF), from his father in 1982 (Assael and Mooneyham 2002) and almost immediately set about changing the business in ways that had positive and, more importantly for this chapter, negative and essentially permanent effects. The wrestling business in North America had always been organized into numerous regional territories, each with its own local promoter and, in some cases, particular style of matches (Assael and Mooneyham 2002; DeGaris 2005). The territory system was governed by a set of informal rules dealing with, among other things, turf disputes. In short, the promoters were generally not motivated to put all of their rivals out of business, because when things functioned properly, everybody made money. Top wrestlers traveled from territory to territory periodically, and each promoter reaped the benefits of new or "fresh" talent drawing fans to the shows. Most wrestling historians, such that they exist, generally agree that most promoters would bend the rules, but not break them. However, when McMahon bought the business from his father in 1982, it took less than a decade for him to buy out, force out, or simply overwhelm other territory owners (Assael and Mooneyham 2002).

McMahon knew that in order to increase revenue for his company, he had to get local media markets to show his product. Dave Meltzer, the publisher of the long-running "insider" newsletter *The Wrestling Observer*, noted that while the practice of promoters buying television time for their shows, which would then theoretically pave the way for live events, was not uncommon, McMahon perfected it (Meltzer 2003). The bond that had existed between local promoters and local stations was no match for what McMahon offered, and eventually local promotions that in some cases had been institutions in the market now had no media outlet and were doomed from that point on. McMahon also mastered the practice of persuading wrestlers in other organizations to jump ship, leaving the promoters without their money-drawing performers. Other organizations, most notably Crockett Promotions in the Carolinas, still turned in hefty profits. However, Meltzer argues that while this allowed them to continue for months, even years, the fact that McMahon's company was based in and around major markets, including New York, and had Hulk Hogan's increasing star power allowed the WWE to monopolize the mainstream media coverage of their product. As he states, even as the first WrestleMania event did poorly in some of the old territory markets, "they were the kings of New York, and New York was where all the decision makers lived" (Meltzer 2003, 5).

One interesting aspect of the WWE's publicly traded status is that the WWE became what amounts to a monopoly by systematically working to put other regional territories around the United States and Canada out of business via ravenous adherence to free-market principles. With the added obligation of turning profits for its shareholders as the utmost priority, the ends seemed to justify the means as far as business dealings were concerned. For example, if World Championship Wrestling (WCW), based in Georgia, ran its inaugural pay-per-view event, then McMahon made sure the WWE had an event on free television to counter and leech viewers away (Assael and Mooneyham 2002). The laws of the free market and the morphing of the company's particular neoliberal agenda allowed McMahon to create his growing global multimedia empire, and yet it also essentially removed what might be termed the occupational subculture of wrestling in the process. While trivial when compared to the massive loss of public services and jobs in the United States over the past decades, the business of pro wrestling and the livelihoods of the wrestlers were dramatically affected by McMahon's WWE.

Indeed, DeGaris (2005) argued that while McMahon's growing monopoly of the business in the late 1980s may have been good for the bottom line of the company, it had several negative effects. For example, one of the functions the "more than twenty-five regional circuits" (197) provided was a kind of informal North American training environment for newcomers to the business. As opposed to the contemporary system, which often requires that interested men and women attend wrestling schools, often at a hefty fee, to even learn the basics of the practice, DeGaris noted that when he (a veteran of more than fifteen years in the business) entered in 1987, few of these schools existed. The formal training would last only several weeks, after which you went out on the circuit, wrestling several times a week until you learned how to "work," or perform. DeGaris and many other veteran performers bemoan the current system because they see the lack of fundamentals of many younger wrestlers. Further, many are disturbed at the shift from an emphasis on live performances in local markets to a television-based product that eventually led to the literal scripting of matches, thereby, ironically and probably not coincidentally, removing individual creativity and ad-lib communication from much of the process. DeGaris elaborates on what amounts to the production line model of wrestling: "I have noticed a trend in locker rooms toward a much more detailed choreography of matches. When I started, scripting matches was a joke. Within the past few years, I have seen detailed written scripts of matches. I have even witnessed 'dress rehearsals' for matches" (210). In the end, young wrestlers "become reliant on the script and never learn to work" (211). Wrestling throughout most of the twentieth century, then, was a public practice that necessitated individual creativity and intimate communication. In addition, it constituted an authentic occupational subculture that, in many ways, was akin to an ontological melding of physical theater and factory work. McMahon's WWE played by the rules of the market, certainly, but in the process it helped eliminate a public pedagogical space and prompted the creation of fee-based services. Further, the subsequent move to matches that are scripted move by move stands as a sharp counter to neoliberalism's claim that, as Farred describes it in this volume, "only the free market can produce the kind of competition that enables individuals in all walks of life to achieve their full potential." What was once a creative, spontaneous practice based on cooperation between performers devolved into mere rote repetition, poesis replaced by mimesis. Again, I am not arguing that this shift is in any way as troubling as the privatization of health care, for instance. What I am arguing is that, when examined in light of larger neoliberal ideologies that gained steam in the 1980s, McMahon's WWE can be seen as part and parcel of a whole host of troubling shifts, from the profound to the merely unfortunate.

In the end, once McMahon had established the WWE as the only game in town, with the exception of WCW in the mid-1990s, and the ad-lib matches were replaced by detailed scripts, performers became, to an extent, interchangeable and disposable. Of course, some wrestlers had more natural charisma and athletic ability than others, but if the "role" called for a big guy who could work a little, then there were certainly many men who could fit that bill. This change in the business was also dangerous from a labor perspective, because with few options left for employment, speaking out against company practices was feared. As far back as the early 1980s, McMahon had proven hostile toward unionization. Meltzer, for example, notes that McMahon fired the popular Sergeant Slaughter in 1984 partly because "he'd gotten wind Slaughter was talking about unionizing the wrestlers" (2003, 3), and even former WWE star and eventual Minnesota governor Jesse Ventura was frowned on when he advocated similar worker organization (H. Jenkins III 2005). Numerous other former wrestlers, as well as a few wrestling writers, have long criticized the business, and WWE specifically, for its resistance to any form of unionization or general workers' rights movement (Assael and Mooneyham 2002; Wilson and Johnson 2003).

Locating the WWE's Politics: Corporate Citizenship, Militarization, and Juiced Corporeality

With McMahon and the WWE's role in the downsizing of the pro wrestling workforce in North America established, what are we to make of the company's current modes of operation as they relate to neoliberalism's market-centered and decidedly antidemocratic directives? What are the politics of the business, how do they market themselves, and how do the wrestlers who have managed to secure a place with the WWE negotiate the demands of the business? While neither the WWE nor any large media conglomerate or outlet is in itself a "neoliberal company," Giroux notes that they can "use their power to simultaneously support neoliberal values, reactionary policies, and the politicians who produce them" (2008, 11). This quote is particularly timely given the recent media attention on wife of Vince McMahon and former WWE CEO Linda McMahon as she stages a campaign for the U.S. Senate seat in Connecticut (Hernandez and Brustein 2010). Numerous articles in the popular press, including the *New York Times* and *Wall Street Journal* (e.g., Frank 2010), have either taken McMahon's treatment of wrestlers to task or praised her keen sense of business acumen, depending on their perspective. Most notably, and amid the current debates over health care, McMahon and the WWE have been taken to task over the longtime practice of designating their performers as independent contractors, thus freeing the company from the economic burdens of traditional employee health insurance.

However, the company, while undoubtedly politically conservative, is not above morphing its product into whatever it sees as the most viable profit-making entity domestically and internationally. In fact, it has a keen sense of when the larger political and cultural tides are shifting. In the first several months of 2008, WWE initiated a move toward a more "family friendly" product, including the restriction of the use of blood (via blading or cutting of the forehead) in live and televised events, the introduction of a *WWE Kids* magazine, complete with word puzzles and so on, and the "improvement" in its television rating to a PG, down from the equivalent of a PG-13 rating ("Overview" 2012). In addition, much of the misogynist and profoundly sexist content that was commonplace in the late 1990s and early 2000s is virtually nonexistent, with the women's matches containing little of the nearly nude spectacle and titillation that used to be part of them. On the surface, the WWE's desire to penetrate and settle into new global markets has led to something akin to not a kinder and gentler product but one that can be consumed more comfortably by more people globally. Indeed, many of these have changes have benefited Linda McMahon in her run for the U.S. Senate seat. While her opponents and many media critics have commented on the "old" WWE and Linda McMahon's role in the creation of it (e.g., Collins 2010), she has repeatedly reminded anyone who will listen that she was (supposedly) instrumental in bringing about the changes to the WWE product, thus framing herself as the "good conservative" she claims to be.

In fact, both Linda and Vince McMahon have, quite slyly, attempted to rebrand the WWE as a conservative-friendly (yet still politically unaligned) and socially minded model for other public companies. Not unlike many other forms of sport and entertainment, the WWE has constructed an image of itself as a responsible corporate entity situated squarely within democratic ideals of political participation. The "Smackdown Your Vote!" campaign, for instance, has been a public relations coup for the WWE, including numerous mentions in the *New York Times* (Stelter 2008). The company had correspondents at both national conventions in 2004, staged a debate between real-life conservative Republican wrestler and MSNBC financial show host John Layfield and Democratic performer Mick Foley, and worked with organizations such as MTV's Rock the Vote campaign and, somewhat surprisingly, the League of Women Voters, to register young voters. The WWE's efforts to register the youth vote, in particular is, in one sense, aimed at the empowerment of their fans and the health of the U.S. democratic process, such that it still exists. A critical read, though, is that the campaign is yet another of Vince McMahon's attempts to gain legitimacy in the eyes of the mainstream and the more affluent public, many of whom have a disdain or indifference toward professional wrestling.

While the WWE claims to be bipartisan in its programs, however, one need only look at an episode of their flagship *Monday Night Raw* show that aired during the 2009 political season to see where their political views lie. The 2008 U.S. presidential primary candidates, Democrats Hillary Clinton and Barack Obama and Republican John McCain, all understood the importance of reaching out to the WWE's audience, as the trio taped scripted promos that aired on the *Raw* program the Monday night before the Pennsylvania democratic primary in April (Schneiderman 2008). Using catchphrases from wrestlers of the past woven into their even-more-simplified-than-usual stump-speech sound bites, the candidates sought to position themselves as Main Street populists rather than Wall Street elitists. Obama, for instance, adapted a catchphrase from former WWE star Dwayne "the Rock" Johnson and with a smile, asked, "Can you smell what Barack is cookin'?" All thee clearly read from a teleprompter, and the sight of John McCain awkwardly uttering the term "McCainiacs" (a play on Hulk Hogan's "Hulkamaniac" fans) would have won few talent auditions. Later in the show, however, the company showed which side of the aisle they were courting, perhaps, when a "match" featured two (poor) impersonators of Obama and Clinton, as well as a Bill Clinton look-alike at ringside who served as Hillary's manager. The crowd booed through this televised trainwreck, but importantly, both Democratic candidates were effectively lampooned, while McCain was spared similar treatment. Again, on the confines of their website, the WWE has allowed for a variety of diverse political voices, with African American wrestler Elijah Burke openly advocating for Obama. Further, at various publicity events related to the "Smackdown your Vote!" campaign, Libertarian Val Venis was an outspoken advocate of third-party candidates. However, the bulk of the WWE's audience on a weekly basis is not on its website, or at gatherings in local communities, but rather tuned into its television shows. Thus while the grassroots attempts to broaden the democratic process may or may not be sincere on the part of the individuals taking part, the corporate headquarters' viewpoints speak loudest. In fact, both Vince McMahon's private business endeavors and the acts of his public, steroid-enhanced doppelganger, the reviled "Mr. McMahon" persona, show an indifference to working-class sensibilities that, ironically, characterize a large portion of its audience.

The WWE has also stood side by side with neoliberalism's practice of militarizing public domains. Militarization, according to Giroux, "is widespread in the realm of culture and functions as a mode of public pedagogy, instilling the values and the aesthetic of militarization through a variety of pedagogical sites and cultural venues" (2004, 216). Indeed, the militarization of public space characterized by the increased presence, and apparent fascination with, military units has been echoed to an extent by the militarization of popular culture as well, with shows such as the Fox network's *24* complete with storylines lambasting such "obstructionist" groups as the American Civil Liberties Union (ACLU). The WWE has also integrated overt jingoist rhetoric into their broadcasts, and their annual Tribute to the Troops show emanating from Baghdad has aired every Christmas for the past several years.

In the "community" section of the corporate wing of their website, an entire page is devoted to the WWE's relationship with the U.S. military, including the numerous awards given to the company and McMahon from military organizations, and organizations related to the military families. In 2008, the company was awarded the first annual Corporate Patriot Award at the GI Film Festival in honor of its service to the military and their families, particularly in the form of their yearly trips to Iraq and Afghanistan. WWE programming regularly features members of the military in the audience as well, and individuals in the armed forces are eligible for free tickets to WWE live events. The WWE's most enduring practice since 9/11 has been its annual "Tribute to the Troops" Christmas show that has been taped every year since 2003 in a location in either Iraq or Afghanistan. The trips are admirable for the simple fact that they still occur, long after many celebrities have ceased going on USO tours and the like, and also because the WWE makes less mention of them and, in fact, loses money because of poor ratings during the holidays. Again, however, while the practice of supporting predominantly young men and women overseas, many of whom are serving extended tours of duty authorized by the military under President Bush, appears both sincere and admirable, my point is that the intersections between the WWE and the U.S. military confirm the fact that pro wrestling, or at least World Wrestling Entertainment, has aided the further militarization of American popular culture, and perhaps even normalized the need for war in the minds of its many young viewers. Indeed, one of the most popular performers in the company, the white, crew-cut, heavily muscled John Cena, made his entrance into the 2010 WrestleMania XXVI show as a U.S. Air Force Guard Drill Team completed their ritualistic routine. As Cena continued to the ring, he performed his standard military-style salute, and the camera panned to the crowd to reveal hordes of young children responding in kind.

A final example of the WWE's propensity to play by the rules of neoliberalism is the way that the company has handled the most recent allegations of steroid abuse by its employees, and its response during the aftermath of the Chris Benoit double murder–suicide case in 2007. A onetime WWE champion, Benoit murdered his wife and child, the latter with a version of his finishing chokehold, and then hung himself, ironically, on his weight machine.

The issue of steroids in pro wrestling is not new, and McMahon nearly went to prison and lost the whole company in the early 1990s on steroid-related charges (Assael and Mooneyham 2002). As many commentators on the business have noted, McMahon always seemed to have a fascination with 'roided-up physiques (he had started a short-lived pro bodybuilding organization in the 1980s, in fact), and in the late 1990s he would chemically alter his own body to more closely resemble that of one of his employees and become a "competitor" himself (Assael and Mooneyham 2002).

The events of the summer of 2007 were different, however, because for the first time the mainstream media, including several pieces in the *New York Times*, began to frame steroids in wrestling not just as a moral or ethical issue, or even a legal one, but rather a public health concern. While the focus in the past had been, for instance, the impact of Hulk Hogan's steroid use on his status as a role model to kids, this time the concern was for the lives of the wrestlers working for McMahon and everyone associated with them. McMahon had allowed the market and the demand, at least his demand, for doped bodies to essentially condone what he and the company knew was a flawed testing program. Now, the media and the medical profession were both asking a new set of questions related to public health (Johnson 2007; Meltzer 2007, 2008, 2009).

The strict drug-testing program that the company instituted in the early 1990s was long gone in November 2005, when former champion Eddie Guerrero was found dead in his hotel room in what was later determined to be heart failure because of, among other things, the prolonged use of steroids and in all probability, human growth hormone. In the media onslaught that followed the Benoit case, numerous former wrestlers appeared on both network and cable television shows, and most made comments regarding steroid use (Johnson 2007). A small number of wrestlers, including former WWE performers Marc Mero and "Superstar" Billy Graham, connected the culture of steroids that McMahon had helped to cultivate with the alarming number of wrestlers who had died "prematurely" in the past decade, many from the use of performance-enhancing and/or recreational drugs. The WWE's wellness policy, instituted after Guerrero's death, was revealed to be something of a sham, as Benoit had received copious amounts of testosterone from a physician who turned out to be a supplier to several WWE wrestlers.

In his book *Ring of Hell: The Story of Chris Benoit and the Fall of the Pro Wrestling Industry*, Randazzo (2008) presents a scathing portrayal of McMahon, the WWE, and the entire global infrastructure of wrestling as a heartless, greedy system with no real compassion for its employees, particularly those who had fallen on hard times. Indeed, numerous writers, from both within and outside the business, began to frame the WWE as an exploitive enterprise that operates under the principle of what Giroux (2008) describes as the politics of disposability. Wrestlers are punished when they are caught, and suspended, sent to rehab, or in extreme cases, fired. The culture of steroid use and abuse, however, and its framing as a poorly thought-out "personal choice" remains. The dozens of performers who have died over the past ten years, McMahon and his "loyal" employees argued on the *Larry King Show*, were the unfortunate victims of their own faulty judgments and excesses.

While I am not arguing that pro wrestlers are at the "frontier-zone of invisibility" (Giroux 2008, 160), many wrestling insiders have argued that if any other population of athletes or entertainers were dying at the rates wrestlers were, the mainstream media and the government would have likely already intervened (Randazzo 2008). Whether this is the case or not, given the notion that wrestling audiences tend to skew lower in socioeconomic status, and the distaste with which many in the mainstream media view the business, it is perhaps not surprising that the health of the individuals who work for the world's largest wrestling organization would not be at the forefront of the public consciousness.

In the end, though, the company took what might be considered a short-term hit, with stocks initially falling and then rebounding by the end of 2007. The company also lost no major sponsors (Schneiderman 2008). In one sense, the company's being featured, albeit negatively, on cable television shows for the entire summer of 2007 may have actually helped the eventual return to corporate normalcy.

As Giroux notes, within the context of neoliberalism, "Financial investments, market identities, and commercial values take precedence over human needs, public responsibilities, and democratic relations" (2008, xvi). While the maintenance of an occupational subculture is certainly not a human need in the same sense as public education or health care, it does constitute a public practice that allowed thousands of men in the United States and Canada to make a decent living, albeit with an often nomadic existence, for decades. More importantly, it is clear that McMahon looked away from the obvious and, apparently, widespread issue of steroid and pain pill use in the company even as some of his most valued employees dropped dead, and in the case of Benoit, took others along as well.

As Randazzo argues, "McMahon had the power to instantly fix pro wrestling's deadly dysfunctional culture with four easy steps that would entail a financially negligible sacrifice for the hugely profitable WWE" (2008, 322). Randazzo's proposed solutions included scheduled "off-season" time for individual performers, a more legitimate drug-testing program, a company policy that restricted the hiring of obviously doped performers, and a comprehensive pension and health care program that would allow wrestlers to retire rather than take immense risks to keep cashing McMahon's paychecks. The public health of professional wrestlers was a central part of the media discourse following the Benoit family tragedy, garnering substantial coverage. Time will tell whether this extremely private, publicly held company alters its practices in any noticeable way. As previously noted, Linda McMahon has had to answer questions related to the company's treatment of its workers during her Senate campaign. In the meantime, the WWE continues to prosper in the global marketplace, to raise its standing in the entertainment business via its charitable and voter registration programs, and to periodically punish a handful of employees who violate its now amended drug policy.

Conclusion

In his description of the WWE as a form of "monster" that, following the work of literary critic Jerome Cohen (1996), works to problematize moral panics, H. Jenkins III states:

> The WWE is a horrifying hybrid—not sports, sports entertainment; not real, not fake, but someplace in between; appealing to the "white trash" working class and the college educated alike; courting kids and appealing to adolescents on the basis of its rejection of family values; existing outside the cultural mainstream and yet a commercial success; appealing to national pride even as it shoots a bird at most American institutions; masculine as hell and melodramatic as all get out. (2005, 299)

This quote speaks to the many tensions I have tried to shed light on in this chapter. The legacy of Vince and Linda McMahon, and their transformation of the WWE and pro wrestling/sports entertainment business, have been etched in stone. What is more interesting, from a critical sport and cultural studies perspective, is the way the company's history and practices from the early 1980s through the present correspond with the rise of neoliberalism and the damage done by it to many of our most treasured democratic ideals. If, as Giroux suggests, neoliberalism "violates the first rule of democratic politics by denying its own historical and contemporary relationship to power and ideology, and shrouding itself in a discourse of objectivity and historical inevitably" (2008, 133), then the McMahon-helmed WWE is a neoliberal poster child.

McMahon and the WWE are, I argue, a perfect company for early twenty-first-century global capitalism and the neoliberal agenda. While they continue to employ a number of international wrestlers, and often create characters that play on racist and xenophobic stereotypes, they are savvy enough to know how to recast these characters in ways most likely to be consumed by local audiences globally (Silk and Andrews 2001). The images and messages can be read according to local politics and cultures and yet still do the ideological work of the conservative corporation. Domestically, the WWE has been able to quell the attacks from both the academic left and the religious right by making changes to its content, again, while still maintaining some of its problematic messages of sexism, an emphasis on drug-induced bodies, and so on. Further, as neoliberal rationality continues to break down the pillars of democracy, seemingly with the consent of the American population, the WWE has *promoted* democratic engagement with other corporate partners far to the left of its own politics. On the surface, the WWE is a shining example of a reformed company looking to "do the right thing" for the country, and while we can applaud the attention to the numerous causes it supports, beneath the veneer of corporate citizenship lies a wealth of problematic values and business practices.

Giroux (2008) and others have rightfully questioned the overall lack of collective outrage over economic policies that favor the wealthiest U.S. citizens, the Orwellian provisions of the Patriot Act and Homeland Security Acts, and numerous other affronts to democratic ideals. On a far smaller scale, those interested in professional wrestling as a cultural form may ask similar questions. Although many of the storylines may appeal to working-class audiences, the company has engaged in practices that run directly counter to the well-being of its own laborers. Further, as previously discussed, while the WWE is certainly worthy of praise for the charitable work it has engaged in, we can still be critical of the messages it sends to children and question the implications of the WWE becoming a global multimedia powerhouse.

Undoubtedly, for scholars interested in the resilient and peculiar cultural phenomenon of professional wrestling and its dominant brand, the WWE, a great deal of academic work remains to be done. Most relevant to this chapter is the need for an ongoing interdisciplinary analysis of the business of pro wrestling, and how the performers make sense of the conflicting message they receive. Methodologically, this type of ethnographic work will be difficult, but the voices of the workers, or former workers, will ultimately provide critical scholars with a better portrait of how the neoliberal agenda has affected a small but enduring form of popular culture. In addition, research is also needed to determine how local cultures read the WWE's encroachment into its cultural space, and how the content of the storylines, including messages related to norms and values, are negotiated (Deeter-Schmelz and Sojka 2004). It will be interesting to see, for example, whether McMahon decides to frame a new incarnation of an all-American Hulkamania character as a villain in certain global markets where anti-American sentiment could, ironically, draw a greater audience response and ultimately ensure the WWE's success as a worldwide multimedia empire. In the meantime, Vince McMahon and the WWE will continue to wrestle with their place as a successful global corporation that exists harmoniously with the larger neoliberal agenda.

REFERENCES

Assael, S., and M. Mooneyham. 2002. *Sex, Lies, and Headlocks: The Real Story of Vince McMahon and World Wrestling Entertainment*. New York: Three Rivers Press.

Atkinson, M. 2002. "Fifty Million Viewers Can't Be Wrong: Professional Wrestling, Sports Entertainment, and Mimesis." *Sociology of Sport Journal* 19:47–66.

Cohen, J. J. 1996. *Monster Theory: Reading Culture*. Minneapolis: University of Minnesota Press.

Collins, G. 2010. "Who Wants to Elect a Millionaire." *New York Times*, May 26. Available at http://www.nytimes.com/2010/05/27/opinion/27collins.html?scp=2&sq=Linda%20McMahon&st=cse.

Deeter-Schmelz, D. R, and J. Z. Sojka. 2004. "Wrestling with American Values: An Exploratory Investigation of World Wrestling Entertainment as a Product-Based Subculture." *Journal of Consumer Behavior* 4:132–143.

DeGaris, L. 1999. "Experiments in Pro Wrestling: Toward a Performative and Sensuous Sport Ethnography." *Sociology of Sport Journal* 16:65–74.

———. 2005. "The 'Logic' of Professional Wrestling." In *Steel Chair to the Head: The Pleasure and Pain of Professional Wrestling*, ed. N. Sammond, 192–212. Durham, NC: Duke University Press.

Frank, T. 2010. "Linda McMahon's Pro Wrestling 'Soap Opera.'" *Wall Street Journal*, July 21. Available at http://online.wsj.com/article/SB10001424052748703724104575379510984766960.html?KEYWORDS=linda+mcmahon.

Giroux, H. 2004. "War on Terror: The Militarising of Public Space and Culture in the United States." *Third Text* 18:211–221.

———. 2008. *Against the Terror of Neoliberalism: Politics beyond the Age of Greed*. Boulder, CO: Paradigm.

Hernandez, R., and J. Brustein. 2010. "A Senate Run Brings Wrestling into the Spotlight." *New York Times*, July 15. Available at http://www.nytimes.com/2010/07/16/nyregion/16mcmahon.html?_r=1&scp=2&sq=linda%20mcmahon&st=cse.

Jenkins, H. 1997. "Never Trust a Snake: WWF Wrestling as Masculine Melodrama." In *Out of Bounds: Sports, Media, and the Politics of Identity*, ed. A. Baker and T. Boyd, 48–78. Bloomington: Indiana University Press.

Jenkins, H., III. 2005. "Afterword, Part I: Wrestling with Theory, Grappling with Politics." In *Steel Chair to the Head: The Pleasure and Pain of Professional Wrestling*, ed. N. Sammond, 295–316. Durham, NC: Duke University Press.

Jhally, S., and J. Katz. 2002. *Wrestling with Manhood: Boys, Bullying, and Battering*. Northhampton, MA: Media Education Foundation.

Johnson, S. 2007. "'Roids, Reporters, and Rasslin': Anatomy of a Feeding Frenzy." In *Benoit: Wrestling with the Horror That Destroyed a Family and Crippled a Sport*, ed. S. Johnson, H. McCoy, I. Muchnick, and G. Oliver, 93–132. Toronto: ECW Press.

Maguire, B. 2005. "American Professional Wrestling: Evolution, Content, and Popular Appeal." *Sociological Spectrum* 25:155–176.

Mazer, S. 1998. *Professional Wrestling: Sport and Spectacle*. Jackson: University Press of Mississippi.

McLaren, P., and G. Martin. 2004. "The Legend of the Bush Gang: Imperialism, War, and Propaganda." *Cultural Studies ↔ Critical Methodologies* 4:281–303.

Meltzer, D. 2003. *Wrestling Observer Newsletter*, April 21.

———. 2007. *Wrestling Observer Newsletter*, July 19, July 23, July 25.

———. 2008. *Wrestling Observer Newsletter*, May 26.

———. 2009. *Wrestling Observer Newsletter*, January 12.

"Overview." 2012. WWE. Available at http://corporate.wwe.com/parents/overview.jsp.

Randazzo. V. M. 2008. *Ring of Hell: The Story of Chris Benoit and the Fall of the Pro Wrestling Industry.* Beverly Hills, CA: Phoenix Books.

Sammond, N., ed. 2005. *Steel Chair to the Head: The Pleasure and Pain of Professional Wrestling.* Durham, NC: Duke University Press.

Schneiderman, R. M. 2008. "Better Days, and Even the Candidates, Are Coming to W.W.E." *New York Times*, April 28. Available at http://www.nytimes.com/2008/04/28/business/media/28wwe.html?scp=6&sq=wrestling&st=nyt.

Show, J. 2006. "WWE Busy Scripting Its Next Moves." *Street and Smith's SportsBusiness Journal* (October 9–15): 21–23.

Silk, M. L., and D. L. Andrews. 2001. "Beyond a Boundary? Sport, Transnational Advertising and the Reimagining of National Culture." *Journal of Sport and Social Issues* 25:180–201.

Spark, A. 1996. "Wrestling with America: Media, National Images, and the Global Village." *Journal of Popular Culture* 29:83–98.

Stelter, B. 2008. "Where People Know the Meaning of the Word 'Smackdown.'" *New York Times*, April 21. Available at http://thecaucus.blogs.nytimes.com/2008/04/21/where-people-know-the-meaning-of-the-word-smackdown/?scp=5&sq=smackdown%20your%20vote%20campaign&st=cse.

Tamborini, R., P. Skalski, K. Lachlan, D. Westerman, J. Davis, and S. L. Smith. 2005. "The Raw Nature of Televised Professional Wrestling: Is the Violence a Cause for Concern?" *Journal of Broadcasting and Electronic Media* 49:202–221.

Wilson, J., and W. T. Johnson. 2003. *Chokehold: Pro Wrestling's Real Mayhem outside the Ring.* Xlibris.

"WWE Breaks Records in Abu Dhabi." 2012. WWE, February 28. Available at http://corporate.wwe.com/news/2012/2012_02_28.jsp.

Afterword

Sport and Neoliberalism

NORMAN K. DENZIN

Cinematic Prelude

Date: September 19, 2010
Place: ESPN Studios
What: "Sunday Night Football" (SNF): Indianapolis Colts versus New York Giants
Sponsor: SNF brought to you by Oliver Stone's *Wall Street: Money Never Sleeps*[1]
Main Event: Peyton Manning (Colts) versus Eli Manning (Giants)— Peyton dominates Manning battle: 38–14

> *A Marriage Made in Heaven:*
> *Sport,*
> *Neoliberalism,*
> *Money,*
> *Greed*
> *Greed is Good*
> *NFL is good,*
> *ESPN is good*

Sunday Night NFL Football and Oliver Stone's new film *Wall Street: Money Never Sleeps*: a marriage made in heaven. Sport never sleeps. Money never sleeps. ESPN never sleeps (24-hour news). Wall Street never sleeps. Sport is greed. Sport is greedy. Sport is a commodity. The sporting body wants it all: *to win*, not lose. The losing body always comes back for more.

GORDON GEKKO: I'm not a loser. I'm back!!
BUD FOX/FRANK SINATRA: Fly me to the moon[2] / Let me play among
the stars.

A physical cultural studies project that matters must speak from the historical present (Andrews 2002, 2008; Silk 2010; Andrews and Giardina 2008; Giardina 2005; Giardina and Newman 2011; Bruce 1998). The attacks of September 11, 2001, on the World Trade Center in New York and the Pentagon in Washington, D.C., and the now nearly decade-old wars in Iraq and Afghanistan have changed the context of global social relations. Consider the facts. Ever since 9/11, we have been living in a perpetual state of terror. Bush's "Global War on Terror" has morphed into a war on people of color from conservative politicians, right-wing media, and prospective presidential candidates (e.g., Palin, Gingrich, Romney, Huckabee). This war, in turn, has morphed into a war on "illegal" immigrants, a war on "aliens," a war on insurgents and global citizens who cross national borders, and white paranoia everywhere (Giardina and Newman 2011).

The Bush administration perpetuated a cycle of state-sponsored terrorism. It created a network of secret prisons and gulags. It violated the Geneva Convention. It abridged basic constitutional rights, including those ensured by the First, Fifth, and Sixth Amendments—that is, the right to freedom of speech, to due process, and to a speedy public trial. The list of legal abuses is endless. The need for public discourse on the nature of personal identity, citizenship, freedom, privacy, patriotism, justice, and democracy in this time of perpetual war has never been greater. And it is made even more difficult, because today we have to write against the complex war policies of a pragmatic, liberal, African American president.[3]

A physical cultural studies project that speaks from the historical present inserts itself into these spaces of violence and global terror: the spaces of nation, neoliberal regimes, identity, self, gender, freedom, justice, and equality. The situation that confronts sports studies scholars is complex and points in two directions at the same time, one inward, the other outward.

Inwardly, conceptually, as Silk and Andrews and their colleagues in this important new book acknowledge, sport studies will learn how to conceptualize in new ways the terms *nation, national identity, citizenship, democracy,* and *neoliberalism.* They will address these terms in more complex and original ways, understanding that traditional British, subcultural models of cultural studies have been exhausted, rendered archaic by the monumental shifting of global conditions and multiple diasporic figurations that exist in the contemporary moment (Giardina and Newman 2011).

Many of the old sport studies narratives, both methodological and interpretive, are exhausted. This is because too much of what passes for scholarship in the field of sport studies has not kept pace with the changing landscape of global social relations, especially as related to neoliberalism and democracy in the post-9/11 era. Nor has it kept step with the new interpretive methodologies that frame a performance cultural studies project. We must redouble our efforts to engage in moral, progressive, interventionist political struggle that should be the hallmark of critical inquiry, sport-related or otherwise. We do this by writing our way into the future (Rinehart 1998; 2010; Bruce 2010; Denison and Markula 2003).

And so this group of scholars offers the field new narratives and new methodologies, new ways of being in the present, new ways of looking inward and outward at the same time. We need a new language and a new way of representing life under violent, global postmodernism. Silk, Andrews, and their coauthors give us the terms of this new language and its concepts and imagery.

A New Language

Here is a sample: sport, neoliberalism and the state, the neoliberal city, perpetual war, financial crises, threats of terror; the logics, ideologies, structures, formations, mechanics, and cultural geographies of neoliberalism; sporting bodies, hard bodies, soft bodies, female bodies, fat bodies; money making as a spectator sport; family, stigma, loss, identity; global capitalism, economic citizenship, getting back in the game; race, class, politics; post-Katrina America, New York City, infrastructures; wild money, consuming pleasures; sporting agents, capitalism-as-a-sporting pedagogy, sport as pedagogy, mud wrestling in the Big Apple. This language allows us to conceptualize sports studies in globalizing times. These key terms allow us to speak of the corporate university, Nike, sports celebrities, immigrants, border crossings, and queer bodies of color; to listen to and hear the voices of oppression, bilingual belongings, discourses of trespassing, public education in globalizing times, and postcolonial intellectuals decolonizing the academy. It's all here, a new language for a new beginning, a new way of speaking from the present, confronting, locating, and doing critical sports cultural studies in violent globalizing times.

The chapters in this book offer insights into how global sport (both sporting agents and sporting institutions) functions, as stated in Chapter 1, "as a component of popular culture" and "acts as a powerful educational force that, through pedagogical relations and practices, organizes identity, citizenship, and agency within a neoliberal present." Thus do the authors untangle the complex relationships between neoliberal ideology, political praxis, critical pedagogy, and sport. Reading outward from the sporting body, situating it always in its historical present, each author opens a space for an utopian imaginary, a place where the inconvenient truths of a global sporting culture are exposed and then reconfigured within a radical democratic present.

Imagine neoliberal society as an ugly, huge, sprawling, multiheaded beast, like a beached whale stranded on the shoals of a rocky island. Think of sport and the sporting body as lovely, sometimes elegant, sometimes disfigured organisms buried deep inside the belly of this grotesque, monstrous beast. The chapters in Part I interrogate the outer economic structures and formations of this beast, moving from sport as commodity and the consuming sporting body to the latent and systematic racism embedded in those massive performance arenas where sporting spectacles are staged. The free sporting body that performs to its fullest potential enacts free-market ideology. Free-market capitalism builds the spaces where this can happen, a beast within a beast.

The chapters in Part II take up the geographic spaces and moral places where an urban sporting imaginary is performed, consumed, and regulated, from new urban glamour zones to health clubs; the Rugby World Cup stadium in Dunedin, New Zealand; and surfing and free-running economies. Part III locates the consumers of the sporting body in the discourses of advertising and consumerism, including celebrity and reality television, basketball, football, stock car racing, hockey, and wrestling.

Together these chapters create a critical dialogue and a radical intervention into the multiple neoliberal worlds that shape and contain the sporting body. They offer the outline of a utopian imaginary, a radical democratic present. This would be a place where the shackles of neoliberalism are cast aside, where consumer culture is held in abeyance, a place safe and sheltered, where the sporting body sets the criteria for a good performance. A place outside the belly of the beast. But how to get there? Or is there even a there to get to? Is it all an illusion, and *is* this simply as good as it gets: critical sports pedagogy scholarship at the very highest level?

Silk, Andrews, and their group of multinational colleagues give us a language for policing the current global crisis. They help us locate, interpret, perform, and represent the lives of a new global citizen on the move. They help us craft a morally centered, critically informed dialogue focused on human rights, history, and politics. They help us imagine a sports cultural studies that will interrupt history. A sports studies that will not stand silent when a nation rushes to war. A sports studies that creates a moral discourse that challenges official versions of political reality. A sports studies that challenges the ways political administrations manipulate information and produce regimes of fear and terror. This is a sports studies that argues for a politics of truth that answers to enduring issues concerning what is just.

It is time for a change. Remaining within the current communication grid is a recipe for failure. Although many scholars offer a language of critique of power, knowledge, and culture, what is often missing "is a language of *possibility*, one that engages what it would mean pedagogically and politically to provide the conditions for rethinking a new type of social agent, one that could individually and collectively imagine a global society that combines freedom and social justice modeled after the imperatives of a radical and inclusive democracy" (Giroux 2003, 58, emphasis added; see also Andrews and Giardina 2008, 402–403).

A Physical Cultural Studies Project That Matters

An embodied sports studies project that matters must locate the body within a radically contextual politics. It must focus on the active, agentic flesh-and-blood human body. It must treat inquiry as embodied performance (Giardina and Newman 2011). Working from within these coordinates, it must take up *at least* four topics at the same time.

First, we must start with the personal and the biographical and our own location within the world around us. We need a critical, humane discourse that creates sacred and spiritual spaces for people and their moral communities—spaces where people can express and give meaning to the tragedies in their lives, including the Bush wars and their aftermath. This project will work back and forth, connecting the personal, the political, and the cultural. It will reject terrorism and the claim that peace comes at any cost. It will help people think critically, historically, and sociologically. It will move to expose the pedagogies of oppression that produce and reproduce oppression and injustice. It will contribute to an ethical self-consciousness that is critical and reflexive, empowering people with a language and a set of pedagogical practices that turn oppression into freedom, despair into hope, hatred into love, and doubt into trust. And it will engender a critical racial self-awareness that contributes to utopian dreams of racial equality and racial justice.

Second, critical discourse must be launched at the level of the media and the ideological, including discourses on war, America, patriotism, democracy, globalization, neoliberalism, and the silences surrounding peace, human rights, and nonviolence. This discourse will call for justice without war. It will ask for calm deliberations. It will plead against rash actions that could erode human rights and civil liberties. It will ask, "Whose democracy? Whose America?"

A new sports media culture is required.[4] This culture operates in three sites at the same time—in a public culture that demands good "good"[5] news grounded in a communitarian ethic (Christians, Ferre, and Fackler 1993, 14); in schools of journalism committed to training sports journalists in the communitarian news framework; and in a new generation of journalists, fiction writers, and sports scholars dedicated to this form of writing practice. This is writing that produces reports and narrative accounts that are deliberately, self-consciously, reflexively ethical, communitarian, and transformative. These are stories that "enable cultural beings to fulfill their civic tasks" (Christians, Ferre, and Fackler 1993, 14). This is news written by those who want to do more than report on history. They want to interrupt and interpret sport cultural history as it is being written.

Third, we need to foster a critical (inter)national conversation on what is happening, a coalition of voices across the political, cultural, and religious spectra: the socialist left; Greenpeace; women's groups; gay, lesbian, bisexual, and transgender communities; African American, Asian American, and Latino movements; libertarians, the young; the old; students; workers; the clergy; people from all religions; and intellectuals. Every era must develop its own theory

of radical politics and social democracy, a place where citizenship is an argument, not a sing-along. This dialogue is one that must stay alive in our conversations, mutterings, and dialogues about peace, justice, war, and the shrinking
of civil liberties and social justice in America and abroad, and must get louder
and continue until we have secured another four years of a progressive president and elected additional progressives to Congress.

We cannot let democratic dialogue be eviscerated in a time of crisis. We
cannot allow discussions of immigration policy to become a justification for
attacks on people of color. Or women. Or gay and lesbian Americans. Or kids.
Or Muslims, Iraqis, Palestinians, and those subjected to genocide in Africa. We
cannot let the political discourse be shaped by the needs and voices of multinational corporations.

Fourth, there has never been a greater need for critical, interpretive methodologies that can help us make sense of life in an age of the hyperreal, the
simulacra, TV wars, and staged media events. These critical methodologies
must exhibit interpretive sufficiency; be free of racial, class, gender, or sexual
stereotyping; rely on multiple voices; enhance moral discernment; and promote
social transformation and critical consciousness. They must help informed citizens to consensually develop rock solid, baseline definitions of political reality,
enabling us to judge a political regime by its actions, not its carefully crafted,
focus-group-tested buzzwords and phrases.

Writing and Interrupting History in the Current Moment

In the present context, there are at least two normative, inscriptive systems,
two ways of telling things about life in a democratic society, two ways of writing history and culture. Journalism operates under the rule that the public has
the right to know certain things; the First Amendment guarantees freedom of
the press. Social science operates under another rule: the cloak of secrecy associated with a state-sponsored project that maintains the illusion of privacy
within the postmodern world.

A public, civic, or everyday life performance ethnography draws on the legacies of the new new journalists. It borrows from the public journalists. Like the
new and old new journalism and like public journalism (Boyton 2005) it willingly breaks with old routines and evidences a desire to connect with people
(citizens) and their concerns and biographical problems. It writes in ways that
move people to action, words that promote serious discussion about democratic
and personal politics. It makes readers actors and participants, not spectators
in the public dramas that define meaningful life in these early years of a new
century.

When modified, then, journalism's and performance ethnography's norms
open the door for a communitarian, everyday life discourse, local critical stories focused on problematic democratic forms. This is a socially responsible
writing that advocates democracy by creating a space for and giving a civic
(public) voice to the biographically meaningful, epiphanal experiences that

occur within the confines of the local moral community. A new generation of sports studies represented in this book leads the way in this project.

An Updike Intervention

And underneath it all there is the sporting body. The accomplishments of this body constitute, even as it ages, an aura, the stuff that myths are made of, the place of fandom, a field of dreams. And we need good writers who tell stories about our sporting legends, even as we understand that these bodies are themselves commodities, celebrities whom we ask to perform on demand.

John Updike offers an example. Here is a *there* to get to, sportswriting in its very finest form: Fenway Park, Boston, Wednesday September 28, 1960.

> [It was the] Red Sox's last home game of the season, and therefore the last time in all eternity that their regular left fielder [Ted Williams] known to the headlines as ted, KID, SPLINTER . . . would play in Boston. . . . [H]e was forty-two. . . . The afternoon grew so glowering that in the sixth inning the arc lights were turned on. . . . Fisher (the pitcher) was wide with the first pitch. He put the second one over and Williams swung mightily and missed. The crowd groaned. . . . Fisher threw the third time, Williams swung again, and there it was. The ball climbed on a diagonal line into the vast volume of air over center field. . . . It was in the books while it was still in the sky. . . . Like a feather caught in a vortex, Williams ran around the square of bases at the center of our beseeching screaming. He ran as he always ran out home runs—hurriedly, unsmiling, head down. . . . [H]e didn't tip his hat. The crowd, the players, the umpires begged him to come out and acknowledge us in some way, but he never did and did not now. Gods do not answer letters. . . . On the car radio as I drove home I heard that Williams had decided not to accompany the team to New York. So he knew how to do even that, the hardest thing. Quit. (Updike 1960; see also McGrath 2010)

It's all here, the embodied sporting presence, ideology, consumption, desire, dignity, identity, records, quitting sporting body performing at the highest level, the reason why we keep coming back, myth. A physical cultural studies must have a place for this kind of writing—lyrical, poetic, performative, autoethnographic. Here is where the flesh-and-blood, sporting body is represented and consumed.

This is a call for a way of writing that interrupts history itself by focusing on interruptions at the epistemological, performative, and moral level. It asks scholars to contest and challenge the models of knowledge, intelligence, and truth that circulate in the conservative news arenas: conspiracy theorists, birthers, Tea Party extremists, conservatives, states' rights constitutional revisionists. The politics of truth and evidence are at issue.

This volume marks an important first step in changing the conversation about how we think about neoliberalism in the historical present. But this first step is not the last step. We need to continually push forward, thinking about, theorizing, and writing ourselves into a present not yet known. We must move away from a "cultural studies of convenience" toward a "cultural studies that matters" (Giardina and Newman 2011). This volume charts this new course for us.

This will not be easy. Robert Penn Warren (1946, 529) reminds us:

> By the time we understand the pattern we are in, the definition we are making of ourselves, it is too late to break out of the box. . . . [T]he definition we have made of ourselves is who we are. To break out of it we must made a new self. But how can the self make a new self when the selfness which it is, is the only substance from which the self can be made?

Is a sports studies that wants to matter up to this challenge? And how will it do so? Where will it start?

To conclude, in this age of global uncertainty, we have a moral obligation to police the global crises created by neoliberalism; to confront the current situation; to speak to the death of lives, culture, and truth; to undo the official pedagogies that circulate in the media. We need testimonials, autoethnographies, performance texts, new stories, plays, and dramas about real people with real lives, the horror of it all. We need stories about what it is like to hate and feel despair, anger, and alienation in a world bursting at the seams as it struggles to reinvent its dominant mythology. We need pedagogical discourses that make these feelings visible, palpable—stories and performances that connect these emotions to wild utopian dreams of freedom and peace. We need to bring about the collapse of the corporate, neoliberal globalization project, the death of old-fashioned imperialism, the death of the new empire before it is too late (Rinehart and Sydnor 2003).

This is what a critical sports cultural studies that matters will do. We must thank the authors and editors of *Sport and Neoliberalism* for showing us how to do this.

NOTES
Acknowledgment: I thank Michael Giardina for his comments on this chapter.

1. *Wall Street: Money Never Sleeps:* director, Oliver Stone; cast: Michael Douglas, Josh Brolin, Frank Langella, Susan Sarandon, Carey Mulligan, Shia LaBeouf; studio: 20th Century Fox (2010). This film revisits the life of Gordon Gekko, the focus of Stone's 1987 *Wall Street.* Of course, Stone has another Sunday Night football film, *Any Given Sunday* (1999).

2. Sinatra's version of this song is heard over the opening credits of *Wall Street.*

3. It was easy to write against Bush, much harder against Obama.

4. The work of progressive sports journalists such as Dave Zirin, Will Leitch, and Michael Lewis is relevant in this context.

5. This is news that carries the voice of justice, hope, and goodwill; it is a voice for reform, a catalyst for community renewal and transformation.

REFERENCES

Andrews, D. L. 2002. "Coming to Terms with Sports Studies." *Journal of Sport and Social Issues* 26 (1): 110–117.

———. 2008. "Kinesiology's Inconvenient Truth and the Physical Sports Studies Imperative." *Quest* 60 (1): 45–60.

Andrews, D. L., and M. D. Giardina 2008. "Sport without Guarantees: Toward a Cultural Studies That Matters." *Sports studies* ↔ *Critical Methodologies* 8 (4): 395–422.

Boyton, R. S. 2005. "Interview." In *The New New Journalism: Conversations with America's Best Nonfiction Writers on Their Craft*, vi–xxxii. New York: Vintage Books.

Bruce, T. 1998. "Postmodernism and the Possibilities for Writing 'Vital' Sports Texts." In *Sport and Postmodern Times*, ed. G. Rail, 3–30. Albany: State University of New York Press.

———. 2010. "Ethical Explorations: A Tale of Preparing a Conference Paper." *Qualitative Inquiry* 16 (3): 200–206.

Christians, C. G., J. P. Ferre, and P. M. Fackler. 1993. *Good News: Social Ethics and the Press.* New York: Oxford University Press.

Denison, J., and P. Markula. 2003. *Moving Writing: Crafting Movement in Sport Research.* New York: Lang.

Giardina, M. D. 2005. *Sporting Pedagogies: Performing Culture and Identity in the Global Arena.* New York: Lang.

Giardina, M. D., and J. I. Newman. 2011. "Sports Studies: Performative Imperatives and Bodily Articulations." In *Handbook of Qualitative Research*, 4th ed., ed. N. K. Denzin and Y. S. Lincoln, 387–401. Thousand Oaks, CA: Sage.

Giroux, H. 2003. *The Abandoned Generation: Democracy beyond the Culture of Fear.* New York: Palgrave.

McGrath, C. 2010. "Tribute to a Hero on Twilight." *New York Times*, Sports Sunday, September 26, 1–2.

Rinehart, R. E. 1998. "Born-Again Sport: Ethics in Biographical Research." In *Sport and Postmodern Times*, ed. G. Rail, 33–48. Albany: State University of New York Press.

———. 2010. "Sport Performance in Four Acts: Players, Workers, Audience and Immorality." *Qualitative Inquiry* 16 (3): 197–200.

Rinehart, R. E., and S. Sydnor, eds. 2003. *To the Extreme: Alternative Sports, Inside and Out.* Albany: State University of New York Press.

Silk, M. L. 2010. "Postcards from Pigtown." *Cultural Studies* ↔ *Critical Methodologies* 10 (2): 143–156.

Updike, J. 1960. "Hub Fans Bid Kid Adieu." *New Yorker*, October 22, 18–25.

Warren, R. P. 1946. *All the King's Men.* New York: Harcourt.

Contributors

David L. Andrews is a professor of physical cultural studies in the Department of Kinesiology and an affiliate faculty member of the Departments of American Studies and Sociology at the University of Maryland, College Park. He is also a visiting professor in the Faculty of Humanities and Social Sciences at the University of Bath in the United Kingdom. His research draws from theories and methods associated with cultural studies, the sociology of culture, body studies, and urban studies, to critically contextualize the relationship between broader sociopolitical structures and the embodied discourses, representations, and experiences of contemporary physical culture. He serves as assistant editor at the *Journal of Sport and Social Issues* and editorial board member for the *Sociology of Sport Journal*, the *International Review for the Sociology of Sport, Leisure Studies*, and the *Kinesiological Review*.

Michael Atkinson is an associate professor in the Faculty of Kinesiology and Physical Education at the University of Toronto. His teaching and research interests center on nonmainstream physical cultures, human rights, and biopedagogical practices in physical cultures and bioethics within global and local sport cultures. He has published on diverse subjects, including ticket scalping, tattooing, transhumanism in sport cultures, Ashtanga yoga, fell running, criminal violence in sport, animal abuse in sport, youth masculinities and health, cosmetic surgery, and athletes with critical illnesses. He has authored seven books, including *Battleground: Sports* (2008), *Deviance and Social Control in Sport* (with Kevin Young [2008]), *Boys' Bodies: Speaking the Unspoken* (with Michael Kehler [2010]), *Deconstructing Men and Masculinities* (2010), and *Key Concepts in Sport and Exercise Research Methods* (2011). He serves as editor of the *Sociology of Sport Journal* and director of the Sport Legacies Research Collaborative. In October 2004, the Social Sciences and Humanities Research Council of Canada awarded him the Aurora Prize, as the outstanding young scholar in the Canadian social sciences.

Ted Butryn is an associate professor of sport sociology and sport psychology in the Department of Kinesiology at San José State University. He also serves as codirector of the department's Qualitative Research Lab. Butryn earned his doctorate in sport psychology and cultural studies from the University of Tennessee in 2000. He currently teaches

graduate courses in qualitative research methods and sport sociology and undergraduate courses in sport sociology and the psychology of coaching. His principal areas of research include the application of cyborg theory and the philosophy of technology to sport
and physical cultures, the subcultural meanings of mixed martial arts/Ultimate Fighting
Championship and professional wrestling, and the emerging area of cultural sport psychology. His articles have been published in the *Sociology of Sport Journal*; the *Journal
of Sport and Social Issues*; *Qualitative Research in Sport, Exercise, and Health*; the *Sport
Psychologist*; and the *Journal of Sport Behavior*.

C. L. Cole is a professor of gender and women's studies, sociology, and communications
research at the University of Illinois, Urbana-Champaign, where she teaches courses in
feminist cultural studies, critical sexuality and race studies, and body studies. She has
published four books as author or editor, including the forthcoming *Good Sports? The
Boundaries of American Democracy*. She is the editor of the *Journal of Sport and Social Issues*, and she serves on the editorial boards of *Cultural Studies ↔ Critical Methodologies*,
Qualitative Research in Sport and Exercise Science, and the series *Biopolitics: Medicine,
Technoscience, and Health in the Twenty-First Century*.

Norman K. Denzin is Distinguished Professor of Communications; College of Communications Scholar; and Research Professor of Communications, Sociology, and Humanities at the University of Illinois, Urbana-Champaign. He is also director of the
International Congress of Qualitative Inquiry. His most recent book is *Custer on Canvas:
Representing Indians, Memory, and Violence in the New West*.

Grant Farred teaches at Cornell University. His published works include *What's My
Name? Black Vernacular Intellectuals* (2003), *Phantom Calls: Race and the Globalization
of the NBA* (2006), and *Long Distance Love: A Passion for Football* (Temple University
Press [2008]). His two forthcoming books are titled *Bodies in Motion, Bodies at Rest* and
Conciliation.

Jessica M. Francombe is a lecturer in the Department of Education in the Faculty of
Humanities and Social Science at the University of Bath. Her research interests revolve
around the theorization of contemporary physical culture and the varied articulations
related to the governance of the body, health, and (in)activity. Her publications have, to
date, worked to interrogate cultural technologies, public pedagogies, gendered subjectivities, and consumer culture. She has recently published articles in *Television and New
Media*, the *Sociology of Sport Journal*, and *Interactions: Studies in Communication and
Culture*. Her current work explores the process and forces of wider culture through particular (lived) experiences. Her ongoing projects include an investigation of the corporeal governance of British girlhood and a critical and methodological exploration of the
healthification of popular culture.

Caroline Fusco is an associate professor in the Faculty of Physical Education and Health
at the University of Toronto. Drawing on poststructuralist, postcolonial, and feminist
theories and cultural geography, her research interrogates the sociocultural study of
play; the geographies of the physical activity and health of children and youth; physical cultural studies of the body, gender, and sexuality; and qualitative research methods.
Fusco teaches undergraduate courses in ethics, equity, and diversity studies in education
and graduate courses in space/place and the body. She earned her doctorate in community health (exercise sciences) from the University of Toronto and her master of science
in physical education from the University of Manitoba. She also holds a certificate in
education and a bachelor of arts degree in sports studies from the University of Ulster,
Northern Ireland. An avid (Toronto) urban cyclist, Fusco also loves walking her dog and
playing (just about anything) with her son, Liam.

Michael D. Giardina, Ph.D., is an assistant professor in the Department of Sport Management at Florida State University. He serves as associate editor of the *Sociology of Sport Journal*, associate director of Florida State University's Center for Physical Cultural Studies, and associate director of the International Congress of Qualitative Inquiry. He has authored or edited a dozen books, including, most recently, *Sport, Spectacle, and NASCAR Nation: Consumption and the Cultural Politics of Neoliberalism* (coauthored with Joshua I. Newman [2011]) and *Qualitative Inquiry and the Politics of Advocacy* (coauthored with Norman K. Denzin [2012]).

Mick Green was senior lecturer in sport management and policy at the Institute of Sport and Leisure Policy at Loughborough University until his death in February 2009. Mick published widely on British sports policy, including elite sport development, school sport and physical education, sport for all, and the "modernisation" of British sport under a New Labour government. He also published research on developments in elite sport systems and policy change in different countries.

Leslie Heywood is a professor of English and sport studies at Binghamton University. Her books include *Dedication to Hunger: The Anorexic Aesthetic in Modern Culture* (1996), *Bodymakers: A Cultural Anatomy of Women's Body Building* (1998), *Pretty Good for a Girl* (1998), *Built to Win: The Rise of the Female Athlete as Cultural Icon* (2003), and *The Proving Grounds* (2005). She has also authored articles that focus on women and sport. Her most recent work on the importance of affect, "Affective Infrastructures: Toward a Cultural Neuropsychology of Sport," was published in *Frontiers in Evolutionary Neuroscience*.

Samantha King is an associate professor in the School of Kinesiology and Health Studies at Queen's University, where she researches and teaches the cultural politics of sport, health, and the body. Her book, *Pink Ribbons, Inc: Breast Cancer and the Politics of Philanthropy* (2006), is the subject of the National Film Board documentary of the same name. King's work has appeared in venues such as *Social Text*, *Cultural Studies ↔ Critical Methodologies*, the *Sociology of Sport Journal*, and *Health Communication*. She is currently writing a book about painkillers in contemporary culture.

Lisa McDermott, Ph.D., is an associate professor in the Faculty of Physical Education and Recreation at the University of Alberta, in Edmonton, Canada. Her research interests include cultural analyses of gender, the body, physical activity and health, and sport and popular culture. Her work has been published in a number of scholarly journals, including the *Sociology of Sport Journal*; *Leisure Studies*; the *International Review for the Sociology of Sport*; *Sport, Education and Society*; and the *Journal of Canadian Studies*.

Mary G. McDonald is a professor in the Department of Kinesiology and Health at Miami University, where she also teaches in the Western Program for Individualized Studies and is an affiliate faculty member within the Women's, Gender, and Sexuality Studies Program. McDonald's teaching and research focus on feminist and cultural studies of sport, the media, and popular culture and explore power relations as constituted through relations of race, class, gender, and sexuality. Her articles have appeared in such journals as the *International Review for the Sociology of Sport*, *Leisure Studies*, *Ethnic and Racial Studies*, *American Studies*, and *Sociological Perspectives*. She has served as guest editor for two special issues of the *Sociology of Sport Journal* and is coeditor of *Reading Sport: Critical Essays on Power and Representation* (with Susan Birrell [2000]). She has also served as president of the North American Society for the Sociology of Sport.

Toby Miller lives in Mexico. Readers can follow his adventures at *tobymiller.org*, where he navigates fair use and copyright to make the majority of his published work available at no charge. He has authored or edited more than thirty books, and his work has been translated into Japanese, Chinese, Portuguese, Spanish, German, and Swedish. His podcast, CulturalStudies, is available free on iTunes and via applications for Android and iPhone.

Mark Montgomery is a professor of English at Cayuga Community College and a lifelong surfer. His creative work has been published in many literary journals, and his essay "'Ambassadors of the Last Wilderness'? Surfers, Environmental Ethics and Activism in America" (coauthored with Leslie Heywood) was published in *Tribal Play: Subcultural Journeys through Sport.*

Joshua I. Newman is an associate professor and the director of the Center for Physical Cultural Studies at Florida State University, where he lectures in the areas of sport and physical culture, qualitative research, cultural studies, and critical pedagogy. His research focuses on social inequalities and the cultural and political economies of the active body. He has authored two books, *Embodying Dixie: Studies in the Body Pedagogics of Southern Whiteness* (2010) and *Sport, Spectacle, and NASCAR Nation: Consumption and the Cultural Politics of Neoliberalism* (with Michael D. Giardina [2011]).

Jay Scherer is an associate professor in the Faculty of Physical Education and Recreation at the University of Alberta. His research interests include globalization, sport and public policy, and cultural studies of sport and leisure. He is the coauthor of *Globalization, Sport and Corporate Nationalism: The New Cultural Economy of the New Zealand All Blacks* (with Steve Jackson [2010]) and the author of a wide range of articles, which have been published in such journals as *Sociology*; *Media, Culture and Society*; *Policy Sciences*; *New Media and Society*; and the *Sociology of Sport Journal.*

Kimberly S. Schimmel, Ph.D., is an associate professor of the sociology of sport in the School of Foundations, Leadership, and Administration and an affiliate faculty member within the Women's Studies Program at Kent State University. She teaches courses on sport and domestic diversity issues, sport in global perspective, and social theory. Her scholarship focuses on the political economy of sport, sport and local/global urban development, and sport and urban politics. Schimmel currently serves on the editorial boards of the *International Review for the Sociology of Sport* and the *Brazilian Journal of Sport and Physical Education* and as a vice president of the International Sociology of Sport Association.

Michael L. Silk is a reader in the Faculty of Humanities and Social Sciences and director of the Sport, Physical Activity and Culture Group (PCS) at the University of Bath. He is the author of *The Cultural Politics of Post-9/11 American Sport: Power, Pedagogy and the Popular* (2011) and coauthor of *Sport and Corporate Nationalisms* (with David L. Andrews and C. L. Cole [2005]), *Qualitative Methods in Sports Studies* (with David L. Andrews and Daniel S. Mason [2005]), and *Qualitative Research for Physical Culture* (with Pirkko Markula [2011]). His interdisciplinary research and scholarship focus on the relationships between sport and physical activity (physical culture), the governance of bodies, cultural pedagogies, and identity politics. He is particularly interested in these relationships as they manifest themselves at a number of public sites (including film, television, and promotional culture) and in transformations of urban space (especially in connection with sporting spectacle). His work pushes the ontological, epistemological, and methodological boundaries of what counts as the critical, social science–oriented study of sport and physical activity.

Brian Wilson is a professor in the School of Kinesiology at the University of British Columbia. He is the author of *Fight, Flight or Chill: Subcultures, Youth and Rave into* *the Twenty-First Century* (2006) and *Sport and Peace: A Sociological Perspective* (2012), as well as articles on sport, social inequality, environmental issues, mass media, social movements, and youth culture. His most recent work focuses on environmentalist practices in the Canadian golf industry and on how the sport of running is used for peace promotion in Kenya.

Index